Amidst widespread approaches to the Bible from the perspectives of the margins in Asia, it is refreshing to read an exploration of the Old Testament by Asian evangelical scholars who delve into both the text and the Asian context. In interpreting the Old Testament with utmost sincerity and sensibly demonstrating its applicability to complex Asian contexts, the contributors have engaged in an authentic Asian reading of the Old Testament.

Chubamongba Ao, DTh
Principal,
Everest Theological Institute, Nepal

I enthusiastically commend this fine collection of essays on the theology of the Old Testament in Asian contexts. How good, as a Westerner who lived in Asia for some years, to see the mature contributions in this book. How helpful to see the deep engagement of the Old Testament with contemporary Asian cultures. In our global village, this book is invaluable wherever in this village we live. My thanks to the editors and contributors for feeding and stimulating the global church in such helpful, relevant, and missional ways.

Paul Barker, PhD
Bishop, Anglican Diocese of Melbourne, Australia
Visiting Lecturer in Old Testament,
Myanmar Graduate School of Theology

This is the volume for which I have been looking for a very long time. It contains the finest collection of evangelical studies in First Testament theology by Asians for Asians that I have encountered. Many of the individual essays are the best on the subject that I have read. This volume aims primarily to advance the kingdom of our Lord in a significant portion of the Majority World. However, if it were required reading in biblical theology and exegesis courses in Western institutions, we might awaken to the myopic and alien presuppositions that plague our readings of Scripture and recognize some unfortunate missiological and ecclesiological consequences for having exported these predispositions abroad.

Daniel Block, DPhil
Gunther H. Knoedler Professor Emeritus of Old Testament,
Wheaton College, Illinois, USA

As the globalization of Christianity continues, so does the need for contextual theology, especially from an evangelical perspective. Focusing on the interpretation and application of the Old Testament in diverse Asian contexts, the articles in this volume repeatedly show the varied interfaces between the Bible and culture, as well as how to engage in thoughtful, constructive dialogue. Not only Asian Christians but also all who love the global church will benefit greatly from this book.

Kevin Chen, PhD
Associate Professor of Old Testament,
Christian Witness Theological Seminary, California, USA

Exploring the Old Testament in Asia is a rare find. An excellent scholarly yet practical book, offering Old Testament theology from the Asian context for Asian communities, and written mainly by Asian authors. There is a rich and comprehensive application of biblical perspectives, covering a wide range of topics relevant to the Asian context, including our views on Yahweh and other gods; gender relations; our understanding of leadership, authority, and power; comparisons between Confucius's concept of spirituality and biblical worship; our understanding of blessings including wealth and healing; and more. I fully agree with the contributors to the book that God still speaks today through the Old Testament in all its fullness through all cultures, including the Asian context. I highly recommend this book to all who want to dig deeper into the Old Testament to understand how it may apply to the Asian context today, helping us to powerfully communicate our Christian faith in diverse contexts.

Rev. Dr. Patrick Fung
General Director,
OMF International

This is a much-needed book for understanding the Old Testament in modern-day Asia, where the maturing Asian church needs a contextualized lens through which to apprehend the marvelous and timeless truths of God's first written revelation to humanity. A special strength is the many chapters' engagement with specific religious traditions in specific countries, like India, the Philippines, Vietnam, Taiwan, and more. It will certainly enrich the church in Asia, but it should be read in the West as well!

David M. Howard, Jr., PhD
Professor of Old Testament,
Bethlehem College and Seminary, Minnesota, USA
Professor Emeritus of Old Testament,
Bethel Seminary, Minnesota, USA

In 2008 I published my book *Why Don't We Read the Book that Christ Read?* in Arabic to help Arab readers understand and appreciate the Old Testament. It has always been my dream to see similar (and better) books written in various contexts by local authors. The publication of this book is a dream becoming a reality! It is an indispensable read for anyone who aims to dig deep theologically and biblically into Asian issues. I am delighted to see several Langham graduates contributing to this volume, thus fulfilling John R. W. Stott's vision for relevant contextual roots of the biblical truth.

Rev. Riad Kassis, PhD
International Director,
Langham Scholars Ministry

How is the Old Testament relevant to contemporary Asian contexts and issues? *Exploring the Old Testament in Asia: Evangelical Perspectives* offers an informative, insightful, and thought-provoking response for interested church leaders, pastors, missionaries, and scholars. In twelve essays, Asian biblical scholars bridge the gap well with such topics as: Old Testament law and ethics, and Asian parallels; Old Testament wisdom compared with Confucian wisdom; and gift-giving and bribery in Asian contexts. These stimulating essays deliver balanced discussions between the Old Testament and Asian contexts. They demonstrate an accurate understanding of Asian issues in their specific contexts, sound exegetical and theological analysis of parallel Old Testament contexts and passages, and careful evaluation of Asian issues with relevant Old Testament beliefs, values, and practices.

Roy Kong Low, PhD
President,
Grace Biblical Seminary, Hong Kong

A wide-ranging collection of essays which consistently draws thought-provoking parallels between the Old Testament and major aspects of Asian culture and religion. These essays are certainly not the last word on their respective subjects – many of them could have been expanded to book-length studies – but they are a welcome word nonetheless, opening up many areas for further research. I wish a book like this had been available twenty-four years ago, when I, a Westerner, first came to Singapore to teach the Old Testament.

Philip Satterthwaite, PhD
Lecturer Emeritus,
Biblical Graduate School of Theology, Singapore

This is a creative book heralding Asian evangelical biblical scholarship at its best with key scholars who not only take the Hebrew Bible seriously, but also resolve difficult, challenging, and relevant issues. The book will definitely be the best resource for thinking Christians in Asia as well as global scholarly communities.

Joseph Shao, PhD
President Emeritus, Biblical Seminary of the Philippines
4th General Secretary, Asia Theological Association

In *Exploring the Old Testament in Asia: Evangelical Perspectives*, the contributors de-center from the Eurocentric perspective and "recenter the narrative of Christianity's rootedness in Asia" (p. 2) in order to provide the basis for theology and ministry. They bring the world of the Old Testament and the world of Asia together to address issues pertaining to diverse Asian contexts such as the challenge of monotheism, the dynamics of gender differences, Confucius spirituality, kinship bonds, etc. In so doing, the word becomes flesh. I highly recommend this book for all who are passionate about the Scripture and its relevance to all people.

Chloe T. Sun, PhD
Professor of Old Testament,
Logos Evangelical Seminary, California, USA

Many have studied the Old Testament for the enrichment of the church, but most of this work has been done in the context of Europe and North America. This excellent collection of essays by scholars across Asia beautifully highlights the relevance of the Old Testament for the church today, showing how these readings can come to life in new ways in Asian contexts. Asian readers will feel at home in many of these discussions, and others across the world will be able to read the Old Testament in new ways that enliven their relationship with the God of the Bible.

Charlie Trimm, PhD
Associate Professor of Old Testament,
Biola University, California, USA
Director,
Every Voice: A Center for Kingdom Diversity in Christian Theological Education

I highly recommend *Exploring the Old Testament in Asia*. The authors intentionally open the "strange" world of the Old Testament by introducing Asian readers to familiar cultural issues. The authors are Asians or have lived in Asia. They critically examine the Old Testament from Asian perspectives. Each chapter bridges the Asian world with the world of the Old Testament. As a Western Christian with intercultural interests,

I found the essays fascinating. They encourage all readers, Western and non-Western, to think critically of assumptions they bring to the Old Testament.

Willem VanGemeren, PhD
Professor Emeritus of Old Testament and Semitic Languages,
Trinity Evangelical Divinity School, Illinois, USA

Exploring the Old Testament in Asia: Evangelical Perspectives is an excellent book to understand the Old Testament from an Asian evangelical perspective. While we Asians are very grateful to our overwhelmingly European saints for bringing the Scriptures to us (though there were some who came from Asia and other continents), the illustrations and metaphors they used to explain and teach the Scriptures came from their culture and community – and that made the word of God geographically distant for most of us.

Junias Venugopal, PhD
Associate Dean and Associate Professor of Evangelism & Leadership,
A. Duane Litfin School of Mission, Ministry, and Leadership,
Wheaton College, Illinois, USA

The Asian theological community comes here into its own and explores what Scripture says to Asian Christian communities. Scholars from different ethnic and national backgrounds explore Old Testament themes in dialogue with pertinent concerns that arise from within their own culture and society, such as polytheism, syncretism, relationships, poverty, leadership, and more. This textbook confirms that the evangelical Asian church is perfectly capable of "self-theologizing." The authors provide not only well-researched models of contextual readings but also contribute fresh insights into Scripture that are of importance to the global church.

Michael Widmer, PhD
Lecturer,
Theological Seminary Chrischona, Switzerland

 FOUNDATIONS IN ASIAN CHRISTIAN THOUGHT

Series Editor: Stephen T. Pardue

The Foundations in Asian Christian Thought series offers accessible and innovative introductions to key topics that are biblically rooted, contextually engaged, and theologically rich. In each volume, a mixture of seasoned and rising scholars from all over Asia with a shared commitment to genuinely contextual reflection and the primary authority of Scripture introduce readers to major issues, identifying the key contributions of Asian Christians to the global theological conversation. In addition to introducing readers to the dynamic landscape of Asian Christian thought, each book also includes constructive proposals regarding how Christians can wisely advance the development of Asian biblical and theological reflection.

Titles in the Series

Asian Christian Theology
2019 | 9781783686438

Asian Christian Ethics
2022 | 9781839730740

Exploring the Old Testament in Asia
2022 | 9781839732799

Exploring the New Testament in Asia
2023 | 9781839737114

 FOUNDATIONS IN ASIAN CHRISTIAN THOUGHT

Exploring the Old Testament in Asia

FOUNDATIONS IN ASIAN CHRISTIAN THOUGHT

Exploring the Old Testament in Asia

Evangelical Perspectives

Editors
Jerry Hwang and Angukali Rotokha

© 2022 by Jerry Hwang and Angukali Rotokha

Published 2022 by Langham Global Library
An imprint of Langham Publishing
www.langhampublishing.org

Langham Publishing and its imprints are a ministry of Langham Partnership

Langham Partnership
PO Box 296, Carlisle, Cumbria, CA3 9WZ, UK
www.langham.org

Published in partnership with Asia Theological Association
ATA
QCC PO Box 1454 – 1154, Manila, Philippines
www.atasia.com

ISBNs:
978-1-83973-279-9 Print
978-1-83973-759-6 ePub
978-1-83973-760-2 Mobi
978-1-83973-761-9 PDF

Jerry Hwang and Angukali Rotokha hereby assert their moral right to be identified as the Author of the General Editor's part in the Work in accordance with sections 77 and 78 of the Copyright, Designs and Patents Act 1988.

All rights reserved. No part of this publication may be reproduced, stored in a retrieval system or transmitted, in any form or by any means, electronic, mechanical, photocopying, recording or otherwise, without the prior written permission of the publisher or the Copyright Licensing Agency.

Requests to reuse content from Langham Publishing are processed through PLSclear. Please visit www.plsclear.com to complete your request.

All Scripture quotations, unless otherwise indicated, are taken from the Holy Bible, New International Version®, NIV®. Copyright ©1973, 1978, 1984, 2011 by Biblica, Inc.™ Used by permission of Zondervan.

British Library Cataloguing-in-Publication Data
A catalogue record for this book is available from the British Library

ISBN: 978-1-83973-279-9

Cover & Book Design: projectluz.com

Langham Partnership actively supports theological dialogue and an author's right to publish but does not necessarily endorse the views and opinions set forth here or in works referenced within this publication, nor can we guarantee technical and grammatical correctness. Langham Partnership does not accept any responsibility or liability to persons or property as a consequence of the reading, use or interpretation of its published content.

CONTENTS

Foreword xv

Acknowledgments xix

Abbreviations xxi

Introduction 1
    Angukali Rotokha and Jerry Hwang

Chapter 1: The Hebrew Bible and Translation as Scripture 7
    Bayarjargal Garamtseren

Chapter 2: Yahweh and Other Gods 25
    Koowon Kim

Chapter 3: Men, Women, and God 41
    Understanding the Male-Female/Husband-Wife Relationship
    through Genesis 1–3
    Havilah Dharamraj

Chapter 4: Israel, The Nations, and the *Missio Dei* 59
    Jerry Hwang

Chapter 5: Leadership, Power, and Authority 81
    Annelle Sabanal

Chapter 6: Old Testament Law and Ethics 101
    Mona P. Bias

Chapter 7: Taiwanese Christian *Li* 123
    The Embodied Worship of the Lord
    Shirley S. Ho

Chapter 8: Education, Learning, and Wisdom 145
    Lady Wisdom Invites Us!
    Elaine Wei-Fun Goh

Chapter 9: Old Testament Narratives 165
    Historiography and Historicity
    Angukali Rotokha

Chapter 10: Exodus and Liberation 185
    Naga Nationalism and the People of God
    Angukali Rotokha

Chapter 11: Kinship, Patronage, and Corruption 205
  Peter H. W. Lau

Chapter 12: Prosperity Theology in Asia 229
  Description and Evaluation in Light of the Old Testament
  Huu-Thien Tran N. and Daniel C. Owens

Contributors 253

Subject Index 259

Author Index 263

Scripture Index 269

FOREWORD

"What difference would it make in India if some of the laws of Leviticus 19 were actual statute legislation in this country?" That was a question I used to ask the class during a lecture course on the Pentateuch at the Union Biblical Seminary, Pune. I taught the Old Testament there between 1983–88. And, as a Westerner from urban Britain, it was a constantly fascinating and challenging mental experience to be studying and teaching the Bible (especially the Old Testament) in a very different cultural and religious environment. I had so much to learn!

Sometimes the hermeneutical distance was very short. It seemed that Baal was alive and well in India, with the ambient polytheism, the sexualized deities, the social oppression, and sexual degradation that accompanied some forms of idolatry – very much as Hosea would have recognized. Amos too would have had strident words for the rampant bribery and corruption – not only in the secular courts and public life, but endemic within the churches and denominations as well. Moses would have wondered how the laws he gave to Israel about mitigating and redressing poverty, dealing systemically with debt so that it did not enslave all future generations, could transform the lives of bonded millions in countries like India.

The response to my question in class, after some silent perusal of the chapter, would often be somewhat embarrassed laughter. These laws from before 1,000 BCE would impact modern India transformatively, as they demand: generosity to the landless (vv. 9–10); fair and prompt payment of wages to day-laborers (v. 13); integrity in the judicial system (v. 15); diligence, not negligence, for other peoples' lives (v. 16b); conservation practices in agriculture (vv. 23–25); ban on the occult (v. 26b, 31); ban on giving daughters into religious prostitution (v. 29); fairness and legal equality for all ethnic groups (vv. 33–34); honesty in the commercial marketplace (vv. 35–36). Who says the Bible is out-of-date?

Sometimes comparisons were ironic. Having studied the Israelite practice of a marriage gift being given by the groom's family to the bride's father and having rejected the common interpretation of the word *mohar* as "bride-price," with the implication that the Israelite wife was simply purchased property, it was (a little) amusing to imagine that the reverse direction in India, where a girl's parents must pay vast amounts to the boy's parents could even remotely be interpreted as the husband being bought, or treated, as the wife's property!

Sometimes it called for deeper thought as the tectonic plates of strong ethical paradigms and assumptions clashed. As a Western academic, I prided myself on the highest standards and demands of integrity and honesty (and I still would, just to reassure). Cheating in exams or plagiarism in assignments were just about top of the list of ethical negatives, reprimands, and disqualification. What then could I say to the student in tears in my office, whom I had failed for some such fault in a way that would mean he could not graduate, pleading with me to reconsider and let him pass since, he said, he simply could not go back to his parents, having failed them, let them down, betrayed their trust, and so on. It was not that he thought his dishonesty was "OK" – he knew it was sinful. But on his inner scale of ethical values, honesty came lower down than honoring his parents by succeeding in what they had paid and prayed for. Loyalty to his parents was, for him, a higher demand than honesty in his studies. Disloyalty would be a worse sin, in his eyes, than dishonesty.

So I found myself wrestling with the way cultural values and imperatives move ethical values (including biblical ones) around in terms of their relative priority on some sliding-scale of what is considered of first importance. Non-Western traditional cultures in general tend to be far more committed to family loyalty and kinship obligations than Western individualized cultures. Is that not a strongly biblical value that we in the West have eroded to our great cost? I found I could not excuse the student's dishonesty as if it had not happened or didn't matter, but at the same time I found myself wondering what I needed to learn from a young Asian lad in his agony about relative ethical values and on what biblical basis I would place one above another.

I have not had the privilege of living in another Asian country for the length of time we lived and worked in India, though I have visited many others for various forms of Christian ministry and teaching. So I have not personally wrestled with the kind of cultural, theological, and ethical issues such as those mentioned above in other cultures. But I have experienced much kindness, politeness, affection, and warm-hearted response in my visits to Pakistan, Myanmar, Thailand, South Korea, Japan, Indonesia, Hong Kong, Taiwan, Singapore, Malaysia, Kyrgyzstan, Mongolia, the Philippines. And in most of these countries, people have honestly shared with me some of the ways the Christian faith and the interpretation of the Bible itself are intertwined with cultural, historical, linguistic, and ethical distinctives of their contexts.

It is so encouraging and welcome, therefore, to see this book exploring the Old Testament and the theological issues it raises through Asian eyes. Of course, Asians have been writing theology for thousands of years, ever since

Foreword

those ancient West Asians wrote all the books we now call the Bible itself. And indeed much of the theological writing of the early centuries of the Christian church was done by Asians (and Africans too, of course) in Syria, Lebanon, Arabia, Turkey, Armenia, Georgia, Persia, and on along the Silk Route to China itself. Vince Bantu's recent book, *A Multitude of All Peoples: Engaging Ancient Christianity's Global Identity* (Downers Grove: IVP Academic, 2020), has the wonderful opening lines: "Christianity is and always has been a global religion. For this reason, it is important never to think of Christianity as *becoming* global" (p. 1). This symposium is a worthy and enriching contribution to the two millennia of global Christian theology – an exploration, rightly so-called, that invites other explorers to engage, comment, critique, and continue the journey together.

It is a privilege for Langham Partnership to walk alongside churches around the world, and in this instance specifically, to partner with ATA and Asian biblical scholars, including a pleasing number of Langham Scholars, in bringing this project to birth. May it be the firstborn of many more!

Christopher J. H. Wright
Global Ambassador and Ministry Director, Langham Partnership
July 2022

ACKNOWLEDGMENTS

This Old Testament textbook from Asia and for Asia and beyond was conceived in its entirety, from planning to publication, during the COVID-19 pandemic. For this reason, the two of us would like to give thanks to God, first and foremost, for the strength to design the book, recruit contributors, and assemble the whole even as we dealt with various challenges ourselves in health and ministry. Besides COVID-19 itself and the related difficulties which all our contributors faced, we would like to recognize the other scholars who had originally planned to pen essays for this volume but needed to withdraw due to sudden and massive upheaval in their home countries (at one point, one contributor was a refugee fleeing from war, while it was unclear if another contributor was even alive). Suffering is universal to the human experience, of course, but many scholars of religion have recognized that suffering is an especially prominent theme in the religio-cultural systems that are native to Asia. Not only this, but the lived reality for many Christian brothers and sisters in Asia is that of persecution and poverty, both of which have been exacerbated by the pandemic.

It is with these realities in mind that we dedicate this textbook to the victims of the pandemic in Asia, especially the bereaved families of Christian ministers who continued to visit the sick and minister to the grieving, even as their own lives ebbed away. We can only echo the words of the psalmist, "Precious in the sight of the Lord is the death of his faithful servants" (Ps 116:15).

Jerry Hwang
Angukali Rotokha
May 2022

ABBREVIATIONS

AAMM	*Asia-Africa Journal of Mission and Ministry*
AB	Anchor Bible
AnBib	Analecta Biblica
ApOTC	Apollos Old Testament Commentary
BA	*Biblical Archaeologist*
BASOR	*Bulletin of the American Schools of Oriental Research*
BBR	*Bulletin for Biblical Research*
BBRSupp	*Bulletin for Biblical Research, Supplements*
BCOTWP	Baker Commentary on the Old Testament Wisdom and Psalms
BDB	Brown, Francis, S. R. Driver, and Charles A. Briggs. *A Hebrew and English Lexicon of the Old Testament*
BECNT	Baker Exegetical Commentary on the New Testament
Bib	*Biblica*
BibInt	*Biblical Interpretation*
BN	*Biblische Notizen*
BSac	*Bibliotheca Sacra*
BT	*The Bible Translator*
BZAW	Beihefte zur Zeitschrift für die alttestamentliche Wissenschaft
BZNW	Beihefte zur Zeitschrift für die neutestamentliche Wissenschaft
CBQ	*Catholic Biblical Quarterly*
ERT	*Evangelical Review of Theology*
GOTR	*Greek Orthodox Theological Review*
GTJ	*Grace Theological Journal*
HALOT	*The Hebrew and Aramaic Lexicon of the Old Testament*
Int	*Interpretation*
JAAR	*Journal of the American Academy of Religion*
JAOS	*Journal of the American Oriental Society*
JBL	*Journal of Biblical Literature*

JETS	*Journal of the Evangelical Theological Society*
JISMOR	*Journal of the Interdisciplinary Study of Monotheistic Religions*
JPSTC	The Jewish Publication Society Torah Commentary
JSOT	*Journal for the Study of the Old Testament*
JSOTSup	Journal for the Study of the Old Testament Supplement Series
LHBOTS	The Library of Hebrew Bible/Old Testament Studies
MARI	Mari: Annales de recherches interdisciplinaires
NAC	New American Commentary
NIB	*The New Interpreter's Bible*
NICOT	New International Commentary on the Old Testament
NIDOTTE	*New International Dictionary of Old Testament Theology and Exegesis*
NIVAC	The NIV Application Commentary
NovT	*Novum Testamentum*
OBT	Overtures to Biblical Theology
OTL	Old Testament Library
PNTC	Pillar New Testament Commentaries
RevExp	*Review and Expositor*
SHCANE	Studies in the History and Culture of the Ancient Near East
SJOT	*Scandinavian Journal of the Old Testament*
TDOT	*Theological Dictionary of the Old Testament*
ThTo	*Theology Today*
TJ	*Trinity Journal*
TynBul	*Tyndale Bulletin*
UNIOCC	*International Journal of Reformed Theology and Life: Unio Cum Christo*
VE	*Verbum et Ecclesia*
VT	*Vetus Testamentum*
WBC	Word Biblical Commentary

INTRODUCTION

Angukali Rotokha and Jerry Hwang

The rapid growth of the evangelical church in Asia during the last century has found a parallel in the rising numbers of Asian Christians enrolling in seminaries to train for ministry. Theological education, however, has often not grown truly Asian roots at a pace comparable with the increase in Asian students with respect to providing resources written by Asians, asking questions relevant to Asians, and offering biblical perspectives on issues of concern to Asian communities. This dearth of contextual theology has meant that seminarians and thinking Christians in Asia are still reliant on Western resources, leaving them at a loss for how to read and apply Scripture faithfully in a manner that connects God's authoritative word to the specific contexts and issues facing their communities.

Although Christianity originated in ancient Near East and is quite established in numerous parts of the Asian continent,[1] it is nonetheless still perceived as a Western religion in much of Asia. This perception of the "Western-ness" of the Christian faith is partly because Christianity arrived along with Western empires relatively late in the history of many Asian nations. Such an association between Christianity and Western colonialism has tended to overshadow

---

1. For example, church tradition indicates that the start of Indian Christianity can be traced back to the second half of the first century CE, and to the evangelistic efforts of the apostle Thomas, who is said to have arrived in Kerala, where the community of Thomas Christians now reside (also called Mar Thoma Christians, Malabar Christians, etc.). Tradition also has it that the apostle Thomas visited and preached at Taxila (also known as Takshashila) in 52 CE, which was a center of learning in ancient India and is now part of Pakistan, before proceeding to other parts of India; similarly in Sri Lanka, where the apostle Thomas is said to have visited around the same time (Theodore Gabriel, *Christian Citizens in an Islamic State: The Pakistan Experience* (Hampshire, UK: Ashgate, 2007), 17–18; R. T. B. Abeysinghe, "Challenges and Opportunities for Theological Education in Sri Lanka," paper presented for the South Asia: Challenges and Opportunities for Theological Education Webinar on February 10, 2022, accessed March 14, 2022, https://www.anglicancommunion.org/media/467000/TEAC_South-Asia-Challenges-and-Opportunities_Rasika-Abeysinghe_0222_en.pdf. Likewise, the origin of Chinese Christianity goes back to the seventh century CE during the T'ang Dynasty through the work of the Nestorian monk Aloben (Peter C. Phan "Living for the Reign of God: Liberation, Cultures, Religions. A Theology of Liberation for Asian Churches," in *Movement Or Moment?: Assessing Liberation Theology Forty Years After Medellin*, Studies in Theology, Society, and Culture, ed. Patrick Claffey and Joe Egan [Oxford: Peter Lang, 2009], 58–60).

Christianity's ancient roots in Asia,[2] a reality often also reinforced by how Christian scholarship, textbooks, and resources used in Asian seminaries come largely from the West. Western-style theological education has certainly shaped and guided the Asian church in laudatory ways, but the maturing of the Asian evangelical church in recent decades has also revealed the limitations of Western scholarship in addressing the diverse concerns and interests of Asian Christian communities. Even in a globalizing world, the exposition of Scripture through Western lenses and cultural categories often struggles to engage with Asian societies outside the walls of the seminary, leaving theologically trained Asians with tools that are less than effective for their ministry work.

For Asians, what counts as *religion* is often synonymous with *culture*, due to the holism of Asian societies in which the usual dichotomies between sacred/secular, physical/spiritual, natural/supernatural, and earthly/heavenly are often blurred. Since the needs of Asian Christians differ from their Western brothers and sisters, theological education in and for Asia must connect Scripture with aspects of life that are not as commonly treated in Western evangelical scholarship. Among these areas are living as a religious minority, poverty, gender, syncretism, familial and societal relationships, superstition, violence, corruption, and others that this book seeks to examine. Silence from the Christian community about these lived realities in Asia leaves a vacuum that the cultures surrounding evangelical Asian Christians are ready to fill using beliefs and practices from their own environments. Further, such an approach not only fails to serve the Asian church, but also impoverishes the global church.

The presence of cultural pluralism in Asia means that the avenues for contextual application of biblical perspectives are also numerous. The Old Testament is particularly relevant in this regard, since many of its themes find special resonance among Asian communities. At the same time, bridges between the OT world and contemporary Asian lived contexts and experiences must be built cautiously in order to maintain the proper cultural and theological distance between ancient Israelites and modern Asians. To this end, then, this book explores how the world of the OT, which is both familiar to us and yet far removed in time and space, can speak today as God's authoritative *and* contextual word. This approach seeks to recenter the narrative of Christianity's rootedness in Asia and take steps towards providing Asian biblical reflections as the backbone of our theology and ministry.

---

2. The Portuguese and Spanish came to Asia as colonizers in the 16th century CE, and other Europeans from the 17th century CE on.

Introduction

Thus, *Exploring the Old Testament in Asia* examines traditional topics in OT theology, but does so for Asia and from Asian perspectives. Chapter 1 begins the book with Bayarjargal Garamtseren's essay that considers how the Hebrew Scriptures become God's word to those who are not descendants of Abraham, by highlighting the case of Bible translation for Mongolian Christians. He observes and contrasts Mongolia's socialist evolutionary narrative, as well as its own traditional narratives, to the biblical creation narrative. In addition, the viability of new Bible translations as God's word is rooted in God's universal mission and self-revelation to ancient Israel in a language they understood.

Chapters 2 and 3 examine two fundamental relationships – between God and human beings, and between man and woman respectively. Koowon Kim's essay on Yahweh and other gods speaks to Asia's highly spiritual and supernatural contexts. By establishing points of contact between East Asia and the OT, Kim demonstrates how Asian Christians in polytheistic cultures can relate to ancient Israelites in their shared struggle to understand how to believe in Yahweh as the one God. The polytheism of the surrounding peoples was the cultural environment out of which Israel eventually came to the light of biblical monotheism. Havilah Dharamraj invites readers to reexamine the man-woman relationship by juxtaposing the biblical narrative of Adam and Eve with Hinduism's cultural and religious understanding of gender relations in Ram and his wife Sita, as found in the *Ramayana*. Going across the biblical canon, she shows how the biblical understanding of gender differs from that of the *Ramayana* in offering a healing solution for the unhealthy state of the man-woman relationship.

In chapter 4, Jerry Hwang explores the theme of God's universal mission and grapples with the OT's apparent contradiction between God's mission to bless the nations via Israel, and God's dealings with the nations which often involved domination and violence, also via Israel. Since the history of Christianity in many Asian countries is entangled with the history of colonialism, it is necessary for Asian Christians to understand how the OT's narrative of divine wrath fits within the *missio Dei* of God's love and care to draw all nations to know him.

Annelle Sabanal's essay in chapter 5 examines the institutions of leadership in the OT and observes similarities in leadership, authority, and power with Asian cultures. Drawing on the holistic worldview common to both the ancient Israelites and contemporary Asian communities, Sabanal demonstrates how the OT's God-centered vision of leadership ought to shape our understanding, standards, and practices. She concludes with biblical reflections on the Filipino context in which the nature of political leadership is a perennial challenge for believers. In chapter 6, Mona Bias examines law and ethics in the OT by focusing on the theme of covenant. She draws particular attention to parallels between the beliefs and practices of ancient Israel and the Philippines. Such similarities mean that OT laws, which Christians often consider too specific or irrelevant, find parallels and resonance in some Asian communities. When these connections are highlighted well, Asian Christians can recover the relevance of the OT and create opportunities for deeper engagement with their communities.

The next two essays, chapters 7 and 8, use Confucian thought as conversation partners. Shirley Ho's essay on worship uses the Confucian concept of *Li* to demonstrate how the Taiwanese spiritual worldview and ritual life provide the cognitive and experiential framework to understand the worship life and ritual practices of the OT, especially as seen in Leviticus and Psalms. Ho highlights the theological rationale behind OT worship rituals which can otherwise be perceived as mindless or repetitive. She also shines a spotlight on common misunderstandings regarding worship rituals that are prevalent in Asian churches, while offering correctives for the same. Elaine Goh examines the pedagogy of biblical wisdom and its goal of "blessedness" that is oriented to building character. Goh situates this discussion of biblical wisdom in the Asian context by bringing in Confucius' *Analects*, a work that has shaped Asian ethics since ancient times and is complementary to biblical ethics. She concludes by suggesting how biblical wisdom can make distinctive contributions to Asian contexts.

Angukali Rotokha addresses the categories of history and historiography, with reference to OT narratives, in chapter 9. After providing a brief overview of the modern and ancient Near Eastern historiographies to highlight the differences between them, she brings in India's historiographical enterprise as represented by the *Mahabharata*. This comparison allows for a greater level of cross-cultural objectivity on the issue of historicity in ancient texts, especially in the task of reassessing the historical value of the OT. In the following chapter, chapter 10, Rotokha also examines what it means to be God's people in the context of a Christian community's struggle for political independence. She investigates theopolitical issues of selective use and "over-appropriation" of the OT promises to the Israelites, and the use of violence while still professing Christ. She proposes that God's promises to the Israelites in the OT are too specific to be indiscriminately appropriated for our use today, thereby requiring a shift from striving to be Israel-like to Christ-like.

Introduction

Peter Lau's essay in chapter 11 discusses how the presence and strength of kinship bonds in collectivist-dominant cultures, like ancient Israel was and Asian cultures today are, impact social and interpersonal interactions. He observes that while gift-giving and reciprocity are inherent and legitimate parts of social interactions, the dynamics of shame and honor at play in Asian societies also inform such interactions. He demonstrates how proper understanding and application of Scripture can deal with favoritism and corruption. Chapter 12 brings Huu-Thien Tran and Daniel Owens' evaluation of the growing influence of prosperity theology in Asia and why it is attractive to many Asians. Drawing on their experiences in Vietnam and beyond, Tran and Owens address prosperity theology's inadequate teachings on issues such as wealth, suffering, and healing. They outline how the biblical understanding of blessing not only affirms God's care for his people, but can also bring hope to Asians undergoing various trials since suffering itself can be a blessing under God's sovereignty, both for innocent and guilty sufferers.

As the Asian theological community slowly but surely comes into its own and explores what Scripture says to Asian Christian communities, our hope is that *Exploring the Old Testament in Asia* will communicate how Christian faith can engage powerfully with diverse contexts, both in Asia and beyond. The editors and contributors to this book can hardly claim to speak for all evangelical scholars in Asia (though a dozen ethnicities and nationalities are represented), but we share the theological commitment that God still speaks today through the Old Testament in all its fullness.

REFERENCES

Abeysinghe, R. T. B. "Challenges and Opportunities for Theological Education in Sri Lanka." Paper presented for the South Asia: Challenges and Opportunities for Theological Education Webinar, February 10, 2022. Accessed March 14, 2022. https://www.anglicancommunion.org/media/467000/TEAC_South-Asia-Challenges-and-Opportunities_Rasika-Abeysinghe_0222_en.pdf.

Gabriel, Theodore. *Christian Citizens in an Islamic State: The Pakistan Experience*. Hampshire, UK: Ashgate, 2007.

Phan, Peter C. "Living for the Reign of God: Liberation, Cultures, Religions. A Theology of Liberation for Asian Churches." In *Movement Or Moment?: Assessing Liberation Theology Forty Years After Medellín*. Studies in Theology, Society, and Culture, edited by Patrick Claffey and Joe Egan, 55–96. Oxford: Peter Lang, 2009.

CHAPTER 1

THE HEBREW BIBLE AND TRANSLATION AS SCRIPTURE

Bayarjargal Garamtseren

The Old Testament (OT), also known as the Hebrew Bible (HB), was Scripture for the Israelites and is likewise for Jews today. How can these Hebrew Scriptures be God's word to us who are not descendants of Abraham? What relevance does their story have to us today? Why is translation of the Bible undertaken and how does that translation become the Scriptures to those receiving them? In this essay, I will attempt to answer these questions with application to Asian contexts.

In the first part, "The Hebrew Bible as Scripture to All Humanity," I will consider certain elements in the HB pertaining to the whole human race. These include humans as the creation of God, the nature of God as revealed to all, the origin of human sin, the mission of God for humanity, the foundation of human moral standards, and the story of Israel in relation to believers in Christ Jesus. In the second part, "Translation as Scripture," I will examine the rationale for Bible translation into other languages and how such translations become God's word to those receiving them. I will discuss how God desires to speak to people in their languages, that all languages are God's ordained recipients of his message, and that God has chosen translation as the means of delivering his message to people. In addition, the work of the Spirit of God and faith in Jesus Christ are central to receiving translations as God's word.

1. THE HEBREW BIBLE AS SCRIPTURE TO ALL HUMANITY

The HB is a collection of books written mainly in ancient Hebrew. Only a small portion of the OT is written in Aramaic, a sister language to Hebrew. Hebrew is a northwest Semitic language, and is closely related to Phoenician and Moabite, forming a Canaanite group of languages. The Hebrew language is not a special heavenly language. Some Christians have a mystical view of the Hebrew language and even claim that there is no other language like Hebrew. Contrary to such claims, Hebrew was an ordinary language which was spoken by the Israelites, changed slowly over time just as other languages do, and had its ups and downs in its degree of usage over centuries (even during biblical times).

The HB has a three-part division, as evident in its compilation as Law, Prophets, and Writings. The Law is the first five books of the HB; the Prophets are divided into the Former Prophets (Joshua, Judges, Samuel, and Kings) and the Latter Prophets (the Major and Minor Prophets). The Prophets are counted as eight books in their Hebrew classification. The Writings include all the other books, eleven in all by their Hebrew classification. The Writings can be further divided into Books of Truth/Wisdom (Psalms, Job, and Proverbs), five scrolls (Ruth, Song of Songs, Ecclesiastes, Lamentations, and Esther), and others (Daniel, Ezra-Nehemiah, and Chronicles). While the Protestant canon of the OT is said to have thirty-nine books, these same books in the HB are counted as twenty-four since numbered books like 1 and 2 Samuel are counted as one, while the twelve books of the Minor Prophets are counted as one, and Ezra and Nehemiah are also a single book. The first Hebrew letters of these three divisions, "T" for Torah ("Law"), "N" for Navi'im ("Prophets") and "K" for Ketuvim ("Writings"), make up the abbreviation TaNaK (or Tanaach), which is the Jewish name for the HB. The books in the HB are sequenced in this three-part division with the Pentateuch followed by the books of the Prophets, with the Writings coming at the end. The Protestant Bible, on the other hand, more or less follows historical-chronological order, ending with the book of Malachi.

This Scripture, written in Hebrew and Aramaic, was initially given to the Israelites. It is also Scripture to all humanity because in its books God reveals his own nature, who we are as his creation, and how we are to live as his people who fulfill his mission for all other humans and creation. In other words, the HB is the word of God to all nations, including those who are not in the bloodline of Abraham, and is thus relevant to how we as the people of God live today. In order to show that the HB is Scripture to all humanity, I will explore the following aspects of the HB: (1) humans as God's creation, (2) the nature of the one true God, (3) the origin of human sin, (4) God's mission for the world, (5) the foundation of morality for humanity, and (6) the story of Israel with whom the non-Israelites later "joined" spiritually.

1.1. Humans as God's Creation

The HB shows that God is the sole Creator. Humans and everything else are his creation. Growing up in a socialist country, Mongolia, we were taught the evolutionary view that humans evolved from apes through a process of random natural selection. In my youth, I used to wonder where I came from and had questions about my existence such as "Is there someone out there greater than humans?," "Is there life beyond death?," "Where does this earth come from?," and "Is there meaning for my life?" My achievements in school and active participation in sports as well as many other activities did not give meaningful, coherent, and satisfying answers to these questions.

Many nations and people groups in Asia have their own stories or myths about how the world and humans came to be. One of the Mongolian myths is as follows. God created the earth and all the inhabitants on it. First, God created birds in their different kinds, *Khan Garuda* as their king, and then land animals, the lion as their king, and then water animals, the whale as their king, and finally insects, with animals bothering God the whole time with their inter-animal conflicts and fights. When the kings of the animals came to God with their complaints, God created a man as a ruler over all the animals. Then, because of the man's harsh character, the whole world turned into a mess and God created a woman with a soft heart. After a while, fights began between the man and the woman which tested God's patience. In response, God created a child, so the man and the woman began to live in harmony, and even animals lived in ways God desired. God was delighted and relieved that he did not create an angel to watch over humans but a child who brings love to man and woman. God lay down to have a long-overdue rest.

In comparison with such a story in Mongolia, it was only when I read the Bible that my questions began to be answered comprehensibly in a way that made sense of the world around me, with all its good and bad, beauties and messes. I cannot agree more with Richard Bauckham, who comments that "the Bible tells a story that in some sense encompasses all other human stories, draws them into the meaning that God's story with the world gives them."[1]

Chapters 1 and 2 of Genesis, the first book of the HB, tell us that "in the beginning God created the heavens and the earth." The phrase "the heavens and the earth" includes everything in heaven and on earth, seen and unseen, spiritual and physical, heavenly, and earthly. This creation story climaxes in the creation of humans, giving the details (in chapter 2) of how God created man and woman and gave functions and roles to each. This chapter also tells of the stewardship role he gave to humans in relation to the land, animals, and nature. In the story of forming the first woman out of the first man (Gen

---

1. Richard Bauckham, *Bible and Mission: Christian Mission in a Postmodern World* (Milton Keynes, UK: Paternoster, 2003), 5.

2:21–25), the OT demonstrates how intricately man and woman are connected and how functionally they are to complete each other. In Genesis 2:24 we see the foundational unit of human society – a family with husband and wife, forming one whole body.

1.2. The Nature of the One True God

The HB reveals to us the nature of the one true God, thus enabling us to see how different he is from the gods that humans create. Here I will attempt to show stark contrasts between the nature and character of the God of the Bible on the one hand, and the gods of the nations on the other.

1.2.1. The Singularity of the God of the Bible versus The Multiplicity of Gods in Asia

In Asia, there are many countries where the dominant religion has multiple and sometimes an almost endless number of gods for different purposes and spheres. Hinduism is said to have millions of gods or deities. Buddhism also has a pantheon of gods and deities, depending on the region, and sometimes includes local animistic spirits. Islam is the exception in this regard.

In contrast, the Bible declares that this Creator God is the only God, with no one else besides him. We can find many references in the OT declaring the singularity of the Creator God. For instance, Deuteronomy 4:35 says, "You were shown these things so that you might know that the Lord is God, besides him there is no other." 1 Kings 8:60 proclaims "that all peoples of the earth may know that the Lord is God and there is no other." The singularity of the God of the Bible is loud and clear throughout the Scriptures. In contrast to this singular and one and only God of the Bible, the gods of the nations are created by human hands (e.g. Isa 44:12–20; Jer 10:3–16; Ps 115:2–8).

1.2.2. The Omnipresent and Omnipotent God versus Local Deities

In Mongolia, every mountain or hill is said to be ruled by a god or spirit of that mountain. Those who live within the vicinity of the mountain or who climb to the top are to follow the ritual of daily offering from their morning tea or give honor to the god by putting food or money on the offering pile at the mountain top. This activity of venerating local gods who are said to exercise dominance over the area becomes intense during the Lunar New Year, births, weddings, funerals, and religious holidays. We can find such local gods or deities almost everywhere in Asia, sometimes represented in city symbols. The fact that such deities have a dominant locality tells us that their power is effective mainly in that area or region, therefore limiting their power since they themselves are controlled by higher powers within their hierarchical system. Calling upon the god of another region may even be problematic, causing conflict between gods of different regions.

In comparison with these local deities, the God of the Bible is presented as the One who is present everywhere and who rules over everything. The omnipresent nature of God tells us that he can be anywhere at the same time. For example, Psalm 139:7–12 reminds us that Yahweh is everywhere; we cannot run away from his presence, and we will find no place where he is not there. The omnipresent nature of this God goes with his almighty power – his omnipotence. Because Yahweh is the God of every locality, he rules over everything, and there is no place that is not under his authority. The omnipresent and omnipotent traits of God are distinct but closely related.

1.2.3. Single-hearted Devotion to God versus Veneration of Multiple Gods

The God of the Bible is the only God in existence.[2] Therefore, he summoned Israel to total commitment and single-hearted devotion. This characteristic of God is expressed in the Bible as his jealousy. For example, in Exodus 20:5 and 34:14, Yahweh calls himself "a jealous God" after commanding the Israelites not to worship any other god. God approves when someone shows such single-hearted commitment and devotion to him. In Numbers 25:11, when Eleazar, the son of Aaron, showed such jealousy on God's behalf, the wrath of God was turned away and the plague stopped among the Israelites. The God of the Bible wants total dedication and devotion from humans.

Conversely in many parts of Asia, there seems to be no limit to the number of gods and deities one can worship and venerate. It is presumed that the greater number of gods one worships, for the sake of one's household, tribal ancestry, ethnicity, region, and even occupation, the better the protection and blessing. Worshiping multiple gods at the same time is not prohibited, but even encouraged for practical purposes.

1.2.4. The Image of God in Humans versus the Image of Humans in Gods

In Genesis 1:27, we are told that God created humans in his own image. In other words, humans reflect God and his nature. Out of the whole creation,

---

2. See chapter 2 by Koowon Kim for further discussion of biblical monotheism.

it is only humans who are created in the image of God, thus making humans distinct from the rest of the creation. This uniqueness of human beings is understood in the capacity of being able to communicate with God spiritually, reflecting the character and nature of God in a limited way in our personality and character, while exercising a degree of dominion and rule over the creation. The exact ways and limitations of humans reflecting the image of God can be debated, but humans are certainly created to be like their Creator God in some way.

Opposing this biblical understanding is the reality that the gods and deities of other religions are depicted, shaped, and molded after the image of humans. The gods of Hinduism and Buddhism (as well as the Greek and Roman gods) have many different shapes and bodies, but the common feature among them is that they basically have human-like bodies with hands and feet, either as male or female. In Tibetan Buddhism in Mongolia, all the eight main gods are depicted with human bodies, complete with all the main extremities, either as a monk, a deity with three eyes, male or female, seated or standing, holding things in their hands, or riding an animal. In these gods we can see the reflection of human beings themselves. These gods have their own hierarchical system and spheres of dominion. While lower-status gods have control over certain functions or regions, they also have other gods who exercise control over them.

The Bible explicitly prohibits creating any image as an idol to worship. For example, in Exodus 20:4, Yahweh commands the Israelites, "You shall not make for yourself an image in the form of anything in heaven above or on the earth beneath or in the waters below." Representing God in any such image or replacing him with any human-made idol is what angers God the most. Such an act of equating Yahweh with any humanly created image is an insult and blasphemy against who he is. Israel's repeated behavior of worshiping images and refusal to stop going after the gods of other nations ultimately led them to the lowest points in their history.

1.2.5. *A God Who Is Worshiped with Service versus Gods Who Serve Man's Needs*

In my observation, people in Mongolia worship gods for pragmatic purposes and have a "consumer mentality" towards them. Gods are supposed to bless or help people in specific situations. For instance, in Buddhism, the god of art is worshiped by singers and artists in Mongolia. They will place a picture of this god on their wall and may also place food offerings before it. Worshipers of this god of art have no specific worship rules to follow, but they expect their god to bless them. In other words, gods serve human needs.

On the other hand, the God of the Bible is to be worshiped with service. One of the Hebrew words for worship, *'ābad,* has a range of meaning, but the main idea is to serve and do certain duties, as in offering sacrifices and obeying commands. This aspect is especially evident in the works of the Levites and priests in connection with the worship of God in the tabernacle or temple. The whole tribe of the Levites was dedicated to serve God in this way. The fulfilment of their service in sacrifices and their duties at the temple were considered their worship to God. God gave clear instructions to priests and the Israelites regarding how they were to serve him.

1.3. The Origin of Sin as Humanity's Fundamental Problem

The HB also portrays the source of the great human problem – sin. Every day of our lives, we see problems such as arguments, anger, violence, divorce, drinking, and drugs in individual lives, as well as corruption, turmoil, conflicts, and war in the society. All these human problems have existed, and humans have always sought to find the source of the problem and offer solutions to it. Religion, with its various forms and shapes in different nations, is one way of trying to find the source and solution to this fundamental problem. According to Buddha, existence itself is considered to be suffering. Therefore, escaping from this endless cycle of rebirth requires entering the state of nirvana as the way of escape. Yet paradoxically, "we cannot definitely say that Gautama brought about his own salvation."[3]

On the other hand, the book of Genesis tells us that all human problems go back to the original sin, depicted in the story of Adam and Eve in the garden of Eden. This story of the Fall (Gen 3) adequately explains all human problems in the world. Furthermore, we can see in the same chapter the indication of God's solution to the problem. The full story of God sending his Son Jesus as the Savior and as the promised Messiah begins in the OT and is fully revealed in the NT.

In animistic and Buddhist contexts in Mongolia, everyone will easily accept that they do wrong things in one way or another, almost as if they must do them to survive in life. When it comes to the idea of sin, however, many think that only acts like stealing in a significant way or killing someone fit

---

[3]. R. Pierce Beaver, "The Enlightened One: Buddhism," in *A Lion Handbook: The World's Religions*, ed. Christopher Partridge (Oxford, UK: Lion Publishing, 1992), 228.

this category. The urgency to have their "sinful" conscience cleared is not great and many, sadly, are indifferent about the consequence of sin. The prevalence of sin in society has made people apathetic to their own sins. The root of the problems in society is largely seen as systemic and not so much an issue of the human heart. This is the kind of society that Christians are in, so we are called to make people aware of their sin according to the biblical understanding and to bring biblical solutions to it.

1.4. The Mission of God for the World and Humanity

Chapters 1–11 of Genesis describe the state of human sin and corruption affecting all human beings in their minds, desires, and actions. This universal state requires a universal solution. The seed of God's rescue for this situation is signaled in his announcement to the serpent in Genesis 3:15. Then in Genesis 15, God demonstrably begins to unfold his mission by calling Abram – to bless all the families, tribes, and nations of the earth through him (cf. Gen 12:3). This is God's great mission for the whole world, not just for the nation of Israel but for every nation and tribe on this earth. The HB shows how this mission of God unfolds through Abraham and his descendants, the Israelites. The purpose of God giving his complete "instruction" (i.e. the Hebrew word *tôrâ*) on how to worship him and live as his chosen and distinct people under his covenant, in contrast to other peoples, is so that God's purpose for all nations might be fulfilled. As Christopher Wright has put it, "[T]here is one God at work in the universe and in human history, and . . . this God has a goal, a purpose, a mission that will ultimately be accomplished by the power of God's Word and for the glory of God's name. This is the mission of the biblical God."[4]

By knowing the mission of God – to bring blessing to all nations, including the very ethnic group and nation that we ourselves belong to – we can see the big picture of God's work. The significance of the coming of Jesus Christ, the promised Messiah, into the world in human form becomes clear and important within this broader mission of God towards all nations. The death and resurrection of Jesus are the pivotal points in the purpose of God, because only through Jesus is salvation possible for all nations.

Realizing the grand mission of God through Jesus Christ encourages us in our efforts to bring the gospel more effectively to our own people and

---

4. Christopher J. H. Wright, *The Mission of God: Unlocking the Bible's Grand Narrative* (Downers Grove, IL: InterVarsity, 2007), 64.

nation. At the same time, we see that we are a part of something big, indeed big enough to be global. The mission of God needs to continue until we see the blessing of God in our societies, workplaces, churches, and individual lives. What God started in Israel in the OT and continued through Jesus Christ and his disciples in the NT needs to continue in every place and nation through us, the followers of Jesus Christ. In other words, the passion and responsibility to see the fulfillment of God's mission is now upon everyone who received the baton of the gospel. As Bauckham puts it, "[T]he universal goal of God's purpose for the world presses upon us with a kind of immediacy that impacts the church's life and mission."[5]

On this note, the needs of God's mission in my home country of Mongolia are urgent since Christians currently stand at about only 2 percent of the population. Considering that this growth came only since 1990, it may seem significant, but the church in Mongolia has already seen stagnation during the last few years. We have challenges in a number of areas, particularly in leadership for churches and Christian organizations, discipleship of believers, theological education in the face of cults and false teaching, and effective evangelistic outreaches in the urban and rural contexts of Mongolia.

1.5. The Foundation of Moral Standards for Humanity

God gave to Israel many laws and commandments, and guidance showing them how to be a well-functioning and healthy society. These laws and instructions clearly demonstrated what is good and what should be avoided. In the same way, in these laws we find moral standards for humanity. Today in many societies what should be deemed wrong is openly approved and praised, while what should be considered right and good is devalued and made fun of.

In Mongolia, for example, seventy years of Communist and atheist ideology have seriously damaged traditional values and moral standards. When God is totally out of the picture and no consideration is given to God or deity, moral standards disappear and what is morally good is reimagined to please a godless ideology. Disorder and chaos occur when human beings are the agents to establish moral standards. During the long years of the oppressive Communist regime, lying and cheating in their various shapes and forms were accepted since they were sometimes necessary even to survive. Human life was not valued, and abortion was not seen as killing a human life. Thousands of innocent people were killed for the sake of ideology. This unhealthy attitude

---

5. Bauckham, *Bible and Mission*, 25.

continues today after the collapse of Communism, so much so that if one is able to cheat the system, one is considered smart. Bribery is a common practice, and it is expected on the part of some government officials, medical doctors, tax officers and many others. Pregnant mothers need to give bribes to midwives, nurses, and even cleaners on shift to receive adequate treatment during birth and postnatal care.

In this regard, Wright correctly asserts, "In the Old Testament, however (as in the whole Bible), ethics is fundamentally theological. That is, ethical issues are at every point related to God – to his character, his will, his actions, and his purpose."[6] Biblical ethics thus derives from God, his nature, and character. In other words, when God is in the picture in relation to ethics, he becomes the one who defines moral standards. From the laws and stories in the OT, we can learn the boundaries for good and evil from God's perspective which form the standards for God's people.

1.6. The Story of God's People with Whom We Are Joined

Much of the OT is the story of the Israelites, starting with their forefathers Abraham, Isaac, Jacob, and Jacob's twelve children, who became the founders of their own tribes. Nearly 2000 years of their history show their movements as a people, deliverance from Egypt, establishment in the land of Canaan, development into a kingdom, tragedy of exile, and their return and re-establishment as a people.

Why and in what way does their story matter to us who are ethnically different from them? Why is knowing their story in the OT important when we already have our own histories? These questions are relevant and must be answered coherently. Especially for new believers in Christ, the relevance of the story of the Israelites is a real question. Teaching them the OT can seem like giving them just a history lesson on ancient Israel. Can we not just skip over those stories of the Israelites and speak of our own lives and stories of today?

The importance and relevance of the story of Israel becomes clear when we realize that those stories manifest the same theological realities in our lives and our own experience reflected in them. Those realities are our inherent sinfulness, stubbornness, selfishness, and lust for self-gratification instead of choosing to please God. We have a tendency to shamelessly forget what God has done for us in his salvation, forgiveness, mercy, and provision. The only

---

6. Christopher J. H. Wright, *Old Testament Ethics for the People of God* (Leicester, UK: InterVarsity, 2004), 23.

real difference is that we live in a different time and place. We are just as sinful as the Israelites, just as quick to forget our gracious and saving God, and just as pitiful without him.

At the same time, those stories in the OT show that when Israel cried out to God, he heard them. When Israel was sinking into sin, God saved his people. When Israel was powerless in the face of their enemies, God was powerful over their enemies. When Israel was hopeless in their exile, God gave them hope and even brought them back to their land. When Israel was at the brink of obliteration, God always orchestrated the course of history to deliver them. These stories of God's grace and mercy give us courage and assurance to seek God's help when we are in trouble. If God patiently acted favorably toward his people of Israel, certainly he will do the same for us as Asians who have joined his covenant people.

Because we are foreigners who spiritually "join" OT Israelites, they are our spiritual ancestors and their stories become our stories (cf. Deut 29:14–15; 1 Cor 10:1–6). A tremendous number of lessons can be applied from this story of Israel to our lives today. As "wild olive shoots," we are grafted into the cultivated olive tree and share the benefits of being nourished by this olive tree, which is OT Israel (Rom 11:11–24).

The young Christian church in Mongolia is drawn to these amazing stories of Yahweh's acts in forming Israel as his people. This history supplies us with powerful tools to strengthen the faith of Mongolian Christians in God and illustrates what God can do in our lives today. At the same time, a lack of maturity in the Mongolian church's theological understanding has inclined some congregations to imitate biblical Israel slavishly and follow OT laws like the Sabbath, and to observe feasts and Jewish calendars. It has even led a few to teach about the significance of numbers according to rabbinic traditions. This situation raises the need for proper biblical teaching on how to translate the story of OT Israel for the present day in a place like modern Mongolia, especially in light of the NT era and how Christ fulfilled those OT laws.

2. TRANSLATION AS SCRIPTURE

The second part of this chapter will explore the rationale for Bible translation and how a translation undertaken by ordinary men and women becomes God's word to those receiving it.

2.1. God's Message to All Peoples and Nations

The Bible is God's message to all peoples, and all nations, not just the Israelites. This belief makes a translation of the Scriptures one of the first and crucial steps in spreading this message among people. For many religions, such as Islam and Buddhism, translation of the holy scriptures is not seen as essential. In fact, the Arabic of the Qur'an is considered a holy language, making it untranslatable to other languages so that attempts to translate it are frowned upon. Similarly, in Tibetan Buddhism (the strand that is dominant in Mongolia), the translation of their scriptures is deemed unnecessary, so all prayers and chanting are done in the Tibetan language.

The essence of God's message, however, is that all languages, peoples, and nations may know that Yahweh alone is God and no other (e.g. 2 Kgs 19:19; Isa 37:20; Ezek 36:23), and only in Christ Jesus is there salvation for all nations (Acts 15:11; Phil 2:9–11). This conviction provides the vision for Bible translators to persevere until they see the final product as a reality in the languages they are working in. Bauckham thus sets out the double role of God's acts as revelation to Israel as well as to the nations:

> God makes himself known *as* the God of Israel, in the particular identity he has given himself in choosing this one people as his own, but his acts on his people's behalf make him known at the same time as the one true God of all the earth, whom the nations themselves must also acknowledge.[7]

In Mongolia, Christianity is known as a religion with a holy book. Since Tibetan Buddhism, which has dominated the Mongolian religious scene for centuries now, has many holy books and prayers are requested from those books, there is an ingrained respect for books in Mongolia, especially religious books. Thus, the Bible as a religious book is generally regarded with honor and esteem by the public. While Mongolia also has rich oral traditions of folk tales, fables, and songs, for a religion such as Christianity to have its own authoritative scripture is typical. The long history of the Mongolian script, going back over seven hundred years, contributes to this proper recognition and respect for ancient religious texts.

---

7. Bauckham, *Bible and Mission*, 37, emphasis original.

2.2. God's Speech in the Language of the People

Despite the loftiness of religious traditions and language, it is significant that God reveals himself in the language that people speak and understand. God's holy and reverent word could have been written in a language that had higher status or was considered more "religious." Instead, God spoke to his people and they wrote down his words in the language they spoke. This principle, that God revealed himself and spoke to his people in their common language, also guides and undergirds the age-old task of Bible translation into other languages.

On this note, the Jews of the second and first centuries BCE could no longer fully understand the Hebrew language when they heard it in the synagogues and at religious gatherings. This practical need was the main reason to translate their Hebrew Scriptures into Koine Greek, the common and everyday language of the Mediterranean region. The Jews needed to understand and comprehend the Scriptures in order to appreciate them and live by them. The same is the case for the NT, which was also written in Koine Greek. This has also been the motivation for all the labor of translating the Bible into other languages since then. As Lamin Sanneh puts it, "Christian missionaries assumed that since all cultures and languages are lawful in God's eyes, the rendering of God's word into those languages and cultures is valid and necessary."[8]

In the translation project for the Mongolian Standard Version of the Bible, it is the translation committee's belief that God also desires to speak to Mongolians in their mother tongue. This means we have a God-given responsibility to translate the message of the Bible into today's Mongolian language using the Cyrillic script. In this task, we use the following five principles: (1) to translate from the biblical languages, (2) to be accurate to the source text, (3) to produce a translation that has natural language, (4) to make it understandable to readers, and (5) to make it good for hearing. Following these principles gives us assurance that God is speaking to Mongolians in their language. Indeed, the fact that God desires to speak to people in their own languages brings to my mind a deaf Mongolian Christian's testimony that God spoke to her in a dream through Mongolian sign language.

2.3. All Languages as Ordained Recipients of God's Message

All languages are capable of transmitting God's message. The story of Babel in Genesis 11 is the first exclusive statement about the use of language for human endeavors. Even though the diversification of languages is God's response to

---

8. Lamin Sanneh, "Pluralism and Christian Commitment," *ThTo* 45 (April 1988): 27.

human arrogance and self-deification, God also uses this instrument to reveal himself. This desire of God can be seen at Pentecost in Acts 2, where multitudes who gathered from different nations heard the disciples speak in their native languages and understood God's message. In discussing the theology of language, Craig Bartholomew comments, "Thus Babel does *not* present the diversity of languages as judgment, but as God-given. The judgment in terms of (mis)communication is given expression through language but derives, not from structural problems with language, but from humans seeking idolatrous centers for their lives."[9]

Because all languages are God-given, they possess the means and sufficiency to be beneficial for God's purposes. In speaking of the use of local languages in mission, Sanneh comments, "It is clear that in employing vernacular languages for translation, missionaries saw these languages as more than arbitrary devices, but as endowed with divine significance, so that they may substitute completely for the language of revelation."[10] All languages are capable of conveying God's message since they were ordained by God to be channels of revelation to speakers of those languages. Following this theological principle, the language that receives a Bible translation becomes a "biblical" language since it conveys and is fully capable of transmitting the message of the Bible.

2.4. Translation as the Means for God's Message to People

God did not demand that all other nations learn the Hebrew language to know him, but in his providence ordained ordinary men and women as translators to be the channel of his message for humanity. As Andrew Walls says regarding the theological foundation of Bible translation, "God chose translation as his mode of action for the salvation of humanity."[11] This underscores the importance and responsibility of the task of Bible translation. Just as God chose a variety of people with their human personality, occupation, education, and linguistic skills to give his word in the Hebrew language, God continues to use ordinary men and women to make himself known in languages through this human but God-ordained process of Bible translation. Although the Bible has been the

---

9. Craig G. Bartholomew, "Before Babel and After Pentecost: Language, Literature and Biblical Interpretation," in *After Pentecost: Language and Biblical Interpretation*, ed. Craig G. Bartholomew, Scripture and Hermeneutics Series, vol. 2 (Carlisle, UK: Paternoster, 2001), 148–49, emphasis original.
10. Sanneh, "Pluralism and Christian Commitment," 30.
11. Andrew F. Walls, *The Missionary Movement in Christian History* (Maryknoll, NY: Orbis, 1996), 26.

most translated book in history, beginning with the Septuagint in the second century BCE, the process of translation will continue endlessly, since when one generation's need is met, the need arises again for the next generation even within the same language. It is wonderful in this regard to see the acceleration of Bible translation in our generation. For example, the United Bible Societies aim to complete one thousand two hundred translations over the next twenty years, making the Scriptures available to six hundred million people.

Translation as the means for God's message can be illustrated by the use of the term for "God" in Mongolian. In the Mongolian language, both our present translation project as well as most of the historic translations and revisions have used the word *Burkhan*.[12] This is a general word meaning "deity" or "God" and can be employed in various religions and contexts. The extent of meaning and usage of the word can be compared to generic words like "God" in English, "Allah" in Arabic, "Theos" in Greek, and "Elohim" in Hebrew. No single faith or religion can claim exclusive ownership of such words since they are naturally a part of a given language. Even when a term was coined by a specific religion, there is no guarantee that the usage of the term will stay only within that religion, since it could evolve to include other meanings over time. The origin of the Mongolian word *Burkhan* is debated, for instance, and the meaning is specified only by the context. While Buddhist lamas use this word to mean "enlightened one," other people use it to refer to a deity (as someone spiritual, great and in authority), or even their mothers for whom they have great respect. Despite some shortfalls, then, Mongolian Christians also use it to refer to the God of the Bible since it is a term that best communicates the notion of God or deity and is understood with that meaning by the Mongolian public. The context makes the reference unmistakably clear. Although the earliest attested translation of the Bible into the Mongolian language dates to over seven hundred years ago,[13] the hiatus of the Christian church in Mongolia (especially in the twentieth century, until 1990) means that we do not have a continuous story of Bible translation which forms our view of the God of the Bible. Instead, we are building anew the foundation for understanding him.

---

12. Bayarjargal Garamtseren, "Re-Establishment of the Christian Church in Mongolia: The Mongolian Standard Version Translation by National Christians," *UNIOCC* 2 (October 2016): 49–66.

13. Bayarjargal Garamtseren, "A History of Bible Translation in Mongolian," *BT* 60 (2009): 215–23.

2.5. Translation Under the Work of God's Spirit and Through Faith in Christ Jesus

Bible translation is both a human as well as a spiritual work of God. This principle is true already for the Bible in its original languages. For the original Bible which was written in Hebrew, Aramaic, and Greek, humans wrote down words in those languages under the inspiration and guidance of the Spirit of God. God used and worked through the humanness of their literary skill and abilities in thinking, speaking, and writing. When Bible translators take their task under the guidance and enabling of the Spirit of God by the same principle, the translated text becomes not just another book, but the Scriptures, the word of God. Bible translators are therefore called to make their best effort in producing a translation that is faithful to the source text, but at the same time understandable, clear, and as effective as the Hebrew Scriptures were for their original readers and hearers. The process of a translation of the Bible becoming Scripture is the outcome of the diligent toil of Bible translators in planning, translating verse by verse, reviewing, checking, testing, revising, more testing, and revising repeatedly until the text is ready to be delivered to the readers and hearers. This whole process never stops because the need for refinements never ends.

Besides the linguistic dimension, the spiritual dimension of faith is crucial in understanding and receiving the translated text as God's word to ourselves. Without faith, the Bible will merely be a collection of good and strange books at best, without much meaning and application to our lives. What is required is faith in the God of the Bible through Jesus Christ, the Son of God. As we Christians read a translation while exercising faith in God, the Holy Spirit opens our eyes to understand the Scriptures and to speak them into our lives. What is more, God gives empowerment through his Spirit to live out what his word calls us to live by and to be his witness in this world. As Raymond Van Leeuwen rightly says, "[O]n the 'heart' level, without the Holy Spirit, Scripture is *de facto* foreign to a humanity in rebellion."[14]

What, then, are the obstacles for Mongolian Christians in accepting the Bible as God's word? I can think of several. First, the lack of a good, literary translation of the Bible in the modern Mongolian language has been a challenge for Christians, and even for non-Christians. While the literal translation

---

14. Raymond C. Van Leeuwen, "On Bible Translation and Hermeneutics," in *After Pentecost: Language and Biblical Interpretation*, ed. Craig G. Bartholomew, Scripture and Hermeneutics Series, vol. 2 (Carlisle, UK: Paternoster, 2001), 298.

currently used often makes the Bible hard to understand, the overly paraphrased alternative translation lacks correspondence with the original languages. We are working to provide a solution to this situation by the production of the Mongolian Standard Version, which is expected to be completed by 2025.

A second factor is the low frequency of Scripture reading by Christians. The general movement in Mongolian society towards digital and visual technologies, the busyness of life in both urban and rural settings, and attraction to other forms of entertainment like social networking and online content all contribute to this unhappy trend. Third, a lack of good resources and reference materials in Mongolian (with only a handful of reference books and a single NT commentary) weakens interest in reading the Bible with understanding and proper application. There is an urgent need to explain Israelite culture and customs as well as the main events in the history of Israel. Fourth, the spiritually young leaders of the growing Mongolian church have much to learn about what it means to take the Bible seriously as God's word, both as a community and as individuals in our everyday spiritual walk with God.

CONCLUSION

The Hebrew Bible, originally written in Hebrew and Aramaic by the descendants of Abraham, can undoubtedly be claimed as the Scriptures, or God's word, to all people from all nations because it reveals all humans as God's creation. The OT proclaims the nature of the one true God whom we otherwise would not be able to know. As this Bible becomes God's word all through translation into various languages, it bears the same message of God to us as well. This is based on the conviction that the Hebrew Scriptures are God's message to all peoples and nations, both Israelites and non-Israelites, and thus translations are God-ordained means to deliver that message through faith in Christ Jesus and by the work of the Spirit. Therefore, both the Hebrew Scriptures as well as their translation into other languages are Scripture for us, God's word in human words, akin to two sides of a coin.

REFERENCES

Bartholomew, Craig G. "Before Babel and After Pentecost: Language, Literature and Biblical Interpretation." In *After Pentecost: Language and Biblical Interpretation*, edited by Craig G. Bartholomew, Scripture and Hermeneutics Series. Vol. 2, 131–70. Carlisle, UK: Paternoster, 2001.

Bauckham, Richard. *Bible and Mission: Christian Mission in a Postmodern World*. Milton Keynes, UK: Paternoster, 2003.

Beaver, R. Pierce. "The Enlightened One: Buddhism." In *A Lion Handbook: The World's Religions*, edited by Christopher Partridge. Oxford, UK: Lion Publishing, 1992.

Garamtseren, Bayarjargal. "A History of Bible Translation in Mongolian." *The Bible Translator* 60 (2009): 215–23.

———. "Re-Establishment of the Christian Church in Mongolia: The Mongolian Standard Version Translation by National Christians." *UNIOCC* 2 (October 2016): 49–66.

Sanneh, Lamin. "Pluralism and Christian Commitment." *Theology Today* 45 (April 1988): 21–33.

Van Leeuwen, Raymond C. "On Bible Translation and Hermeneutics." In *After Pentecost: Language and Biblical Interpretation*, edited by Craig G. Bartholomew, Scripture and Hermeneutics Series. Vol. 2, 284–311. Carlisle, UK: Paternoster, 2001.

Walls, Andrew F. *The Missionary Movement in Christian History*. Maryknoll, NY: Orbis, 1996.

Wright, Christopher J. H. *Old Testament Ethics for the People of God*. Leicester, UK: InterVarsity, 2004.

———. *The Mission of God: Unlocking the Bible's Grand Narrative*. Downers Grove, IL: InterVarsity, 2007.

CHAPTER 2

YAHWEH AND OTHER GODS

Koowon Kim

The Old Testament declares its belief in Yahweh as the one and only God (Deut 4:35, 39; 6:4; 32:39). The prophet Isaiah proclaims the truth of monotheism in a statement of God himself: "I am the Lord, and there is no other; apart from me there is no God" (Isa 45:5). Judaism and Christianity both accept the OT as the word of God and thus are monotheistic religions. The Talmudic sages also say, "Anyone who denies the existence of other gods is called Jewish" (Babylonian Talmud, *Megillah* 13a.). Likewise, the Christian doctrine of the Trinity has been affirmed and understood as a form of monotheism despite heretical efforts to interpret it otherwise. Hence, it is no wonder that the cessation of ancestor sacrifice has been regarded in Korea (among other places in East Asia) as the mark of true conversion ever since the very first generation of Christians.[1]

A close reading of the Hebrew Bible shows, however, that some biblical authors and ancient Israelites seem to have acknowledged the existence, if not the power, of other gods. It may thus be argued that the divine Author himself accommodated the polytheistic environment of the ancient Near East in some respects while guiding the Israelites toward the truth of monotheism. For example, what is the identity of the heavenly beings (*běnê 'ĕlōhîm*, lit. "the sons of God"; Ps 29:1; Job 1:6, often translated "angels"), who recall the Canaanite pantheon that includes the sons of El and Asherah? This goes to show that the question of monotheism is not as simple as it might seem at first.

Two caveats are in order before we delve into the surprisingly complicated matter of monotheism. First, the term *monotheism* is actually of modern origin and originally served as a contrast to *polytheism* and *atheism* rather than being merely a term for belief in the existence of a single God.[2] However, the

---

1. Bae Choon Sup, "Ancestor Worship in Korea and Africa: Social Function of Religious Phenomenon?" (PhD diss., University of Pretoria, 2004), 71.
2. The term *monotheism* was first coined by Henry More in the seventeenth century. In the early nineteenth century, the term appeared in print for the third time to refer to "pure" monotheism as opposed to Trinitarian monotheism (Laurel C. Schneider, *Beyond Monotheism: A Theology of Multiplicity* (New York: Routledge, 2008), 19, 211).

OT's own understanding of "monotheism" does not necessarily exclude the existence of other beings with some sort of divine or semi-divine status, since the vast differences between Yahweh and other deities are still portrayed more as a matter of quality than number (without precluding the latter). Benjamin Sommer defines the monotheism of the Hebrew Bible in the following terms which will be adopted in our discussion:

> What distinguishes the Bible from other religious texts known from the ancient world is not that the Bible denies that Marduk and Baal and Zeus exist – it does not – but that it insists that Yhwh is qualitatively different from all other deities: Yhwh is infinitely more powerful. Monotheism, then, is the belief that one supreme being exists, whose will is sovereign over all other beings. These other beings may include some who live in heaven and who are in the normal course of events immortal; but they are unalterably subservient to the one supreme being, except insofar as that being voluntarily relinquishes a measure of control by granting other beings free will.[3]

As we will see, this definition of monotheism on the Hebrew Bible's own terms differs in important ways from the modern definition of "the doctrine of belief that there is only one God,"[4] which can be anachronistic when applied to ancient Israel's faith in Yahweh.

Second, our discussion of monotheism will pay attention to its historical development in the OT as well. This should not, however, be a stumbling block to anyone with a high view of Scripture since God's revelation has always been a gradual and progressive process. Though the OT clearly portrays the God of Israel as a singular sovereign deity, it also affirms that the actual practice of monotheism took a long time to take root in the lives of ancient Israelites. God may be compared in this regard to a patient teacher who is willing to stand in his students' shoes to impart a critical but difficult lesson. The OT reveals not only God's plan of redemption, but also the nature of God, gradually and progressively. In our presentation of OT monotheism, we will seek to do justice both to the canonical presentation of Israelite monotheism (Sections 1 and 3) and to the process of its historical development (Section 2). Similarly, Asian

---

3. Benjamin D. Sommer, "Monotheism," in *The Hebrew Bible: A Critical Companion*, ed. John Barton (Princeton, NJ: Princeton University Press, 2009), 241.
4. This is the first entry given by the *Oxford English Dictionary* ("Monotheism, *n.*," OED Online, May 2022, Oxford University Press, https://www.oed.com/view/Entry/121673).

Yahweh and Other Gods

Christians who live in polytheistic cultures can relate to ancient Israelites in a polytheistic environment who also struggled to understand what it meant to believe in Yahweh as the one God.

1. WORSHIP OF ONE SUPREME GOD

As noted earlier, monotheism in the OT is a belief in and worship of one supreme God, who is ontologically distinct from and rules with ultimate power over other divine or mortal beings. The most celebrated passage for this doctrine is found in the so-called "Shema" of Deut 6:4–5: "Hear, O Israel: Yahweh is our God, Yahweh is one. You shall love Yahweh your God with all your heart and with all your soul and with all your might" (author's rendering).

Scholars observe that "love" in the Shema conveys the idea of loyalty, as in the Hittite treaty documents.[5] Also, the confession that "Yahweh is our God, Yahweh is one" seems to provide two related reasons for the Israelites to stay loyal to Yahweh alone. First, it denotes a special relationship between Yahweh and the Israelites. Note that the clause "Yahweh is our God" recalls the covenant formula, "I will be your God, and you shall be my people" (Jer 7:23).[6] The concept of covenantal loyalty assumes choice, which in turn assumes multiple options – just as Yahweh chose Israel out of many nations, so Israel should choose Yahweh instead of other gods. This supports the idea that OT monotheism cannot be reduced to denying the existence of other gods. Hence, the clause "Yahweh is one" is better taken as connoting Yahweh's uniqueness.[7] It may refer to Yahweh's special relationship with Israel, one in which Israel is "the one nation on earth" for Yahweh (cf. 2 Sam 7:23). Alternately, it may refer to the ontological differences, qualitatively speaking, between Yahweh and other gods.

---

5. William L. Moran was the first scholar to propose a political meaning for "love" in ANE treaty documents. Cf. Moran, "The Ancient Near Eastern Background of the Love of God in Deuteronomy," *CBQ* 25 (1963): 77–87. For the affective dimensions of the term "love," see Susan Ackerman, "The Personal is Political: Covenant and Affectionate Love (*'āhēb, 'ahăbâ*) in the Hebrew Bible," *VT* 52 (2002): 437–58; and Jacqueline E. Lapsley, "Feeling Our Way: Love for God in Deuteronomy," *CBQ* 65 (2003): 350–69.

6. The covenant formula is also reminiscent of God's promise, "I will be with you" (Exod 3:12; Josh 1:5; Judg 6:16; Isa 43:2). For the study of the formula itself, see Seock-Tae Sohn, "'I Will Be Your God and You Will Be My People': The Origin and Background of the Covenant Formula," in *Ki Baruch Hu: Ancient Near Eastern, Biblical, and Judaic Studies in Honor of Baruch A. Levine*, eds. Robert Chazan, William W. Hallo, and Lawrence H. Schiffman (Winona Lake, IN: Eisenbrauns, 1999), 355–72.

7. Hebrew *'eḥād* can be glossed as "unique."

Deuteronomy 32:8–9 repeats the same idea in mythopoetic language. Yahweh is here described as the "Most High" (*'elyôn*), namely, the head of the heavenly council who assigns "the sons of God" to the nations. Each nation is permitted to worship the one god that Yahweh assigns to them. As for the Israelites, however, Yahweh makes himself available as their one God.[8] The verses read as follows:

> When the Most High gave the nations their inheritance,
>   when he divided all mankind,
> he set up boundaries for the peoples
>   according to the number of the sons of God.[9]
> For the LORD's portion is his people,
>   Jacob his allotted inheritance.

What is significant here is that Israel's *monolatrous*[10] worship of Yahweh is not on par with that of the other nations' monolatrous worship of their gods, because Yahweh is not only Israel's national god, but also the supreme deity of the universe who determines the fates of other nations and their gods. As shown in detail below in Section 2, it is in this sense that Israel's monolatrous worship of Yahweh is also monotheistic for recognizing a singular supreme deity, whereas that of other nations is polytheistic. A monotheistic monolatrist "worships only one God because that God is unique in holding ultimate power."[11] A polytheistic monolatrist, on the other hand, worships a single deity while recognizing the genuine, though not always superior, powers of other gods. The creation story in Genesis 1 underscores the supreme power of Yahweh as the Creator.

The creation account in Genesis culminates with the Creator resting on the seventh day (Gen 2:2). This divine rest confirms that the God worthy of Israel's worship is indeed the king of the universe, and also provides a theological justification for instituting Sabbath worship in ancient Israel (Exod 20:11). On the basis of ancient Near Eastern parallels, John Walton demonstrates that the Creator's rest is equivalent to his enthronement as the ruler of the universe

---

8. Cf. "Yahweh is our God" in Deuteronomy 6:4.
9. On the rationale for this rendering which follows the Septuagint, see Michael S. Heiser, *The Unseen Realm* (Bellingham, WA: Lexham Press, 2014), 113.
10. This term refers to worship offered to a single deity, as opposed to the traditional emphasis of monotheism as the *existence* of a single deity.
11. Sommer, "Monotheism," 242.

that he has just created.¹² The six-day creation account is, at the same time, crafted in a manner that underscores the absolute chasm between the Creator and his creatures in both ontology and power.

The notion of creation by *fiat* (the Latin term for "let there be") is a case in point. First, it affirms the Creator's sovereignty. Unlike Egyptian Ptah's creation by speech¹³ or a Chinese creator's act of creation by shouting, creation by *fiat* is couched in the command-obedience structure of Genesis 1. In other words, it is designed to proclaim that the universe came into being in obedience to God's sovereign will. No such theology is found in Egyptian or Chinese myths. Ptah's creation by speech is nothing more than what may be called "divine naming" by which the fates of individual creatures are determined. The creation by shouting in a Chinese myth is intended as a veiled criticism of incest between a mother and son.¹⁴ In one myth prevalent among the Miao people in Yunnan province, a mother and son who survive the primeval flood are said to shout the rest of humans into existence.¹⁵ Second, *fiat* creation, which assumes God's incorporeality, emphasizes the ontological gulf between the Creator and the creature. The Creator in Genesis 1 is not described as a physical being with vocal cords or hands; rather, he is Spirit (cf. Gen 1:2). His words, or his disembodied voice, may be imagined as a movement of his *rûaḥ* ("breath/spirit").¹⁶ In summary, monotheism in the OT has two sides to it. The first is the idea that a single God rules everything in the world with ultimate power, and the second is the notion of God's incorporeality.¹⁷ The *fiat* of creation manifests both these two aspects of monotheism.

God's ontological uniqueness and power that inform biblical monotheism are best reinforced in some of the passages that critical scholars tend to (mis)interpret as examples of polytheistic features in Israelite religion. For instance, Psalm 29:1 and Job 1:1 mention the heavenly beings (*bĕnê 'ĕlōhîm*, "the sons of God") as members of the *divine council*, a concept that recalls the Canaanite

---

12. John H. Walton, *Ancient Near Eastern Thought and the Old Testament* (Grand Rapids, MI: Baker Academic, 2006), 157–58.
13. James P. Allen, "From the 'Memphite Theology' (1.15)," in *Context of Scripture*, vol. 1, *Canonical Composition from the Biblical World*, eds. W. W. Hallo and K. L. Younger Jr., vol. 1 (Leiden: Brill, 1997), 21–23.
14. A similar taboo against incest appears in another Chinese myth of human creation by a brother-sister marriage. Cf. Lihui Yang and Deming An, *Handbook of Chinese Mythology* (Santa Barbara, CA: ABC-Clio, 2005), 68.
15. Yang and An, *Handbook of Chinese Mythology*, 21.
16. For the relationship between spirit and word, see Section 4 below.
17. James L. Kugel, *The Great Shift: Encountering God in Biblical Times* (Boston, MA: Houghton Mifflin Harcourt, 2017), 163–69.

pantheon which is also composed of the sons of El. However, the divine council in the OT differs from its Canaanite counterpart at crucial points. On the one hand, El, the head of the Ugaritic pantheon, shares the trait of divinity with other members of the council. This is intimated by the fact that they are literally El's children born of Asherah, his consort. Further, El's children challenge and even threaten their father to do their bidding.[18]

On the other hand, Yahweh stands in a totally different relationship with the divine members of his council. Yahweh does not consult with them but rather commands them; he never allows the "sons of God" to challenge him. Further, they are ontologically different from Yahweh. They are much closer to humans than to Yahweh. The fact that prophets are allowed to be present alongside the heavenly beings in the divine council (cf. 1 Kgs 22; Isa 6) underscores that humans and these gods are essentially on par with one another in their ontological distance from Yahweh.[19] Furthermore, God casts out from his council the gods who do not uphold his just and good ways and even relegates them to the status of mere mortals (Ps 82:6–8).

The polytheistic motif of *Chaoskampf* (Germ. "chaos-struggle") is also redirected in the Hebrew Bible to accentuate monotheistic belief in Yahweh. The author of Genesis 1, for instance, diminishes the common Canaanite motif of a cosmic battle between gods to a distant allusion. It is as if to say that either there are no other gods that Yahweh must defeat, or that the power of Yahweh is so overwhelming that the other gods dare not challenge him. Even the poems that are more explicit about Yahweh's conflict with sea monsters (Isa 27:1; Ps 74:13–15; Job 41:1–11) stand apart from their ancient Near Eastern counterparts – they do not describe a genuine battle between gods of equal status, but a doomed revolt against a supreme deity who is already in charge. Unlike Baal and Marduk who struggle with their enemies to ascend to the top of the pantheon, Yahweh suppresses his enemies without difficulty.[20] Psalm 104:26 extends this idea to the extreme by saying that Yahweh created Leviathan the sea-monster to play with it like a toy.

As has been shown, OT monotheism concerns one supreme God who is ontologically distinct from other beings and rules over them with absolute power. The Israelites are commanded to render their loyalty exclusively to him

---

18. See the episode in the Baal Cycle where Anat, Baal's sister, threatens El to build Baal's temple (Dennis Pardee, "The Ba'lu Myth" in *Context of Scripture*, 1:241–74).
19. Pardee, 167.
20. Sommer, "Monotheism," 257.

alone. Archaeological evidence shows that most Israelites did indeed solely worship Yahweh. According to J. H. Tigay, the names of ancient Israelites found in the Hebrew inscriptions are mostly Yahwistic in having a shortened form of "Yahweh" as a *theophoric* element such as Abi*yahu*, Beni*yahu*, and Hanani*yahu*.[21] This preponderance of Yahwistic names indicates that monolatrous, if not exclusively monotheistic, Yahwism was the normative religion in ancient Israel. Although the implications of these theophoric names are not always conclusive (since a name with a form of "Yahweh" may not reflect its owner's actual practice of religion), prophetic warnings against idolatry clearly betoken the widespread prevalence of idolatry and syncretism among the Israelites.

2. THE HISTORICAL DEVELOPMENT OF YAHWISM

The Bible depicts Yahweh as ontologically unique. He is the God of eternity (Gen 21:33). Unlike his creatures, his being has no beginning or end (Isa 40:18; cf. Rev 1:8). But this may not always have been how Yahweh was conceived and perceived by ancient people such as the Israelites, since historians of religions have found traces of Yahwism in other parts of the ancient Near East.[22] The Hebrew Bible, for example, says that the Israelites were ignorant of the personal name "Yahweh" (usually translated "the LORD") until Moses introduced it to them (Exod 6:2–3). Hence, it might seem contradictory to say that Yahweh is both an *eternal* deity but also that the *historical* understanding of "Yahweh" underwent development as he revealed himself.

2.1. Convergence of Divine Aspects in the OT's Portrayal of Yahweh

On this note, the OT's portrayal of Yahweh incorporates various names, titles, and attributes of El, the Canaanite deity who was known as the creator of the universe, the patriarch of gods as well as humans, and the head of the divine council. Like El, Yahweh is also characterized as being old and wise, kind and compassionate.[23] Yahweh's mobile shrine, the Tabernacle, also recalls depictions

---

21. J. H. Tigay, *You Shall Have No Other Gods: Israelite Religion in the Light of Hebrew Inscriptions* (Atlanta, GA: Scholars Press, 1986), 37–41.
22. For a survey of this topic, see Theodore J. Lewis, *The Origin and Character of God: Ancient Israelite Religion Through the Lens of Divinity* (Oxford: Oxford University Press, 2020), 227–34.
23. For El's various characteristics as incorporated by Yahweh, see Mark Smith, *The Early History of God: Yahweh and the Other Deities in Ancient Israel* (Grand Rapids, MI: Eerdmans, 2002), 32–43.

of El's house as made of cloth. In fact, the patriarchal narratives of Genesis characterize Yahweh as a local manifestation of El when he reveals himself in different places such as El Olam (Beersheba), El Elyon (Salem = Jerusalem), El Bethel (Bethel), etc.[24] This rich convergence of features must have occurred long before the time of the earliest biblical authors, since Yahweh and El (= Elohim) are never described as separate deities in the OT.

Indeed, it seems that early Israelites may have been El worshipers. Notice, first, that the eponymous name of "Isra*el*" has El rather than Yahweh as its theophoric element. Also, Jacob named Shechem, the city of his residence, as "El, Elohe Israel" (Gen 33:20). Even God tells Moses that he had been known as "El Shaddai" (typically translated "God Almighty"), not Yahweh, at the time of patriarchs (Exod 6:3). This is puzzling at first since there are many passages in Genesis where biblical characters directly mention Yahweh (Gen 3:1; 14:22; 26:22). However, they are likely to be a sort of anachronism since all the biblical texts were edited at a time when Yahweh was already worshiped as the only God of Israel. It was natural for the final compilers of the OT to retroject the worship of Yahweh to the earliest time, even to Adam and Eve, in order to reinforce the theological continuity of belief in Yahweh as the singular supreme deity.[25]

Finally, Yahweh is not only the patron God of Israel who meets the needs of the Israelite clan, but also a righteous god over the nations. Yahweh identifies himself frequently in the OT as the deity who had brought them out of slavery (e.g. Exod 20:2). This act of liberation was done before he reestablished any formal relationship with Israel. He did it out of compassion for the oppressed (cf. Exod. 2:23–24). Noteworthy is that this act "became indicative of how Israel was to treat slaves and other groups outside the fixed structures of power."[26] In other words, Yahweh has been an ethically oriented god since his appearance in redemptive history. No wonder that Yahweh was the only

---

24. Further, Israelite place-names, mostly dating from the second millennium BCE, appear to confirm that the early Israelites worshiped God by the name "El" until Yahweh was fully identified with El. These place-names are constructed with various divine elements, such as El, Baal, Anat, but never with Yahweh. See Thomas Römer, *The Invention of God* (Cambridge, MA: Harvard University Press, 2015), 86.
25. Lewis, *The Origin and Character of God*, 83–85. Also see R. W. L. Moberly, *The Old Testament of the Old Testament: Patriarchal Narratives and Mosaic Yahwism*, OBT (Minneapolis, MN: Fortress, 1992), 36.
26. Patrick D. Miller, *The Religion of Ancient Israel* (Louisville, KY: Westminster John Knox, 2000), 7.

god in the ancient Near East who promulgated the law, and that Yahweh's law reflects his enduring concern for the marginalized and powerless.[27]

Yahweh's story of moving with a new people to a new land is echoed by a story of the Japanese storm god Susanowo. Just like their ancient Near Eastern counterparts, storm gods in East Asia were the most dynamic and ambitious of gods. Not content with the status quo, they dared to challenge the hierarchy of their pantheon. In Japanese mythology, Susanowo was not satisfied with his inheritance and defied his father Inazagi's command to rule the coastal plain. This disobedience led to his exile from the divine realm. Once he arrived at a certain place called Torikami, he rose to the occasion to slay an evil serpent with seven heads who had harassed an old couple by asking for their daughters as sacrifice. As a way of thanking Susanowo, the old couple, later found to be patron gods of that town, built a palace for him so that he could rule in their city. Interestingly, it is unclear if Susanowo's rule was just and fair. After all, the reason he killed the serpent was not because of his sense of justice, nor out of compassion, but only because he had fallen in love with one of the daughters. Unlike Yahweh, Susanowo was not a righteous god.

In sum, there is both biblical and archaeological evidence to warrant the hypothesis that Yahweh was first identified as the personal deity of the patriarchs who incorporated aspects of El and Baal, the chief gods of Canaanite religion. More than this, however, Yahweh also manifested himself both as a distinct national god of Israel as well as an ethical deity who cares for the underprivileged.

3. MONOTHEISM IN PRACTICE

We have thus far examined the theological framework of monotheism in the OT and traced the historical development of the Israelites' understanding of Yahweh. It is now time to reflect upon the practical implications of monotheism on both the theological and historical levels.

3.1. Word and Spirit

Monotheism in the OT is characterized by the ontological gap between Yahweh and other divine or mortal beings. Yahweh's righteous rule with ultimate power is the consequence of this absolute distinction between Creator and creature. In order that the almighty God may rule justly, however, he should be all wise, and for him to know everything, he should be present everywhere all

---

27. The typical lawgivers in the ancient Near East were kings rather than deities.

the time. That is why God in a monotheistic system is typically characterized with three kinds of *omni-* (Lat. "all") attributes: *omnipotence, omniscience* and *omnipresence*. However, the idea of an omnipresent god was probably unheard of for ancient people who always imagined their gods to be present in the form of images enshrined in their city temples. In other words, divine presence was always manifested as physical and local.

This idea is reflected in ancient myths where gods appear in human or animal forms. For example, Pangu was a Chinese creation deity who was a giant and who emerged from the cosmic egg. When he died, his giant body formed the world, each part becoming one of its elements. Yu, founder of the first civilized state, Xia, in China, is said to have lived among the people while assuming a human form. Sometimes, he changed his shape to that of a bear so that no one could recognize him. If gods must assume a physical form in this world, however, they cannot be present everywhere, and they certainly cannot be present in a city where their images are not enshrined.

However, one of the fundamental tenets of monotheism is that of divine omnipresence. This means that Yahweh's mode of presence must be non-physical; in other words, spiritual. Yahweh can be everywhere all the time because of his spiritual mode of presence in the world. Hence, Yahweh's omnipresence demands that the mode of his presence be spiritual. It is interesting to note that references to the Spirit of God occur predominantly in the oracles of the OT prophets who were strong advocates of monotheism (e.g. Isa 42:1; Ezek 36:27; Hag 2:5; Zech 4:6; cf. Joel 2:29).

All this has important implications for the practice of monotheism. The *spiritual* mode of Yahweh's presence is closely related to the *verbal* mode of his revelation. This synergy is beautifully illustrated in 1 Kings 19 when Yahweh reveals himself neither as wind, nor as earthquake, nor as fire, but as the sound of thin silence (vv. 11–12). Yahweh stands apart from the gods of polytheistic religions who reveal themselves through the various elements of nature. The Hebrew phrase rendered "the sound of thin silence" (*qôl děmāmâ daqqâ*, "still small voice" in KJV) is an oxymoron that the biblical author uses to express both the non-physical, spiritual mode of divine presence ("silence") as well as the verbal mode of divine revelation ("sound").

In OT monotheism, then, God is with his people in spirit and communicates with them in word. It is noteworthy that there is more than a metaphorical association between God's spirit and the words breathed out by God, because Hebrew *rûaḥ* can mean both "breath" and "spirit." It is no coincidence, therefore, that the final forms of biblical books began to be fixed in writing during the exilic period of monotheism. Thus, the full turn toward monotheism coincides with the dawn of the religion of the book. Since God reveals himself in words, the practical piety of monotheism devotes itself more to the study of God's words rather than attending to temple rituals. In other words, godly living is no longer a matter of attending to images in the temple. In a monotheistic system, the temple is not the house of images any longer, but it functions as a "house of prayer" where words go up to the heaven like the smoke of sacrifice (Isa 56:7; cf. 1 Kgs 8:29–30). Instead of icon- or temple-related rituals, piety is equated to studying the words breathed out by God and living by God's spirit who equips his people for every good work (cf. Exod 31:3; Num 14:24; see also 2 Tim 3:16–17). This shift in the idea of religious piety was ideal for a Jewish diaspora in exile that lived in places far removed from the temple. Hence, it is unsurprising that the first time in biblical history the people of Yahweh met in one place for the sole purpose of studying his laws was when the entire community met in Persian Judea (Neh 8).

Asians familiar with the Chinese classics may relate to this sort of monotheism. Mencius (ca. 372–289 BCE), the Chinese philosopher and political thinker, said that there were two virtues that distinguished him from his contemporaries. One is *zhi yan* ("knowing the words") and the other is *hao ran zhi qi* ("very broad spirit"). Although what Mencius meant by *zhi yan* is to discern other people's words, one may justifiably apply *zhi yan* to studying God's words as well since God is the ultimate "Other." *Hao ran zhi qi,* by contrast, was explained by Mencius as a state of mind that can be gradually achieved by accumulating small but righteous deeds every day. This may also be applicable to the monotheistic life of daily obedience to the Spirit. Thus, there are certain points of similarity between the piety of biblical monotheism and Asian moral virtues.[28]

---

28. According to James Legge (1815–1897), a Victorian missionary to China, the Chinese were originally monotheists before they succumbed to idolatrous worship and divination. He held that the God whom the Chinese served was the same as the God of Christianity. Legge went on to argue that the name *Shangdi* does not simply refer to the highest deity but to the personal God who "created heaven and earth, ruled the world, endowed human beings with good nature, revealed himself to the ancient Chinese, heard their prayers and was worshipped by the Chinese people." For this citation and the debates about Chinese names for God, see Sung-Deuk Oak, "Competing Chinese Names for God: The Chinese Term Question and Its Influence upon Korea," *Journal of Korean Religions* 3 (2012): 89–115 (97).

3.2. Covenant for All Humanity

Most *monolatrous* systems are informed and yet limited by the exclusive relationship between a god and its patron nation. Most of the gods in these systems have national or territorial jurisdictions beyond which they have no power. Ashur and Marduk, who became quasi-monotheistic gods in the Assyrian and Babylonian empires, are the exceptions that prove the rule.[29] *Monotheistic* systems, by contrast, are universal for including all nations. Yahweh is both an omnipotent God whose jurisdiction has no limits and a compassionate God who allows all nations to come, relate to, and be blessed by him. In this regard, the question then turns to why the special patronage relationship between Yahweh and Israel arose in history. We will see that God's election of Israel is not for bestowing privileges on a particular nation, but for his universal purpose of bringing salvation to all nations.

This is best demonstrated by the covenants that Yahweh respectively makes with Abraham, the nation of Israel, and David. First, note that these covenants were made before monotheism was fully understood and took root in Israel. Hence, God's vision of universal salvation is couched in Israel's understanding at those times, namely, the language of a monolatrous covenant. These covenants all appear to establish a patronage relationship between Yahweh and a particular person or nation. Although the *perception* of Yahweh by the Israelites may have changed over time, the *nature* of Yahweh has never changed. Even so, Yahweh's act of giving covenants to the Israelites was meant to expand their monolatrous understanding of the covenant into his vision of universal salvation.

One could add that these covenants are all particular in that each is made with a particular nation and a particular king, but the same covenants are also universal because a particular nation and king are merely divine instruments to bring salvation to all humanity. Much as Abraham was chosen to be a blessing for all nations (Gen 12:1–3), the nation of Israel was chosen to be "a kingdom of priests" that leads other nations to the true God of monotheism and "a holy nation" that represents God's presence in their life of love and justice (Exod 19:6). The descendant of King David was chosen to be Yahweh's special "son" who will bring the kingdom of God on earth (2 Sam 7:14; cf. Ps 2:7; Mark 1:1).

---

29. During the peak of Assyrian and Babylonian imperial power, Ashur and Marduk incorporated aspects of all other gods, relegating other gods to the status of their subordinates. See Miller, *The Religion of Ancient Israel*, 26.

Yahweh and Other Gods

All this demonstrates that monotheism, rightly understood, is far from the prosperity gospel in which God has an exclusive relationship of blessing with one person, clan, or nation. The goal of religious piety is not to attain health and wealth, but to be of service to God by becoming a blessing for all humanity. Traditional religions in Asia are mostly prosperity-oriented in this regard.[30] Multitudes of people regularly visit their temples to get their wishes granted, whether it is Sensoji Temple on New Year's Day in Japan, or the Renzu temple complex on Fuxi's birthday festival in China. Of course, the temptation to make gods a means to our own prosperity is not limited to Asians. All humans easily fall prey to the desire of using God or gods to build their own kingdoms. The universalistic vision of monotheism may rein in our egocentric nature by reminding us of God's purpose for all humanity.

3.3. Human Responsibilities

The human desire for blessing also brings its converse of the theological problem of evil. Strictly speaking, this question occurs only in monotheistic religions, for if there is but one Creator God, he must be responsible for evil in the world (cf. Isa 45:7). Biblical monotheists nonetheless cannot accept this position because Yahweh is depicted in the OT as not only omnipotent but also as righteous. The existence of evil is not problematic in polytheism, because power struggles between rival gods or criminal acts of some gods may account for the evil in the world. According to the Japanese book *Nihon Shoki*, for instance, Susanowo, a child of Inazagi and Inazami, was evil from birth unlike other sibling gods; he killed people and caused plants to wither. Further, his violence scared Amaterasu the sun goddess into hiding in a rock cave, leaving the world in pitch darkness and out of balance.[31]

How then does OT monotheism solve the problem of evil? Ironically, part of the solution is connected to the development of angelology in the post-exilic period. Despite the threat they may apparently present to monotheism, angelic beings start to be identified with proper names in some of the latest written texts of the Old Testament, as is the case with Gabriel (Dan 8:16) and Michael (Dan 10:13). As angelic beings gain prominence, it becomes easier to impute evil to some angelic beings. However the real reason that biblical monotheists,

---

30. See chapter 12's discussion of prosperity theology in Asia by Huu-Thien Tran N. and Daniel Owens.
31. Robert Borgen and Marian Ury, "Readable Japanese Mythology: Selections from Nihon Shoki and Kojiki," *Journal of the Association of Teachers of Japanese* 24 (1990): 77–79.

whether Jewish or Christian, chose what might be called a *quasi-polytheistic* solution to the problem of evil is that they were more interested in a practical solution to the evil in the world. In their opinion, evil is undeniably real in the world regardless of its mystical origin; and if evil is a result of a free moral agent (e.g. Satan, some demons), one may argue that it cannot go away until another free moral agent confronts it (God or his image-bearer, that is, humans). In other words, the imputation of evil to angelic, semi-divine beings was a necessary premise for biblical monotheists in order to underscore the human responsibility as God's image-bearers to fight the evil in God's name. The story of Yahweh defeating a sea monster before creation (Ps 74:12–17) reminds the Israelites of their responsibility to stand up to the evil in the world.[32]

The Chinese people have a similar concept of human responsibility in their flood myth. When the flood destroyed the earth, Gun wanted to stop the destruction and stole Xirang, a magical soil that was able to grow by itself, without the permission of the Supreme Divinity in heaven. Because of this, he was killed by the fire god Zhurong, dispatched by the Supreme Divinity. Undeterred, his son Yu continued his father's efforts to stop the flood. He changed the terrain of the earth and channeled all the flood waters into the seas. Chinese flood heroes had no help from the gods in overcoming the destruction by the flood, in contrast to both Noah and Utnapishtim, the Mesopotamian hero of the flood. The Chinese flood myth shows how evil was removed by a great human effort that straddled two generations.[33] Be that as it may, it is a helpful surprise to see a point of contact between Asian mythological solutions to the problem of evil and the monotheistic teaching that God counts on his image-bearers to fight evil and bring God's blessing for all humanity.

CONCLUSION

The picture of monotheism painted by the OT is rich and complex. Yahweh is unique as "one" and never changes in his being, but the biblical authors not only depict Yahweh in the cultural concepts of their time which relates Yahweh to Canaanite gods such as El and Baal, they also do justice to the long historical process through which ancient Israelites came to conceive and receive Yahweh as he truly is. In other words, there were vestiges of polytheism out of

---

32. For the general treatment of the problem of evil in Judaism, see Jon D. Levenson, *Creation and the Persistence of Evil: The Jewish Drama of Divine Omnipotence* (San Francisco, CA: Harper & Row, 1994).
33. For the impact of ancient myths on the Chinese spirits, see Yang and An, *Handbook of Chinese Mythology*, 54–56.

which ancient Israelites eventually came to the light of biblical monotheism. This dynamic picture of Yahweh in the OT underscores Yahweh's loving patience in guiding his people to the fullness of truth. This encourages us to be humble, loving, and wise in representing the truth of monotheism to those yet immersed in a polytheistic or atheistic worldview. The nature of God is ultimately a mystery.

REFERENCES

Ackerman, Susan. "The Personal is Political: Covenant and Affectionate Love (*'āhēb, 'ahăbâ*) in the Hebrew Bible," *Vetus Testamentum* 52 (2002): 437–58.

Allen, James P. "From the 'Memphite Theology' (1.15)." In *Context of Scripture*. Vol 1, Canonical Composition from the Biblical World, edited by W. W. Hallo and K. L. Younger Jr., 21–23. Leiden: Brill, 1997.

Borgen, Robert, and Marian Ury. "Readable Japanese Mythology: Selections from Nihon Shoki and Kojiki." *Journal of the Association of Teachers of Japanese* 24 (1990): 61–97.

Choon Sup, Bae. "Ancestor Worship in Korea and Africa: Social Function of Religious Phenomenon?" PhD diss., University of Pretoria, 2004.

Heiser, Michael S. *The Unseen Realm: Recovering the Supernatural Worldview of the Bible*. Bellingham, WA: Lexham Press, 2015.

Kugel, James L. *The Great Shift: Encountering God in Biblical Times*. Boston, MA: Houghton Mifflin Harcourt, 2017.

Lapsley, Jacqueline E. "Feeling Our Way: Love for God in Deuteronomy." *Catholic Biblical Quarterly* 65 (2003): 350–69.

Levenson, Jon D. *Creation and the Persistence of Evil: The Jewish Drama of Divine Omnipotence*. San Francisco, CA: Harper & Row, 1994.

Lewis, Theodore J. *The Origin and Character of God: Ancient Israelite Religion Through the Lens of Divinity*. Oxford: Oxford University Press, 2020.

Miller, Patrick D. *The Religion of Ancient Israel*. Louisville, KY: Westminster John Knox Press, 2000.

Moberly, R. W. L. *The Old Testament of the Old Testament: Patriarchal Narratives and Mosaic Yahwism*. Overtures to Biblical Theology. Minneapolis, MN: Fortress, 1992.

Moran, William L. "The Ancient Near Eastern Background of the Love of God in Deuteronomy." *Catholic Biblical Quarterly* 25 (1963): 77–87.

"Monotheism, *n*." *Oxford English Dictionary*. OED Online, May 2022. Oxford University Press. https://www.oed.com/view/Entry/121673.

Oak, Sung-Deuk. "Competing Chinese Names for God: The Chinese Term Question and Its Influence upon Korea." *Journal of Korean Religions* 3 (2012): 89–115.

Pardee, Dennis. "The Baʻlu Myth." In *Context of Scripture*. Vol 1, Canonical Composition from the Biblical World, edited by W. W. Hallo and K. L. Younger Jr., 241–74. Leiden: Brill, 1997.

Römer, Thomas. *The Invention of God*. Cambridge, MA: Harvard University Press, 2015.

Schneider, Laurel C. *Beyond Monotheism: A Theology of Multiplicity*. New York, NY: Routledge, 2008.

Smith, Mark. *The Early History of God: Yahweh and the Other Deities in Ancient Israel*. Grand Rapids, MI: Eerdmans, 2002.

Sohn, Seock-Tae. "'I Will Be Your God and You Will Be My People': The Origin and Background of the Covenant Formula." In *Ki Baruch Hu: Ancient Near Eastern, Biblical, and Judaic Studies in Honor of Baruch A. Levine*, edited by Robert Chazan, William W. Hallo, and Lawrence H. Schiffman, 355–72. Winona Lake, IN: Eisenbrauns, 1999.

Sommer, Benjamin D. "Monotheism." In *The Hebrew Bible: A Critical Companion*, edited by John Barton, 239–270. Princeton, NJ: Princeton University Press, 2009.

Tigay, J. H. *You Shall Have No Other Gods: Israelite Religion in the Light of Hebrew Inscriptions*. Atlanta, GA: Scholars Press, 1986.

Walton, John H. *Ancient Near Eastern Thought and the Old Testament*. Grand Rapids, MI: Baker Academic, 2006.

Yang, Lihui, and Deming An. *Handbook of Chinese Mythology*. Santa Barbara, CA: ABC-Clio, 2005.

CHAPTER 3

MEN, WOMEN, AND GOD

Understanding the Male-Female/Husband-Wife Relationship through Genesis 1–3[1]

Havilah Dharamraj

Stories are the way the Old Testament does theology. That is why we turn to the stories of Genesis 1–3 to understand the topic before us – the relationship between male and female. The Genesis narratives will give us a good start with figuring out the desperate condition of the man-woman relationship in the world we live in.

We know that traditionally stories start at the very beginning. So, a story might start: "Once upon a time there was . . ." In storytelling now, though, the storyteller might start anywhere in the sequence.[2] That is what we will do. First, we will look at the state of affairs after the Fall (Gen 3) – a state that continues into the present day. This will set up the "problem," one so sadly familiar to us, and give us good reason to spend time on the topic. Then, we will go back and look at how things were before the Fall (Gen 1–2). After that, we will move forward to when time ends and eternity commences, and see if the Bible gives us any idea of how the human male and female will relate in that age to come. We will do more than read a story. We will watch a drama in three acts, but not in the serial order featured in Genesis 1–3, and probably not what you would generally expect in a theology textbook.

Before we settle into our seats, a word on what we will be looking out for. We will not simply give all our attention to our main actors, Adam and Eve. We must take note of the stage on which they play out their parts, which is

---

1. I am indebted to Francis Mathew, my MTh student, for assisting with the research necessary for this essay, which is adapted from a lecture delivered at the Annual Meeting of Christians for Biblical Equality in Houston, Texas (USA) in August 2019. Due to the oral nature of that occasion, the present essay uses phonetic transliteration of Hebrew rather than the academic style used elsewhere in this book.
2. "In media Res," 8 Classic Storytelling Techniques for Engaging Presentations, https://www.sparkol.com/en/blog/8-classic-storytelling-techniques-for-engaging-presentations.

the created world of earth and sky, of trees and serpents and thistles. We will also keep an eye on the third and all-important actor in the drama, God. We might find that humans, the created world, and God interlace in surprising ways. Somewhere in that intermeshing lies the theology of male-female relationships – what they were meant to be, what they have become, and why.

As the curtains rise, there is one other thing: this story has odd bits. There is a tree whose fruit confers immortality on its eaters; a mud sculpture will come alive; there is a tree whose fruit will bring death on its eaters; a piece of bone will get built into a woman; and there is a speaking snake. Discussions on how to understand these odd bits we will leave to others. Now, on to Act 2, before we come back to Act 1 and then go on to Act 3. In each act, we will add in a parallel scene from the *Ramayana* to bridge Genesis' narrative theology into our everyday Asian stories.[3]

1. ACT 2: RELATIONSHIPS IN PARADISE LOST

Everything that can go wrong has gone wrong. This is what theologians call "the Fall." Standing before God are the first humans, Adam, and Eve, and presumably, the Serpent as well. Now God speaks, and he is clearly angry (Gen 3:14–15).

Here is the first of the penalties pronounced on the perpetrators of the Fall. This penalty is in the form of a curse. The serpent, introduced as the craftiest of all creatures, is brought low – literally so. Crawling along the ground and eating dust is vocabulary that describes an inferior existence, much reduced from what has been thus far; but that's not all. He now has something to be afraid of. He must watch his back, for, from now on, he has an adversary; an adversary whom he may wound, but whom he can never defeat.

The second of the penalties is not a curse, but is just as grim and concerns the woman (3:16). Again, the penalty is in two parts. One part describes the offender's condition from this point on, and the other describes a new status in relationships. If the serpent had been reduced to a groveling existence, the woman must forever submit to labor pangs intensified well beyond what would

---

3. The *Ramayana* is an epic poem composed in Sanskrit, with early layers dating from the 7th to the 4th centuries BCE. Besides being adapted into other religions such as Buddhism, Jainism and Sikhism, its versions are seen in the Cambodian, Indonesian, Filipino, Thai, Lao, Burmese, and Malay cultures. What makes this story relevant to our study here is that it is popularly understood to depict Rama as the ideal husband and Sita as the ideal wife. Here, I use a version by Arshia Sattar, a translator of Valmiki's *Ramayana* who is known globally as a Sanskrit translator. The text is found in *Ramayana for Children* (New Delhi: Juggernaut, 2019).

have been normal. But what is worse is that she has something to be afraid of. She too must watch her back, for from now on she has an adversary. She will "desire" a husband who will rule over her. What does that mean?

Traditionally, interpreters have postulated two possible readings. In line with the childbearing function mentioned in the same verse (3:16a) and consonant with the sexual overtone of the same word "desire" (*teshuqa*) when used in Song of Songs 7:10, it is possible to interpret the word as "sexual desire." The woman will be sexually dependent on the man. The other view is to see this as an economic and emotional dependence of the woman on her man for her livelihood. In both cases, the man will take advantage of her by dominating over her.[4]

But there is a third reading: Identical vocabulary and phrasing occurs in the very next story, that of Abel and Cain. There, God cautions a disgruntled Cain that sin lies in wait for him. It "desires" him, but he must rule over it – that is, he must master it. Similarly, the woman will now "desire" control over her husband, but he will turn around to overpower her, and will lord it over her. The woman has an adversary she can never defeat.

Similarly in the *Ramayana*, the idyllic devotion between the king, Rama, and his queen, Sita, is also in tatters at the end of the story. The beautiful Sita has been abducted by Ravana, the ruler of Lanka. Rama has marshalled a great army and marched on to Lanka, consigning the capital city to flames. Ravana has been slain on the battlefield and even given a royal funeral befitting his birth and rank. Still standing on the battlefield, Rama asks that Sita be brought to him. His warrior brother Lakshmana is puzzled. Would Rama not wish to be reunited with his queen more privately? Unquestioning, Lakshmana does as he is bidden. Sita comes to the battlefield, eager to see Rama again. She is hardly prepared for what awaits her. "You were abducted," Rama says. "I cannot take you back. You are free to go wherever you wish, Sita!" To Rama, Sita is "damaged goods." Even if she has remained unmolested, her long captivity raises doubts about her chastity.

The burden of proof of purity lies on Sita. She orders a fire to be built and undertakes an ordeal by fire. Emerging unharmed, she is able to prove to her husband and to the army of witnesses that she is chaste. There is a reunion, even if somewhat sobered by this test, and Rama and Sita return to Ayodhya to

---

4. Nahum M. Sarna, *Genesis*, JPSTC (Philadelphia: The Jewish Publication Society, 1989), 28; Kenneth A. Mathews, *Genesis 1–11:26*, NAC, vol. 1A (Nashville, TN: Broadman & Holman, 1996), 250.

resume their interrupted reign. However Rama's need to keep his public image unsullied by gossip again wins over his love Sita. The queen is with child, and not all the citizens of Ayodhya are entirely sure of its paternity. Soon it comes to Rama's ears that his subjects are unimpressed that the king should take back a wife who has lived in the house of another man, even if as a captive. "I must banish Sita from the city," he decides. "The people must respect their queen; she cannot be the subject of their suspicions." With that, the pregnant Sita is abandoned in the forest close to the ashram of the sage Valmiki in the hope that she will be found and taken care of. Whether in the Genesis story or in the *Ramayana*, readers find a mirror to their own sad world – "happily ever after" is more a hope than a reality.[5]

The third and the last of the penalties continues in the same desolate strain (Gen 3:17–19). Once more, we notice that the penalty is in two parts. Humanity had been given the gift of work. In reflection of God's exultation in the work of creating the world, man had the opportunity to enjoy the work of tending to that creation. That work now turned into labor – tedious labor, sweaty and unrelenting, from which there was to be no respite. This is because, like the serpent and the woman, he too has an adversary. The ground has been cursed into becoming his opponent. This is only poetic justice. Five times in these three verses, the verb "to eat" is repeated. He who *ate* what was forbidden will henceforth *eat* only through painful toil. The land he tends will fight him. The earth from which he was formed, the earth for which *adam* was named – *adamah*, the earth he was given to rule – looks down at it with helplessness and frustration, as it waits to triumphantly gobble him into itself. Man has an adversary he can never defeat.

Standing back from this section of Genesis 3 and reading it at the level of the whole story, we notice a thrice-repeated pattern.[6] In each case, there is a reduction in the quality of life – the snake will crawl, the woman will bear

---

5. Sattar, *Ramayana*, 183–209. Victim blaming happens regularly in cases of rape in India. In a shame-honor culture, this can lead to the rape victim having no future as far as marriage is concerned. See Annie Gowen, "Why an Indian Judge Thinks Rapists Should Marry their Victims," *The Washington Post*, 9 July 2015, https://www.washingtonpost.com/world/asia_pacific/why-an-indian-judge-thinks-rapists-should-marry-their-victims/2015/07/08/606f8998–23e5–11e5-b621-b55e495e9b78_story.html; "Indian Woman Marries her Alleged Rapist," *BBC News*, 16 Feb 2015, https://www.bbc.com/news/world-asia-india-31483956.
6. For Mathews, the pattern is: "divine penalty followed by a description of consequence – defeat" (*Genesis 1–11:26*, 243). For Hamilton, the divine pronouncement affects both "a life function and a relationship" (Victor P. Hamilton, *The Book of Genesis: Chapters 1–17*, NICOT [Grand Rapids, MI: Eerdmans, 1990], 196).

children in great pain, and the man's work has turned into toil. In each case, there is a breakdown of an existing harmonious relationship. There is hostility between the animal and the human, there is hostility between the human and his mate, and there is hostility between the human and the land. Where once the created order was "very good," now each is at the throat of the other: animal against human, human against human, land against human.

2. ACT 1: RELATIONSHIPS IN PARADISE

What did this world look like before things went so badly wrong? What did the whole look like before it collapsed into these warring parties, each intent on overpowering the other?

As the climax of his creative venture, God resolved to create humanity in his image (*tselem*) and likeness (*demuth*; Gen 1:26). Although some early Christian interpreters distinguish between these two terms, the interchangeable use of these expressions in Genesis 5:3 leads us to conclude that they are one and the same and repeated to clarify the precise nature of *imago Dei* as the "likeness of God."[7] What does being created in the likeness of God mean? Some of the dominant interpretations of *imago Dei* throughout history have laid stress on a resemblance with God on either a spiritual, relational, or non-physical level such as "moral, intellectual and personality."[8] However, reading the Genesis 1 creation story in light of its own ancient Near Eastern counterparts, we may safely conclude that beyond the material and immaterial attributes shared with the deity, humanity created in the image of God is also God's way of setting up his vice-regents on earth to "act like him."[9]

The resultant act of the creation of humanity (1:27) is described by the narrator in a poetic fashion that has both chiastic and parallel structures:

> A So, God **created** mankind
>   B in **his** own ***image***;
>   B' in the image ***of God***
> A' he created them;
>   B" ***male*** and ***female***
> A" he **created** them.[10]

---

7. Gordon J. Wenham, *Genesis 1–15*, WBC, vol. 1 (Waco, TX: Word Books, 1987), 29–30.
8. Mathews, *Genesis 1–11:26*, 164–68.
9. John H. Walton, *Genesis*, NIVAC (Grand Rapids, MI: Zondervan, 2001), 106.
10. Adapted from the structural analysis in Phyllis Trible, *God and the Rhetoric of Sexuality*, OBT (Minneapolis, MN: Fortress, 1978), 16–17.

Thus, while the chiastic panels (AB–B'A') emphasize the centrality of the divine image in humanity, the parallel panels (B'A'–B"A") stress that this divine image is borne by both male and female. In Genesis 1, the only distinction between humans is based on gender, unlike other created beings that are distinguished based on their species (1:11, 12, 21, 24–25). Unlike other living creatures, there is "only one sort of humanity" bearing "only one image of God."[11] The Jewish sages perceived a divine intention in this act so that "no person [would] have claim to unique ancestry as a pretext for asserting superiority over others."[12] This idea could be extended by observing that just as the distinction of species within living creatures does not imply hierarchy, the gender distinction within humanity need not imply any one gender being superior to the other. The narrator of Genesis 1 portrays male and female humans as image-bearers of God without gender distinctions implying any precedence.

The creation of male and female bearers of the divine image is followed by the divine blessing and the divine commands to increase in number, spread over the earth, subdue it, and rule over every living creature (1:28). Both male and female are the recipients of this blessing and command. The divine provision of food is made for both of them (1:29). At no point do we observe any gender-based distinction in this creation story. As beneficiaries of the divine image, they stand undifferentiated.

In that world on which God's signature had barely dried, in that world yet un-smudged with sin, the elements of the created order segued into each other in perfect harmony (Gen 2:5, 7, 15). The man was to work it and take care of it. Genesis 1 used the verbs "subdue" and "rule over" in describing the function of humankind (1:28). Far from being an "unbridled exploitation and subjugation" of the created order,[13] Genesis 1, when read alongside the Garden Narrative (Gen 2–3), transposes these verbs onto a benign monarch, and shows us how such an authority would rule and exercise dominion. A benign monarch would tend and care for. The Garden Narrative began with the description of untended land: "no plant had yet sprung up, for . . . there was no one to work the ground." That situation is now reversed. There is someone to till the ground and attend to its needs. The ground and the human are so deeply bound to each other that they even share the same name: one is

---

11. David W. Cotter, *Genesis*, Berit Olam (Collegeville, MN: The Liturgical Press, 2003), 17–18.
12. Sarna, *Genesis*, 13.
13. This is the coinage of Wenham, *Genesis 1–15*, 33, to describe a common (mis)interpretation of Genesis 1.

adamah and the other is *adam*. The day has not yet come when one will turn against the other.

This tying together of the living and the non-living, the sentient and the non-sentient, resonates with the worldview in several Asian religions. A textual example comes from the last scenes of the *Ramayana*. Rama asks that Sita, the wife he abandoned at Valmiki's ashram, be brought to his court so that she can prove her innocence before the people of Ayodhya and all the dignitaries of the world gathered at the royal sacrifice for which he has invited them. Sita comes, clothed not as the queen she is, but as the forest-dweller she has been these last many years. At Rama's instruction to prove herself virtuous, she steps forward. "If I am innocent, let the goddess accept me into the earth," she whispers. The ground at Sita's feet opens up and a throne emerges, borne on the hoods of two great bejeweled serpents. Sita seats herself on the offered throne, and the serpents slide back into the earth taking her with them into the womb of the goddess Earth. Though the parallel with Genesis is inexact since in the *Ramayana* it is the earth that is deified, the cooperation between the living and the non-living is a shared idea.

Next, in the creation story, we notice the harmony between humans and the animal world (Gen 2:19–20). In the OT, naming something or someone has significance. One names that which belongs to oneself, that which one has ownership of. The act of naming confers on the one who names authority over that which is named.[14] Thus, in Genesis 1, God creates and then names that which he creates, demonstrating authority over what is his – day and night, sky, land, and sea. Having transferred that ownership to humankind, God offers the man an opportunity to name his subjects – the animals and birds. Humankind and the animal world coexist in harmony. The day has not yet come when the serpent will seek to strike the man's heel, who in turn will crush its head. That was the animal world in Eden before the Fall.

Finally, the narrator says of the man and his wife, "That is why a man leaves his father and mother and is united to his wife, and they become one flesh" (2:24). The prescription derived from the incident is culturally odd.[15] In a patriarchal culture such as existed in ancient Near East, the woman leaves

---

14. Wenham, *Genesis 1–15*, 68. In the immediate context, this idea is implied in 1:5, 8, 10; 3:20; 4:17.
15. A variant reading of Genesis 2:24 points to a marriage tradition where the husband leaves his family to settle down with his wife's household. See C. H. Gordon, "*Erēbu* Marriage," in *Studies on the Civilization and Culture of Nuzi and the Hurrians. In Honor of Ernest R. Lachemann*, ed. M. Morrison and D. Owens (Winona Lake, IN: Eisenbrauns, 1981), 155–61. An alternate

her father and mother to join the family of her husband. We recall Rebekah leaving her maternal home with much ceremony to travel to another country to become the wife of Isaac and a member of Abraham's household.

That is how it is also told in the *Ramayana* as the popular Indian guide to the contours of the ideal male, Rama. Rama's tutor, the sage Vishwamitra, brings Rama to Mithila, where the king Janaka has announced a contest for the hand of his daughter Sita. The suitor must string the mighty bow of Shiva, an object of veneration in the royal family. It needs the labors of five hundred men and an iron cart with eight wheels to be brought into the town square, but Rama is able to string it in a trice. Marriage celebrations ensue, with the four daughters of Janaka given in marriage to Rama and his three brothers. "The multiple weddings lit up Mithila for days and nights but finally it was time for the young princesses to leave their home and go with their husbands to Ayodhya, a city very different and very far away from their own."[16]

In South Asia, this sending away of the bride is so much the norm that there are proverbs on the futility of investing in a girl child. Investing in a girl child is like watering your neighbor's garden, it is thought. In a joint family system, in which the bride becomes part of the man's family, the girl's family loses their daughter to the groom's family. Her skills, her capacity to earn an income – all of these benefit her husband's household. She is a non-permanent member of her biological family. At marriage, her surname will change. In some communities, she will even change her first name, taking on a name that her in-laws decide for her. Her loyalties henceforth are to her new family. Even if she is mistreated in her new home, social pressure demands that she should not return to her parental home. Her place is by the side of her husband, whether or not he treats her well. In the *Ramayana*, Janaka asks Rama for assurance of his future care of Sita: "Whoever wins her hand must treat her exceptionally well because she is special. Will you promise to do that?"[17]

That is why Hindu weddings end with the ceremony called the *vidaai*, the farewell. After the wedding rituals are completed, and as the bride leaves the maternal home, she stops to throw three handfuls of rice or wheat over her head towards the home she is leaving. This is her symbolic repayment of the care she has received from her family. She may even throw a few coins over her

---

interpretation argues that the verse only reflects the need for the man to cut off all emotional ties from his parents and be attached to his wife. See M. M. Bravmann, *Studies in Semitic Philology* (Leiden: Brill, 1977), 593–95.
16. Sattar, *Ramayana*, 19.
17. Sattar, 18.

head to symbolize her gratitude. There is much shedding of tears here, making this the most sentimental part of the wedding. The bride is then escorted by her father and brothers to the vehicle that will carry her to her new home, the home of her husband and her in-laws. This is why the daughter of the house is called *paraaya dhan*, "someone else's wealth." Except in a few matriarchal societies in the south and northeast of India, this is the common perception of the girl child, whether she be born in a Hindu, Muslim, or Christian household – she is a temporary member of the family.

This is why the South Asian reader finds the prescription of Genesis 2:24 just as odd as the ancient reader might have found it. Why would a *man* leave his father and mother on taking for himself a wife? It is because he becomes one flesh with her. What does it mean, "becoming one flesh"? We need to go back to the poem that precedes this prescription. "Bone of my bones and flesh of my flesh," the man says of the woman. To make sense of this phrase in the culture in which it is used, we should look for its other occurrences. In the Jacob story, Laban will use the phrase on his sister's son. "You are my own bone and flesh" (Gen 29:14, my translation) Laban tells Jacob, warmly welcoming him as a family member. Most English versions render this into our cultural equivalent: flesh and blood. In Judges 9:2, Abimelek negotiates with the elders of Shechem to see if they will make him their leader on the grounds that he is their "bone and flesh" (author's literal rendering). In 2 Samuel 5:1, the tribes of Israel come to Hebron, where David reigns as king over Judah. "We are your bone and flesh" (lit.), they say, inviting him, on that basis, to become king over them.

With that as cultural context for the idiom "bone and flesh," we return to why a newly married man must leave his father and mother and cleave to his wife. In the culture in which the stories of the OT are set, the highest obligation is to those who are related to you by blood. Relationship by marriage comes a poor second, even if that were to be your wife. In Indian families, the son walks a tightrope between his parents and his wife. It is not uncommon for his mother to say something like this: "Haven't I borne you nine months in my womb and cared for you these last thirty years? And yet, my word counts for nothing before the word of your wife who came into this family barely a year ago!"

It is also not uncommon for a cousin one has never met to turn up at one's door asking for help. "Of course we have to take him in and help him," the head of the house would say. "If we don't, what will our relatives say? He's our flesh and blood!" The priorities here lie clearly in favor of those related by blood. How countercultural for Asian societies, then, is the prescription in Genesis 2. A man is to treat his wife as if she were his flesh and blood, his kin, rather than as someone from a different family who has been imported into his.[18] His obligation to her must be no less than the obligation he feels to his blood relatives. Rather, he must prioritize her over the blood relations that have the greatest claim over his loyalty, namely, his father and mother. *A man leaves his father and mother* – in terms of ordering his obligations – *and is united with his wife and they become one flesh.* That is, they enter a relationship that is to be valued on par with a kinship relationship.

There is one other piece in this text that is not immediately apparent. Is the injunction to the man only, and not to the woman? To answer this, we should look at two other places in the garden narrative. In Genesis 2:16, "And the LORD God commanded the man, 'You are free to eat from any tree in the garden; but you must not eat from the tree of the knowledge of good and evil, for when you eat from it you will certainly die.'" There is no separate instruction given to the woman. Yet in Genesis 3:2, the woman says, "We may eat fruit from the trees in the garden, but God did say, 'You must not eat fruit from the tree that is in the middle of the garden.'" It appears that the command given to the man is binding on the woman also.

This inclusion of the woman into the treatment of the man is seen again at the end of the garden narrative. According to Genesis 3:23, "So the LORD God banished him from the Garden of Eden to work the ground from which he had been taken." Was not the woman driven out along with the man? It is understood that she was. Based on these two cases, we could argue that the prescription that a man should leave his father and mother to cleave to his wife includes the prescription that the woman should likewise leave her father and mother and cleave to her husband.

This said, we are in a good position to make up our minds on how best to render the Hebrew word *ezer*[19] which describes the woman in relationship to the man: "And the LORD God said, 'It is not good for the man to be alone. I will make a helper (*ezer*) suitable for him'" (Gen 2:18). We have submitted

---

18. Wenham, *Genesis 1–15*, 71.
19. Traditionally, the word *ezer* was rendered as "help meet/helpmate," leading to a view prescribing the inferiority of woman in relation to man. For a brief survey see LeAnn Snow Flesher, "What the @#$! is a Helpmate?," *RevExp* 115 (2018): 457–59.
 The complementarian view, while challenging the idea of inferiority and claiming equality, proposes a sense of the subordination of woman to male headship implied in the word *ezer*. See Raymond C. Ortlund, Jr., "Male-Female Equality and Male Headship: Genesis 1–3," in *Recovering Biblical Manhood and Womanhood*, ed. Wayne Grudem and John Piper (Wheaton,

that: (a) The marriage bond is to sit at the top of the pyramid of kinship relationships, and (b) The marriage partnership requires that *both* the man and the woman *leave* their prior order of loves and *cleave* to each other in a radically reconstituted prioritization of affections. As such, we should render *ezer* in a manner which best fits the Edenic state. An *ezer*, then, is one who stands alongside the other, shoulder to shoulder. A comrade, a soul mate, a companion. One who is of common bone and flesh. One who is – as Asians understand it – kin.

In this reading of *ezer*, might it be possible to infer that the man is as much an *ezer* to the woman as the woman is to him?[20] If the two are each other's bone and flesh, if the two are to mutually cleave at the cost of leaving behind kinship obligations, it could well be that they end up as *ezer* to each other. That would be mutuality that affirms their affinity – both creatures of clay, but both, according to the first Creation account in Genesis 1, stamped with the likeness of God and so, authorized to rule over creation. Both *mutually* committed, with an unswerving commitment, to the good of the other.

Now we understand why the creation of the woman takes the route it does. The woman is extracted out of the man, out of his bone and flesh. It does not matter so much that the bone in question should be the rib because a rib is close to the heart.[21] What matters most here is that she is his bone and flesh, or as English idiom would have it, his flesh and blood. That is the deep and demanding kinship relationship that the man's poem celebrates. There was no one else in all of creation that could be a suitable match for him but

---

IL: Crossway, 1991), 95–112; Richard N. Longenecker, "Authority, Hierarchy and Leadership Patterns in the Bible," in *Women, Authority & the Bible*, ed. Alvera Mickelsen (Downers Grove, IL: InterVarsity, 1986), 67.

Setting aside any notion of inferiority or subordination is a third view that argues that *ezer* emphasizes equality here. When read alongside the adjoining word *kenegedo* – "a helper who is a counterpart" – this view insists that the woman should be seen as equal to Adam, as compared to God who is superior and the animals who are inferior, all relationships described in the immediate context of the creation narrative. See Phyllis Trible, "Depatriarchalizing in Biblical Interpretation," *JAAR* 41 (1973): 35–42. Other occurrences of *ezer* in the OT do not imply subservience (e.g. God – Exod 18:4; Ps 70:5; humans – Ps 20:2; 89:19; Isa 30:5).

20. For setting me thinking about this, I am obliged to Christina Martin, a student in my Master's-level Introduction to the Old Testament class at SAIACS in Bengaluru, India.

21. *Genesis Rabbah* 18.2 has this comment: "He [God] thought to himself: 'We should not create her beginning with the head, so that she not be frivolous, nor from the eye, that she not be a starer [at men], not from the ear, that she not be an eavesdropper, nor from the mouth, that she not talk too much [as a gossip], nor from the heart, that she not be jealous, nor from the hand, that she not be light-fingered, nor from the foot, that she not be a gadabout, but from a covered up place on man. For even when a man is standing naked, that spot is covered up.'" Jacob Neusner, *Genesis Rabbah*, vol. 2 (Atlanta, GA: Scholars Press, 1985), 149.

his own flesh and blood. The day has not yet come when he will turn against his own in a blame game.

3. ACT 3: RELATIONSHIPS IN PARADISE REGAINED

Standing back from the Garden Narrative, we can admire the interconnectedness between the various parts and the multiple actors – an interconnectedness that undergirded the Edenic ideal and operated at various levels. Here is the human physically linked to the earth by being formed out of the dust of the ground. Here is the animal world also created out of the same substance, loosely connecting humankind with that lower order of creation. Here is the woman extracted out of the substance of the man, binding them to each other with bonds that cannot be broken; and here is humankind given life by the very breath of God. In Eden, the earth, the animal world, and humankind are interconnected in perfect harmony. Humans are to relate among themselves and with God in deep and perfect kinship. That world, of course, is now lost. We wait with eager anticipation for the day when it will be restored in all its former glory, and perhaps even superseded.

Before we talk about what we may hope for in Eden regained, let us finish our parallel reading of the *Ramayana*. When that epic ends, "Sita had gone forever."[22] A distressed Rama returns to the task of governance, which he does wisely and well – with a gold statue of his lost queen standing by him at all ceremonial events. Time did not heal the loss. Rather, Rama grew sadder as the years rolled on. And finally, Rama set his kingdom in order, and scheduled his departure from the earth. As his family and subjects looked on, he walked into the waters of the Sarayu and was received into godhood in a blinding flash of light.[23] The ideal husband is never reunited with his ideal wife. Devotees continue to celebrate their marriage annually as *vivaha panchami*. In Nepal's Janakpurdham, supposedly where the wedding took place, it is a major festival. However, when Valmiki's story ends, Rama and Sita are each separately subsumed into eternal existence, their earthly relationship dissolved forever.[24]

---

22. Sattar, *Ramayana*, 208.
23. Sattar, 208–13.
24. Indian viewers tearfully (re-)watched the *Ramayana's* ending when Ramanand Sagar's 1987 TV series was re-telecast over the COVID lockdown in March-April 2020. https://timesofindia.indiatimes.com/tv/news/hindi/viewers-call-ramayans-last-episode-as-most-painful-and-get-teary-eyed-a-look-at-such-emotional-reactions/photostory/75515396.cms.

This said, in the worship of Rama, it is the ideal marriage of Rama and Sita that is celebrated. To this end, he is commonly portrayed standing between Sita and his brother Lakshmana. The couple are even invoked with their names meshed: Sitaram.

In the biblical new heavens and new earth, marriage too ceases, but hardly for the same reasons as in the *Ramayana*.

What does the biblical canon say about the new heavens and the new earth? Let us look at the warring categories we have been talking about. First, earth and humankind: the day will come when the earth and humankind will be reconciled to each other (Rom 8:20–22). Second, the animal world and humankind: Isaiah's vision for the new world order (Isa 11:7–9) reads, "The cow will feed with the bear, their young will lie down together, and the lion will eat straw like the ox. The infant will play near the cobra's den, and the young child will put its hand into the viper's nest." This is poetic and metaphorical language – we do not know how exactly it will play out; but it is a text that looks forward to the day when the created orders will be reconciled to each other.

Third, man and wife. Will the marriage bond continue into the world beyond the veil? The text that immediately comes to mind is Jesus's sharp response to the Sadducees. This was a group that did not believe in the resurrection of the dead and were attempting to trap Jesus with a hypothetical case of levirate marriage – that is, the widow marrying her brother-in-law to propagate the name of the dead (Matt 22:23–28).

This encounter between the Sadducees and Jesus is reported in all three Synoptic gospels. In Matthew and Mark, Jesus replies, "At the resurrection/when the dead rise, people/they will neither marry not be given in marriage; they will be like the angels in heaven" (Matt 22:30; Mark 12:25). Luke expands on this by contrasting the temporal with the eternal. Luke 20:34–35 records, "Jesus replied, 'The people of this age marry and are given in marriage. But those who are considered worthy of taking part in that age to come and in the resurrection from the dead will neither marry nor be given in marriage.'"

Most scholars agree that these words of Jesus mean what they seem to mean on first reading: the institution of marriage is a temporal one.[25] Even though it is the first and most solemn of the institutions established in Genesis 1–11, and even though it is a universal institution that transcends religions

---

25. Bradley R. Trick, "Death, Covenants, and the Proof of Resurrection in Mark 12:18–27," *NovT* 49 (2007): 241–44; Robert H. Stein, *Mark*, BECNT (Grand Rapids, MI: Baker Academic, 2008), 550.

On the other hand, Ben Witherington argues that Jesus's remark implied a dissolution of only levirate marriages and not every marriage bond. See Ben Witherington III, *The Gospel of Mark: A Socio-Rhetorical Commentary* (Grand Rapids, MI: Eerdmans, 2001), 328–29.

and cultures and stretches across known time and geographic space, marriage belongs in time. It will not carry over into eternity.

If that is to be the case, what happens to sex, something we understand as a gift of the Creator? C. S. Lewis answers: "The letter and spirit of Scripture . . . forbid us to suppose that life in the New Creation will be a sexual life."[26] If that draws the exclamation: What?!, then here is how Lewis helps us understand the situation:

> I think our present outlook might be like that of a small boy who, on being told that the sexual act was the highest bodily pleasure, should immediately ask whether you ate chocolates at the same time. On receiving the answer "No," he might regard absence of chocolates as the chief characteristic of sexuality. In vain would you tell him that the reason why lovers in their raptures don't bother about chocolates is that they have something better to think of. [But] the boy knows [only] chocolate: he does not know [any] positive thing that excludes [chocolate]. We are in the same position. We know the sexual life; we do not know, except in glimpses, the other thing which, in Heaven, will leave no room for it.[27]

What is this "other thing . . . in Heaven" which Lewis says will leave no room for the sexual life? It is the consummation of relationship between Christ and his bride, the church. This is an end-time event that the whole of the canon looks forward to. In the OT, a dominant metaphor for the special relationship between Yahweh and Israel is that of husband and wife. Our familiarity with the metaphor probably comes from the prophetic texts that deploy it, such as Hosea and Ezekiel, but we recall that the imagery goes back as far as Deuteronomy, when Israel, newly covenanted to Yahweh, is cautioned not to go whoring after other gods. The metaphor invariably shows up Israel in a less than favorable light – she is a wanton wife. Here is where the Song of Songs becomes relevant.

When read as allegory, the Song of Songs presents a picture of Yahweh's ideal wife, an ideal that remains unrealized in the pages of the OT. Where the prophetic texts dramatize the breakdown of human-divine marriage, the Song enacts the satisfaction of it; if the other texts present the ferocity of a

---

26. C. S. Lewis, *Miracles: A Preliminary Study* (London: Centenary Press, 1947), 190.
27. Lewis, 190–91.

thwarted deity, the Song pictures one who delights in his beloved; if in the other texts the human remains sullenly silent, in the Song, the human voice is the first and last we hear. In the NT, the metaphor of divine-human marriage is transposed on to Christ and his bride, the church. Paul speaks of it in his letters, but more gloriously, the book of Revelation ends with it.

Literal, physical marriage as we know it on earth is sublimated into the perfect relationship between the church and Christ. Meanwhile, the members of the church relate with each other in kinship – the family of God, the children of God, brothers and sisters in Christ, bound together by and unified in perfect and harmonious love – the love that remains and continues on when faith and hope have outlived their use and are needed no longer.

So then, we have arrived at an unpacking of the "other thing" that Lewis refers to. "We do not know," Lewis says, "except in glimpses, the other thing which, in Heaven, will leave no room for [the sexual life]." The "other thing" has two dimensions: one dimension is the kinship communion of the saints, its fractures healed by kinship love perfected; the other dimension is the consummation of the marriage of this collective with her bridegroom, Jesus, in a bond that transcends even the deepest love that a blood relationship can enjoy. We will see then that our earthly partnerships in marriage were a pale shadow of this ultimate unimaginably intimate and inconceivably ecstatic reality. The day will come when humans will be forever reconciled to each other and to God.

CONCLUSION

That is where our three-part drama concludes. We have placed the man-woman relationship into the great whole of the creation of Genesis 1. Act 1 established a world humming with harmony between humans and the earth, and between humans and the orders of living things. Man and woman held each other in a bond that mirrored the deepest of all relationships, that of kinship. It was a bone and flesh bond, the convoluted subtleties of which we Asians so well understand, one that renders irrelevant questions of equality and mutuality and complementarity.

In Act 2, human recklessness destroyed the peace. The earth turned against humankind, animals, and humans against each other. As for the man and woman, they remain locked into a bitter contest to gain domination, a war as thoughtless and ugly as that between blood brothers, one in which there can be no winner. Act 3 waits to unfold, bright with the promise of the consummation of the very institution of marriage. The Lamb will wed his bride, which is humankind – man and woman – resplendent in restored kinship, never to be violated again.

In between Eden lost and Eden regained, the institution of marriage keeps afloat, as best as it can, on the stormy waters of human systems. We recall that it was after the Fall that the man gives his wife a name, Eve. If, as we said earlier, naming is the act of marking territory and establishing authority over, then here is the first indication of things to come. From here onwards, the institution of marriage accommodates the push and pull of fallen cultures and sinful systems – including polygamy, for the twelve tribes of Israel are born from four mothers, two wives and two surrogates. However, we notice how the accommodation decreases as we move further away from the Eden of the Fall towards the Eden of the Future. For example, the Song of Songs celebrates exclusive, dedicated love – "I am my beloved's and my beloved is mine." The NT requires monogamy. Even Ephesians 5, in which Paul recommends that the wife submit to the husband, may be but a staging post on the relentless movement towards the Eden of the future, for Paul goes on in that same section to exhort slaves to obey their earthly masters.[28] The human story and its institutions move slowly, but surely, towards the Eden to come, shedding all that entangles, all that detracts from what *should* be and what *will* be.

In the ages since the Fall, marriage at its best has been an idyllic world of two that mirrors – even if dimly and imperfectly – the Edenic world-made-whole-again. It will be a world in which the earth will be reconciled with humankind; in which the animal world and humankind will be at peace; in which men and women will enjoy among themselves kinship perfected; when humankind will be finally restored in relationship with God. When we have not merely returned to Eden, but transcended it to go – as C. S.

---

28. I acknowledge my colleague Joshua Kenneth George for this point of view.

There are two dominant interpretations to this verse. One view argues for mutual submission of both partners in a marriage in line with the general principle advocated in the previous verse that calls for "submitting to one another" (Eph 5:21), thus making all hierarchical distinctions trivial. The opposite camp opts for a unidirectional submission of the wife to her husband based on the asymmetrical relationship implied in the verb "submit."

For a detailed presentation of both views, see Peter T. O'Brien, *The Letter to the Ephesians*, PNTC (Grand Rapids, MI: Eerdmans, 1999), 398–404. O'Brien concludes in favor of the unidirectional subordination view.

A slightly more nuanced position attempts to reconcile the above extremes. See Andrew T. Lincoln, *Ephesians*, WBC, vol. 42 (Grand Rapids, MI: Zondervan, 1990), 21–22. Referring to a similar exhortation in 1 Peter 5:5, Lincoln argues that the verse appeals to an idea where "mutual submission coexists with a hierarchy of roles within the household." Such a view, although it may appear conflicting to modern readers, would not have been incompatible for a first-century family in light of their new faith and practice.

Lewis puts it – "further up and further in"[29] into ascending spirals of everlasting contentment.

REFERENCES

Bravmann, M. M. *Studies in Semitic Philology*. Leiden: Brill, 1977.

Cotter, David W. *Genesis*. Berit Olam. Collegeville, MN: The Liturgical Press, 2003.

Flesher, LeAnn Snow. "What the @#$! is a Helpmate?," *Review and Expositor* 115 (2018): 453–66.

Gordon, C. H. "*Erēbu* Marriage." In *Studies on the Civilization and Culture of Nuzi and the Hurrians. In Honor of Ernest R. Lachemann*, edited by M. Morrison and D. Owens, 155–61. Winona Lake, IN: Eisenbrauns, 1981.

Gowen, Annie. "Why an Indian Judge Thinks Rapists Should Marry their Victims." *The Washington Post*, July 9, 2015. https://www.washingtonpost.com/world/asia_pacific/why-an-indian-judge-thinks-rapists-should-marry-their-victims/2015/07/08/606f8998–23e5–11e5-b621-b55e495e9b78_story.html; "Indian Woman Marries her Alleged Rapist." *BBC News*, February 16, 2015. https://www.bbc.com/news/world-asia-india-31483956.

Hamilton, Victor P. *The Book of Genesis: Chapters 1–17*. New International Commentary on the Old Testament. Grand Rapids, MI: Eerdmans, 1990.

"In media Res," 8 Classic Storytelling Techniques for Engaging Presentations, https://www.sparkol.com/en/blog/8-classic-storytelling-techniques-for-engaging-presentations.

Lewis, C. S. *Miracles: A Preliminary Study*. London: Centenary Press, 1947.

———. *The Last Battle*. London: Lions, 1990. Original pub. London: Bodley Head, 1956.

Lincoln, Andrew T. *Ephesians*. Word Biblical Commentary 42. Grand Rapids, MI: Zondervan, 1990.

Longenecker, Richard N. "Authority, Hierarchy and Leadership Patterns in the Bible." In *Women, Authority & the Bible*, edited by Alvera Mickelsen, 66–84. Downers Grove, IL: InterVarsity, 1986.

Mathews, Kenneth A. *Genesis 1–11:26*. New American Commentary 1A. Nashville, TN: Broadman & Holman, 1996.

Neusner, Jacob. *Genesis Rabbah*. Vol. 2. Atlanta, GA: Scholars Press, 1985.

O'Brien, Peter T. *The Letter to the Ephesians*. Pillar New Testament Commentaries. Grand Rapids, MI: Eerdmans, 1999.

---

29. C. S. Lewis, *The Last Battle* (London: Lions, 1990; original pub. London: Bodley Head, 1956), 162.

Ortlund Jr., Raymond C. "Male-Female Equality and Male Headship: Genesis 1–3." In *Recovering Biblical Manhood and Womanhood*, edited by Wayne Grudem and John Piper, 95–112. Wheaton, IL: Crossway, 1991.

Sarna, Nahum M. *Genesis*. The Jewish Publication Society Torah Commentary. Philadelphia: The Jewish Publication Society, 1989.

Sattar, Arshia. *Ramayana for Children*. New Delhi: Juggernaut, 2019.

Stein, Robert H. *Mark*. BECNT. Grand Rapids, MI: Baker Academic, 2008.

Trible, Phyllis. "Depatriarchalizing in Biblical Interpretation." *Journal of the American Academy of Religion* 41 (1973): 35–42.

———. *God and the Rhetoric of Sexuality*. Overtures in Biblical Theology. Minneapolis, MN: Fortress, 1978.

Trick, Bradley R. "Death, Covenants, and the Proof of Resurrection in Mark 12:18–27." *Novum Testamentum* 49 (2007): 232–56.

"Viewers Call Ramayan's Last Episode as 'Most Painful' and Get Teary-eyed; A Look at Such Emotional Reactions." *Times of India*, May 3, 2020. https://timesofindia.indiatimes.com/tv/news/hindi/viewers-call-ramayans-last-episode-as-most-painful-and-get-teary-eyed-a-look-at-such-emotional-reactions/photostory/75515396.cms.

Walton, John H. *Genesis*. NIV Application Commentary. Grand Rapids, MI: Zondervan, 2001.

Wenham, Gordon J. *Genesis 1–15*, Word Biblical Commentary 1. Waco, TX: Word Books, 1987.

Witherington III, Ben. *The Gospel of Mark: A Socio-Rhetorical Commentary*. Grand Rapids, MI: Eerdmans, 2001.

CHAPTER 4

ISRAEL, THE NATIONS, AND THE *MISSIO DEI*

Jerry Hwang

Ancient Israel was a dwarf among giants. Since the Old Testament focuses on Israel it is easy to think of Egyptians and Babylonians as merely part of the scenery. The result is not unlike when Australians (jokingly) produce maps of the world with their nation in the middle, splitting the major continents on either side of the page. The Australian sense of humor reflects an awareness of their small country's standing on the world stage. But it is not as innocent when readers of the OT imagine tiny Israel to be a superpower that lies at the center of its world.

Why does the OT spotlight such a modest nation, humanly speaking? Does God's choice of Israel mean that other nations are incidental or even despised in his purposes? These questions are expressed pointedly by the "new atheist" Richard Dawkins in his influential book *The God Delusion*:

> The God of the Old Testament is arguably the most unpleasant character in all fiction: jealous and proud of it; a petty, unjust, unforgiving control-freak; a vindictive, bloodthirsty ethnic cleanser; a misogynistic, homophobic, racist, infanticidal, genocidal, filicidal, pestilential, megalomaniacal, sadomasochistic, capriciously malevolent bully.[1]

Dawkins is being melodramatic, of course. The stakes are rather low for his post-Christian perspective since the OT is "fiction" which can be easily dismissed. However, for Asian Christians, the frequent use of the OT by Western empires to justify colonialism underscores the importance of reexamining Israel's relationship to other nations.[2] It was commonplace in this

---
1. Richard Dawkins, *The God Delusion* (London: Black Swan, 2007), 31.
2. The Puritan pastor John Winthrop concluded his famous "city upon a hill" sermon with an exhortation from Deuteronomy 30. On their ship bound for the New World, Winthrop and his hearers saw themselves mirrored in Moses's audience on the verge of the promised land (Mark Charles and Soong-Chan Rah, *Unsettling Truths: The Ongoing, Dehumanizing Legacy of*

regard for the armies of Christendom to characterize themselves as chosen "Israelites" and colonial peoples as pagan "Canaanites." Their battle cry in wars of expansion naturally became the familiar words of Joshua 1:9, "Have I not commanded you? Be strong and courageous. Do not be afraid; do not be discouraged, for the LORD your God will be with you wherever you go."[3] Christian missionaries have similarly viewed this verse as a triumphal OT counterpart to Jesus's promise that "surely I am with you always, to the very end of the age" (Matt 28:20).[4] Thankfully, the OT has plenty to say about the disputed relationships between Israel and the nations as well as between mission, culture, and imperialism.

This chapter proceeds in three parts. First, we will explore the nature of Israel's missional calling in the world. Since the Torah includes both this responsibility toward the nations (Gen 12:1–3) and the mandate to "show them no mercy" (Deut 7:2), our second section will address the OT's apparent contradiction between blessing the nations and destroying them. Does the *missio Dei* include conquest, given how missionaries and conquerors traveled some of the same paths in church history? Third and finally, the prophetic book of Jeremiah will provide a case study on the dynamic relationship between Israel and its much larger neighbors in the OT. Since Yahweh is both the God of Israel and the God of all the earth, Jeremiah depicts the *missio Dei* as a cosmic drama of love and wrath, with Israel and the nations playing the roles of both subjects and objects in Yahweh's redemptive purposes.

1. ISRAEL'S CALLING TO BLESS THE NATIONS

What kind of gospel did Israel possess in the Old Testament? Did Israel have a missionary mandate to the nations? Attention has usually focused on whether Israel had a Great Commission like the command of Jesus to "go and make disciples of all nations" (Matt 28:19), often with the proposal that the calls of Abraham or the prophet Jonah to "go" (Gen 12:1; Jonah 1:2; 3:2) serve as

---

the *Doctrine of Discovery* (Downers Grove, IL: IVP Academic, 2019), 70–73. The "Doctrine of Discovery" that undergirded European settlement in the Americas resulted in tens of millions of deaths among indigenous peoples.

3. Hélène Dallaire, "Taking the Land by Force: Divine Violence in Joshua," in *Wrestling with the Violence of God: Soundings in the Old Testament*, ed. M. Daniel Carroll R. and J. Blair Wilgus, BBRSupp 10 (Winona Lake, IN: Eisenbrauns, 2015), 53–56.

4. Protestant missions describe recruitment and strategy in terms of *mobilization*, while missionary conferences routinely use the martial language of Psalm 2:8 ("Ask of me, and I will make the nations your inheritance, the ends of the earth your possession") as a theme.

models for *centrifugal* mission.[5] Most of the OT, however, describes the *missio Dei* less as the obligation for Yahweh's people to "go and tell" and more as a *centripetal* pattern in which the nations are invited to "come and see."[6] In other words, Israel is mainly called to embody a counterculture among the nations that brings honor to Yahweh due to its "missional magnetism."[7]

The special identity of Israel is evident in its first official event as a nation. In the Sinai narrative of Exodus 19–20, Yahweh directs Moses to tell a newly redeemed people: "You yourselves have seen what I did to Egypt, and how I carried you on eagles' wings and brought you to myself" (19:4). The priority of divine grace rather than law in establishing this relationship is critical, for the next verse's command to "obey me fully and keep my covenant" (19:5a) is not a matter of Israel earning its salvation (which it already has; cf. Exod 14:30; 15:2; 20:2). Instead, obedience to Yahweh has the aim that "you shall be my treasured possession among all peoples, for all the earth is mine; and you shall be to me a kingdom of priests and a holy nation" (19:5b–6a ESV).[8] Later OT passages do set aside a special class of priests within Israel (e.g. Num 3). But at this formative point in Israel's history, it is "all the earth" that Israel will serve as "a kingdom of priests and a holy nation." That is, the quality of Israel's holiness *before* Yahweh has a direct impact on the quality of Israel's testimony among the nations *about* Yahweh.

The book of Deuteronomy gives special attention to Israel's calling to reflect the glory of Yahweh. In chapter 4, Moses emphasizes that the nations are an eager audience that will envy three distinctive blessings of Israel. First, they will marvel at the depth of Israel's insight, "Surely this great nation is a wise and understanding people" (4:6). Second, the singular God of Israel is nearer to his people than the gods of other nations are to theirs (4:7). Third, the law of Yahweh surpasses the laws of other nations because of its righteousness (4:8). This emphasis on the goodness of Yahweh's revelation to his people at Mount Sinai stands in contrast to the view among many Christians that law, being the supposed opposite of grace, is a hindrance to one's relationship with God.

---

5. E.g. Walter C. Kaiser, Jr., *Mission in the Old Testament: Israel as a Light to the Nations*, 2nd ed. (Grand Rapids, MI: Baker Academic, 2012).
6. Michael W. Goheen, *A Light to the Nations: The Missional Church and the Biblical Story* (Grand Rapids, MI: Baker Academic, 2011), 49–73.
7. Christopher J. H. Wright, *The Mission of God's People: A Biblical Theology of the Church's Mission* (Grand Rapids, MI: Zondervan, 2010), 129.
8. Cf. NIV's "*although* the whole earth is mine" which assumes a contrastive relationship between Israel and the nations.

A closer look at some of Deuteronomy's laws will reveal why the nations will find them to be unusual but appealing. Before doing this, however, Moses preempts the common view among the people of God that law itself is the problem. He anticipates a conversation "in the future, when your son asks you, 'What is the meaning of the stipulations, decrees and laws the LORD our God has commanded you?'" (6:20). It is striking that the son in this story acknowledges that Yahweh is "*our* God." But he evidently finds Yahweh's revelation at Sinai to be tedious since he describes it as "the stipulations, decrees and laws . . . [that he] commanded *you*." The son is preoccupied with law at the expense of grace, so Moses directs the father to reorient the conversation: "[T]ell him: 'We were slaves of Pharaoh in Egypt, but the LORD brought us out of Egypt with a mighty hand'" (6:21). This unexpected answer shifts the focus from Yahweh's expectations of his people back to Yahweh's commitment to them, as seen in both the exodus from Egypt (6:22) and the gift of the land (6:23). Moses concludes that Israel's obedience will result in a long tenure in Canaan (6:24–25), a strategically located but vulnerable land that lies at the junction of two continents. Canaan's combination of centrality and vulnerability in the ancient Near East provides an ideal platform for other nations to gaze at Yahweh's dealings with his "treasured possession" (14:2; 26:18; cf. Exod 19:5). Israel is a marginal people that has uniquely heard the voice of its mighty God and experienced his salvation (4:32–34, 36–38), so the gods of the nations cannot compare with him (4:35, 39).

The rest of Deuteronomy emphasizes Yahweh's delight in small and weak things rather than big and strong ones (e.g. 7:7–8). In the Deuteronomic law code (chs. 12–26), the inversion of the usual authority structures is closely tied to Israel's distinctiveness as a marginal but blessed people.[9] With Yahweh as the father of the nation (1:31; 8:5; 14:1), every member of Israel is therefore a "brother/sister" (the Hebrew term *'āḥ* is collective rather than solely masculine). Let us examine how chapters 15 and 17 use familial language to summon Israel to be countercultural in the areas of social justice and spiritual leadership.

Deuteronomy 15 is a passage about the poor in Israel, not so much as a socioeconomic category, but as members of a larger community that can and should help them. In most societies, however, the economic structures in place mean that the rich get richer and the poor get poorer, especially through the

---

9. Peter Machinist, "The Question of Distinctiveness in Ancient Israel," in *Essential Papers on Israel and the Ancient Near East*, ed. Frederick E. Greenspahn, Essential Papers on Jewish Studies (New York: NYU Press, 2000), 433–34.

problem of accumulating debts that cannot be repaid. This is true whether the economic system is capitalist, socialist, or anywhere in between. Whether in a democracy or dictatorship, the poor often become trapped in deepening cycles of poverty from which they cannot escape. This is the reason Deuteronomy 15 says Israel is a family that must differ from other nations in its treatment of the poor:

> At the end of every seven years you must cancel debts. This is how it is to be done: Every creditor shall cancel any loan they have made to a fellow Israelite. They shall not require payment from anyone among their own people, because the LORD's time for canceling debts has been proclaimed. You may requirement payment from a foreigner, but you must cancel any debt your fellow Israelite owes you. (Deut 15:1–3)

In these verses, English Bibles tend to render *'āḥ* as "fellow Israelite" (NIV) or "member of your community" (NRSV). But the literal meaning of the Hebrew word is "brother/sister." According to Moses, the most important thing about a debtor in Israel is not the money they owe but the fact that they are the creditor's "brother/sister." In this ancient, clan-based society without banks and little savings or surplus beyond one's daily bread, it is amazing that Moses can say that "there need be no poor people among you, for in the land the LORD your God is giving you to possess as your inheritance, he will richly bless you" (v. 4). When people matter more than money in Israel, such a countercultural nation will only lend to other nations but never need to borrow (v. 6). Debt release among Israelites is directly connected to the survival and flourishing of weak Israel among much stronger nations (v. 5) – the link here between caring for the weak and being strong is simply astounding!

Perhaps because this promise seems too idealistic, Moses acknowledges that the society of Israel will not be perfect. He foresees the reality that there will still be poor people in Israel: "If anyone is poor among your fellow Israelites [brothers/sisters] in any of the towns of the land the LORD your God is giving you, do not be hardhearted or tightfisted toward them. Rather, be openhanded and freely lend them whatever they need" (vv. 7–8). The ideal of no poverty is expressed in verse 4, but verse 7 also adds the reality that poverty will still exist. Yet, the existence of poor people is cause for neither fatalism nor tightfistedness, but for the people of Yahweh to be softhearted and lend freely.

This command may still seem too impractical until we see how Moses addresses the plight of the poor. Instead of focusing on *why* they are poor,

Moses again focuses attention on *who* the poor are. In verse 7, the poor person is "one of your brothers/sisters who should become poor, in any of your towns within your land that the LORD your God is giving to you" (my translation). These are family members in any place who happen to be poor, not a category to keep at a distance as strangers or outsiders. Even if you do not know this person who is poor, Moses says, that person is your brother or sister rather than a stranger. No exceptions and no excuses, because Israel dwells in "*your* land that the LORD your God is giving to *you*." Similarly, the Hebrew pronouns of verse 11 emphasize that the needy in Israel are "*your* needy" and "*your* poor" rather than an abstraction or someone else's problem.[10] Since all must be honored as equal members of God's family, social justice in Israel will be like no other nation in the ancient world. To be poor, marginalized, and vulnerable in the rest of the ancient world was practically a death sentence – but not in this extended family!

Deuteronomy 17 also uses the concept of family to address the other end of the economic spectrum. It is not only the weak, but also the strong who must be one of the "brothers" in the family of Israel. In verse 14, Moses knows that Israel will seek to have powerful kings: "When you enter the land that the LORD your God is giving you and have taken possession of it and settled in it, and you say, 'Let us set a king over us like all the nations around us.'" The problem in days to come will not be kingship as an institution, for Yahweh had already promised kings for his people (e.g. Gen 17:6; 35:11). Instead, the issue lies in how Israel wants a ruler "*like the nations around us.*" Much like Pharaoh in Egypt, kings in the ancient Near East viewed their people as pawns for their royal projects and plans. In response to this kind of autocratic leadership, Moses offers a rather different model which centers on Yahweh as the head of the family: "be sure to appoint over you a king the LORD your God chooses. He must be from among your fellow Israelites [brothers]. Do not place a foreigner over you, one who is not an Israelite [brother]" (Deut 17:15).

> The Israelite king will be denied several privileges that ancient kings usually possessed: The king, moreover, must not acquire great numbers of horses for himself or make the people return to Egypt to get more of them, for the LORD has told you, "You are not to go back that way again." He must not take many wives, or

---

10. Compare "the needy" (NIV) and "the poor" (ESV).

his heart will be led astray. He must not accumulate large amounts of silver and gold. (vv. 16–17)

Firstly, kings in Israel should have no horses, because possessing them would draw the people toward military strength and alliances rather than trusting in God. In that time, not having horses and chariots was like trying to defend a nation today without any automobiles, tanks, or airplanes. Secondly, accumulating wives would not be allowed for kings in Israel, though ancient kings typically kept a harem of concubines both for sexual gratification as well as to boast to other leaders how powerful they were. In the book of Esther, for example, the king of Persia sought to parade his wife in front of others as a sign of his stature. But the king of Israel is a "brother" who cannot exploit his "sisters" in this way. And thirdly, the king of Israel must not accumulate the precious metals of silver and gold. One of the benefits of kingship elsewhere was the ability to gain at the expense of others, but Israel's king must not use his position to enrich himself.

If a king in Israel cannot live as other ancient Near Eastern kings, what way will he live by? In verses 18–19, Moses tells the Israelite king what he must do instead:

> When he takes the throne of his kingdom, he is to write for himself on a scroll a copy of this law, taken from that of the Levitical priests. It is to be with him, and he is to read it all the days of his life so that he may learn to revere the LORD his God and follow carefully all the words of this law and these decrees.

The king is forbidden from delegating the copying of the law to the priests or anyone else. Rather, he must do so himself in the presence of the priest and read it continually. He must fear Yahweh his God instead of trying to get his people to fear him. In fact, Israel is unique in the ancient Near East since kings are not only equal with their people but are in fact lower than priests. The king in Israel may not assume the typical role of high priest who supervises other priests, for the priest in Israel will oversee the copying of the law and hold the king accountable.

When the king faithfully copies the law given to every Israelite (cf. Deut 4:1–2), he will remember his ordinary status and receive the blessing of a long reign (Deut 17:20). This is a rather strange royal dynasty in that the key to keeping power is to give it away! Ultimately, this kind of countercultural leadership stresses that the human king is not truly the king in Israel, for Yahweh is both the King who has chosen a vice-regent over his family as well as a Father who appoints one of the "brothers" as the head of his household. Those who were powerful and mighty in other empires, like Babylon and Egypt, would be like everyone else since Israel must be a truly special family.

In short, Yahweh gives such laws in Deuteronomy to form a countercultural community that is a blessing to the whole world. The family of Yahweh was supposed to be a sanctuary of countercultural social justice and spiritual leadership. Sadly, the later history of Israel failed to reflect this special identity. Deuteronomy 15 was violated by kings like Ahab, who failed to consider Naboth one of his brothers but killed him instead and stole his vineyard. Other kings were like Solomon, who accumulated all three things – horses, wives, and precious metals – that Moses had forbidden in Deuteronomy 17. The sins of these kings eventually led to the punishment of exile, far from the land that God had given to his people.

2. THE *MISSIO DEI* AS BLESSING OR DESTROYING THE NATIONS?

Deuteronomy's call to embody a counterculture among the nations soon encounters another problem besides Israel's own sinfulness. There is also the issue of Israel's conflicted relationship with those same nations – how could the call of Israel to be a blessing to other peoples also involve dominating them under the guise of possessing a superior culture? It is one thing to recognize that, in church history, the "Golden Age of Missions" coincided with the height of colonialism, as in the Opium Wars in China or the "Scramble for Africa" during the 19th century. This is the mixed legacy of Christendom and imperialism that our third section will address from an OT perspective. It is another thing and far more disturbing to find that the *missio Dei* and conquest overlap to some degree in the OT itself. The theological stakes are well expressed by Hélène Dallaire:

> Because God told Abraham (Gen 12:1–3) that, through him, all the families of the earth would be blessed (including the Canaanites), how could God instruct his people to kill all Canaanites or anyone else indiscriminately? A literal interpretation of the conquest narrative [of Joshua], that includes the annihilation of all foreigners of the land, corresponds neither to the greater mission of God for the world nor to the true character

of the God of heaven and earth as revealed in the full extent of the Bible.[11]

Dallaire writes as an evangelical OT scholar who recognizes the authority of Scripture. Her sincerity about these difficulties in the OT stands in contrast to Richard Dawkins and his dismissiveness toward all things biblical. It is important to note, then, that a high view of Scripture does not entail denying that Joshua's narrow focus on conquest sits uneasily within the OT's bigger narrative of the *missio Dei*.

Besides this ethical challenge from within the Bible's pages, the history of interpretation for Joshua is also controversial because the label of "holy war" is often used to characterize the conquest of Canaan. This English term was first used to translate Arabic *jihad* (i.e. a religiously motivated war to acquire converts and territory). The frequent label of "holy war" given to Joshua is misleading, however.[12] "Holy war" does not accurately describe the storyline of Joshua, nor the "Christian" conquests that were wrongly based on this OT book (e.g. the medieval Crusades).[13] Since the question of Joshua and Canaanite genocide has already received detailed attention from Christian archaeologists, exegetes, theologians, and ethicists, the reader is directed to those resources for a full treatment of the issues.[14]

---

11. Dallaire, "Taking the Land by Force," 71–72.
12. This happened especially through Gerhard von Rad's German study from 1952 (*Der heilige Krieg im alten Israel*), published in English as *Holy War in Ancient Israel*, trans. Marva J. Dawn (Eugene, OR: Wipf & Stock, 2000).
13. Stephen B. Chapman, "Martial Memory, Peaceable Vision," in *Holy War in the Bible: Christian Morality and an Old Testament Problem*, ed. Heath Thomas, Jeremy A. Evans, and Paul Copan (Downers Grove, IL: InterVarsity, 2013), 47–51.
14. Several features of the OT storyline challenge the notion that the conquest was a genocide of innocents: (1) Canaanites and Israelites are held by Yahweh to the same moral standards, with both nations being justly cast out from the land for their sins (Lev 18:24–30; Deut 9:5; 2 Kgs 16:3–4; 17:7–8); (2) Yahweh gives ample opportunities to Canaanites to repent and trust in him (Gen 15:16; Josh 2:9–11; 9:24–25); (3) The Hebrew root *ḥrm* has a metaphorical meaning of "separation, place under the ban" which may take precedence over the literal sense of "destroy totally," since otherwise Deuteronomy's prohibition on intermarriage with the Canaanites is self-contradictory (Deut 7:2–3); (4) OT conquest narratives alternate between the Hebrew terminology of "separate, destroy totally" (*ḥrm*; Deut 11:23; and "drive out, dispossess" (*hdp, yrš* Hiphil; e.g. Deut 6:19; Josh 23:5; Judg 1:33), problematizing the singular notion of conquest as extermination; (5) The book of Joshua has a hyperbolic literary element since both Joshua's farewell speeches to the people and the book of Judges refer to Canaanites remaining in the land (e.g. Josh 23:3–13; Judg 1–2) even though earlier passages say that they were all subject to *ḥrm* (e.g. Josh 10:39–40); and (6) God has an ultimate plan to bring peace and salvation to all nations (Ps 46:8–10; Isa 2:1–4).

For detailed discussion of these issues, see Charlie Trimm, *The Destruction of the Canaanites: God, Genocide, and Biblical Interpretation* (Grand Rapids, MI: Eerdmans, 2022); John H. Walton

Dallaire's other observation about the consistency of God's character is nonetheless pertinent for our purpose of examining the *missio Dei*. Even more urgently than the issue of unity between Joshua and the rest of the OT, the unity of Yahweh's personality also comes into question. How does one reconcile his twin postures of kindness and harshness toward those who are not his chosen people? The common stereotype of a bipolar God is captured by David Lamb, an OT professor and ethicist, in a trick question that he poses to unsuspecting students:

> How does one reconcile the loving God of the OT with the harsh God of the New Testament? When I ask this question of students, at first they are shocked, and then most assume that I have simply misspoken, . . . I then observe that God in the OT is consistently described as slow to anger and abounding in steadfast love, but Jesus speaks about hell more than anyone else in Scripture.[15]

Indeed, the challenge of relating love and wrath to one another is of utmost relevance for the *missio Dei*. The trend among Christians, however, has been to view these attributes of God as opposites. This is evident in missionary literature of the nineteenth century, for example, as in the pamphlet *China's Spiritual Need and Claims* by J. Hudson Taylor, the founder of the China Inland Mission (now OMF International). This influential work, which went through several reprintings, pits love and wrath against each other as alternating motivations for preaching the gospel to sinners. It is the love of God that compels believers to participate in missionary efforts to save the people of China from the wrath of God. The unstated assumption is that God's attributes are at odds with themselves so that believers and unbelievers experience them in diametrically opposite ways. While Taylor's intentions in writing were devotional rather than theological,[16] his laudable efforts to inspire Christians to missionary service

---

and J. Harvey Walton, *The Lost World of the Israelite Conquest: Covenant, Retribution, and the Fate of the Canaanites* (Downers Grove, IL: IVP Academic, 2017); Paul Copan and Matthew Flannagan, *Did God Really Command Genocide?: Coming to Terms with the Justice of God* (Grand Rapids, MI: Baker Books, 2014); Christopher J. H. Wright, *The God I Don't Understand: Reflections on Tough Questions of Faith* (Grand Rapids, MI: Zondervan, 2008), 76–108.

15. David T. Lamb, *God Behaving Badly: Is the God of the Old Testament Angry, Sexist, and Racist?* (Downers Grove, IL: IVP Academic, 2011), 9.

16. For an insider's sympathetic critique of Taylor's "evangelical empiricism," see Christopher E. M. Wigram, "The Bible and Mission in Faith Perspective: J. Hudson Taylor and the Early China Inland Mission" (PhD diss., University of Utrecht, 2007).

are nonetheless a form of *implicit theology* which reveals a deep anxiety about the relationship between God's love and wrath toward the nations.

The British-Canadian theologian J. I. Packer addresses the angst about God's character that underlies a theological dichotomy like Taylor's. Packer writes in his book *Knowing God*,

> The root cause of our unhappiness seems to be a disquieting suspicion that ideas of wrath are in some way unworthy of God. To some, for instance, "wrath" suggests a loss of self-control, an outburst of "seeing red" which is partly, if not wholly, irrational.... Surely, it is said, it would be wrong to ascribe to God such attitudes as these? The reply is: indeed it would, *but the Bible does not ask us to do this*.[17]

Most of Packer's Scripture references in his chapter on "The Wrath of God" come from the NT, however.[18] His otherwise helpful discussion leaves open the question of how the OT does not support the frequent accusation that it portrays only a God of wrath.

A major way forward in explaining the relationship between God's wrath and love has come from the celebrated Asian theologies by Kazoh Kitamori and Kosuke Koyama. Each brings his Japanese heritage to bear on a more holistic understanding of God's wrath in the OT. For Kitamori, Yahweh's declarations about his yearning for Israel that is nonetheless under his judgment (Jer 31:20; cf. Isa 63:15; Hos 11:8–9) express how "[t]he 'pain' of God reflects his will to love the object of his wrath."[19] God willingly takes on the heavy burden of feeling love and wrath simultaneously toward his people, making the pain of God an essential theological category to understand how these divine emotions work together. Both feelings of God are genuine and intense toward those he has made, rather than balancing or canceling each other out. The pain of God is thus a major part of the Bible's testimony which provides an alternative to Western understandings of God that draw on Greek Stoicism's idea of *apatheia* – a freedom from passions which views aloofness and rationality as the height of virtue.[20]

---

17. J. I. Packer, *Knowing God* (Downers Grove, IL: InterVarsity, 1973), 136, italics added.
18. Packer cites Nahum 1:2–8 (*Knowing God*, 135). He does supply numerous OT references in other chapters, but it is a bit surprising that his chapter on God's wrath does not.
19. Kazoh Kitamori, *Theology of the Pain of God*, trans. M. E. Bratcher (Richmond, VA: John Knox, 1965), 21.
20. Interestingly, a similar emphasis on radical transcendence at the expense of divine emotions and immanence is found in Islam's understanding of Allah.

Building on Kitamori, Koyama shows that Asian Christians often struggle to understand divine wrath since Buddhist ideas have influenced people to see emotions and desires as vices. In Thailand, for example, where Koyama served as a missionary, "[p]erturbation of soul is to be eschewed. So the Christian doctrine of the wrath of God, the divine loss of tranquility, perturbation of soul, has been soft-pedaled or avoided."[21] The Eastern stoicism that results is not unlike its Western counterpart in Greek philosophy for valuing divine love (in its coolheaded forms) at the expense of divine wrath. Yet, Koyama regards this clash of worldviews as even more reason to emphasize the Bible's conflict with Asian culture:

> A head-on collision between Thai tranquility theology and the wrath of God presents an opportunity for a fresh and more relevant study of the doctrine of God. . . . *it is essential to preach on the wrath of God boldly to the Thai audience, historicizing God in the way the Bible does.*[22]

Changing the metaphor from calmness to temperature, Koyama goes on to explain that "the 'hot' God heats the cool outlook by placing it in the context of covenant relationship. The life in the covenant relationship is experienced basically not as decaying (direction toward 'coolness'), but as healing and renewing (direction toward 'hotness')."[23]

The Western and Eastern theologies of Packer, Kitamori, and Koyama pave the way to reconsider the flaming *pathos* of Yahweh – his "divine relatedness to humanity"[24] – which burns passionately in salvation history for both Israel and the nations. This aspect of the OT's portrayal of God has been explored most comprehensively by Abraham Joshua Heschel, the Jewish-American rabbi who explored the divine pathos in his classic book *The Prophets*.[25] Heschel also put this theology into practice by "praying with my feet," joining his friend Martin Luther King, Jr. in the American civil rights marches of the 1960s.

In a renowned chapter on "The Meaning and Mystery of Wrath," Heschel shows how the Hebrew Bible defies both Western and Eastern worldviews by joining together divine wrath and love: "The secret of anger is God's care.

---

21. Kosuke Koyama, *Water Buffalo Theology*, 25th anniversary ed. (Maryknoll, NY: Orbis Books, 1999), 69.
22. Koyama, 74, italics added.
23. Koyama, 108.
24. Dennis Ngien, "'The Most Moved Mover': Abraham Heschel's Theology of Divine Pathos in Response to the 'Unmoved Mover' of Traditional Theism," *ERT* 25 (2001): 138.
25. Abraham J. Heschel, *The Prophets*, 2 vols. (New York: Harper and Row, 1962).

There is nothing greater than the certainty of His care. Anger brings about destruction and distress, but not despair. The prophet's response is not only acceptance, but also gratitude. This is the climax of faith."[26] Divine anger, in other words, is essential to pathos. To encounter apathy when jealousy is demanded would show that God has no real commitment to his people. Indifference toward oppression when righteous indignation is necessary would likewise prove that God is unjust.

As he works through various prophetic texts, Heschel demonstrates that "[t]he anger of God must not be treated in isolation, but as an aspect of the divine pathos, as one of the modes of God's responsiveness to man . . . God's concern is the prerequisite and source of His anger. . . . Anger and mercy are not opposites but correlatives."[27] Israel's experience of wrath and mercy is simultaneous so that lament for Yahweh's delays in restoration, such as "in wrath remember mercy" (Hab 3:2), are not only possible but expected. In Israel's experience, the close relationship between divine wrath and love is why arguing with Yahweh about the justice of his ways, as Abraham and Moses do (e.g. Gen 18:23–33; Exod 32:11–14), eventually gives rise to the Jewish cultural tradition of "arguing with God."[28]

Even for nations under condemnation, the intent of God's wrath is that of ultimate redemption when "the LORD will strike Egypt with a plague; he will strike them and heal them. They will turn to the LORD, and he will respond to their pleas and heal them" (Isa 19:22).[29] In fact, punishment against Israel's traditional enemies is just an intermediate step on the way to Yahweh welcoming them as his family members alongside Israel: "The LORD Almighty will bless them, saying, 'Blessed be Egypt my people, Assyria my handiwork, and Israel my inheritance'" (Isa 19:25). Here the familial language of "my people" applied to Egypt echoes the *covenant formula* that Yahweh repeatedly spoke to Israel (e.g. Lev 26:12; 2 Sam 7:7–8; Hos 1:9–10).

The divine pathos thus invites Israel and the nations to rejoice in Yahweh's judgments, even though these must run their course before ultimate good can result. Prior to the people of Yahweh suffering the sentence of exile in Assyria, the prophet Isaiah foretells that the manifestation of divine anger will be the turning point in Israel's spiritual awakening: "In that day you will say,

---

26. Heschel, 2:72.
27. Heschel, 2:62–63.
28. Anson Laytner, *Arguing with God: A Jewish Tradition* (Lanham: Rowman & Littlefield, 2004).
29. Heschel, *The Prophets*, 2:72.

'I will praise you, LORD. Although you were angry with me, your anger has turned away and you have comforted me'" (Isa 12:1). Similarly, the whole earth rejoices in Yahweh's kingship, even as his just rule over all means that his adversaries must be punished (Ps 97:1–6; cf. Ps 9:15–20).

Herein lies the biblical paradox that Zion/Jerusalem is both the place where all nations are subdued under the great King who rules from there (Ps 47) as well as the joy of all the nations (Ps 48). Such OT passages about all nations echo the Exodus narrative in which both Israelites and Egyptians must come to "know that I am the LORD" (e.g. Exod 6:7; 7:5; 10:2; 14:4). Distinctively in the Judeo-Christian tradition, then, suffering takes on the purposefulness of knowing God better in the present life and not just as a legal act of punishment (as in the West) or the *karma* of accruing merit for the next life (as in the East). Within such a strongly relational system, repentance and restoration with a personal Deity become a theological possibility for the first time.

It has always been easier, though, to conceive of God as a mechanistic moralist rather than having a relational and sometimes unpredictable pathos. The prophet Jonah, for example, voices his displeasure that Yahweh will no longer follow through the original threat of judgment, "Forty more days and Nineveh will be overthrown" (Jonah 3:4). When the king of Nineveh directs his city to repent and Yahweh relents, Jonah dares to say that he knows his God's covenantal nature, but detests it: "Isn't this what I said, LORD, when I was still at home? That is what I tried to forestall by fleeing to Tarshish. I knew that you are a gracious and compassionate God, slow to anger and abounding in love, a God who relents from sending calamity" (Jonah 4:2; cf. Exod 34:6–7). The reality of the divine pathos means that the threat of judgment always has repentance as its best outcome, even when judgment might seem unconditional and irreversible.[30] In other words, punishment is a temporary, necessary, but often mysterious part of Yahweh's plan to bless the nations.

3. THE *MISSIO DEI* AND IMPERIALISM IN THE PROPHECY OF JEREMIAH

As noted already, Western Christian powers have historically often engaged in "mirror reading" that regards the OT's conquest narratives and judgment

---

30. Paul R. Raabe, "Why Prophetic Oracles against the Nations?," in *Fortunate the Eyes That See: Essays in Honor of David Noel Freedman*, ed. A. B. Beck et al. (Grand Rapids, MI: Eerdmans, 1995), 244.

oracles as a template for colonial rule over other peoples, lands, and resources in the non-Western world. Despite this frequent use of pseudo-biblical reasoning, it is of crucial importance that the OT represents a form of protest literature against tyranny of all kinds, no matter its source, and especially when the target are those who profess to be God's people.[31] On the one hand, the OT subverts the prideful empires and kings of the nations since Yahweh is the God who "brings princes to naught and reduces the rulers of this world to nothing" (Isa 40:23). On the other hand, the OT treats the leaders of Yahweh's own people as *round* characters with flaws and foibles rather than extolling them as *flat* heroes and role models. The *missio Dei* involves a strong God who often accomplishes his redemptive purposes through (and not merely despite) the weak and sinful. This demonstrates Yahweh to be both sovereign and wise in a manner that raw power never could on its own.

The OT is thus realistic for granting the fact of empire in the world, while at the same time assuming the prophetic posture of speaking truth to power. In other words, the OT's depiction of the relationship between Israel and the nations reflects a certain kind of *postcolonialism* which opposes and dethrones the abuses of power that have frequently characterized (mis)readings of it. But since critiques of Western hegemony can sometimes be perceived by evangelical Christians as Marxism, socialism, or other postmodern assaults on biblical authority,[32] the book of Jeremiah will supply a case study of how the OT contains anti-imperial dynamics that differ from other contextually oriented theologies which tend to read against the grain of the text, among them the liberation theologies and reader-response approaches to the Bible that are common in Asia today. It is natural, in fact, that postcolonialism is a contested area of study due to its focus on conflict settings – namely, when imbalances between size and power lead smaller but stronger entities to exercise disproportionate control over larger but weaker ones. As perhaps the most contentious book in the OT, the prophecy of Jeremiah is uniquely suited to draw together the strands of the *missio Dei*, Israel's relationship to the nations, and postcolonial themes.

---

31. Cf. Michael Prior, *The Bible and Colonialism: A Moral Critique*, The Biblical Seminar 48 (Sheffield: Sheffield Academic Press, 1997), 46.
32. Brazilian evangelical theologian João Chaves helpfully catalogues such theological disagreements between Latin American liberationists (some of whom are evangelical) and North American conservatives in *Evangelicals and Liberation Revisited: An Inquiry into the Possibility of An Evangelical-Liberationist Theology* (Eugene, OR: Wipf & Stock, 2013), 36–69.

Before examining Jeremiah, it is noteworthy that colonial theologies have generally focused on the OT's depiction of the land as a *gift* to Israel to the neglect of land as *obligation* and *temptation*.³³ In Christian Zionism, for example, Yahweh's covenantal promise to Abraham that "I will bless those who bless you, and whoever curses you I will curse" (Gen 12:3a–b) is often taken as an unconditional statement that anyone who opposes (ancient/modern) Israel's occupation of Canaan comes under divine judgment.³⁴ Already in Genesis, however, the land promise is clearly contingent upon the obedience of Abraham and his family to Yahweh's ways (17:1; 22:16). This element of conditionality is unpacked in the rest of the Pentateuch, which presents Israel's disobedience as the eventual cause of deportation from its land. Particularly in Deuteronomy, Moses emphasizes that Israel is not only just as unrighteous as the land's original inhabitants (9:4, 5), but is already plotting apostasy so that punishment in exile is inevitable even before the conquest begins (chs. 29–32).

The book of Jeremiah links the Pentateuch's covenant theology to the *missio Dei* in several ways.³⁵ Most obviously, Jeremiah is "a prophet to the nations" (1:5) whom Yahweh appoints "over nations and kingdoms to uproot and tear down, to destroy and overthrow, to build and plant" (1:10). It then comes as a surprise that the book bearing Jeremiah's name mostly records his ministry among his own idolatrous "nation" that needs to repent (e.g. 2:11, 28; 7:6) before it can be a blessing to other "nations" (4:2).

Yahweh's people in Judah regarded the Temple in Jerusalem as a good-luck charm that supposedly protected the chosen city from Assyria in the eighth century BCE (7:9–10; cf. 26:2–6), as opposed to the northern kingdom that went into exile. The Zion theology of Isaiah, which had made Jerusalem's blessing to the nations conditional upon repentance, had been distorted into an unconditional superstition that the city of David was invulnerable to its enemies among the nations, Babylon the latest among them. With the centuries-long failure of Israel and Judah to participate in the *missio Dei*, Jeremiah warns that the nations will assume a new role in Yahweh's purposes. They will change from being an audience of his gracious ways to being witnesses

---

33. These categories are from Walter Brueggemann, *The Land*, 2nd ed., OBT (Philadelphia, PA: Fortress, 2002).
34. This theological view became British foreign policy under Lord Shaftesbury, a leading nineteenth-century proponent of a Jewish homeland in Palestine (Gerald R. McDermott, "A History of Christian Zionism," in *The New Christian Zionism: Fresh Perspectives on Israel and the Land*, ed. Gerald R. McDermott [Downers Grove, IL: IVP Academic, 2016], 67).
35. For details, see Jerry Hwang, "The *Missio Dei* as an Integrative Motif in Jeremiah," *BBR* 23 (2013): 481–508.

and instruments of his righteous judgment against his people (27:3–5). For both Yahweh and his prophet, however, the confluence of wrath and love for a beloved but rebellious people brings intense anguish. This pathos is fully on display when a voice cries out, "Oh, that my head were a spring of water and my eyes a fountain of tears! I would weep day and night for the slain of my people" (9:1). Jeremiah is often known as the "weeping prophet," but here and elsewhere in the book, "Yhwh weeps more often than Jeremiah does, and even Jeremiah's tears embody the tears of Yhwh."[36]

Judah also becomes a model for how Yahweh deals with all nations (18:7–11). When the people in Jerusalem wonder if Yahweh will deliver them from Babylon, Yahweh responds that he is no longer fighting for his people as he did in the past:

> I am about to turn against you the weapons of war that are in your hands, which you are using to fight the king of Babylon and the Babylonians who are outside the wall besieging you. And I will gather them inside this city. *I myself will fight against you with an outstretched hand and a mighty arm* in furious anger and in great wrath. (21:4–5)

Tragically, the God of the exodus has switched sides because his kings are acting like Pharaoh and other emperors of the nations (22:1–10). In response, Yahweh commissions King Nebuchadnezzar of Babylon as "my servant" (27:6; compare this Davidic title in 2 Sam 7:5–9; Jer 33:21, 22, 26) to exercise *ḥrm* ("totally destroy, place under the ban") against both Judah and other evil nations (25:9), much as Joshua did to the Canaanites (Josh 2:10; 6:17; 10:1).[37] In sum, the abuses of power by Judah's kings toward their people requires the homeopathic remedy of imperialism to cleanse its sins.

The *missio Dei* continues in unexpected ways while Yahweh is disciplining Judah. As Babylon's siege of Jerusalem worsens, the prophet is rescued from his own people's clutches by Ebed-Melek the Ethiopian, a foreign official who was serving in the palace of King Zedekiah (ch. 37). Strikingly, an outsider like Ebed-Melek turns out to be one of Jeremiah's most loyal friends while the king of Judah hands him over to the Judahite conspirators who attempt to kill him for advocating submission to Babylon (chs. 38–39). After Babylon sacks Jerusalem in Jeremiah 40, Nebuzaradan, the Babylonian guard, is another

---

36. David A. Bosworth, "The Tears of God in the Book of Jeremiah," *Bib* 94 (2013): 24.
37. See n. 14 on pp. 67–68 for discussion of *ḥrm*.

foreigner who takes the prophet Jeremiah more seriously than Judah ever did. He not only makes special arrangements for Jeremiah, his prisoner, but also voices the keen insight that "the LORD your God decreed this disaster for this place. And now the LORD has brought it about; he has done just as he said he would. All this happened because you people sinned against the LORD and did not obey him" (40:2–3). In sum, Ebed-Melek and Nebuzaradan anticipate the *missio Dei*'s harvest of foreigners on the day when "all the nations will gather in Jerusalem . . . No longer will they follow the stubbornness of their evil hearts" (3:17).

The conclusion of Jeremiah turns to salvation for Judah and judgment for other nations. The OT's lengthiest oracles concerning the nations in this book might seem at odds with Jeremiah's calling as "a prophet to the nations" (1:5). Keeping the whole book in mind, though, offers a better sense of literary and theological perspective: "The eye of Yahweh falls on his own, and rests there in discomfort. So the entire first part of the book lingers over the theme – judgment against the chosen. No lengthier, more detailed, and passionate diatribe exists."[38]

In fact, Yahweh's wrath not only burns more hotly against Judah than any other nation, he expresses the same kind of grief about judging the nations that he felt toward Judah. At the turning point of the oracle concerning Moab (ch. 48), the conjunction "therefore" joins anger and compassion in a riveting way: "'I know her insolence but it is futile,' declares the LORD, 'and her boasts accomplish nothing. *Therefore* I wail over Moab, for all Moab I cry out, I moan for the people of Kir Hareseth'" (48:30–31). Here as elsewhere, the book of Jeremiah portrays Yahweh as simultaneously a God of wrath and compassion. This is the reason the *missio Dei* in Jeremiah concludes with Yahweh's promise to Moab and several other nations that their judgment is only a prelude to restoration (46:26; 48:47; 49:6, 39) on the same terms as Yahweh's chosen people (chs. 30–33).

CONCLUSION

Indeed, the exile to Babylon inaugurates a new phase of the *missio Dei*. Since the settledness of Israel's centripetal calling eventually led to internal tyranny (despite being a small nation), the punishment of exile even becomes a short-term mission trip of sorts. The people of Yahweh experience Babylon as a

---

38. Daniel Berrigan, *Jeremiah: The World, The Wound of God* (Minneapolis, MN: Fortress, 1999), 179–80.

refuge that preserves them from destruction and renews their commitment to be a blessing to the nations. As refugees such as Daniel and his friends are wrenched from their comfort zone, the book of Daniel records how this centrifugal journey away from Israel provides them with access to Babylon's courts of power to testify of Yahweh in a manner that a merely centripetal mission never would have. King Nebuchadnezzar himself comes to "praise and exalt and glorify the King of heaven, because everything he does is right and all his ways are just. And those who walk in pride he is able to humble" (Dan 4:37). In this way and even after the return from exile, the marginality of Jews (and later Christians) as strangers and exiles becomes an identity to be embraced for the sake of the *missio Dei* (Jer 29:4–7; Heb 11:13; 1 Pet 1:1) and not merely a burden to be tolerated.

God continues to use the weakness of his people to shame the strong among the nations and bring them to himself. This has been the theological pattern of mission in both Testaments, culminating in the countercultural message of "Christ crucified" (1 Cor 1:23). The OT paradox of power in lowliness is what led the apostle Paul to summarize the NT gospel in terms of Jeremiah's ancient wisdom: "Let the one who boasts boast in the Lord" (1 Cor 1:31; cf. Jer 9:23–24).

REFERENCES

Berrigan, Daniel. *Jeremiah: The World, The Wound of God*. Minneapolis: Fortress, 1999.

Bosworth, David A. "The Tears of God in the Book of Jeremiah." *Biblica* 94 (2013): 24–46.

Brueggemann, Walter. *The Land*. 2nd ed. Overtures in Biblical Theology. Philadelphia: Fortress Press, 2002.

Chapman, Stephen B. "Martial Memory, Peaceable Vision." In *Holy War in the Bible: Christian Morality and an Old Testament Problem*, edited by Heath Thomas, Jeremy A. Evans, and Paul Copan, 47–67. Downers Grove, IL: InterVarsity, 2013.

Charles, Mark, and Soong-Chan Rah. *Unsettling Truths: The Ongoing, Dehumanizing Legacy of the Doctrine of Discovery*. Downers Grove, IL: IVP Academic, 2019.

Chaves, João B. *Evangelicals and Liberation Revisited: An Inquiry into the Possibility of An Evangelical-Liberationist Theology*. Eugene, OR: Wipf & Stock, 2013.

Copan, Paul, and Matthew Flannagan. *Did God Really Command Genocide?: Coming to Terms with the Justice of God*. Grand Rapids, MI: Baker Books, 2014.

Dallaire, Hélène. "Taking the Land by Force: Divine Violence in Joshua." In *Wrestling with the Violence of God: Soundings in the Old Testament*, edited by M. Daniel Carroll R. and J. Blair Wilgus, 51–73. Bulletin for Biblical Research Supplement 10. Winona Lake: Eisenbrauns, 2015.

Dawkins, Richard. *The God Delusion*. London: Black Swan, 2007.

Goheen, Michael W. *A Light to the Nations: The Missional Church and the Biblical Story*. Grand Rapids, MI: Baker Academic, 2011.

Heschel, Abraham J. *The Prophets*. 2 vols. New York: Harper & Row, 1962.

Hwang, Jerry. "The *Missio Dei* as an Integrative Motif in Jeremiah." *Bulletin for Biblical Research* 23 (2013): 481–508.

Kaiser Jr., Walter C. *Mission in the Old Testament: Israel as a Light to the Nations*. 2nd ed. Grand Rapids, MI: Baker, 2012.

Kitamori, Kazoh. *Theology of the Pain of God*. Translated by M. E. Bratcher. Richmond, VA: John Knox, 1965.

Koyama, Kosuke. *Water Buffalo Theology*. 25th Anniversary Ed. Maryknoll, NY: Orbis Books, 1999.

Lamb, David T. *God Behaving Badly: Is the God of the Old Testament Angry, Sexist, and Racist?* Downers Grove: IVP Books, 2011.

Laytner, Anson H. *Arguing with God: A Jewish Tradition*. Northvale, N. J.: J. Aronson, 1990.

Machinist, Peter. "The Question of Distinctiveness in Ancient Israel." In *Essential Papers on Israel and the Ancient Near East*, edited by Frederick E. Greenspahn, 420–42. Essential Papers on Jewish Studies. New York: NYU Press, 2000.

McDermott, Gerald R. "A History of Christian Zionism." In *The New Christian Zionism: Fresh Perspectives on Israel and the Land*, edited by Gerald R. McDermott, 45–75. Downers Grove, IL: IVP Academic, 2016.

Ngien, Dennis. "'The Most Moved Mover': Abraham Heschel's Theology of Divine Pathos in Response to the 'Unmoved Mover' of Traditional Theism." *Evangelical Review of Theology* 25 (2001): 137–53.

Packer, J. I. *Knowing God*. Downers Grove: InterVarsity, 1973.

Prior, Michael. *The Bible and Colonialism: A Moral Critique*. The Biblical Seminar 48. Sheffield: Sheffield Academic Press, 1997.

Raabe, Paul R. "Why Prophetic Oracles against the Nations?" In *Fortunate the Eyes That See: Essays in Honor of David Noel Freedman*, edited by A. B. Beck et al., 236–57. Grand Rapids, MI: Eerdmans, 1995.

von Rad, Gerhard. *Holy War in Ancient Israel*. Translated by Marva J. Dawn. Eugene, OR: Wipf & Stock, 2000.

Trimm, Charlie. *The Destruction of the Canaanites: God, Genocide, and Biblical Interpretation*. Grand Rapids, MI: Eerdmans, 2022.

Walton, John H., and J. Harvey Walton. *The Lost World of the Israelite Conquest: Covenant, Retribution, and the Fate of the Canaanites*. Downers Grove: IVP Academic, 2017.

Wigram, Christopher E. M. "The Bible and Mission in Faith Perspective: J. Hudson Taylor and the Early China Inland Mission." PhD diss., University of Utrecht, 2007.

Wright, Christopher J. H. *The God I Don't Understand: Reflections on Tough Questions of Faith*. Grand Rapids, MI: Zondervan, 2008.

———. *The Mission of God's People: A Biblical Theology of the Church's Mission*. Grand Rapids, MI: Zondervan, 2010.

CHAPTER 5

LEADERSHIP, POWER, AND AUTHORITY

Annelle Sabanal

The Old Testament portrays leaders as key players in the life of Israel who headed its different sectors and institutions. Israel's leaders played a major role in the formation of Israel's identity as a community as it underwent the different stages of its history.

In this chapter, I will examine the various forms of leadership in the OT and explore salient themes in leadership which enrich our understanding of community dynamics vis-à-vis authority and politics. Whenever applicable, I will also call attention to realities in the Asian context that resonate with these themes. This will show points of similarities and parallels between conceptions unique to Asian culture and the OT notions of leadership, authority, and power, as well as how such shared notions open up the possibility of bringing the OT's political ethics to bear on our own notions of leadership, power, and politics.

1. A COMMUNITY UNDER THE RULE OF YAHWEH

One of the OT's main assumptions behind all aspects of leadership is that Yahweh is the supreme leader of the community. To him, every member owes personal loyalty. The combination of the oft-repeated phrase "my people" (e.g. Exod 5:1; Isa 1:3) and "the LORD your God" (e.g. Deut 1:10–11; Isa 41:13) point to this idea. This notion of Yahweh's kingship and all its attendant implications are celebrated in the kingship psalms most of all (e.g. Pss 9; 99). These hymns about Yahweh's reign portray him as an active participant in the day-to-day affairs of the community – he saves people from the enemy, he goes with them day and night, follows them into a foreign land, and returns back with them to their homeland. This concrete understanding of Yahweh can be quite different from modern theological conceptions of a God whose presence is expressed more in metaphysical and abstract terms.[1]

The goal of Yahweh's kingship is the *shalom*, or well-being, of the community. This implies abundant and long life in the land for the people as Yahweh's

---

1. See the first volume of Jaroslav Pelikan, *The Christian Tradition: A History of the Development of Doctrine,* 5 vols. (Chicago, IL: University of Chicago Press, 1987–1994).

presence dwells with them. The gift of Yahweh's rule and all its benefits are expressed in the covenant which also comes with its requirement of obligation for Israel to show absolute loyalty to Yahweh. This creative purpose for God's rule is not exclusive to Israel since Israel was to model this unique relationship with Yahweh to the whole world, with all its corresponding benefits and privileges.[2]

The communal notion of a supreme deity who is nonetheless active in community affairs is one that Israel shares with its neighbor nations in the ancient Near East. It is also not foreign to Asian cultures. Some indigenous communities and major world religions in Asia continue to believe that the deity takes a direct role in the life of the community. I am part of such a minority indigenous tribe in the northern Philippines which holds this belief. Each of our deities is in charge of at least one important aspect of community life: war, peace, planting and harvesting, family matters, etc.[3] They determine the success and failure of each endeavor and the well-being or downfall of people and families. For each significant occasion in the life of an individual, a family, or the entire community, the elders of the family or clan will perform a ritual to ensure that deities are appeased and not act in a harmful manner toward anyone in the community.

From the notion of Yahweh's rule over the community comes the expectation that human leaders must lead with a loyalty that acknowledges Yahweh's jurisdiction over them, as expressed in their faithful obedience to the covenant. The leadership of human agents is therefore intermediary between Yahweh and the people. This arrangement means that institutions of leadership answer to Yahweh on the basis of how well they perform their roles.

Traditional Asian cultures resonate with this leadership dynamic in which the deity is the sovereign leader of the land, with human leaders acting according to the deity's mandate. In ancient China, for instance, the king is perceived as the "collective man" representing all humans on earth and serving as the mediator between heaven and earth. This relationship finds justification in the doctrine of the "Mandate of Heaven," which regards the ruler as the recipient of a divine mandate to rule. As in the OT, this relationship between

---

[2]. J. G. McConville, *God and Earthly Power: An Old Testament Political Theology, Genesis-King–* (London: Bloomsbury, 2008), 69–70, makes a strong exegetical case for the universality of the benefits and responsibility accorded to Israel.
[3]. Francis Lambrecht, "The Missionary as Anthropologist: Religious Belief Among the Ifugao," *Philippine Studies* 5 (1957): 271–86. See also Margaret Palaghicon Von Rotz, "Ifugao Identity: The Retention of Indigenous Religion and Rituals Despite Colonialism," *Philippine Quarterly of Culture and Society* 46 (2018): 114–23.

the supreme deity and the ruler is tangible and not just symbolic,[4] providing impetus for the ruler to maintain a good and just government.[5]

1.1. Leadership and Worldview

Life under the leadership of Yahweh lacks explicit demarcations between worship, morality, and law. In the modern world, these areas of communal existence are usually classified under either politics or religion, with politics regarded as secular and religion as sacred. However, this distinction does not exist in the ancient world of the OT. Instead, these areas are parts of a single system which are under the jurisdiction of Yahweh.[6]

The leadership positions and institutions to be explored in this chapter belong to such a holistic system of norms. While no sharp divisions between religion and politics exist in the OT, it is still possible to discern the distinctions in the roles of the leaders in the various institutions which they serve. Sometimes, however, a human leader will play multiple roles in different institutions. Examples include Kings David and Saul, who also exercised prophetic roles for a short while (1 Sam 10:11; 18:10), or the priests who became the primary civic and political leaders of the community during the post-exilic period. Israel still distinguished between institutions such as kingship and priesthood, but they also overlapped in ways that we are not accustomed to as modern readers.

Many Asian cultures arose from a similarly holistic notion of community.[7] One such community that still insists on having its own laws and rules as prescribed by their faith is that of Muslims in Asia, who collectively represent the different sects and traditions of Islam. Islamic law, or *Shari'ah*, is recognized in a number of places in Asia. In the Philippines, for example, Presidential Decree No. 1083 partially implements Shari'ah for the sake of Islamic communities in the country, especially in the south. Likewise in other parts of Asia, a synthesis between religious precepts and democracy persists despite the attempts of Western colonizers to do away with such "religious" worldviews.[8]

---

4. Julia Ching, "Son of Heaven: Sacral Kingship in Ancient China," *T'oung Pao* 83 (1997): 15.
5. Luke Glanville, "Retaining the Mandate of Heaven: Sovereign Accountability in Ancient China," *Millennium* 39 (2010): 328–34.
6. John H. Walton, *Ancient Near Eastern Thought and the Old Testament* (Grand Rapids, MI: Baker Academic, 2006), 87.
7. Ishtiaq Ahmed, "The Politics of Religion in South and Southeast Asia," in *The Politics of Religion in South and Southeast Asia*, ed. Ishtiaq Ahmed (Milton: Routledge, 2011), 4.
8. Ahmed, 5.

2. POLITICAL INSTITUTIONS IN THE OT

The following section explores the OT's holism towards politics and religion as expressed through the dynamics of human leadership and institutions. *Politics* is taken here to mean the public life by which Israel managed its order, power, and aspects of law and justice.[9]

2.1. Political Structures

The OT is witness to the evolution of political leadership and structures in Israel. None of these lasted or adhered satisfactorily to the full scope of Yahweh's rule. Is there something to learn from this seeming unpredictability of politics in the OT?

We first encounter Israel as a community with a discernible political structure in the stories of Exodus and Deuteronomy, featuring it as a loosely organized confederation of tribes under the one-man leadership of Moses and eventually Joshua. It seems that the leadership position of Moses and Joshua was merely temporary and for very specific crises (Exod 3; 1 Sam 12:6–8), as when Moses brought the community out of bondage from Egypt and Joshua led the conquest. Although a successor is promised before Moses dies (Deut 18:15–18), continuity of leadership is missing as Joshua also bids the people goodbye (Josh 23–24). The end of the book of Joshua leaves the foreboding impression that the community will not receive another charismatic leader who can lead the community into multiple successful feats as previous leaders have done.

What follows are short-term "judges" who fumble their way through the responsibility of delivering the community from enemies during the struggle to possess the land. Few of them are near-remarkable, no one is exceptional, and most are portrayed with a tinge of irony. As such, the end of each short narrative cycle depicts a community that has "done what is evil in the sight of Yahweh" and forgotten his sovereign leadership over them. Towards the end of the book of Judges, the community is at its worst state and far from the ideals of a community that manifests Yahweh's rule.

Following the leadership of the judges is the institution of kingship. Its very inception, as depicted in 1 Samuel 8, came with Yahweh's warnings to the elders of Israel who came together to demand a king. The OT is thus ambivalent towards kingship. On the one hand, hints of disapproval are expressed in

---

9. See also Lester L. Grabbe, *Priests, Diviners, and Sages: A Socio-Historical Study of Religious Specialists in Ancient Israel* (Valley Forge, PA: Trinity International, 1995), 20–40.

passages like Deuteronomy 17:14–20, 1 Samuel 8:10–18, and Judges 8:22–23. Moreover, many of the judgment oracles in the Prophets are directed towards kings. On the other hand, there are passages that suggest that kingship was necessary and inevitable. An example is the phrase in the book of Judges, "In those days Israel had no king; everyone did as they saw fit" (Judg 17:6; 21:25; cf. 18:1; 19:1).[10] At the same time, the kingship of the Davidic line in particular is central to the narrative of 2 Samuel. This theme later becomes a key element in OT passages elsewhere about the idea of a future Messiah (e.g. Isa 9:7; Jer 23:5–6; Ezek 34:23–24). Ambivalence towards monarchy became moot as Israel and Judah went into exile and lost their identity as states.

This brief sketch of Israel's political structures in different periods underscores the equivocal attitude that the OT holds towards them. This may suggest that there is no ideal kind of political or social leadership, or that the structures described in the OT are merely provisional and transitory. However, it is this same impermanence that creates space for reflection on how the ethos of God's rule might work in our own leadership.

The exile which removed monarchy, land, and temple in Israel raises questions about the future of political structures as described in the OT. The survival of a much smaller community than before, trying to make sense of its tragic experience, exhibits a leadership that is volatile and subservient to another empire. Nonetheless, some preliminary hints of the political future of the community are given to us in the messianic passages and salvation oracles of the Prophets. These passages anticipate a future for political governance in which Yahweh's rule will be realized again through a remnant community overseen by a messiah.[11] Concomitant to the realization of this vision is the role of the people in the political process and whose participation is marked by service to the community, as modeled by the suffering servant (Isa 42:1–4; 52:13–53:12).

2.2. Human Leaders and Power

The OT insists that the right use of power must characterize human leaders. Despite its expectation for power to be used responsibly for the wellness of

---

10. For contrasting approaches to these statements, see Gale Yee, "Ideological Criticism: Judges 17–21 and the Dismembered Body," in *Judges & Method: New Approaches in Biblical Studies* (Minneapolis, MN: Fortress, 1995), 157–58; and William J. Dumbrell, "'In Those Days There Was No King in Israel; Every Man Did What Was Right in His Own Eyes,' The Purpose of the Book of Judges Reconsidered," *JSOT* 25 (1983): 130–32.
11. McConville, *God and Earthly Power*, 151–67, makes a similar analysis of the future of the political structures, but using 1–2 Kings.

the community, the OT also grapples with the fact that human leaders are prone to abuse power. To counter this, checks and balances were instituted at significant junctures of Israel's political history. Even Moses, whom the OT considers a paradigmatic leader, did not hold absolute power. Under his leadership, Yahweh acts as a counterpoise to Moses's authority by taking on a very active role in the decision-making process, with Moses relying heavily on Yahweh's orders.

Before crossing to the promised land, Moses democratized his power by delegating judicial tasks to tribal leaders. Before his death, the community inherited the Torah, which functions not just as a guide to how the Israelites should live out their citizenship in the land, but also as a counterbalance in mitigating the concentration of power in one person. The non-familial succession of leadership from Moses to Joshua and the consequent success of Joshua in administering his office demonstrate the wisdom of a non-dynastic transfer of power. This also serves as an implicit critique of dynastic succession within the later Israelite monarchy.

In contrast to Moses's story, the stories of Israel's monarchs are a testament to the tyranny of leaders when they have too much power. The lengthy narratives of the first three kings of Israel – Saul, David, and Solomon – are troubling examples of the potential for kings to consolidate and corrupt power, with Solomon as perhaps the worst expression of what Deuteronomy 17 warned about. In addition to the Torah, the institution of prophets also emerged as a check on the power of the kings. Even so, the Israelite monarchy failed and passed into history, along with the temple and the land. The assessment of 1–2 Kings and the Prophets is that various abuses of power were responsible for the demise of the nation and the exile of the people. Was this tragic outcome for the Israelite kingship an inevitable one, however? The OT's ambivalence toward kingship needs a closer look in light of kingship in other ANE civilizations.

2.3. Kingship in the OT

In the ancient Near East, kingship was the central institution of society.[12] The same was true of Israel, given the number of textual materials pertaining directly or indirectly to kingship. For in both the ANE and the OT, kings

---

12. John Baines, "Ancient Egyptian Kingship: Official Forms, Rhetoric, Context," in *King and Messiah in Israel and the Ancient Near East*, ed. J. Day, JSOTSup 270 (Sheffield: Sheffield Academic Press, 1998), 16.

were chosen by the god/s of the nation. This concept of divine sponsorship was essential within the ideology of kingship to provide legitimation for the authority that the kings held (see Pss 2; 72).

The people of the ANE typically also believed that kings shared in some measure of divinity with the deities. The OT departs notably from this belief in that only Yahweh has divine status and human kings are merely his vice-regents or administrators. Yahweh's supreme and unique kingship is articulated well by Psalm 24:8–10 in its repeated reference to "the King of glory . . . the Lord, strong and mighty."

As noted above, divine legitimation of leaders is not foreign to the history of politics in Asia. Besides ancient China, which was mentioned earlier, pre-modern Japan had a similar phenomenon in the establishment of Shinto as the state religion. Shinto, or the *Kami-no-michi*, is conventionally translated as "the Ways of the Gods." In this understanding, the emperors were regarded as *kami* ("ancestors of the nation") and therefore divine.[13] While Japan was forced to repudiate the divine status of the emperor at the conclusion of World War II, the ascension of Akihito to the imperial throne in 1990 still included a *Daijosai*, the ceremony where the divine status of an emperor is ritualized. And though the Japanese constitution now mandates the separation of church and state, government officials still worship at Yasukuni Shrine, the Shinto shrine to war heroes. This and other practices which involve Japan's other religious memorials of war are remnants of state Shinto and its religious support for the state.[14]

On this note, divine legitimation of political power can easily become an excuse for abuse of power and oppression of one's subjects. By contrast, in the OT's conception, it is this very idea of divine legitimation that serves as the primary check and balance to the power of the king. Divine legitimation instead demands that the king be accountable to Yahweh and must therefore lead the people in accordance with Yahweh's own kingship.

2.4. Functions of the King

In both the ANE and the OT, kings were mediators between the divine and human worlds and were thus expected to discern the divine will and facilitate its execution. The ideals of this mediating function of kings are well captured

---

13. Randall L. Nadeau, *Asian Religions: A Cultural Perspective* (Hoboken, NJ: John Wiley and Sons, Inc., 2013), 210–11.
14. Nadeau, 212–13.

by the use of the shepherd metaphor to depict kings of the OT and the larger ANE. By drawing associations from the nurturing image of the shepherd who tends, guards, and saves the flock, royal ideology presents the king as the deity's chief redistributor of material and symbolic good for the community.[15]

Ezekiel 34 exemplifies a passage that utilizes the shepherd metaphor and captures ideas such as the functions of a king, the dynamics of his rule, and the implications of his failure. According to this passage, the king must act as the mediator of divine authority and the channel by which Yahweh's rule is realized. He accomplishes this mediating role by providing means of wellness and welfare, ensuring an abundance of resources, offering protection, and administering justice and righteousness in the community so that its more powerful members cannot oppress the weak. In this sense, the community finds its embodiment in the person of its king. When the king successfully administers his duties, his political authority is upheld and his subjects flourish. On the other hand, the failure of the king to administer his responsibilities according to the bounds of Torah will lead not only to his own destruction, but that of the entire nation.

Contrary to this ideal political scenario in the imagery of the shepherd, Ezekiel 34 also illustrates how kings generally failed to maintain the ideal power structures that Yahweh instituted. They exercised power instead for their own gain and failed to perform their responsibilities. This reality is elaborated in other parts of the prophetic corpus as well. According to these passages, the people perished, the community crumbled, and the weak were exploited when kings lost sight of their subordinate roles within the hierarchy of power. The exile was the most severe consequence of the kings' failure to perform their duties.

This interplay of power of the kings of Israel in relation to God is a dominant concern outside of the Latter Prophets as well. It is found even in passages portraying the inception of the monarchy, especially in the lengthy stories of the first two kings of Israel, Saul, and David. Their narrative cycles categorically point to the fact that the highest power granted to humans is still subject to divine mandate. Moreover, their stories show the tendency of kings to overstep the boundaries imposed by Yahweh. Consequently, kings are criticized and rejected whenever they exhibit a hint of desire to accumulate power that serves their own interest rather than those of Yahweh. In the case

---

15. Annelle Sabanal, "The Motif of 'Shepherd' and Politics in the Hebrew Prophets" (PhD diss., University of Edinburgh, 2017), 34–35.

of Saul, this is markedly shown in the passages portraying his rejection as king (1 Sam 13; 15) after he commits a series of rash acts in a bid to keep the throne.

David also exhibits this tendency to cling to power in some of the ambiguous characterizations of him as leader, especially in the narratives about his accession as king.[16] One of the notable hints of his interest in power lies in the curious narrative about his effort to bring the ark to Jerusalem, resulting in the death of Uzzah (2 Sam 6). Consequently, Yahweh rejects his desire to build a temple (2 Sam 7). These two events suggest that David is attempting to consolidate his power with Yahweh as the legitimator. In the first incident, David attempts to move the ark from Baal-Judah to mark his victory over the Philistines (cf. 2 Sam 5). Among others, Donald F. Murray reads this particular narrative as expressing David's misguided motive to bring all authority under his sway.[17] The return of the ark symbolizes the return of the warrior-king Yahweh, with the ark as booty liberated by David himself. Unfortunately, the perplexing incident of Uzzah's death happens, causing David to be angry. The implicit message is that David does not have the control over the ark that he thought he had, and consequently of Yahweh as well.[18]

As for 2 Samuel 7, this is the narrative in which Yahweh refuses David's request to build the temple. Explanations for the rejection are given elsewhere in the OT (1 Kgs 5:3–4; 1 Chr 22:8). However, within the context of the Davidic stories of 2 Samuel and especially chapter 6, the emphasis falls on Yahweh's response to David as a refusal to be controlled by the usual ANE expectation of kings celebrating their victory by building a temple for their patron deity.[19] In turning back David's request and offering to build David a "house" instead, Yahweh seems to be hinting at his dissatisfaction with David's aspiration to be like other ANE monarchs.

In summary, what underlies Yahweh's rebukes against Saul and David is the OT's rejection of concentrating power in a single human entity, particularly kings. This is largely due to the potential of the monarchy to absolutize its hold on power and claim possession of kingship rather than submit to the kingship

---

16. McConville provides a very useful summary, along with counteropinions, of these ambiguous moments in David's life that show hints of his personal interest in power (*God and Earthly Power*, 140–41).
17. Donald F. Murray, *Divine Prerogative and Royal Pretension: Pragmatics, Poetics and Polemics in Narrative Sequence about David (2 Samuel 5.17–7.29)* (Sheffield: Sheffield Academic Press, 1988), 19–20, 247–48.
18. Murray, 113–31.
19. McConville, *God and Earthly Power*, 142–43. See also Murray, *Divine Prerogative*, 252–64, who provides parallel examples of ANE kings building temples for their deities.

of Yahweh. The OT's many rebukes against abuses of power by kings support this inference. What is more, the OT's warnings about disproportionate power underlie the basis for "separation of powers"[20] in modern democratic societies and their systems of checks and balances. The OT does not necessarily impose a strict separation of roles,[21] but employs various correctives to prevent leaders from accumulating more power than necessary.

3. THE PROPHETS

The prophets in the OT were those called by Yahweh to be the direct bearers of his message and intentions to his people, usually as a response to contemporary circumstances. Since their message was mainly that of calling people back to faithful observance of the covenant, they were not the fortunetellers that modern readers tend to envision. Instead, they would assess concrete historical situations based on what Yahweh had done in the past, and may pronounce predictions for an immediate future only as a response to a present situation.

As other major leaders of the community, prophets were chosen by Yahweh, though their positions were not necessarily permanent. This is evident, for example, in the cases of Saul and David, who each prophesied for only a brief time. Prophets could also be elected against their will, as with Moses, the first in a line of prophets (Deut 18:15–18) and whose resistance to his prophetic calling (Exod 3–4) may be paradigmatic of a true prophet.

The clear connection between prophecy and kingship in the OT is difficult to miss. The stories of the first two kings of Israel, Saul and David, clearly demonstrate the close association between the prophetic and royal institutions. Prophets anointed kings, castigated them for their mistakes, and pronounced judgment when leaders failed to repent and change their ways. Prophets, therefore, provided a tangible counterbalance from Yahweh to the power of leaders. When a king overreached his authority and power, it was the prophet's task to expose the king's claim to authority that belonged to Yahweh alone.

Prophecy in Israel had numerous similarities with that of other ANE cultures, most notably the close connection between the deity, prophets, and

---

20. The term was coined by the eighteenth-century French philosopher Montesquieu and elaborated in his book, *The Spirit of the Laws*.

21. Clear delineations of roles do not necessarily preclude overlaps between the roles themselves, nor the jostling for position that is well attested in the OT's pages. The former is evident, for example, when kings offer sacrifices to God (Theodorus C. Vriezen, *The Religion of Ancient Israel*, trans. Hubert Hoskins [London: Lutterworth Press, 1967], 83–99) and serve as the *de facto* high priest of the state (Ps 110:4).

kings. However, one noticeable difference between OT and ANE prophecy is the relative lack of criticism against abuses of leaders in the latter.[22] It is unrealistic to infer that this is due to the absence of injustice in other ANE cultures, and the more plausible explanation is that prophetic oracles and other literary materials pertaining to kings and leaders were formulated elsewhere in the ANE to provide divine legitimation for their kings. The departure of the OT from this ideological tendency in ANE prophecy reflects the importance that the OT puts on prophets keeping other leaders in check.

Interestingly, the notion that deities hold leaders accountable for how they use their power is also found in ancient China. Mencius, a Confucian scholar, developed a political philosophy based on the Confucian idea of the Mandate of Heaven, which claimed that the ruler possessed divine approval to rule only when he retained the support of the people. This philosophy assumes that the people's will would be the means by which Heaven also made known its will. As a consequence, the people could rightfully hold their rulers to account. Although a similar "prophetic mandate" of keeping rulers in check was given to China's people, this philosophy shares the OT's assumption that powerful kings tended towards tyranny and thus needed to be kept accountable.[23]

Similarly to kings in the OT, some prophets also behaved contrary to their calling and were deemed to be false prophets for their deviations from biblical ideals. Some prophets were co-opted by the royal institution as the monarchy progressed. A true prophet, however, did not bow to human power and proclaimed Yahweh's message even when it went against the view of the king, the majority, or even fellow prophets. Since the messages of true prophets were usually directed against foreign policy and/or contrary to the whims of the powerful, prophets gradually found themselves on the periphery. In fact, most of the prophets whose words were preserved in the biblical canon were most likely peripheral rather than royally sponsored.

The prophetic task, however, was not only that of pronouncing criticism and judgment of kings. They also brought the pain and hurt of leadership abuses to public expression through offering laments and complaints. Prophets were also tasked to energize the community, point them to a vision of a better future, to assert that Yahweh is on the side of the weak and will act on their

---

22. This lacuna in the prophetic oracles in the ANE is noted by John W. Hilber, "Prophecy, Divination, and Magic in the Ancient Near East," in *Behind the Scenes of the Old Testament: Cultural, Social, and Historical Contexts*, eds. Jonathan S. Greer, John W. Hilber, and John H. Walton (Grand Rapids, MI: Baker Academic, 2018), 371–72.

23. Glanville, "Retaining the Mandate of Heaven," 324, 328.

behalf, and to institute praise to Yahweh as an assertion of the freedom that his kingship would bring, especially in times of crisis. It was this last prophetic task that became especially crucial during the difficulties of the exile.

The role of the prophets, especially concerning leadership, abuse of power, and justice and righteousness, may find some parallel expression in our contemporary time. Recent history provides us with examples of people of faith or faith communities opposing abuses of power, such as those in totalitarian regimes. A recent example is the witness of the Christian church in Myanmar in response to the military's takeover of the government. Numerous Christian churches have taken to the streets alongside other faith communities to express their solidarity with the people. Pastors of evangelical churches who took part in peaceful demonstrations have indicated that they are doing this as an expression of their belief that God is on the side of the oppressed, in this case, the Burmese people.[24] In lower-profile ways and places as well, prophetic acts have often played a positive role in inspiring charity and philanthropy which impart *shalom* in the community. All of these are acts that mirror the forthtelling spirit of prophecy that we find in the Bible.

4. PRIESTHOOD AND WORSHIP

Besides political institutions, other institutions in ancient Israel also played an important role in the OT's conception of power. Both in principle and practice, Israel was primarily a worshiping community. One might say that Israel's politics was subsumed under its worship life, as shown by the psalms that highlight the interplay of politics and worship. Psalm 20 is a classic example for depicting the temple as the locus of the community's life of worship. This was where Yahweh, the glorious king of the community, resided. It was also where human kings directed their appeals for help towards King Yahweh, and from it, King Yahweh granted victory. In this way, the worship life of Israel became a corrective to the potential of human kings to absolutize their power.

We first come across the worship life of Israel in the pages of the Pentateuch that showcase its sacrificial system and rituals. These rituals were led by ministers from the priestly families who performed the same rituals annually, following a steady pattern of sacrifices and practices that sought to ensure the maintenance of holiness. They became a tangible way of actualizing a sense of

---

24. Kate Shellnut, "After Military Coup, It's 'Time to Shout' for Myanmar Evangelicals," *Christianity Today*, February 9, 2021, https://www.christianitytoday.com/news/2021/february/myanmar-coup-burma-christian-pastors-protest-pray-yangon.html.

community since rituals require the participation of each member in common commitment to maintenance of holiness. To a certain extent, the community's shared participation in rituals served to democratize power. For example, the case of ritual sacrifices shows that even those with few resources were given the opportunity to take part according to what they could give.

While the worship life of the community required the participation of all its members, priests stand out as exemplars since they were descendants of designated tribes and families,[25] with positions assigned by Yahweh himself. In this regard, Yahweh chose the priests to perform mediatory roles by offering sacrifices on behalf of the members of the community. They also served as gatekeepers, embodying Yahweh's holiness and ensuring that the Torah's requirements for holiness were properly facilitated in each custom and practice. Since holiness was not confined to rituals, both the Pentateuch and the Prophets remind their readers that holiness also needed to be expressed in right and just living.

In Israel's later history and particularly after the Babylonian exile, the abolition of kingship meant that priests such as Ezra took on both the religious and political aspects of leadership. This underscores the significance of priests in providing leadership for the community in times of crisis.

5. THE SAGE

The final group of leaders in the OT was that of the sages. They represented ancient Israel's *wisdom tradition* which deals with the application of knowledge, intellect, and superior discernment to the many facets of community life. Our concern in this section is the implications of this tradition for the politics and governance of Israel, particularly the roles of sages in managing the community and the relationship between divine and human power.

Unlike kings, prophets, and priests, the sages were usually peripheral figures who were the least institutionalized among Israel's leaders.[26] Despite this, it is not difficult to see the importance of their role as intellectual figures in the community. The witness of both OT narrative and wisdom books highlights

---

25. There is variation in the way priests are chosen or how they relate to the house of Levi or the house of Aaron. For a more detailed discussion, see Menahem Haran, *Temples and Temple-Service in Ancient Israel* (Winona Lake, IN: Eisenbrauns, 1985), 58–111.

26. The notion of wisdom as embodied by a class of professionals practicing wisdom in ancient Israel is explored in Joseph Blenkinsopp, *Sage, Priest, Prophet: Religious and Intellectual Leadership in Ancient Israel*, Library of Ancient Israel (Louisville, KY: Westminster John Knox, 1995), 9–11; contra R. N. Whybray, *The Intellectual Tradition in the Old Testament*, BZAW, vol. 135 (Berlin: de Gruyter, 1974), 15–32.

the importance of wisdom and the indispensability of intellectuals for influencing the community at every level – from its most basic unit in the family to the highest structure of power in the monarchy. The need for wisdom and discernment can also be seen in the earlier phase of Israel's existence when the tribes were to settle in the promised land, under the leadership of men who were wise, discerning, and reputable (Deut 1:13–15). These traits were also to characterize the leaders after occupying the land, as when they settled disputes (Deut 22:15; Ruth 4:1–12), negotiated as diplomats (1 Sam 11:1–4; 16:4b), administered justice, and decided what was best for the community.

Solomon's example in 1 Kings 3 highlights the OT's emphasis on wisdom as a more important trait of the king than might or riches. The case of Rehoboam, who favored the advice of his friends over the advice of the wise elders, underscores the tragedy that may befall the community when the leader fails to exercise enough discernment (1 Kgs 12:1–19). His story inadvertently shows that the community had certain leaders whose main task was to serve as "thinkers" for the community and lend support by being advisers to other leaders. During the Israelite monarchy, the sages were considered regular members of the royal court, as well as leaders in their own right (Ezek 7:26–27; Lam 4:16) much like prophets, priests, and kings. Such wisdom traditions are also found in certain Asian cultures, as in the teachings of Confucianism, which continue to exert influence in politics or political thinking across many parts of Asia today.[27]

6. SOME REFLECTIONS

In what ways can the OT speak about leadership, or authority, or power to our own contemporary world? The politics of Israel resonates with many of our Asian experiences that continue to exert their influence on how we view politics, power, and authority. Highlighting the commonalities between the OT world and Asia – the active role of the deity in community processes, the deity as the sovereign ruler of the land, lack of clear demarcation between religion and politics, divine legitimation of leaders, leaders as mediators between god(s) and people, the relevance of prophetic witness, politics as worship, and the continuing relevance of the wisdom tradition – is a useful starting point for thinking through our own community experience in light of biblical realities and not merely cultural ones.

---

27. For more discussion of OT wisdom's relationship to Asian cultures, see the essays by Shirley Ho (ch. 7) and Elaine Goh (ch. 8) in this volume.

Leadership, Power, and Authority

While many of the OT's political norms, structures, and realities described in this chapter are culturally bound, the OT's social vision of a healthy community are instructive for us today. OT themes such as justice, upright leadership, the wise use of power, politics as a continuity of worship, wisdom's importance in nation-building, and *shalom* as the goal of right governance supply values to strive for in modern Asian communities. The many stories, oracles, and wisdom teachings on leadership help us imagine moral possibilities by providing potential frameworks for examining social issues from the standpoint of biblical ethics. By way of illustration, allow me to bring the political story of the Philippines, particularly during the Martial Law period, into conversation with the OT's political ideas.

The Martial Law period in the Philippines covered the two decades of authoritarian rule by Ferdinand Marcos during the period from 1965 until 1986. His administration was characterized by corruption so massive that it was recognized by Guinness World Records as "The Greatest Robbery of a Government."[28] Marcos' lengthy rule was enabled not only through the consolidation of powerful allies, but also through the support of a huge part of the population, especially from the grassroots level.

Early in his term as president, Marcos was able to garner widespread support by capturing the imagination of a people long formed by folk tradition and religion, as well as the subsequent influence of the Catholic church during Spanish colonialism. Some of the efforts to mythologize the Marcoses are expressed in the symbolism captured by portraits of the president, his wife, or their family.[29] A good example of this is the painting of the president and his wife as characters in the well-known Filipino folktale, "Si Malakas at Si Maganda" (*The Strong and the Beautiful*). *Malakas* and *Maganda* are two mythological characters in the primordial story of the Filipino people. In the folktale itself, the origin of the two characters is unmistakably divine. Banking on its popularity, the Marcoses commissioned an artist to paint the two characters in the likeness of the president and his wife. This motif appeared in the different versions of the painting which were prominently displayed around

---

28. Peter Matthews, *The Guinness Book of Records* (1995 Edition), (New York: Bantam Books, 1994), 440.
29. See Vicente L. Rafael, "Patronage and Pornography: Ideology and Spectatorship in the Early Marcos Years," *Comparative Studies in Society and History* 32 (1990–04), 282–304, that traces the emergence of some of these myths and the ways by which it captivated the Philippine society given the prevalent ideas about conception and display of power in postcolonial Philippine society.

the country. Moreover, the imagery was popularized to ensure that when the folktale was told, it would be the Marcoses who would come to mind.[30] This widespread use of the myth preyed on the tendency of Filipinos to submit to anything or anyone that is supposedly sanctioned by God.

In another set of portraits commissioned by the family, they were even portrayed as gods and goddesses. This may seem to be mere self-aggrandizement, but this self-conception as divinity was mentioned by Imelda Marcos herself in several interviews. In one of them, she explicitly admitted that the Marcoses were like gods on a divine mission to make the Philippines a paradise. In her own words, "And I don't just believe in God – I make God real."[31]

These efforts to solidify the support of the people for their authoritarian rule partly explains how the Marcoses managed to stay in power for two decades until Ferdinand was forced out of his office through the peaceful "EDSA Revolution" of 1986. It is common knowledge that support for this uprising was propelled by the Roman Catholic Archbishop of Manila, Jaime Cardinal Sin. At his urging, around 2 million people flocked to EDSA (the name of a significant highway in Manila) to express discontent against the administration's oppressive acts and policies.[32]

However, the extremely deep damage that the dictatorship inflicted on the country was difficult to undo. As such, although the revolution brought back democracy, subsequent administrations in the Philippines failed to deliver drastic changes that would lift up the lives of ordinary people. The people grew in resentment against those who led the revolution and who consequently took part in the new leadership. This eventually opened the opportunity for another strongman, Rodrigo Duterte, to gain power in 2016. His rise capitalized on presenting himself as a common man, deepening the rift between the elite and the masses, and ushering in a strongly anti-intellectual mood among the people.

---

30. Marco Sumayao, "Painting the Marcos Myth with Ferdinand as Malakas, Imelda as Maganda," *Esquire Magazine Philippines*, Sept. 24, 2018, https://www.esquiremag.ph/culture/lifestyle/marcos-malakas-maganda-a2239-20180924-lfrm.
31. Regine Cabato, "4 Takeaways from Playboy's 1987 Interview with Ferdinand and Imelda Marcos," *CNN Philippines*, Oct. 12, 2017, https://cnnphilippines.com/life/culture/politics/2017/10/11/marcos-playboy-1987.html.
32. Portia L. Reyes, "Claiming History: Memoirs of the Struggle against Ferdinand Marcos's Martial Law Regime in the Philippines," *Sojourn: Journal of Social Issues in Southeast Asia* 33 (2018): 457–98.

Leadership, Power, and Authority

Despite serious accusations of human-rights violations against Duterte by civil society[33] and a pending investigation by the International Criminal Court of the crimes committed by his administration, he continues to enjoy popular support from a large portion of the population, including the evangelical Christian community.[34] Many justify this support by citing passages like Romans 13:1, implying that the president was installed in his position by God himself.

Meanwhile, for the past few years, members of Marcos' immediate family have managed to return and occupy key positions in government by playing on the resentment of the people. This has opened opportunities for them to build and propagate false narratives that downplay the stories of plunder by their family and the suffering of the people, especially those who resisted the dictatorship. At this writing, the Philippines has just had another national election which has culminated with the son of the former dictator being elected president. Interestingly and as with Duterte, evangelical Christians have again been among the supporters of the younger Marcos, some of whom justify their support through questionable readings of the Bible, such as claims that God powerfully used sinful leaders like David and Saul.

This political story shows how certain political realities in the OT continue to be reflected in contemporary Asian experiences. Similarities include the clear interplay of religion and politics, the political possibilities of divine legitimation, the constant potential of power-wielders to abuse their power and the damage this inflicts on people, the need for checks and balances, and the power of prophetic rebuke by God's people and leaders, among others. The experience of the Philippines also highlights how the Bible itself can unfortunately be used to perpetuate abuses of political power. However, this kind of receptiveness to Scripture may also create opportunities for discerning an alternative view that is more aligned with the political and social vision of the OT and its powerful critique against abuses of power. Indeed, there are growing communities of Filipino evangelicals (including scholars and theologians) who have been collaborating to promote a better reading of Scripture

---

33. Catholic News Service, "In Dispute with Catholic Leaders, Duterte Tells Filipinos to Quit Church," *National Catholic Reporter*, November 28, 2018, https://www.ncronline.org/news/world/dispute-catholic-leaders-duterte-tells-filipinos-quit-church.
34. Jayeel Cornelio and Ia Marañon, "A 'Righteous Intervention': Megachurch Christianity and Duterte's War on Drugs in the Philippines," *International Journal of Asian Christianity* 2 (2019): 211–30.

which counters prevailing political narratives and claims, including those that misuse the Bible to justify oppressive politics and injustice.

In conclusion, the OT's confession that God reigns empowers us to see the continuity of biblically shaped leadership with our own experience of community life. We must therefore advocate for just governance, call leaders to account, live as a church that actively participates in the political process, and provide prophetic critique of unjust rulers. These acts are part of our worship of God since they model to the world what it means to live under the sovereignty of God and participate in God's redemptive work. What is more, this is the same ethos that Jesus lived by even as he challenged his disciples to seek the will of God and his kingdom, not just in heaven but here on earth as well (Matt 6:10).

REFERENCES

Ahmed, Ishtiaq. "The Politics of Religion in South and Southeast Asia." In *The Politics of Religion in South and Southeast Asia*, edited by Ishtiaq Ahmed, 1–12. Milton: Routledge, 2011.

Baines, John. "Ancient Egyptian Kingship: Official Forms, Rhetoric, Context." In *King and Messiah in Israel and the Ancient Near East*, edited by J. Day, 16–53. JSOTSup 270. Sheffield: Sheffield Academic Press, 1998.

Blenkinsopp, Joseph. *Sage, Priest, Prophet: Religious and Intellectual Leadership in Ancient Israel*. Library of Ancient Israel. Louisville, KY: Westminster John Knox, 1995.

Cabato, Regine. "4 Takeaways from Playboy's 1987 Interview with Ferdinand and Imelda Marcos." *CNN Philippines*, October 12, 2017. https://cnnphilippines.com/life/culture/politics/2017/10/11/marcos-playboy-1987.html.

Catholic News Service. "In Dispute with Catholic Leaders, Duterte Tells Filipinos to Quit Church." *National Catholic Reporter*, November 28, 2018, https://www.ncronline.org/news/world/dispute-catholic-leaders-duterte-tells-filipinos-quit-church.

Ching, Julia. "Son of Heaven: Sacral Kingship in Ancient China." *T'oung Pao* 83 (1997): 3–41.

Cornelio, Jayeel, and Ia Marañon. "A 'Righteous Intervention': Megachurch Christianity and Duterte's War on Drugs in the Philippines." *International Journal of Asian Christianity* 2 (2019): 211–30.

Dumbrell, William J. "'In Those Days There Was No King in Israel; Every Man Did What Was Right in His Own Eyes,' The Purpose of the Book of Judges Reconsidered." *Journal for the Study of the Old Testament* 25 (1983): 23–33.

Glanville, Luke. "Retaining the Mandate of Heaven: Sovereign Accountability in Ancient China." *Millennium* 39 (2010): 328–34.

Grabbe, Lester L. *Priests, Diviners, and Sages: A Socio-Historical Study of Religious Specialists in Ancient Israel*. Valley Forge, PA: Trinity International, 1995.

Haran, Menahem. *Temples and Temple-Service in Ancient Israel*. Winona Lake, IN: Eisenbrauns, 1985.

Hilber, John W. "Prophecy, Divination, and Magic in the Ancient Near East." In *Behind the Scenes of the Old Testament: Cultural, Social, and Historical Contexts*, edited by Jonathan S. Greer, John W. Hilber, and John H. Walton, 368–74. Grand Rapids, MI: Baker Academic, 2018.

Lambrecht, Francis. "The Missionary as Anthropologist: Religious Belief Among the Ifugao." *Philippine Studies* 5 (1957): 271–86.

Matthews, Peter. *The Guinness Book of Records* (1995 Edition). New York: Bantam Books, 1994.

McConville, J. G. *God and Earthly Power: An Old Testament Political Theology, Genesis–Kings*. London: Bloomsbury, 2008.

Murray, Donald F. *Divine Prerogative and Royal Pretension: Pragmatics, Poetics and Polemics in Narrative Sequence about David (2 Samuel 5.17–7.29)*. Sheffield: Sheffield Academic Press, 1988.

Nadeau, Randall L. *Asian Religions: A Cultural Perspective*. Hoboken, NJ: John Wiley and Sons, Inc., 2013.

Pelikan, Jaroslav. *The Christian Tradition: A History of the Development of Doctrine*. 5 vols. Chicago, IL: University of Chicago Press, 1987–1994.

Rafael, Vicente L. "Patronage and Pornography: Ideology and Spectatorship in the Early Marcos Years." *Comparative Studies in Society and History* 32 (1990–04): 282–304.

Reyes, Portia L. "Claiming History: Memoirs of the Struggle against Ferdinand Marcos's Martial Law Regime in the Philippines." *Sojourn: Journal of Social Issues in Southeast Asia* 33 (2018): 457–98.

Rotz, Margaret Palaghicon Von. "Ifugao Identity: The Retention of Indigenous Religion and Rituals Despite Colonialism." *Philippine Quarterly of Culture and Society* 46 (2018): 114–23.

Sabanal, Annelle. "The Motif of 'Shepherd' and Politics in the Hebrew Prophets." PhD diss., University of Edinburgh, 2017.

Shellnut, Kate. "After Military Coup, It's 'Time to Shout' for Myanmar Evangelicals." *Christianity Today*, February 9, 2021. https://www.christianitytoday.com/news/2021/february/myanmar-coup-burma-christian-pastors-protest-pray-yangon.html.

Sumayao, Marco. "Painting the Marcos Myth with Ferdinand as Malakas, Imelda as Maganda." *Esquire Magazine Philippines*, September 24, 2018. https://www.

esquiremag.ph/culture/lifestyle/marcos-malakas-maganda-a2239-20180924-lfrm.

Vriezen, Theodorus C. *The Religion of Ancient Israel*. Translated by Hubert Hoskins. London: Lutterworth Press, 1967.

Walton, John H. *Ancient Near Eastern Thought and the Old Testament*. Grand Rapids, MI: Baker Academic, 2006.

Whybray, R. N. *The Intellectual Tradition in the Old Testament,* Beihefte zur Zeitschrift für die alttestamentliche Wissenschaft 135. Berlin: de Gruyter, 1974.

Yee, Gale. "Ideological Criticism: Judges 17–21 and the Dismembered Body." In *Judges & Method: New Approaches in Biblical Studies*, 138–265. Minneapolis, MN: Fortress, 1995.

CHAPTER 6

OLD TESTAMENT LAW AND ETHICS

Mona P. Bias

During a recent teaching stint of mine in Nepal, the students admitted to a general lack of interest in the Old Testament. Many pastors in the class acknowledged that they did not know how to handle the OT, so they never ventured to study or preach from it, and that most churches preach mainly from the NT. Although this instance is anecdotal, it does reflect the general relation of Christians and churches in Asia to the OT. As such, there is an urgent need to reclaim the authority of the OT for the Asian church and kindle a new interest for it. This essay will attempt to do just that in the area of OT law and ethics. Since this topic is broad, discussion will focus on the book of Deuteronomy and Deuteronomic law and ethics. The general approach will include a brief explanation of the Deuteronomic law and a distillation of its message within the OT, with a selection of interweaving Asian analogues. It must be mentioned that most of the cultural observations are drawn from the Filipino culture, specifically the Ifugao, Kalinga, Ibaloy, and Kankana-ey people groups of northern Luzon.[1]

1. BRIEF OVERVIEW OF THE OT LAW

Several approaches have been put forward for studying OT law. In contrast to the traditional view of Mosaic authorship, the critical scholar Richard Hiers argues that it developed in several stages over many centuries: (1) the Deuteronomic Code (Deut 5; 20–26) was codified as early as 1000 BCE; (2) the Holiness Code (Lev 17–26) around the middle of the seventh century BCE; and (3) a few decades later, the revised Deuteronomic Code (Deut

---

1. The Philippines comprises three main islands: Luzon, Visayas, and Mindanao. Each of these has its respective provinces. The provinces of Ifugao, Kalinga, and Benguet are located in the north of the Philippines. The *Ifugaos* belong to Ifugao province, the *Kalingas* to Kalinga province while the *Ibaloys* and *Kankana-eys* to Benguet province. These people groups share common cultural practices which pre-date the Spanish colonial era, but differ in some finer points such as traditional clothing and funeral practices. I belong to both the *Ibaloy* and *Kankana-ey* people groups, although I am also of Hispanic and Chinese descent. For a quick review of these people groups, see L. P. Verora, *Unreached Peoples '82: Reaching the Igorots* (Makati: World Vision Philippines, 1982).

12–19) came into being around the time of the Babylonian exile.[2] A bit differently, Douglas Knight sees the four legal collections as "written products of the Persian period, probably well after Darius's initial stimulus to write laws."[3] In focusing more on content than dating, Philip Jenson proposes three levels of law in Deuteronomy which he calls *The Triangle of Generality*:[4] Level 1 (highest): the *Shema* – the most comprehensive, stressing inward assent; Level 2 (middle): Decalogue – which includes inward assent, but focuses on the "outer limits of allowed moral and religious behavior"; and Level 3 (lowest): statues and ordinances – the detailed law code of Deuteronomy 12–26 which "works out its implications of the revealed law in a reasonable range of contexts."[5] Christopher Wright moves beyond Albrecht Alt's categories of law as *apodictic* (unconditional and universal principles) and *casuistic* (conditional case laws) to include categories such as criminal law, family law, cultic law, and compassionate law, among others.[6]

This study will consider the laws as an integral part of the covenant between God and Israel and as presented in the book of Deuteronomy.[7] Thus the OT law is a unified and non-fragmented document in several respects:

(1) It bears the pattern of a second-millennium BCE Hittite treaty.[8] It includes a historical prologue and blessings section which is usually absent in neo-Assyrian treaties of the first millennium.[9] Moshe Weinfeld nonetheless argues that the latter treaties influenced Deuteronomy and the absence of a prologue and blessings section in the Assyrian treaties is partly due to the arrogance of neo-Assyrian kings.[10]

---

2. Richard H. Hiers, "The Death Penalty and Due Process in Biblical Law," *Univ. of Detroit Mercy Law Review* 81 (2004), 751–843, here 753. Online at //school.law.ufl.edu/facultypub/741.
3. Douglas A. Knight, "Israelite Law and Biblical Law," in *Law, Power, and Justice in Ancient Israel* (Louisville, KY: Westminster John Knox, 2011), 9–29.
4. Philip Jenson, "Snakes and Ladders: Levels of Biblical Law" in *Ethical and Unethical in the Old Testament: God and Humans in Dialogue*, ed. Katherine J. Dell (London: Bloomsbury, 2010), 191–93.
5. Jenson, "Snakes and Ladders," 205.
6. Christopher J. H. Wright, *Old Testament Ethics for the People of God* (Leicester, UK: InterVarsity, 2004), 288–314.
7. The laws cannot be extricated from the covenant. The covenant is parallel to law in texts such as Psalm 78:10; 105:10; Jeremiah 31:33; Hosea 8:1; Malachi 2:8. Also, the "Bible itself does not conceive of a law code without a covenant at its base" (Moshe Weinfeld, "berit," *TDOT*, 2:273).
8. George E. Mendenhall, "Covenant Forms in Israelite Tradition," *BA* 17 (1954): 61; Victor Korošec, *Hethitische Staatsvertäge* (Leipzig: T. Weicher, 1931), 12–14.
9. Moshe Weinfeld, *Deuteronomy 1–11*, AB, vol. 5 (New York City: Doubleday, 1991), 8.
10. Moshe Weinfeld, *Deuteronomy and the Deuteronomic School* (Oxford: Clarendon, 1972), 116–22; Dennis J. McCarthy, *Treaty and Covenant: A Study in Form in the Ancient Oriental*

(2) Evangelical OT scholarship is generally more interested in synchronic reading of biblical books as they now exist, rather than reconstructing the underlying sources or history of composition, which can be highly speculative.[11]

(3) Deuteronomy, as a covenant document, presents Yahweh's laws and "is also cast in the form of a narrative."[12] As such, it is a story that may also be conceived as a journey: From Egypt to Horeb, Kadesh to Moab, dwelling in the land itself, Shechem (one possibility for the "chosen place"), exile (Deut 28:63–68), and back to the land (Deut 30:1–10).[13]

2. THE DEUTERONOMIC LAW

The phrase "this law" (Heb. *hattôrâ hazzō't*) refers to the whole book of Deuteronomy (1:5; 4:8; 17:18; 27:3; 28:61; 29:29; 31:11; 32:46),[14] and is chosen as the object of this study since it presents the text of the whole covenant document and acknowledges its ethical and religious nature.[15] Wright explains that the "whole book has the form of a 'covenant renewal' document (see Deut 29:1). Moses and the first generation of Israelites from Egypt had entered into a covenant with Yahweh at Sinai itself (Exod 24). Now, Deuteronomy portrays Moses renewing the covenant with and for the succeeding generation."[16]

Regarding Deuteronomy 29–30, however, Luciano Chianeque and Samuel Ngewa offer two other views. The first is that chapters 29–30 are a summary of Deuteronomy 1–28, or that chapter 29 is a summons preceding the final taking of a covenant oath in 30:11–20. Either way, they take chapter 29 as being patterned on a Near Eastern treaty.[17] In this regard, Daniel Block thus views Deuteronomy 29:1 (28:69 in the Hebrew versification) as a colophonic conclusion to Deuteronomy 28, and explains that the phrase *in addition to*

Documents, AnBib, vol. 21 (Atlanta, GA: John Knox, 1972), 217–40.
11. Raymond B. Dillard and Tremper Longman III, "Deuteronomy" in *An Introduction to the Old Testament*, 2nd ed. (Grand Rapids, MI: Zondervan, 2009), 102–19.
12. J. G. McConville, *Deuteronomy*, ApOTC, vol. 5 (Downers Grove, IL: IVP Academic, 2002), 36.
13. McConville, 36.
14. The expression "Book of the Law" also appears in Deuteronomy 28:61; 30:10; 31:26.
15. OT critical scholarship has long concluded that Moses could have not written the book. Clements mentions that King Josiah and Jeremiah may have been among the authors. See Ronald E. Clements, "The Book of Deuteronomy: Introduction, Commentary, and Reflections," *NIB*, ed. Leander E. Keck, vol. 1 (Nashville: Abingdon, 2015), 861.
16. Wright, *Old Testament Ethics*, 287.
17. Luciano C. Chianeque and Samuel Ngewa, "Deuteronomy" in *Africa Bible Commentary*, ed. Tokunbah Adeyemo (Nairobi: WordAlive Publications, 2006), 247.

the covenant is "elliptical and should be interpreted 'in addition to [the terms of] the covenant he made with them at Horeb.'"[18]

As we deal with the Deuteronomic Law, it becomes clear that the traditional approach of categorizing OT laws as moral, civic, or ceremonial/cultic is not so fruitful.[19] As Wright notes, it is better to classify them "against their own social background in ancient Israel, and then discuss what significant moral features or principles emerge within *every* kind of law they had."[20] It must be acknowledged that Israel had customary laws and their oral laws were later codified in the *Mishnah*.[21] Unlike most nations in postmodern times, there was no separation between the sacred and the secular since the Law made all things subject to Yahweh, who set the standard for morality.

In Asia, there is usually a separation between religious law and secular law (except for Muslim nations), together with a mixture of civil, common, and customary laws, and in the Philippines, there is the addition of Islamic *Shari'ah* Law. Customary laws reflect the deep structures in the culture which, among the Ifugao people group in northern Luzon, include "the norm of conduct of the people based on what their ancestors did in the past,"[22] and belief in a local god or for some, yet-unknown God.[23]

Consistent with the form of a Hittite treaty, the Deuteronomic Law can be divided into basic (5:1–11:32) and detailed (12:1–26:15) stipulations.[24] The following sections will examine the Deuteronomic Law under these two main headings.

---

18. Daniel I. Block, *Deuteronomy*, NIVAC (Grand Rapids, MI: Zondervan, 2012), 662–63.
19. Wright, *Old Testament Ethics*, 288.
20. Wright, 288, italics original.
21. Knight, "Israelite Law and Biblical Law," differentiates biblical law (written laws) from Israelite law (customary laws).
22. Lourdes S. Dulawan, *Ifugao: Culture and History* (National Commission for Culture and the Arts, 2001), 6. For the *Ibaloys*, see C. R. Moss, "Nabaloi Law and Rituals," *American Archaeology and Ethnology* 15 (1920): 207–342.
23. Consider the works of Steven Carter, *The Unknown God* (Murrells Inlet: Covenant Books, 2020) and E. Acoba, *Naming the Unknown God* (Quezon City: OMF Literature, 2006).
24. Eugene H. Merrill, *Deuteronomy*, NAC, vol. 4 (Nashville, TN: Broadman & Holman), 30–32. Kline refers to these as the Great Commandment (5:1–11:32) and Ancillary Commandments (12:1–26:15), respectively. See also Meredith Kline, *Treaty of the Great King: The Covenant Structure of Deuteronomy: Studies and Commentary* (Grand Rapids, MI: Eerdmans, 1963), 48–49.

2.1. The Basic Stipulations (5:1–11:32)

The basic stipulations include the Decalogue (5:6–21),[25] the *Shema*-kernel of the covenant (6:4–9), followed by the parenthetical homilies (7:1–11:32).

The Decalogue is comprised of two parts. The first pertains to Yahweh and Israel's relationship to him (5:6–15). These are the requirements for Israel as Yahweh's vassal: (1) to have no other God (5:7); (2) not to set up manmade idols (5:8); (3) not to wrongfully use Yahweh's name (5:11), and (4) to observe the Sabbath (5:12). Combined, all of these make Israel a distinct nation. The second part concerns the responsibilities of Israel in relation to others (5:16–21). Among these, the command to honor fathers and mothers (5:16) is the only one that is stated positively. Respect for parental authority, and therefore for the leaders of the society, is the basis for social peace. As the only command with a promise, it serves both as an incentive and warning. The Commandments 6–10 are couched in negatives: a definite "no" to murder (5:17), adultery (5:18), stealing (5:19), bearing false witness (5:20), and coveting what belongs to someone else (5:21).[26] William Dyrness rightly summarizes, "Notice that these laws deal with one's attitude both to God and to one's neighbor. No provision is made for the enforcement of these laws . . . for it is of the nature of the relationship that it expresses the free, personal response of the person involved."[27]

The *Shema* is the heart of the law and covenant, centered on Yahweh. It states, "Hear, O Israel: The Lord our God, the Lord is one. Love the Lord your God with all your heart and with all your soul and with all your strength" (6:4–5).[28] Hence, the heart of the Deuteronomic Law is the requirement for Israel to love and worship Yahweh wholeheartedly. This is followed by the injunction to teach (Heb. *šānan* in the Piel stem) his commands (6:6–9), to fear him (6:10–15), to do what is good (6:16–19), and not to forget his awesome deeds (6:20–25).[29] Although Weinfeld argues that "the primary

---

25. The Decalogue is the middle level in Jenson's classification (Jenson, "Snakes and Ladders," 193–94).
26. William Dyrness, *Themes in Old Testament Theology* (Downers Grove, IL: InterVarsity, 1979), 131.
27. Dyrness, 131.
28. The *Shema* is, by Jenson's classification, the highest level. See Jenson, "Snakes and Ladders," 194–95.
29. Deuteronomy 7:1–11:32 presents what the next generation needs to do to remain loyal to Yahweh: (1) remove rival gods (7:1–26); (2) remember Yahweh's tests and provisions (8:1–20); (3) review ancient promises (9:1–29); (4) renew commitments to Yahweh (10:1–22); and (5) recite the blessings and curses (11:1–32).

aim of the Deuteronomic author is the instruction of the people in humanism. . . . The law serves to concretize the moral and humanist principles,"[30] Israel's ability to comply with the commandments was dependent on this basic foundation – relationship with Yahweh. It impinged on every facet of their lives, so that their morality can in no way be simply humanistic.

Covenant making has been practiced since time immemorial among individuals, groups, and countries. For instance, in 1898 by the Treaty of Paris the Philippines was transferred from Spain to the U.S. until 1946, when it was granted independence from foreign domination. The covenant that Yahweh made with Israel is no ordinary agreement, however, as it was Yahweh himself who initiated it, and loved and chose Israel to be his own people (7:7–8). This covenant lay behind the basic stipulations covering the Decalogue and the *Shema* as well as the more detailed stipulations which we will deal with shortly.

2.2. The Detailed Stipulations (12:1–26:15)

Known as the Deuteronomic Code,[31] Deuteronomy 12:1–26:15 concerns the application of the basic stipulations in Israel's relationship with Yahweh (chs. 12–14) and fellow Israelites, dealing with specific cases to ensure order and justice in the land (chs. 15–26). The following are some of the salient features of the detailed stipulations that express Yahweh's expectations of Israel in relating with him.

The Exclusivity of Yahweh: It was explicit that Yahweh alone was to be the object of Israel's worship. As Israel was about to enter the Promised Land, they were commanded not to worship Yahweh in the same way the Canaanites worshiped their many gods (12:4).[32] Moreover, they were not to inquire about serving these gods, or sacrificing their children to them (12:31). Hiers explains that false prophets (13:1–5) and anyone secretly inciting a family member (13:6–11) or a city to worship other gods (13:12–18) is liable for capital punishment.[33] So, should an Israelite be found worshiping other gods, that person must be stoned to death (17:2–7).

On this note, Asia is home to four of the world's major religions and thus many gods. Such multiplicity of gods is a reality in places like Nepal, where

---

30. Moshe Weinfeld, "The Origin of Humanism in Deuteronomy," *JBL* 80 (1961): 242.
31. The statutes and ordinances, by Jenson's classification is the lowest level ("Snakes and Ladders," 195).
32. John Day, *Yahweh and the Gods and Goddesses of Canaan*, JSOTSup 232 (New York: Sheffield Academic Press, 2010), 151–52.
33. Hiers, "The Death Penalty and Due Process," 778–81.

there are as many gods in Nepal as there are households. It is no small feat to introduce the living God there, so that he does not simply become one of the many gods, but the one personal God of every household to whom is owed exclusive allegiance.

Forbidden Occult Practices: Several occult practices that were part of the lives of Israel's neighbors were forbidden in Israel. It included practices such as divination, witchcraft, acting as a medium, and consulting the dead (18:9–12). Though less common in the West, consulting the dead is frequently found in people groups in both Africa and Asia. An African student shared recently that their culture communicates with a dead relative because they believe that when a person dies, he or she becomes a spirit and is therefore nearer to God. The spirit can therefore mediate for living relatives. Similarly in Asia, although belief in the ancestral spirits is an issue that is often brushed aside, it is real in many parts of the continent. Along with animism, this is at the core of native religions and part of the deep structure of the culture.

In the northern mountains of the Philippines, when someone becomes sick, one who believes in *Kabunian*[34] will visit a native priest to inquire about a possible cause. The latter consults the client's dead relatives, who then communicate their message to the native priest through a dream or trance (*sheppo*).[35] Once the probable cause is known, the native priest prescribes the appropriate animal sacrifice. These instances highlight the fact that practices similar to those forbidden in Deuteronomy are still prevalent today. To address such situations, the negotiables and non-negotiables of faith and practice need to be made explicit, and their implications discussed in light of biblical truth so that believers can decide which path to take.

Just Society and Governance: Hugh Williamson proposes that "when we read of 'justice and righteousness' in the OT, we should think primarily of social justice."[36] The word pair *justice* and *righteousness* (Heb. *mišpāṭ* + *ṣĕdāqâ*) may refer to "just rule, to God's just ordering of the world, and in the human realm to just social and political relationships, or what we would call social justice."[37] A just society displays "just and generous relationships, honesty

---

34. *Kabunian* literally means "whom we pray to" and is usually equated with the Judeo-Christian God.
35. Eufronio L. Pungayan and Isikias Picpican, "Rituals and Worship among the Benguet Igorots," *Saint Louise Research Journal* 9 (1978): 485.
36. H. G. M. Williamson, "The Task in Hand" in *He Has Shown You What is Good* (Cambridge: Lutterworth Press, 2012), 18.
37. Walter J. Houston, *Amos: An Introduction and Study Guide* (London: Bloomsbury, 2017), 35.

and integrity, freedom from corruption and violence, the legal, political, and religious means by which these may be ensured."[38] To attain this, the process is equally important as the goal, whether on the family or community level.

The family, as the smallest unit of society, had a judicial role in Israel. Wright explains that family law takes precedence over domestic matters relating to discipline, marriage arrangements, divorce, levirate marriage, inheritance, and as the chief educational agency.[39] The case of a rebellious son is one instance when civil authority would intervene in family matters (Deut 21:18–21). At the community level, the priests and Levites were the teachers and guardians of the Law (18:1–8). In time, Yahweh would choose a king to govern the people (17:14–20). He would also raise up prophets to communicate his message so that anyone refusing to listen to them would be held accountable for disrespecting authority, as in the fifth word of the Decalogue (18:9–22).

The judges were expected to adjudicate cases without partiality (16:18–20). Difficult cases could be appealed to a "higher court" (17:8–13). However, what happens when there is miscarriage of justice? Nothing is said about this in Deuteronomy, but a conventional law prescribed that a judge who rendered a decision and reversed it would pay twelve times the fine set on the case and be permanently removed from office.[40]

The concept of elders and judges in the Deuteronomic Law finds its Filipino counterpart in the *barangay*, the smallest unit of governance in the Philippines, with its council of elders. This is called "the seat of judges,"[41] and nationally, "the council of peacekeepers."[42] When this institution was established, "the *Barangay* Chairman became chair of the *Lupon* or council and could appoint members, elected on the grounds of age, experience, and standing in the community."[43] Unsettled civil disputes are transferred to the regular or criminal courts.[44] A principle involved in all these provisions across

---

38. Houston, 35–36.
39. Wright, *Old Testament Ethics*, 191.
40. See section 5, Martha Roth, "Laws of Hammurabi" in *The Context of Scripture: Monumental Inscriptions from the Biblical World*, ed. William W. Hallo, vol. 2 (Leiden: Brill, 2000), 337.
41. "Seat of judges" is a free translation of the *Subanen* phrase, *Phenguhuman* or *Ginghuran nga Guhum*. Jani Hapalla, questionnaire-interview via messenger with the author, August 28, 2021.
42. This is a free translation of the Filipino phrase, *Lupon Tagapamayapa*.
43. Marco Bias, questionnaire-interview via messenger with the author, August 16, 2021.
44. Marco Bias.

time and culture is the pursuit of good and just governance from the family to the highest seat of government – a task involving the whole community.[45]

Administration of Just Punishment: Under the Deuteronomic Law, the cases liable for death penalty include defying the decisions of the judges or priests, worship of other gods, false prophecy (18:20), perjury (19:16–19), disobedience to parents (21:18–21), adultery-fornication (22:22–23), and kidnapping (24:7). Hiers summarizes, "Although many biblical texts and traditions commonly cited do not in fact, advocate capital punishment, greater biblical laws do enumerate capital offenses. Additionally, various narratives, including a few trial scenes, report executions with evident approval."[46] Capital punishments are meant to vindicate the image of God (19:4–13), purge the land and Israel of guilt and evil (19:13; 21:1–9), and act as a deterrent to crime (21:21).

In administering punishments for crimes, there is a possibility of the miscarriage of justice. For instance, an innocent person may be convicted, or worse, executed. Alternatively, the guilty may be acquitted or disproportionate penalties may be applied.[47] What, then, ensures due process in the Deuteronomic Law? Hiers lists the following requirements that help prevent such a miscarriage: knowledge of the law by the person charged; a chance to escape to a city of refuge in cases of homicide or non-premeditated killing (19:1–13), and diligent investigation and cross examination with implicit procedure and explicit requirements (22:13–21). Moreover, a minimum of two witnesses are called for (17:6) and false testimony is severely punished (19:19–20).[48] Who executes the punishment? In cases of capital punishment, execution is entrusted to the community. Knight explains that "at a minimum, the community as a whole has a certain accountability for justice in the case of a capital offence, which could scarcely be more effectively presented than it is in the extended text of Deut 21:1–9."[49]

Absolute justice in a fallen world remains elusive, but this should not prevent believers from pursuing in their respective contexts what godly leaders in previous generations longed for, "a society so structured that justice was

---

45. Block, *Deuteronomy*, 399–401.
46. Hiers, *Justice and Compassion*, 86–87.
47. Tim Prenzler, "Misconduct and Miscarriages of Justice in the Criminal Courts," in *Ethics and Accountability in Criminal Justice: Towards a Universal Standard*, 2nd ed. (Samford Valley, Australia: Australian Academic Press Group, 2013), 101–21.
48. Hiers, *Justice and Compassion*, 127–44.
49. Knight, "Law in the Villages," in *Law, Power, and Justice*, 143.

its essence."[50] One way to gauge the exercise of justice is how a community treats the marginalized.

The Marginalized and Vulnerable: The Deuteronomic Law extends "loyal love" (*ḥesed*)[51] to the marginalized by allocating for them an amount in produce from the collected tithes every three years (14:27–29). The vision of Deuteronomy, as Peter Vogt explains, is to

> care for one another, and to share the bounty of blessings with the entire community. For this reason, the Levites, aliens, orphans, and widows were not to be considered poor. Their provision was not a charitable act, but was, as we have seen, a normal means of providing for people who had no other means of sustenance.[52]

The provisions in the Deuteronomic Law also ensure that no one takes advantage of the poor and needy. Hearts and help must not be withheld from them (15:7, 8). The source of livelihood must not be taken from a debtor as security, nor a cloak as pledge for a loan (24:6; 10–11). Wages must be paid daily whether to a foreigner or fellow Israelite (24:15). To curb poverty, landlords were to provide for the vulnerable by leaving sheaves of grain and not harvesting the grapes and olives a second time (24:19–22). Being indentured on account of debt, even for debt owed by one's parents or grandparents, is not uncommon in some parts of Asia. In the southern Philippines, when one plantation owner attempted to improve the plight of his workers and increase their wages, he had to contend with the customary laws and anger of other plantation owners; but that did not deter him from helping his workers.[53] There is no poverty in the society that Deuteronomy envisions, but reality shows that unforeseen and extreme circumstances may lead one to poverty and slavery.

Slavery: Whatever the cause of slavery, Deuteronomic legislation puts a limit to it. Israelite slavery "was not a permanent situation; but would end every seventh year."[54] And upon release, the former slave had to be provided for. Further, run-away slaves who took refuge among the Israelites were not to be handed back to their masters but were free to live anywhere they wished

---

50. Houston, "Doing Justice."
51. D. A. Baer and R. P. Gordon, "*ḥesed*," *NIDOTTE* 2:211.
52. Peter T. Vogt, "Social Justice and the Vision of Deuteronomy," *JETS* 51 (2008): 40.
53. This information came from a personal interview that I conducted in Negros Occidental, Philippines, in September 2014. The name of the interviewee is omitted for security reasons.
54. Chianeque and Ngewa, "Deuteronomy," 232.

(23:15–16). This law was against the practice in the ancient Near East,[55] making Israel distinct from other nations.

In the contemporary setting, world-wide slavery has taken on many forms such as forced labor, child labor, and human trafficking. This can be observed in many, if not most Asian countries. According to the *Global Slavery Index Report* in 2018, North Korea tops the list with over 10% of the population, while Japan is at the bottom with only 0.03%.[56] The problem of slavery and many other problems call for the people of God to extend *ḥesed* to the marginalized: widows, orphans, foreigners, refugees, and those who have fallen into hard times due to unforeseen circumstances, like COVID-19 and the devastation it brought with it.

Business Transactions: The Deuteronomic laws relating to business prohibit the use of dishonest weights and measurements in transactions (25:13–16). These verses specify the use of accurate and honest instruments. Honesty and integrity were to be distinct characteristics of one who reverentially feared and obeyed God in practical business matters as in all other areas of life.

Thus, the basic stipulations locate the heart of the Deuteronomic Law as a relationship between God and his covenant people, while the detailed stipulations spell out the various ways in which this special relationship is to be applied in practice towards God and towards fellow Israelites. At this juncture, we will continue dealing with the Deuteronomic Law, but do so in relation to ethics. Law and ethics are closely intertwined, but the Law by itself has limitations in addressing ethics, for "righteousness is more than living by the Decalogue and other laws in the Pentateuch."[57] To help clarify the issue, we propose an operational definition of ethics and then consider "Ethics as Prescribed," followed by "Ethics in Practice."

3. THE DEUTERONOMIC LAW AND ETHICS

Ethics is a system of moral principles or *beliefs* about what is *right* and *wrong*, and which controls or influences a person's behavior. This is true in relation to one's attitude toward others. And almost all ethics systems and laws are closely

---

55. Sections 16–17 of the Laws of Hammurabi would put to death anyone who harbors a fugitive slave; but rewards one who returns the slave to his master (Roth, "Laws of Hammurabi," 338).
56. "Prevalence," in *Asia and the Pacific Region: Global Slavery Index 2018*, accessed September 22, 2021, https://www.globalslaveryindex.org.
57. Gordon J. Wenham, *Story as Torah: Reading Old Testament Narrative Ethically* (Grand Rapids, MI: Baker Academic, 2000), 80.

bound to the religious beliefs of the people. In this regard, Dyrness explains that "cult and piety grow out of the covenant relationship defined in the law. But piety does not stand alone; it naturally expresses itself in the moral life of the community."[58] Moreover, the "health of the community depends quite directly on the health of the people's relationship with God."[59]

3.1. Ethics as Prescribed

Ethics as prescribed in the Deuteronomic Law were conceptualized for Israel in relation to the sanctity of life, of human dignity, fair punishment, and of property. In Asia, to "human dignity" we could add personal and social honor. These are values we respect and firmly hold today. Yet these are not merely postmodern ethical perspectives for they are embedded in the Deuteronomic Law as well.

The Sanctity of Life: The sixth commandment acknowledged the sanctity of human life and care for human beings. No one can commit murder and go unpunished. Death penalty existed for deliberate murder, and the "guilt of bloodshed" is on the head of a household for death on account of negligence (22:8). To protect the innocent there was the provision of the cities of refuge where individuals who had accidentally killed someone could escape to (19:1–13; 4:41–43). In this way God dealt graciously with cases of homicide and non-premeditated killing. Just as there were cities of refuge to preserve life in Israel, so also among the Kalinga people group in northern Luzon, Philippines, there are areas called the "zone of life" (*Matagoan* in the Kalinga language). These are necessary as "revenge and retaliation are the main driving force of tribal and clan warfare and it is deeply rooted in the Kalinga law of 'equal justice,' demanded when a life is taken or blood spilt."[60] However, whereas in the Deuteronomic Law, the death of the confirmed murderer settled the case, in the Kalinga Law, this was not so. It was seen as an honor to avenge the death of a family member, and so the killing did not stop until a new law was passed providing sanctuaries of no harm.[61]

---

58. Dyrness, *Themes*, 171.
59. Jacqueline E. Lapsley, "Historical Books: Ruth" in *The Old Testament and Ethics: A-Book-by-Book-Survey*, ed. Joel B. Green and Jacqueline E. Lapsley (Grand Rapids, MI: Baker Academics, 2011, 2013), 72.
60. Delia Ayabo, questionnaire-interview via Messenger with author, August 16, 2021.
61. This equally refers to the designated "Zone of Life" or *Matagoan* city. To honor the *matagoan* principle, members of the tribes committed not to take revenge or do any crime in this city. Tribal wars are not allowed so that the city does not become a battleground (Ayabo).

Respect for Human Dignity: The Deuteronomic Law sought to preserve respect for human dignity, which is reflected in the commandments against stealing, giving false witness, and coveting a neighbor's property. Taking interest on loans from fellow Israelites is forbidden as it exploits and profits from one who is already poor and vulnerable (23:19–20). In the same vein, kidnapping and selling, or using fellow Israelites as slaves was forbidden for the victim would have been taken against his will and treated like merchandise. Travelers are allowed to eat, hand to mouth, from the produce of a field provided they do not put these into their pockets or baskets (23:24–25). The "freedom to eat the neighbor's produce is a strong depiction of the teaching that the fruitfulness of the land is Yahweh's gift to the whole people."[62] The restrictions are to prevent the exploitation of a neighbor.[63] Related to human dignity is the limit on punishment for non-capital offences.

A Ceiling to Punishment: Excessive punishment was regulated by setting a maximum of forty lashes (25:1–4). Going beyond this would degrade (Heb. *qālâ*) the person, so "warning is given against excessive form of shaming that violates the essential dignity of a person."[64] This is liberating in a culture where shaming is acceptable, if not the norm. The Filipino language has a related term *hiya* which, as Narry Santos writes, "has been seen as both 'shame' and 'shyness'"[65] and hastens to add that it also "has been viewed as neither of them, but as 'propriety.'" Taken positively as propriety, it regulates how one relates with others, whereas taken negatively it can express an inferiority complex,[66] which is especially true when one comes from a small nation or one with a history of foreign domination. This concept of shame along with honor,[67] prominent in the Philippines and much of Asia, was common in the ANE, although couched in different words or pairs. For instance, Dominik Markl believes that Moses on festive occasions used the rhetoric of "praise and

---

62. McConville, *Deuteronomy*, 352.
63. McConville, 353.
64. Philip J. Nel, "qālāh," *NIDOTTE* 3:924–925.
65. Narry F. Santos, *Turning our Shame into Honor: Transformation of the Filipino Hiya in Light of Mark's Gospel* (Quezon City: Life Change Publishing, 2003), 18.
66. Santos, 18.
67. Consider the works of Jayson G. Georges, *Ministering in Honor-Shame Cultures* (Downers Grove, IL: IVP Academic, 2016), 36–37; and E. Randolph Richards and Richard James, *Misreading Scripture with Individual Eyes* (Downers Grove, IL: InterVarsity, 2020), 138–39.

blame" in his discourse in the book of Deuteronomy to deliver a message of both encouragement and warning.[68]

The Sanctity of Property: The Deuteronomic Law respects the right to own property and forbids stealing. Of primary importance to Israel was the land that had been allotted to each of the tribes. As such, moving a neighbor's boundary stone, prohibited by law (19:14), was "cursed" (27:17). Moreover, the firstborn son had the right to inherit a "double portion" of his father's properties (21:15–17). The *Ibaloys* in northern Luzon do not necessarily subscribe to the "double portion," but the eldest boy or girl sometimes receives more of the inheritance whereas all the other children, receive an equal value of the land – with the boys more animals, and the girls more money.[69] Indeed, to leave an inheritance to children and grandchildren is a commendable act (Prov 13:22). The aforesaid values are to be pursued toward life in a fair and just society.

3.2. Ethics in Practice

The moral principles prescribed by the Deuteronomic Law worked out in varying degrees of success in practice in the centuries that followed its institution. The following sections will briefly comment on the period of the judges, examine the story of Ruth and Boaz, and make an assessment of two pre-exilic prophets, Amos and Hosea, concerning their valuation of Israel.

Ethics in the Period of the Judges: Joshua and the elders who survived him lived exemplary lives (Josh 24:31). The generation after them, however, including the judges who periodically led them, lived lives that reflected the nation's morality, which is summed up in the statement: "Israel did evil in the eyes of Yahweh." The statement, repeated seven times in the book, emphasized their moral deterioration and a pattern emerged: Yahweh is provoked to anger; oppressors attack Israel; they cry out to God; Yahweh raises a deliverer; and Israel experiences peace (Judg 2:11–22). In the midst of all this turmoil Yahweh raised up a couple who lived out his expectations, as we will see in the book of Ruth.

An Exceptional Model: The book of Ruth does not explicitly engage in ethics, but rather one can discern ethics espoused and affirmed within the

---

68. Dominik Markl, "Moses' Praise and Blame – Israel's Honour and Shame: Rhetorical Devices in the Ethical Foundations of Deuteronomy," *VE* 34 (Jan 2013): 1–4. http://dx.doi.org/10.4102/ve.v34i2.861.
69. Moss, *Nabaloi Law and Ritual*, 252.

narrative itself.[70] For instance, each of the main characters in Ruth exercised *ḥesed* ("lovingkindness"). Ruth's *ḥesed* refreshed Naomi and Boaz (2:11–12), transformed Naomi's life from bitterness to hope (1:20–21; 4:14–16), and offered a solution to her problem of an heir (3:9–12; 4:17). Further, Naomi also invoked Yahweh to show kindness to Ruth and Orpah (1:8), and Boaz accepted Ruth's marriage proposal as kindness greater than her caring for Naomi (3:10). Wenham suggests criteria to determine when a behavioral pattern is "virtuous": it is repeated in a number of positive contexts and affirmed by the legal codes and psalms.[71] Applying these criteria, the expected values of a believer in Yahweh, which we failed to see in Judges, were exemplified by Ruth and Boaz.[72]

Continuing, virtue can be revealed by the narrator himself or a character's description, words, and actions.[73] Boaz is described by the word *ḥayil*, indicating excellent character, power, and wealth.[74] He was generous and allowed Ruth to gather grain with his workers (2:8–9), prayed that Yahweh reward Ruth for her deeds (2:11), and described Ruth as a "woman of noble character [*ḥayil*]" (3:11). On that decisive night, he acted with respect and promised to do all that Ruth asked (3:11–16). Moreover, he showed respect for the law by informing the nearer kinsman of Naomi's problem. These actions of provision and protection foreshadow the role that he would play to extend *ḥesed* to Ruth and Naomi when he officially became their kinsman-redeemer. Boaz went beyond the requirements of the Deuteronomic Law in his gracious care for Naomi, his marginalized relative, and Ruth, a Moabite refugee. Such demonstrations of lovingkindness by Ruth and Boaz in difficult situations were one bright moment in these dark times.

Pre-Exilic Prophets: The rampant injustice and idolatry in the time of Amos and Hosea signaled a much deeper problem. During the time of the prophet Amos, the covenant had been broken so that the order of blessings and curses had been reversed, with curses invoked time and again. A pattern of judgment speeches emerged: three reasons for judgment, its announcement,

---

70. Lapsley, "Historical Books: Ruth," 72.
71. Wenham, *Story as Torah*, 88–89.
72. Consider the work of Peter H. W. Lau, *Identity and Ethics in the Book of Ruth: A Social Identity Approach*, BZAW, vol. 416 (Berlin: de Gruyter, 2010).
73. Leland Ryken, *How to Read the Bible as Literature* (Grand Rapids, MI: Zondervan Publishing House, 1984), 37–40; Adele Berlin, *Poetics and Interpretation of Biblical Narrative* (Sheffield: Almond Press, 1983; rep. ed., Winona Lake, IN: Eisenbrauns, 1994), 33–39; J. Daniel Hays, "An Evangelical Approach to Old Testament Narrative Criticism," *BSac* 116 (2009): 3–18.
74. HALOT, "*ḥayil*."

the intervention of God, and its results.[75] Due to a corrupt legal system (Amos 2:7), social injustice (3:9–10), bribery and living at the expense of the poor (5:12), disrespect of God's prophets, and idolatry, Yahweh demanded that "justice roll on like a river, righteousness like a never-failing stream!" (5:24). But this divine flow of justice was "obstructed by the refusal of those with power to behave justly."[76] They "turned/changed" (Heb. *hāpak*)[77] justice into poison and the fruit of what is right into something bitter (6:12), so that judgment would be as appropriate (8:11–12) as it was inescapable (9:1–4).[78]

Similarly, through the prophet Hosea, Yahweh informed Israel that he had a covenant lawsuit (Heb. *rîb*, "dispute," "legal case")[79] against them. Using the tumultuous marriage of Hosea, Yahweh revealed in concrete ways Israel's faithlessness, loss of love, and betrayals toward him. Cursing, lying, murder, stealing, and adultery characterized the nation where priests and people alike were bent on idolatry. Hosea did not mince his words when he accused the people of breaking the covenant and rebelling against God and his laws (Hos 8:1). These sins would be the cause for the impending exile (8:13), thus fulfilling the ultimate curse (Deut 28:36–37; 64–68).

Israel and Judah broke the covenant and its accompanying laws in the time of the judges and of the pre-exile prophets and thus failed to live up to Yahweh's standard. Consequently, the Northern Kingdom fell to Assyria in 722 BCE, while Jerusalem fell to Babylon in 586 BCE. In this we see the realization of the covenant curses and the fulfilment of punishments for sins committed, which Yahweh's justice demanded.

3.3. Covenant Blessings and Curses

The blessings (28:1–14) and curses (28:15–68) in Deuteronomy were given in the context of a covenant, which was also rooted in Yahweh's *ḥesed*. Obedience would bring blessings, while disobedience the curses. A related principle is "reaping what you sow," which is not uncommon in Asia. For some people groups in northern Luzon, it can be summed up with the word *inayan*.[80] When

---

75. Claus Westermann, *Basic Forms of Prophetic Speech* (Louisville, KY: Westminster John Knox, 1991), 171.
76. Houston, "Doing Justice."
77. *HALOT*, "*hāpak*."
78. Robert B. Chisholm, Jr., *Interpreting the Minor Prophets* (Grand Rapids, MI: Zondervan Academic, 1990), 107.
79. *HALOT*, "*rîb*."
80. A free translation of *inayan* is "be cautious or warned." It is usually accompanied by *laton*, which can be translated, "all is well."

this word is invoked, it carries with it the idea of a warning or even a curse. Taken positively, it can be an encouragement to do what is right, so that all will be well. Maurice Malanes describes *inayan* as "much like the law of *karma*, or law 'of cause and effect,' or action and reaction which is common among Asian religions."[81] He relates the story of a former mayor who took *inayan* so seriously, that when asked why, after many years of government service, he still live in a simple, grass-thatched, one-room house, he replied that it was for proof he had not misused the taxpayer's money and that it would be *inayan* to break one's oath.[82] By this he meant it would be inviting the curses inherent in the oath when it was made – and curses are taken seriously in this part of Asia as it is in most of Africa.[83] What hope is there for a nation under divine curse or experiencing punishment on account of sin?

3.4. Reconciliation and Restoration

Yahweh saw into the future and made provisions for the eventual exile. When the curses come on Israel, they need to return to Yahweh who promised to restore their fortunes and return them to the land (Deut 30:1–9). Indeed, through the pre-exilic prophets, Yahweh sent messages of hope. For instance, Amos 9 made the pronouncement that the "nation is to be destroyed, but not totally (v. 8). Thus an element of hope is introduced at this point."[84] Moreover, he prophesied the restoration of the Davidic dynasty (9:11, 13–15). Hosea, as well, called on the people to be reconciled to Yahweh. Salim Munayer explains that Hosea 14 "is one of the most sublime expressions of God's compassion, forgiveness, and love for His people when they truly repent and are reconciled with Him in the intimacy of marriage-covenant bond."[85] Yahweh would heal and love them and they would again experience the covenant blessings (14:4–8).

---

81. Maurice Malanes, *Power from the Mountains: Indigenous Knowledge Systems and Practices in Ancestral Domain Management* (Geneva: ILO, 2002), 8.
82. Maurice Malanes, "Putting Igorot Ethics at the Heart of Governance," *Baguio Midland Courier*, August 22, 2021, accessed August 28, 2021, http://baguiomidlandcourier.com.ph.
83. See Passmore Hachalinga, "How Curses Impact People and Biblical Responses," *Journal of Adventist Mission Studies* 13 (2017): 55–63. Available at https://digitalcommons.andrews.edu/jams/vol13/iss1/7/.
84. Thomas E. McComiskey and Tremper Longman III, "Amos," in *The Expositor's Bible Commentary: Daniel–Malachi*, rev. ed., ed. Tremper Longman III and David E. Garland (Grand Rapids, MI: Zondervan, 2017), 416.
85. Salim J. Munayer, *Hosea*, Asia Bible Commentary, ed. Bruce Nicholls (Quezon City: Asia Theological Association, 2010), 291.

Yahweh punished the Israelites for their sins; but equally he sought reconciliation and exercised restorative justice, and brought them back to the land.[86] We might ask the question if, in the sphere of human-to-human relationships, this is possible. Mary Constancy Barrameda writes, "Postmodern Western jurisprudence finally had come to its senses that the punitive justice system is dehumanizing and is detrimental to both individual and society. It now espouses restorative justice."[87] Referring to the justice system of the Kalingas, a people group mentioned earlier, she explains, "In essence and in practice restorative justice is exemplified by the Kalingas who have held their society together creating institutions, customs, and traditions."[88] And for a culture that is holistic, as ancient Israel was, "justice for them is the restoration of peace, order and harmony in the community."[89]

CONCLUSION

This chapter examines OT law and ethics, in particular the book of Deuteronomy, which is itself a document of the covenant between Yahweh and ancient Israel. The Law in Deuteronomy contains both basic (5:1–11:32) and detailed stipulations (12:1–26:15). The former's core message is to love and serve Yahweh alone, while the latter cites specific cases on how one might relate to Yahweh and fellow citizens in pursuit of life in a just society.

The limitations of the law to deal with ethical issues led us to examine ethics as prescribed and envisioned for ancient Israel, and how this was practiced and lived out. In Ruth and Boaz we found exceptional models, who lived beyond the letter of the Law by loving Yahweh and exercising *ḥesed* in their web of relationships. On the whole, however, Israel continued to break the covenant and violate God's laws. On account of this, God warned through the prophets that the nation would experience the ultimate curses of the covenant – exile. Yet Yahweh also promised that when the punishment had run its course, he would exercise restorative justice (Isa 40:1–2), and Israel would be restored to the land (Deut 30:1–9; Hos 14:4–8).

---

86. The exile and return to the land, to some degree, completes the story as presented in the book of Deuteronomy: Egypt–Horeb–Kadesh–Moab–land–Shechem–the "chosen place"–exile–back to the land (McConville, *Deuteronomy*, 36).
87. Mary Constancy Barrameda, "Mainstreaming *Bodong* through *Matagoan*," in *Agham Tao: Journal of Ugnayang Pang-Aghamtao, Inc. (UGAT)/ Anthropological Association of the Philippines* 17 (2009): 1.
88. Barrameda, 2–3.
89. Barrameda, 2–3.

While it is true that we are far removed from the times of ancient Israel, the issues confronting the church in Asia today find many similarities with those that the people of Yahweh faced then. Just as wholehearted commitment to Yahweh was required, so today the same holy God deserves our unreserved love and worship, along with the pursuit of holiness in every aspect of life. Following in the tradition of passing God's word on to the next generation, there is a need to teach and proclaim these truths clearly. Moreover, in relating with others, God expects his people to respect his declared care for life, human dignity, of property, the exercise of restorative justice, and to show *ḥesed* to everyone, especially the marginalized and vulnerable in our midst.

For cases that have no parallels with those identified in Deuteronomy 12–26, there are the Ten Commandments, and especially the *Shema* with its emphasis on loving God and our neighbor, that could serve as the overarching ethical principle.[90] The task of reclaiming the authority of the OT for the Asian church, which was stated in the introduction of this study, is not easy, but nonetheless one which urgently needs to be tackled. There is a need to dig deeper and unveil the existing structures in a given culture, as we did by drawing parallels from Asian culture with select cases in the Deuteronomic Law. Such connections can be maximized as entry points or dynamic equivalences to introduce the living God where he remains unknown and unnamed.

REFERENCES

Acoba, E. *Naming the Unknown God*. Quezon City: OMF Literature, 2006.

Barrameda, Mary Constancy. "Mainstreaming *Bodong* through *Matagoan*." In *AghamTao: Journal of Ugnayang Pang-Aghamtao, Inc. (UGAT)/ Anthropological Association of the Philippines* 17 (2009): 1–13.

Berlin, Adele. *Poetics and Interpretation of Biblical Narrative*. Sheffield: Almond Press, 1983. Rep. ed., Winona Lake, IN: Eisenbrauns, 1994.

Block, Daniel I. *Deuteronomy*. NIV Application Commentary, edited by Terry Muck. Grand Rapids, MI: Zondervan, 2012.

Carter, Steven. *The Unknown God*. Murrells Inlet: Covenant Books, 2020.

Chianeque, Luciano C., and Samuel Ngewa. "Deuteronomy." In *Africa Bible Commentary*, edited by Tokunbah Adeyemo, 209–254. Nairobi: WordAlive Publications, 2006.

---

90. Jenson suggests for interpreters of OT to search for ways to relate the three levels with subtlety and wisdom. See Jenson, "Snakes and Ladders," 205. Consider also the work of Roy Gane, *Old Testament Law for Christians: Original Context and Enduring Application* (Grand Rapids, MI: Baker Academic, 2017).

Chisholm Jr., Robert B. *Interpreting the Minor Prophets*. Grand Rapids, MI: Zondervan Academic, 1990.

Clements, Ronald E. "The Book of Deuteronomy: Introduction, Commentary, and Reflections." *NIB* 1: 2271–87.

Day, John. *Yahweh and the Gods and Goddesses of Canaan*. JSOTSup 232. New York: Sheffield Academic Press, 2010.

Dillard, Raymond B., and Tremper Longman III, "Deuteronomy." In *An Introduction to the Old Testament*, 2nd ed. 133–157. Grand Rapids, MI: Zondervan, 2009.

Dulawan, Lourdes S. *Ifugao: Culture and History*. National Commission for Culture and the Arts, 2001.

Dyrness, William. *Themes in Old Testament Theology*. Downers Grove, IL: InterVarsity, 1979.

Gane, Roy. *Old Testament Law for Christians: Original Context and Enduring Application*. Grand Rapids, MI: Baker Academic, 2017.

Georges, Jayson. *Ministering in Honor-Shame Cultures: Biblical Foundations and Practical Essentials* Downers Grove, IL: IVP Academic, 2016.

Hachalinga, Passmore. "How Curses Impact People and Biblical Responses." *Digital Commons* 13 (2017): 55–63. https://digitalcommons.andrews.edu/jams/vol13/iss1/7/.

Hays, J. Daniel. "An Evangelical Approach to Old Testament Narrative Criticism." *Bibliotheca Sacra* 116 (2009): 3–18.

Hiers, Richard H. "The Death Penalty and Due Process in Biblical Law." *Univ. of Detroit Mercy Law Review* 81 (2004): 751–843. Accessed October 7, 2021. https://scholarship.law.ufl.edu/cgi/viewcontent.cgi?article=1757&context=facultypub.

Houston, Walter J. *Amos: An Introduction and Study Guide*. London: Bloomsbury, 2017.

Jenson, Philip. "Snakes and Ladders: Levels of Biblical Law." In *Ethical and Unethical in the Old Testament: God and Humans in Dialogue*, edited by Katherine J. Dell, 187–207. London: Bloomsbury, 2010.

Kline, Meredith. *Treaty of the Great King: The Covenant Structure of Deuteronomy: Studies and Commentary*. Grand Rapids, MI: Eerdmans, 1963.

Knight, Douglas A. *Law, Power, and Justice in Ancient Israel*. Library of Ancient Israel. Louisville, KY: Westminster John Knox, 2011.

Korošec, Victor. *Hethitische Staatsverträge*. Leipzig: T. Weicher, 1931.

Lapsley, Jacqueline E. "Historical Books: Ruth." In *The Old Testament and Ethics: A-Book-by-Book-Survey*, edited by Joel B. Green and Jacqueline E. Lapsley, 72. Grand Rapids, MI: Baker Academic, 2013.

Lau, Peter H. W. *Identity and Ethics in the Book of Ruth: A Social Identity Approach.* Beihefte zur Zeitschrift für die alttestamentliche Wissenschaft 416. Berlin: de Gruyter, 2010.

Malanes, Maurice. "Putting Igorot Ethics at the Heart of Governance." *Baguio Midland Courier*, August 22, 2021. Accessed August 28, 2021. http://baguiomidlandcourier.com.ph.

———. *Power from the Mountains: Indigenous Knowledge Systems and Practices in Ancestral Domain Management.* Geneva: ILO, 2002.

Markl, Dominik. "Moses' Praise and Blame – Israel's Honour and Shame: Rhetorical Devices in the Ethical Foundations of Deuteronomy." *Verbum et Ecclesia* 34 (Jan 2013): 1–4. http:/dx.doi.org/10.4102/ve.v34i2.861.

McCarthy, D.J. *Treaty and Covenant: A Study in Form in the Ancient Oriental Documents.* Analecta Biblica. Vol. 21. Atlanta, GA: John Knox, 1972.

McComiskey, Thomas E., and Tremper Longman III. "Amos." In *The Expositor's Bible Commentary: Daniel–Malachi.* Rev. ed., edited by Tremper Longman III and David E. Garland. 347–420. Grand Rapids, MI: Zondervan, 2017.

McConville, J. G. *Deuteronomy.* Apollos Old Testament Commentary, edited by David W. Baker and Gordon J. Wenham. Vol. 5. Downers Grove: IVP Academic, 2002.

Mendenhall, George E. "Covenant Forms in Israelite Tradition." *Biblical Archeologist* 17 (1954): 49–76.

Merrill, Eugene H. *Deuteronomy.* The New American Commentary, edited by E. Ray Clendenen. Vol. 4. Nashville, TN: Broadman & Holman, 1994.

Moss, C. R. "Nabaloi Law and Rituals." *American Archaeology and Ethnology* 15 (1920): 207–342.

Munayer, Salim J. *Hosea.* Asia Bible Commentary, edited by Bruce Nicholls. Quezon City: Asia Theological Association, 2010.

Prenzler, Tim. "Misconduct and Miscarriages of Justice in the Criminal Courts." In *Ethics and Accountability in Criminal Justice: Towards a Universal Standard*, 2nd ed, 101–21. Samford Valley, Australia: Australian Academic Press Group, 2013.

"Prevalence." In *Asia and the Pacific Region: Global Slavery Index 2018.* Accessed September 22, 2021. https://www.globalslaveryindex.org.

Pungayan, Eufronio L., and Isikias Picpican, "Rituals and Worship among the Benguet Igorots," *Saint Louise Research Journal* 9 (1978): 460–493.

Richards, E. Randolph, and Richard James. *Misreading Scripture with Individualist Eyes: Patronage, Honor, and Shame in the Biblical World.* Downers Grove, IL: IVP Academic, 2020.

Roth, Martha. "Laws of Hammurabi." In *The Context of Scripture: Monumental Inscriptions from the Biblical World*, edited by William W. Hallo. Vol. 2, 335–53. Leiden: Brill, 2000.

Ryken, Leland. *How to Read the Bible as Literature*. Grand Rapids, MI: Zondervan Publishing House, 1984.

Santos, Narry F. *Turning our Shame into Honor: Transformation of the Filipino Hiya in Light of Mark's Gospel*. Quezon City: Life Change Publishing, 2003.

Verora, L. P. *Unreached Peoples '82: Reaching the Igorots*. Makati: World Vision Philippines, 1982.

Vogt, Peter T. "Social Justice and the Vision of Deuteronomy." *Journal of the Evangelical Theological Society* 51 (2008): 35–44.

Weinfeld, Moshe. "The Origin of Humanism in Deuteronomy." *Journal of Biblical Literature* 80 (1961): 241–47.

———. *Deuteronomy 1–11*. Anchor Bible 5. New York: Doubleday, 1991.

———. *Deuteronomy and the Deuteronomic School*. Oxford: Clarendon, 1972.

Wenham, Gordon J. *Story as Torah: Reading Old Testament Narrative Ethically*. Grand Rapids, MI: Baker Academic, 2000.

Westermann, Claus. *Basic Forms of Prophetic Speech*. Louisville, KY: Westminster John Knox, 1991.

Williamson, H. G. M. "The Task in Hand." In *He Has Shown You What is Good*, 9–21. Cambridge: Lutterworth Press, 2012.

Wright, Christopher J. H. *Old Testament Ethics for the People of God*. Leicester, UK: InterVarsity, 2004.

CHAPTER 7

TAIWANESE CHRISTIAN *LI*

The Embodied Worship of the Lord

Shirley S. Ho

Asian theology has two major trajectories for theological reflection. The first is the theme of liberation from economic poverty and social oppression. This is fertile soil for reflection especially in, by, and for southeast Asians, many of whom suffer from variegated forms of socio-economic poverty. People in these contexts suffer the devastating effects of social injustice, political and social corruption, and the ongoing consequences of colonization by foreign powers. The second distinctive characteristic of Asian theology is in matters of transcendent reality, more precisely, religious pluralism and polytheism.[1] There are three major religions native to Asia: Hinduism, Daoism, and Buddhism. As Lien-Hua Chow states, "People in the East . . . recognize a hidden ruler who controls the universe and human affairs. Many of them also believe that they are never more than three feet away from a god (*touding sanchi youshenming*)."[2] Beyond these organized religions, there is Chinese folk religion which, though lacking unified and robust doctrinal propositions, is an incorporation of different elements of supernatural reality and ritual practices (e.g. ancestor worship, shamanism, divination, belief in ghosts, sacrificial rituals to the spirits of sacred objects and places). Since this essay deals with worship, ritual, and sacrifice in the Old Testament, it will also seek to offer a corrective to polytheism in Asia.

This essay will demonstrate how the supernatural worldview, deep spirituality, and vibrant practice of religious rituals and sacrifice of Taiwanese people provide experiential knowledge and a relevant conceptual framework for grasping Israel's worship life and ritual practices as depicted in the Old Testament. As post-resurrection worshipers of God the Father through Jesus

---

1. Aloysius Pieris, *An Asian Theology of Liberation*, Faith Meets Faith Series (Maryknoll, NY: Orbis Books, 1988).
2. Lien-Hwa Chow, "Towards Evangelical Theology in Buddhist Cultures," in *The Bible & Theology in Asian Contexts: An Evangelical Perspective on Asian Theology*, eds. Bong Rin Ro and Ruth Eshenaur (Taichung: Asia Theological Association, 1984), 315–26.

Christ the Son, who dwell in the Holy Spirit, Asian Christian worshipers (whether Taiwanese or not) are in a better position to appreciate the cognitive and experiential dimensions of Yahwistic worship rituals and sacrifices than Western brothers and sisters in Christ. Having said that, this essay will not subscribe to a blanket acceptance of Asian spiritualist worldviews. I am cognizant of the complexity and necessity of tracing a critical relationship between the Bible and Asian cultures.[3]

I will first describe the Confucian concept called *Li* as the most important resource for Taiwanese spirituality and ritual worship life. A critical and principled appropriation of Confucian *Li* will aid our contextual theological reflection and reading of the relevant biblical texts. Second, I will discuss the supremacy of Yahweh against the backdrop of ancient Near Eastern polytheism which is akin to the Taiwanese spiritualist worldview. This discussion will explore how the superiority of Yahweh underlies the rigorous worship rituals and meticulous sacrificial system of the OT. Third, we will consider the detailed worship rituals and sacrifices of Israel recorded in Leviticus and the Psalms, which summon worshipers into holistic and embodied worship of the Lord of all lords. This will be followed by a discussion of the common contemporary misunderstandings of worship rituals that are found in Taiwanese churches. We will end this essay with the correctives that are necessary to avoid such misunderstandings.

1. TAIWANESE SPIRITUAL WORLDVIEW AND RITUAL LIFE: THE CONFUCIAN *LI*

Whenever Western tourists come to visit Taiwan, places of worship or religious temples appear on their top-five list of must-visit places. Many of these are Taoist or Buddhist temples which are impressive works of architecture. They are typically constructed with massive bricks and slabs of marble, countless stairwells, and long hallways with ancient wall inscriptions. They are decorated with impressive sculptures of intricately carved images in red, gold, or silver.

At such sites, travel vloggers often take video recordings or photographs of local Taiwanese worshipers on bended knee, hands holding their incense, their bodies slightly slanted, their heads nodding front and back, and mouthing

---

3. Wing-Hung Lam, "Patterns of Chinese Theology," in *The Bible & Theology in Asian Contexts*, 327–42, speaks of five patterns in how ethnic Chinese Christians do theology: (1) presence of classical precedents, (2) harmonization of cultures, (3) to fulfill not to destroy, (4) cultural dualism, and (5) Christianity judges culture.

prayers to the images in front of them. Videos abound online of burning joss paper or spirit money which is folded in half before being burned in an earthenware pot. Another common ritual that is filmed is the casting of moon blocks and fortune sticks for divination. Worshipers place their offerings of fruits, sweets, and food at home altars as a form of ancestral worship. These food sacrifices are also offered outside business establishments to keep away bad spirits during the "Hungry Ghost" month or for the birthday of a deity.

Another religious event to behold is the Mazu pilgrimage in celebration of Mazu's birthday, held in the month of March on the Lunar calendar. Mazu is a deified woman in Chinese folk religion who is the goddess of the sea. This pilgrimage involves walking 340 km over eight nights and nine days, and millions of believers welcome the Mazu sedan chair by presenting tables of offerings along the route. Wherever Mazu's colorful sedan chair or carriage passes through on her long tour, worshipers kneel down and bow their heads in two rows along the road, waiting to obtain the blessing of Mazu as the sedan chair passes above them.[4]

Arguably, these are numerous instantiations of the Confucian notion of *Li*.[5] The concept of *Li* may be translated as "ceremony," "ritual," "decorum," "good form," "custom," "etiquette," "rules of propriety," "civility," "conduct," etc. At the risk of oversimplification, we define Confucian *Li* as an abstract moral concept, which is deep-seated in the Taiwanese psyche concerning proper decorum, manners, and behavior in relation to the *other*. More precisely, the concept of *Li* is complemented by Confucianism's five sets of human relationships (*wulun*): ruler and subject, father and son, elder brother and younger brother, husband and wife, and friend to friend. The range of Confucian *Li* can vary from using both hands when receiving something from an elder, respect for leaders and elders,[6] removing shoes before entering a house, bringing a gift to a host, serving food into a guest's bowl, reciprocating gifts and gestures, worshiping and offering sacrifices to dead ancestors, and offering food to hungry ghosts (or spirits) to maintain auspicious relationships with the *other*, to cite a few examples.

---

4. Hsiao-Ming Chang, Ching-Hui Lin, and Yen-Chen Huang, "A Study of Mazuism Religious Tourism in Taiwan: An Example of Dajia Jenn Lann Temple," *International Journal of Religious Tourism and Pilgrimage* 8 (2020), 47–59.
5. For a discussion of Confucian *Li* in dialogue with OT wisdom traditions, see the next essay by Elaine Goh (ch. 8).
6. As with any hierarchy of powers, the Confucian *Li* between elders and young people has regrettably witnessed numerous forms of abuses and manipulations, not only in churches, but also in other social spheres and interactions.

Our taxonomy of the *other* in Confucian *Li* covers both the non-transcendent *other* as well as the transcendent *other*. *Li* is the overarching cultural concept in how Taiwanese engage in bodily interactions with both kinds of the *other*. The non-transcendent "other" denotes fellow human beings who mutually perform *ritualized* acts of practical etiquette. Under this category, *Li* might include the proper decorum in relating with the natural physical world (e.g. geomancy, *fengshui*), including animals.[7] More relevant to my essay, however, is how one behaves morally and ritually in relation to supernatural beings or spiritual ancestors who are dead – the spiritual "other." Filial piety is one such form of propriety, rendered by the young toward their parents. This piety is observed not only while the parents are living, but continues after the parents have passed away. Thus, Confucian Li encompasses two realms, spiritual and non-spiritual, both of which are expressed explicitly in *Analects* 6:22.[8] In this dialogue, Fan Chi asks about the nature of wisdom. Confucius responds, "Working to give the people justice and paying respect to the spirits, but keeping away from them, you can call wisdom."

Confucian *Li* thus defines proper behavior towards other human beings as "justice," while "respect" (i.e. reverence) is to be rendered to spiritual beings. Since it is "wisdom" to avoid spirits, proper behavior towards human beings has been the main focus of Confucian *Li*, usually relegating the spiritual realm to a secondary position. Having said this, although Confucian *Li* is limited in its discourse on spiritual matters, there are still sufficient materials on transcendence for the purposes of theological reflection. In fact, improper behavior towards the transcendent is censured in *Analects* 2:24: "To worship other people's ancestral spirits instead of one's own is to show off unnecessary piety and excessive service." This is a subtle critique against practicing ancestral worship rituals in a preposterous and hypocritical manner.

Although spiritual beings in Confucian *Li* are obscure and better avoided, there is evidence of a ritual-like prayer that involves the non-human realm. As recorded in one dialogue:

> The Master was very sick, and Zi Lu said that he would pray for him.

---

7. Donald N. Blakeley, "Listening to the Animals: The Confucian View of Animal Welfare," *Journal of Chinese Philosophy* 30 (June 2003): 137–57.
8. Unless indicated, all English translations of the *Analects* in this essay are based on the translation of Confucius' *Analects* by A. Charles Muller. Online at http://www.acmuller.net/con-dao/analects.html.

Confucius said, "Is there such a thing?"

Zi Lu said, "There is. The Eulogies say: 'I pray for you to the spirits of the upper and lower realm.'"

Confucius said, "Then I have been praying for a long time already." (*Anal.* 7:35)

Thus, when Confucius speaks of praying in relation to sick people, he is speaking of a ritual performance to seek for spiritual help, revelation, intervention, and blessing, although the prayer is not directed to Yahweh, of course.

Additionally, Confucius considers a person to have "flawless character" based on the following characteristics. Here, he praises a person named Yu:

> The Master said: "Yu was flawless in character. Surviving on the simplest food and drink, yet perfect in his piety to the ancestral spirits. Normally wearing coarse clothing, he looked magnificent in his ceremonial cap and gown. Living in a humble abode, he exhausted himself in the excavation of drainage ways and canals. I cannot find a flaw in his character!" (*Anal.* 8:21)

Confucian *Li* thus defines a virtuous person by the three characteristics of the practice of modesty, service towards other, and, remarkably, piety towards ancestral spirits.

What, then, is the purpose of teaching, behaving, conducting, and living in Confucian *Li*? Xiaohong Wei and Qingyuan Li summarize *Li* (which they render "harmony") as follows:

> As the cardinal cultural value in Chinese society, the Confucian harmony presupposes the coexistence of different things and implies a certain favorable relationship among them. In social interaction, Confucianism puts weight on "harmony but not sameness," "harmony without mindlessly following others" and "harmonization of various kinds of people by observing rituals of propriety," under the influence of which Chinese interpersonal relationships are characterized by emphasis on group orientation, the Doctrine of the Mean, giving or making face for others, *guanxi* (social connections), and reciprocity.[9]

---

9. Xiao-hong Wei and Qingyuan Li, "The Confucian Value of Harmony and its Influence on Chinese Social Interaction," *Cross-Cultural Communication* 9 (2013): 60–66.

In sum, the fundamental purpose of *Li* is to enforce and maintain harmony among and between relationships. This web of relationships can be regulated either by *Li* or by violence. In *Analects* 15:1, when asked about his view on military tactics, Confucius is unapologetic in his expertise on *Li*, over and against military strategy.[10] Arguably, Confucian harmony is analogous to Hebraic *shālôm* ("harmony, welfare, well-being"). The OT worldview entails a commitment to *shālôm* not only with oneself and with fellow human beings, but with the whole cosmos as well, and most importantly, being in harmony with Yahweh himself. However, in Hebraic *shālôm*, Yahweh is the front, center, and goal of harmony, while Confucian harmony is decidedly humanistic in its orientation.

As such, Confucian harmony cannot be accepted indiscriminately for Christians. Although this often happens, unfortunately, we seek in the ensuing discussion to appropriate Confucian harmony critically as a cultural resource for our own reflection on worship and rituals. *Shalomic* harmony with Yahweh and worship of Yahweh are in complementary relationship, with each fulfilling the other. For without *shālôm* with Yahweh, how can one worship him?

The interest of Westerners in Taiwan's worship places and rituals is perhaps due to the absence of these phenomena in their contexts, at least in such elaborate shapes and forms. Howard Curzer writes how rituals are absent from contemporary Western studies, while they are pervasive in Asian and Chinese philosophies:

> Contemporary Western ethicists do talk about habits, practices, and ceremonies, but while these are related to rituals in complex ways, they are not rituals. Overall, Western ethicists are simply ignoring rituals! As the Confucian tradition rightly takes rituals to have an important role in moral development and practice, and because discussion of rituals is completely absent from contemporary Western ethics, Confucians seem poised to make a major contribution to Western philosophy.[11]

---

10. "Duke Ling of Wei asked Confucius about military strategy. Confucius answered, 'I have, indeed, heard something about the use of sacrificial vessels, but I have never studied the matter of commanding troops'" (the translation of D. C. Lau, *Confucius: The Analects* Chinese-English ed. Taipei: Penguin Books, 2009). In a different passage, "Duke Ling of Wei asked Confucius about military tactics. Confucius said, 'I know about the handling of ritual sacrifices, but I have not studied strategy'" (Muller's translation of *Anal.* 15:1).
11. Howard Curzer, "Contemporary Rituals and Confucian Tradition: A Critical Discussion," *Journal of Chinese Philosophy* (2012): 290–309.

While such was surely the situation in the past, it is striking that increasing numbers of Western theologians are rediscovering the importance of rituals and liturgies in their theological reflection. Moreover, whereas for Westerners, rituals and places of worship are objects of interest and curiosity, for the Taiwanese these places and rituals represent everyday aspects of cultural, social, psychological, and religious life. Compared to their Western counterparts, the Taiwanese are by nature deeply ritual-oriented in both religious and non-religious forms of expression.

2. THE SUPREMACY OF YAHWEH AND HIS WORSHIP-WORTHINESS

2.1. Yahweh Above Other Supernatural Deities and Beings

A comparative study of ancient Near Eastern religions, the Yahwistic faith of the Hebrew Bible, and Asian religious pluralism shows that ancient Near Eastern religions and Taiwanese polytheism have many similarities. A common spiritualist worldview is shared between ancient Near Eastern worshipers and the Taiwanese, in contradistinction to the Western scientific worldview. Modern Western epistemology and understandings of reality are deeply influenced by Enlightenment rationality. Spiritual beings and the spiritual realm are deemed void, mythically false, or merely a product of human imagination. Reality is construed only in material terms in light of what may be empirically grasped and verified. Thus, any claims of spiritual beings in the non-physical realm are viewed as a product of primitive, superstitious beliefs, which lack the superior illumination of modernity.

However, the Taiwanese experience tells a more compelling narrative than its Western counterparts.[12] They know that the physical and spiritual worlds are real, as both the OT and the NT portray. In this regard, Michael Heiser's *The Unseen Realm* and John Walton's *Demons and Spirits in Biblical Theology*

---

12. Unfortunately, some Taiwanese Christians have consciously or unconsciously embraced a form of Western dualism – the separation between the spiritual and physical world – due to an Enlightenment orientation and education, despite being Asians. They have accepted physical material realities while abandoning spiritual realities. One wonders at times how these Taiwanese Christians are capable of recognizing Yahweh and the Holy Spirit as spiritual being(s) while simultaneously ignoring the possibility of other spiritual beings, like angels and demons, despite scriptural evidence.

demonstrate the clear existence of a spiritual realm in the Old Testament.[13] Though Enlightenment rationality is hard-pressed to find evidence of it, the unseen spiritual realm includes the presence of spiritual beings, both benevolent and malevolent, gods and goddesses, as well as angels and demons in functional, hierarchical relationships which are both in support of and in competition with each other. These gods and goddesses possess a limited sphere of influence and control over the physical geographical world (which Heiser's book summarizes as "the Deuteronomy 32 worldview"). The unseen realm is not the product of human imagination, but is empirically true and experienced, as evidenced by the Taiwanese lived experience in numerous authentic records of spirit mediums, demon possession, and exorcism. These powers are in conflict and competition against Yahweh. They deceive and lure human beings to be subservient to them instead of directing the latter to worship the most high God.

2.2. Yahweh is Worship-Worthy: Creator and Savior

Human beings are worshipers by nature. Worshiping an entity outside of oneself is characteristic of both ancient and modern as well as Eastern and Western worshipers. Humans are innately conditioned to worship someone bigger and greater than themselves. Worship is a combination of human admiration and a desire for an "other." Consequently, the issue is not whether human beings will worship or not, but rather whom and what they will worship.

Worship of Yahweh in the OT is grounded in the truth claim that he is the divine Creator of the heavens and earth (Gen 1:1; Ps 96:5; 115:15; 136:5–9). As Creator, the whole world exists to serve and worship him. Human beings are the pinnacle of his creative work and have inherited the status of image-bearers of Yahweh (Gen 1:26–27). Human beings are thus created to represent and lead the rest of creation to worship the Creator (Ps 148:1–14). Failure to worship the true and living Yahweh is tantamount to worshiping oneself, as in Western humanism, or worshiping wooden gods and silver idols, as in Asian polytheism. Thus, in the same manner that Yahwistic faith censured ancient near Eastern practices of polytheism, witchcraft, and shamanism, Christianity also speaks against Asian polytheism today.

---

13. Michael S. Heiser, *The Unseen Realm: Recovering the Supernatural Worldview of the Bible.* (Bellingham, WA: Lexham Press, 2015); John H. Walton and J. Harvey Walton, *Demons and Spirits in Biblical Theology: Reading the Biblical Text in Its Cultural and Literary Context* (Eugene, OR: Cascade Books, 2019).

In this connection, Psalm 96 redirects worship towards Yahweh by declaring that he is worthy of worship and praise because of his marvelous works of salvation (vv. 2–3). He delivers from the bondage of sin, darkness, death, and false claims because he is splendid and holy (v. 9). He reigns as king and judge over all things (vv. 10, 13). Climactically, Yahweh is the God whose coming in righteousness and faithfulness leads all creation to rejoice (vv. 11–12). Like ancient Israel, Taiwanese worshipers are exhorted by this psalm to be liberated from the heavy yoke of pagan polytheism and to worship only the true and living God.

2.3. Other Supernatural Beings Worship Yahweh

Embedded in the book of Psalms are countless references to Yahweh as the God of all gods and Lord of all lords. The *divine council* in Psalm 82 denotes these gods and lords as a group of corrupt spiritual beings who have failed in their created role and purpose to serve Yahweh. Instead of judging the competing gods and goddesses as non-existent, the psalm vilifies these competing spiritual beings, labeled as so-called "gods," as inferior in nature, origin, morality, status, sovereignty, and power. The comparative language that is adopted by the psalmist affirms the incomparability and supremacy of Yahweh over other supernatural beings. Moreover, these gods and goddesses themselves are summoned in other passages to submit to and worship Yahweh:

> All who worship images are put to shame,
>   those who boast in idols – worship him, all you
>   gods! (Ps 97:7)

> For great is the Lord and most worthy of praise;
>   he is to be feared above all gods.
> For all the gods of the nations are idols,
>   but the Lord made the heavens. (Ps 96:4–5)

Although Confucianism's understanding of the spiritual realm is ambiguous, minimal, and mostly refers to ancestral spirits, that there is nevertheless a plurality of spiritual beings may be safely assumed. Consequently, they also exist in a hierarchy, as presupposed in the following dialogue:

> Wang Sun Jia asked: "What do you think about the saying 'It is better to sacrifice to the god of the stove than to the god of the family shrine.'?" Confucius said, "Not so. If you offend Heaven, there is no one you can pray to." (*Anal.* 3:13)

Hence, just as the god of heaven is superior to the god of the household stove, Taiwanese worshipers are confronted and exhorted by the Psalms to name the God of heaven as Yahweh and direct their faith and worship to him as the superior spiritual being. Israelite faith asserts the supremacy of Yahweh over all other supernatural beings, such as the ancestral spirits worshiped by Asian people. This superiority must be translated not merely into a worshiper's sense of loyalty, allegiance, and submission, but also into the conducting of proper worship rituals.

2.4. The Nations and the Natural World Worship Yahweh

The scope of biblical worship is not limited to one location or culture. Instead, the biblical vision of worship encompasses the whole heaven and earth so as to recognize the superiority of Yahweh. Non-Israelite nations are summoned to worship him:

> Praise the LORD, all you nations;
> extol him, all you peoples. (Ps 117:1; cf. 86:8–10)

Moreover, even the whole natural world including the heavens, the seas, and the trees of the forests are enjoined to worship the incomparable Yahweh. Indeed, Psalms 96 and 148 summon all creation to praise Yahweh without placing humanity in a privileged position.

Therefore, Taiwanese Christians who are situated in their natural geographical location are exhorted to worship the most high God. Consequently, worship of the natural world such as the local god of the earth (*tudigong*), city god (*chenghuangye*), and god and goddess of the oceans (*hailongwang* and *mazu*) is rendered antithetical to Yahwistic faith. The natural world and non-Israelite nations alike must worship Yahweh.

3. WORSHIPERS' WORSHIP RITUALS TOWARD YAHWEH

The worship-worthiness of Yahweh demands and explains the rigorous ritual directives and highly intricate sacrificial instructions for the worship life of Israel. Biblical worship is all-encompassing in a manner that includes and is expressed with religious sacrifices and rituals. We can refer to these as *worship rituals*. In fact, what are worship, sacrifice, and rituals? Catherine Bell's phenomenological study on ritual provides a working definition which characterizes rituals using the elements of sacral symbolism, formalism, traditionalism, invariance, rule-governance, and performance.[14] Our analysis will show how these six traits are observable in Israel's worship and ritual life.

3.1. Symbols of Sacral Presence and Communion with Yahweh in Leviticus

The detailed instructions and prohibitions regarding rituals and the sacrificial system can easily distract readers from the main point of Leviticus. However, underlying the meticulous sacrifice and ritual instructions in Leviticus are the assumptions of the spiritual reality of Yahweh and his sacred presence.

Worship rituals take place in the place chosen by Yahweh. Before the existence of Israel's temple, Yahweh's presence and dwelling with people was located in the Garden of Eden (Gen 2:8, 10, 15). Later, there were solitary altars (Gen 8:20; 12:7, 8), followed by the tabernacle (Exod 25–40), and later the Solomonic Temple (1 Kgs 8–9). All these were microcosms of Yahweh's sacred presence – the holy place where the heavens and earth meet. It is where Yahweh and his people encounter each other in communion.

Meeting the divine being evokes different feelings from worshipers. Some worshipers desire to commune with the divine, while others are afraid to approach the divine being and prefer to avoid the place of worship. As observed above, the Confucian *Li* teaches that "keeping away from them [spirits], you can call wisdom" (*Anal.* 6:22b). The line "keeping away from them" is Confucian anxiety towards the spirits (i.e. fear of the unknown). Since divine and spiritual beings are reckoned the transcendent *other*, they appear to be capriciously beyond human grasp and understanding. Their unknowability makes them dangerous and taboo. It is thus wisdom to maintain distance so as not to unwittingly disrespect them and incur unnecessary trouble, or even death.

This stands in contrast to Judaism and Christianity, which teach the doctrine of *Immanuel*, a Hebrew term that means "God [is] with us." The Bible espouses drawing near to Yahweh and nearer still to experience his divine presence. Moreover, Yahweh proactively desires to dwell and commune with his people. "Then have them make a sanctuary for me [Yahweh], and I will dwell among them" (Exod 25:8). Yahweh's presence is differentiated in this way from the manifestation of pagan spiritual beings, which required conjuration through religious rituals of incantations and spells.

---

14. Catherine Bell, *Ritual Theory, Ritual Practice* (Oxford: Oxford University Press, 2009).

3.2. Rule-Governed Worship Performance in Leviticus

Leviticus serves as a normative and descriptive handbook for worship rituals. More importantly and similarly to the function of the Confucian *Li*, Leviticus is instructive for proper behavior in relation to the *other*. Levitical *Li*, as we might call it, is about proper decorum when worshiping and communing with the Holy One of Israel.

The three elements of rule-governance, invariance, and performance are all discernible in the Levitical *Li* described in what follows. For example, the sacrificial system mandates different sacrifices according to different purposes and interior motives for offering them (Lev 1–7). The purposes and motives correspond to appropriate feasts and festivals and associated calendrical dates (23:37). Sacrifices are differentiated by the kind of animal offered and its prescribed manner of slaughter (Lev 1–7). Rituals are performed repeatedly and in a disciplined way, whether at regular times or on special holy days. The performance of these rituals involves unvarying rules in the washing and the burning of the animals (1:9, 13; 2:9, 16; 6:27; 8:21), the use of blood in sprinkling (1:5, 11; 4:5, 6, 25; 5:9; 7:14, 26, 27; 8:24), the eating or non-eating of the parts of offerings (3:17; 6:16, 18, 23, 29; 7:16, 23), the waving of the offering (7:30, 34), and the laying of the worshiper's hands on the animal (1:4; 3:2, 8, 13; 4:15, 24, 29, 33).

Also, rule-governance can be seen in the purification laws for clean and unclean or taboos in Leviticus 11–15. The directives involve the worshiper's diet, physical health, sexual life, garments, and even living quarters (Lev 12–15). Leviticus 18–20 provides supplementary instructions on moral and civil purity. The worshiper's bodily uncleanness disqualifies him or her from participating in the worship ritual.

Furthermore, and insofar as worship rituals are performative, they are embodied in nature. The worshiper cannot but use their whole being in communing with Yahweh through the worship rituals. These worship rituals are intended to be passed from the earliest generation of Israel to each one thereafter as traditions. The book of Leviticus thus concludes, "These are the decrees, the laws and the regulations that the LORD established at Mount Sinai between himself and the Israelites through Moses" (Lev 26:46; cf. 27:34). That said, worship rituals in Leviticus leave little room or space for variation and improvisation. The proper steps are to be observed to the fullest and highest degree. To alter the regulation is discouraged, if not prohibited. Failure to observe the proper rituals may result in death, like the fates of Nadab and Abihu (Lev 10:1–20) and Eli's wicked sons (1 Sam 2:12–17).

Worship is the sacred communion between Yahweh and his worshipers. If communion between two human beings is prescribed by the practice of Confucian *Li*, this is all the more so in communion with Yahweh. The Levitical *Li* is a product of two theological realities. First, God is the transcendent holy *Other*. Second, human beings are sinful, finite, and profane. Divine holiness demands wholeness, order, and the absence of chaos. According to Mary Douglas, rituals by nature are concerned with creating and maintaining order, as contrasted with chaos.[15] Worshiping Yahweh requires meticulous observance of Yahweh-ordained religious rituals, sacrifices, and moral living. Contrary to Confucian avoidance of the danger of the spirits, Levitical *Li* provides the proper means to avoid danger in the pursuit of communing with Yahweh.

The actions, movements, and materials in Levitical *Li* symbolize the spiritual realities of order and holiness which are antithetical to chaos and the profane. Likewise in Taiwanese folk religion, sacrifices are offered to gods and spirits in a transaction of sorts. The sacrifices are meant to appease and to provide food to the spirits, and to gain something through reciprocity. Levitical *Li*, however, has three kinds of sacrifices designed to atone for the sins and guilt of the people of Israel – burnt offerings, sin offerings, and guilt offerings. Cleansing of sin is the prerequisite to worshiping Yahweh. In the New Testament, the sins and guilt of worshipers are dealt with by the continuing efficacy of Jesus Christ's work on the cross. Strikingly, the book of Hebrews defines Jesus as both the sacrifice and the priest.

3.3. Performative Worship Rituals in the Psalms

As in Leviticus, worship rituals in the Psalms include rule-governance, performative activity, and sacral symbolism (Ps 141:2). The following fleshes out the performative and embodied dimensions of worship rituals in the Psalms – we might call these Psalmic *Li*.

The Psalms reveal that worship involves worshipers *physically* drawing near to enter the holy presence of Yahweh. Ancient Israelites needed to embark on a difficult pilgrimage, presumably on foot, to the centralized place of worship at the Temple, as evidenced in the Songs of Ascents (Pss 120–134). Psalm 84:5–7 captures how the journey to Zion is painful yet joyful:

---

15. Yahweh is often depicted as fighting against the powers of primordial chaos like the sea monster (Isa 27:1; 51:9–11; Ps 24:1–2; 29:3–4, 10; 74:12–17; 89:9–10).

> Blessed are those whose strength is in you,
>   whose hearts are set on pilgrimage.
> As they pass through the Valley of Baka,
>   they make it a place of springs;
>   the autumn rains also cover it with pools.
> They go from strength to strength,
>   till each appears before God in Zion.

Later in the same psalm, verse 10 says, "Better is one day in your courts than a thousand elsewhere; I would rather be a doorkeeper in the house of my God than dwell in the tents of wickedness." The worshiper thus depicts the choice and longing to worship Yahweh in his dwelling place. Additionally, the psalmist speaks of how he goes to the temple and stands on solid and level ground: "My feet stand on level ground; in the great congregation I will praise the LORD" (Ps 26:12). This shows that public worship occurs together with the worshiping community.

Moreover, worshipers not only deploy their mouths and lips to speak audibly of the worthiness of Yahweh, but their hands are employed as well. They shout, clap, and lift their hands (47:1; 119:48; 141:2) to give their praises and prayers (28:2; 88:9). Psalm 134:2 is representative:

> Lift up your *hands* in the sanctuary
>   and praise the LORD (italics added).

Lifting hands is the ritual manner of worshiping and offering prayers. This action symbolizes human receptivity and the surrendering of authority, power, and glory to Yahweh, for he alone deserves the utmost praise and worship. If applause is rendered to fellow human beings for exceptional achievement, Yahweh deserves even more for his incomparable works of creation, salvation, and sanctification!

Similar to upraised hands, the eyes of the worshipers are lifted up towards the mountain of Zion, where Yahweh establishes his sanctuary. The worshiper declares in Psalm 121, "I lift up my eyes to the mountains – where does my help come?" (Ps 121:1). The lifting of one's visual perception also serves to express one's adoration, trust, and hope, as in the poignant confession from Psalm 123:1, "I lift up my *eyes* to you, to you who sit enthroned in heaven" (italics added).

While human eyes are prone to rove around to seek alternative objects of worship, the Psalmic *Li* models fixing one's eyes upon Yahweh, the author and perfecter of one's faith (118:23; 119:18, 82; cf. Heb 12:2). This desire for focused eyes can also be seen in the worshiping community's prayer: ". . . as the eyes of a female slave look to the hand of her mistress, so our eyes look to the Lord our God, till he shows us his mercy" (Ps 123:2).

Worshiping Yahweh also compels one to bow one's head and come on bended knees. This posture is emblematic of one's prostration and sense of unworthiness before a holy God (Ps 35:13). The following two excerpts from the Psalms are evidence of this:

> Come, let us *bow down* in worship,
>> let us *kneel* before the Lord our Maker. (Ps 95:6,
>>> italics added)
>
> I will *bow down* toward your holy temple and will
>> praise your name
> for your unfailing love and your faithfulness,
>> for you have so exalted your solemn decree
>> that it surpasses your fame. (Ps 138:2, italics added)

Bowing in ritual worship is especially meaningful when viewed in the context of a sovereign-vassal covenant relationship. In such a setting, prostration is a sign of humility, service, obeisance, and fear of Yahweh (e.g. Ps 5:7).

Finally, worship ritual encompasses not solely the external physical body but the heart, soul, and spirit of the worshiper as well. Three psalms illustrate this well:

> Gladden the *soul* of your servant,
>> for to you, O Lord, I lift up my soul. (Ps 86:4 NRSV,
>>> italics added)
>
> Let me *hear* of your steadfast love in the morning,
>> for in you I put my trust.
> Teach me the way I should go,
>> for to you I lift up my soul. (Ps 143:8 NRSV, italics added)
>
> My sacrifice, O God, is a broken *spirit*;
>> a broken and contrite heart
>> you, God, will not despise. (Ps 51:17, italics added)

The Psalmic *Li* stipulates the participation of one's soul and heart in worship through the hearing of the ears. The broken spirit, that is, the repentant spirit, is a sacrifice acceptable to Yahweh. Lifting up one's heart and soul is symbolic of surrendering oneself to Yahweh. It is exposing one's innermost being in authentic vulnerability before Yahweh, so that one worships without reservations.

In conclusion, worshiping Yahweh in the Psalms is a set of bodily and cultic activities with ritual and spiritual connotations. As religious acts performed in sacred space and time, they include, but are not limited to, physically offering sacrifices, singing joyful songs of salvation, uttering words of prayer, and declaring the praiseworthiness of Yahweh:

> Let them sacrifice thank offerings
>   and tell of his works with songs of joy. (Ps 107:22)
>
> I will sacrifice a thank offering to you
>   and call on the name of the Lord. (Ps 116:17)
>
> May my prayer be set before you like incense;
>   may the lifting up of my hands be like the evening
>   sacrifice. (Ps 141:2)

4. CONTEMPORARY TAIWANESE MISUNDERSTANDINGS OF CHRISTIAN WORSHIP RITUALS

The holistic and embodied worship of Yahweh in the OT, as described above, is instructive for the worship life of the contemporary church. It is in this vein that I seek now to address the misunderstandings and excesses of worship rituals that are common in Taiwan's churches.[16] The worship rituals referred to are Christian religious practices common in most Taiwanese churches, namely, the Lord's Supper, baptism, prayer meetings, fasting, and corporate Sunday worship services (including the singing of hymns and spiritual songs, prayers, financial offerings, meditation, etc.).

4.1. Disembodied Worship Rituals

There are three common misunderstandings of worship rituals in local Taiwanese churches. The first is to limit worship to a matter of the heart and not the body. More precisely, this is the misunderstanding that what the worshiper thinks and feels in the mind and heart are the very essence of worshiping Yahweh. This form of theological reductionism maintains that worship does not need to be performed ritually and bodily. Physicality is optional, if not superfluous. Worship is thus a mode of being, provided one is constantly "in

---

16. Other cultures and regions may encounter the same misunderstandings and excesses, of course.

the mode" of worship. Every day is a day for worship, and not just certain holy days. Worship may be practiced anywhere, anytime, and anyhow. It may be done alone at home at one's convenience, in front of one's computer and with breakfast coffee in hand.[17] Partaking of the Lord's supper is optional, provided one is worshiping the Lord in spirit and in truth (to [mis]quote John 4:24). This kind of rationalization is even applied to Christian baptism, whether through sprinkling or immersion. The ritual of baptism is conceived as a merely physical performance since what truly matters is the confession of the heart.

Another misconception is to construe liturgical worship rituals as an unwise use of time. This view regards worship rituals such as worship services, prayer, and fasting as dispensable. They supposedly accomplish nothing for the kingdom of God. Worship rituals produce little that is tangible for the local church, unlike evangelism, helping the poor and needy, engaging in public life, or adding numbers to church membership. Worship rituals, prayer meetings, solitude and meditation, fasting, and prayer are taken lightly in exchange for spending more time in planning and doing various church ministries. Evangelism and the work of justice and mercy are presumed to be superior to worship rituals offered to Yahweh.

The third and last misunderstanding is to practice worship rituals, yet devoid of the human body and affections. Intellectual knowledge of the Christian faith over and against worship rituals is the emphasis. For cerebral-oriented worshipers, heartfelt singing with outstretched hands, tears and beating one's chest, listening to long homilies, kneeling, and fasting are deemed personal preferences. Such expressiveness is considered to be sentimentalism and emotionalism. Affective-driven worship rituals are viewed suspiciously as feeding one's own narcissistic and pietistic tendencies. Instead, it is intellectual study of the Scripture or academic study of theology which is the sole legitimate form of worshiping Yahweh.

The first misunderstanding above unfortunately teaches Taiwanese Christians to become worship spectators rather than worshipers themselves. Worship rituals become a matter of mental assent or observation rather than an embodied participation in the worship community. The two subsequent misunderstandings have one thing in common – they have adopted an overly broad definition of worship as *ritualized Christian life and practice* (i.e. generalized worship ritual). However, insofar as our theological reflection is based on Leviticus and Psalms, while being informed by Bell's taxonomy, the

---

17. This rationalization is not due to the COVID-19 pandemic.

worship rituals under discussion belong to the narrow, particular, and cultic understanding of worship rituals. Worship rituals in this regard are a deliberate "setting apart" of a liturgical time and space, in a self-conscious mode of being, to perform sacred symbolic activity for the purpose of encountering, communing, and worshiping Yahweh in public space with other members of the worship community.

By contrast, ritualized Christian life and practice is pragmatic rather than cultic-oriented. The complementarity of these two forms of worship is reminiscent of Mary's embodied encounter with Jesus at his feet and Martha's service in the kitchen (Luke 10:38–42). Nevertheless, it is noteworthy that Confucius privileges *Li* over anything economically valuable, expedient, and practical. When someone wants to do away with the sacrifice of the sheep, Confucius responded, "You love the sheep, I love the ceremony" (*Anal.* 3:17).[18] Pragmatism is antithetical to Confucian *Li*.

These two views of worship ritual represent opposite ends of the continuum of worship ritual. At one end are the rituals that adhere to Bell's taxonomy of what constitutes worship in its full cultic power and ritual density. On the other side are the practical, utilitarian, and realistic forms of worship. We do not want to pit the two forms of worship rituals against each other since this would create a false dichotomy. It is unnecessary to flatten the Bible's rich teaching, which comprises both *ritualized Christian life and practice* (i.e. generalized worship ritual) and *cultic worship ritual* (i.e. specialized worship ritual).

Generalized worship ritual may be evidenced by the work done by the priests and Levites. Presumably, whenever the Levitical priest executed and performed rituals and sacrifices on behalf of, and together with, the worshipers, the priest also carried out his own set of *ritualized* worship, which was part and parcel of his priestly work and service to Yahweh. In this instance, the priest and Levites *technically* performed both the generalized and specialized worship ritual in a single set of ritual performances. As far as evangelism and discipleship, acts of justice and mercy, and academic study of Scriptures are ritually performed and construed as acts of work and service to Yahweh, they are effective expressions of the general understanding of worship ritual. We may call this form of worship as the "ritualization" of acts of evangelism, discipleship, and acts of justice and mercy. They are performed with distinct

---

18. Lau's translation of *Analects* 3:17 reads as follows: "Tzu-kung wanted to do away with the sacrificial sheep at the announcement of the new moon. The Master said: 'Ssu, you are loath to part of the price of the sheep, but I am loath to see the disappearance of the rite.'"

forms and regularity. In this essay, we endorse both forms of worship rituals to shape the worship life of Taiwanese worshipers in a comprehensive manner.

4.2. Embodied Worship Rituals Devoid of the Heart, Soul, and Mind

Legalism and ritualism are two ways in which embodied worship rituals become devoid of the heart, soul, and mind. Legalism, the first of these, is an excessive emphasis on the performance of worship rituals. Worship ritual becomes merely about fulfillment of the *letter* of the ritual. Worshipers unreasonably elevate certain kinds of worship rituals for their exact day and time, manner of worship (e.g. seated, standing up, kneeling, heads bowed), dress code, proper partaking of the Lord's Supper elements (e.g. unleavened bread only, red wine only), strict observance of fasting, immersion-only baptism, officiation only by an ordained minister, etc. Even baptism can sometimes become a sign of one's status in Jesus Christ. Additionally, one's Christian spirituality is ideologically assessed based on one's attendance at church's worship services, participation in prayer meetings, or similar measures. These rituals can become social and spiritual identity markers that separate the holy from the unholy, the people of God from those not yet God's people. Proper bodily performance of religious rituals is overestimated and becomes the sole principle for judging the worship life of believers.

Another case of missing the meaning of worship is ritualism, an outgrowth of the above excesses in which worship rituals become a habit. It becomes merely a routine action or unthinking motion, which becomes an ingrained and automatic movement devoid of sacral meaning. Closing one's eyes and/or clasping both hands together or stretching out one's hands when praying becomes a reflexive action without a prayerful heart, worshipful mind, and humble posture. For instance, hand clapping in worship becomes irreverent when it is done aimlessly and only to satisfy personal merry-making proclivities instead of truly applauding the greatness and superiority of Yahweh. As time passes, worship rituals can easily slide into such ritualism so that later generations of worshipers become oblivious to their spiritual and theological meaning.

Due to the need for correctives, legalism and ritualism were both vehemently censured by the prophets of Israel. They criticized Israel for worshiping Yahweh ritualistically without circumcised hearts of repentance and obedience. Israel had performed bodily rituals without the proper attitude, as Yahweh asserts: "For I desire mercy, not sacrifice, and acknowledgment of God rather than burnt offerings" (Hos 6:6). Their worship rituals came at the expense of the ritualized, faithful practice of love, mercy, justice, and righteousness, leading prophets such as Isaiah to call out their spiritual hypocrisy and duplicity (Isa 1:11–17). In response to such imbalances, the Psalms also emphasize the importance of heart and mind without jeopardizing that of animal sacrifices and offerings: "Sacrifice and offering you did not desire – but my ears you have opened – burnt offerings and sin offerings you did not require" (Ps 40:6).

Simply put, legalism and ritualism are performative activities bereft of sacral symbolism and meaning. Legalistic and ritualistic worshipers fail to recognize that inherent in biblical worship rituals is a profound theological reality and strong sacral meaning – rituals are done in and for the purpose of encountering and communing with Yahweh. In the process of mere public performance, the sacredness of the worship ritual is lost. Unfortunately, such a body/heart (the latter includes mind-spirit) dichotomy in worship ritual is indicative of the fragmented and disintegrated self of the worshiper.

Similarly, in the Confucian *Li*, the ritual of sacrifice to the deities is understood to include the whole person so that the worshiper is to be physically present at Mt. Tai (*Anal.* 3:6).[19] Sacrificing to the spirits is to be taken as ontologically real. *Analects* 3:12 records Confucius' assertion on this:

> "Sacrificing as if present" means sacrificing to the spirits as if they were present.
> Confucius said, "If I do not personally offer the sacrifice, it is the same as not having sacrificed at all."[20]

Remarkably, both the Confucian *Li* and the biblical *Li* espouse performative, holistic, and embodied worship ritual. Romans 12:1 exhorts worshipers to "offer your bodies as a living sacrifice, holy and pleasing to God – this is your true and proper worship." The Confucian *Li* and the biblical *Li* envision the unity of body and heart, working in integrity and unity. In the *Analects*, the nature of *Li* is that of "a general category, [which] is clearly defined in a relationship with *ren*, where *ren* is the inner, substantial goodness of the human being, and *li* is the functioning of *ren* in the manifest world."[21] We observe the

---

19. Mt. Tai is a sacred mountain in China where various sacrifices are offered.
20. Translation by Muller, *Analects*. Lau translates 3:12 as "'Sacrifice as if present' is taken to mean 'sacrifice to the gods as if the gods were present.' The Master, however, said, 'Unless I take part in a sacrifice, it is as if I did not sacrifice.'" Confucian *Li* provides no details on who has the capacity to determine if the practice is done insincerely.
21. This quote is based on the translator's editorial comment in A. Charles Muller, *The Analects of Confucius* 論語 (2020). http://www.acmuller.net/con-dao/analects.html.

confluence of the internal and external self in worship attitude and posture. To put it more poignantly, to merely aim at the performative facet of worship rituals, or to be fixated only on the disembodied theologizing of worship ritual, is not only foreign to biblical worship ritual, but to the Confucian *Li* as well.

Both the embodied and disembodied forms of worship listed above, with all their various flaws and imperfections, coexist in Taiwanese churches.[22] Each denomination or congregation, or even individual worshiper, may have wittingly or unwittingly perpetrated these misunderstandings and excesses in one form or another, at different times and spaces, or in various stages. Who is a perfect worshiper, in any case? These phenomena, though unfortunate, reveal that worshiping Yahweh is a lofty endeavor and pursuit. It is about fallible worshipers worshiping the most high God, after all. One can only pray and hope that one's worship is acceptable to God.

CONCLUSION

By God's grace and compassion, the biblical instructions on worship rituals invite worshipers to enter an authentic, continuous, and lifelong reformation of their worship theory, life, and practice. On this note, it is appropriate to end with Deuteronomy 6:5: "Love the LORD your God with all your heart and with all your soul and with all your strength." This command is indicative of the manner in which the whole self of the worshiper engages in worshiping Yahweh. It is noteworthy that the Hebrew word translated "strength" is *mĕ'ōd*. It is actually an adverb which lexically and literally means "very" or "much," rather than a noun. The Septuagint (Greek translation of the Old Testament) rendered it *dunamis* ("strength, power") while the Aramaic translation rendered it as "wealth." All things considered, we take this line of the *Shema* to mean loving Yahweh with our "everything" (i.e. capacity, opportunities, wealth, strength). The human body is the basic and necessary condition to speak of "everything." Yahwistic faith thus asserts that divine-ordained worship rituals must be performed by loving Yahweh with one's heart, mind, soul, and *body*.

REFERENCES

Bell, Catherine. *Ritual Theory, Ritual Practice*. Oxford: Oxford University Press, 2009.

---

22. I am a Filipino-Chinese Christian residing in Taiwan. These misunderstandings are also common among Filipino-Chinese churches in the Philippines.

Blakeley, Donald N. "Listening to the Animals: The Confucian View of Animal Welfare." *Journal of Chinese Philosophy* 30 (June 2003): 137–57.

Chang, Hsiao-Ming, Ching-Hui Lin, and Yen-Chen Huang. "A Study of Mazuism Religious Tourism in Taiwan: An Example of Dajia Jenn Lann Temple." *International Journal of Religious Tourism and Pilgrimage* 8 (2020): 47–59.

Chow, Lien-Hwa. "Towards Evangelical Theology in Buddhist Cultures." In *The Bible & Theology in Asian Contexts: An Evangelical Perspective on Asian Theology*, edited by Bong Rin Ro and Ruth Eshenaur, 315–26. Taichung: Asia Theological Association, 1984.

Confucius' *Analects* by A. Charles Muller. http://www.acmuller.net/con-dao/analects.html.

Curzer, Howard. "Contemporary Rituals and Confucian Tradition: A Critical Discussion." *Journal of Chinese Philosophy* (2012): 290–309.

Heiser, Michael S. *The Unseen Realm: Recovering the Supernatural Worldview of the Bible*. Bellingham, WA: Lexham Press, 2015.

Lam, Wing-Hung. "Patterns of Chinese Theology." In *The Bible & Theology in Asian Contexts: An Evangelical Perspective on Asian Theology*, edited by Bong Rin Ro and Ruth Marie Eshenaur, 327–42. Taichung: Asia Theological Association, 1984.

Lau, D. C. *Confucius: The Analects*. Chinese-English ed. Taipei: Penguin Books, 2009.

Pieris, Aloysius. *An Asian Theology of Liberation*. Faith Meets Faith Series. Maryknoll, NY: Orbis Books, 1988.

Walton, John H., and J. Harvey Walton. *Demons and Spirits in Biblical Theology: Reading the Biblical Text in Its Cultural and Literary Context*. Eugene, OR: Cascade Books, 2019.

Wei, Xiao-hong, and Qingyuan Li. "The Confucian Value of Harmony and its Influence on Chinese Social Interaction." *Cross-Cultural Communication* 9 (2013): 60–66.

CHAPTER 8

EDUCATION, LEARNING, AND WISDOM

Lady Wisdom Invites Us!

Elaine Wei-Fun Goh

In the Old Testament, personified Wisdom invites people to follow her ways. Her path is a path of learning, which leads one to attain knowledge, discretion, and insight; to procure perception of what is right, just, and fair; and most importantly, to grasp the fear of the Lord (Prov 1:2–7). On the one hand, the voice of a father is heard in the books of Proverbs (e.g. Prov 1:8) and Ecclesiastes (Eccl 12:12) in teaching "my son."[1] On the other hand, Proverbs also contains the voices of a mother (31:1–9) and Lady Wisdom (1:20–33) who impart wisdom. In short, OT sapiential literature imparts the urgency of gaining education, learning, and wisdom.[2]

In this essay, I introduce the pedagogy of biblical wisdom – pursuing it and following its learning methods as unfolded in the OT. The concept of "blessedness," which is the intended outcome of the way of wisdom, will then be studied and examined in Asian contexts. This will entail a discussion on character formation since, biblically speaking, the state of "blessedness" concerns one's inner character rather than the outward appearance of success. Confucian wisdom is particularly relevant in this discussion for two reasons. First, Confucian wisdom has shaped Asian ethics since ancient times. Second, Confucian ethics is complementary to biblical ethics with reference to shaping character. Finally, I will offer some suggestions on wisdom's contributions to Asian contexts by illustrating several further points of contact between biblical wisdom and Confucian wisdom.

---

1. In this essay, "Ecclesiastes" will refer to the book and "Qoheleth" to the author of the book of Ecclesiastes (cf. Eccl 1:1; 7:27; 12:9).
2. Hereafter, I will use "Proverbs" for the book of Proverbs, while "proverbs" will refer to the short sayings or wise words found in the biblical book.

1. WISDOM AND PEDAGOGY

Proverbs 1:2–7 makes clear the objectives of learning by virtue of pursuing wisdom. In this vein, our first section will begin by defining biblical wisdom and elucidating the wisdom traditions and learning loci that are instrumental for wisdom pedagogy. This section will also explore how the ultimate purpose of pursuing wisdom is to embrace the fear of God. On the methods to achieve this purpose, we will examine the ways of memorization, the rhetoric of personification, and an adaptable way of learning.

1.1. The Pursuit of Wisdom

1.1.1. Defining Wisdom

The adjective "wise" (*ḥākām*) and its corresponding noun "wisdom" (*ḥokmâ*) primarily connote a person's "skill," "expertise," or "competence."[3] As such, in biblical wisdom, various kinds of "skill" are predicated of goldsmiths and artisans (e.g. Exod 31:3–6; Jer 10:9), sailors (Ezek 27:8), skilled women who spin with their hands (Exod 35:25), construction workers for the sanctuary (Exod 36:1–2), political advisers (Isa 19:12), and kings (Prov 20:26; Isa 10:13; 1 Kgs 10:6). These are each described by some form of the Hebrew root *ḥkm* ("to be wise") since they put their skills and competence to good use. The root is also associated with people in religious affairs with reference to faithfulness to the Lord (Deut 4:6; Ps 107:43). Even animals are sometimes considered "wise" because of their survival instincts (Prov 30:24). Yet, being "wise" can also have a negative connotation in the OT for denoting that which is shrewd, crafty, or cunning, as in the case of Jonadab (2 Sam 13:3–5). In OT wisdom literature, the terms "fool" (Prov 29:11; Eccl 2:15) and "simple" (Prov 1:22; 21:11) are opposites for those who are "wise." All of these are primarily used as moral terms rather than referring to one's intelligence or level of education.

In addition to skills and professions, biblical wisdom expresses the ability to gain comprehension and insight. Universally across cultures, discernment and an understanding of human behavior are attributes of wisdom traditions.[4] Confucian wisdom lays particular accent on this intellectual capacity of wisdom. Furthermore, biblical wisdom as a way of life involves pursuing the means to ensure personal well-being, for instance in the state of blessedness.[5]

---

3. BDB, s.v. "*ḥākām*" and "*ḥokmâ*."
4. Gerhard von Rad, *Wisdom in Israel*, trans. James D. Martin (Nashville, TN: Abingdon, 1972), 8.
5. James L. Crenshaw, *Old Testament Wisdom: An Introduction* (Louisville, KY: Westminster John Knox, 1998), 1, 3.

In sum, wisdom is "the art of steering," "the ability to cope," and "the quest for self-understanding and for mastery of the world."[6] Therefore, wisdom is not confined within the Israelite community since it is a universal idea. Ancient sages in all cultures impart their teachings through a combination of verbal pedagogy and wisdom literature.

1.1.2. Wisdom Traditions and Tradents

The counsel of the wise, who are also known as *sages*,[7] represents one of the three centers of Israelite tradition – the other two being the priestly law and the prophetic word (Jer 18:18). Each of these three groups wrote literature that shaped Israelite faith in their own ways throughout biblical history. The traditions of the sages have produced biblical wisdom literature – the books of Proverbs, Job, and Ecclesiastes. Interestingly, the wisdom tradition exhibits an absence of the themes that characterize other strands of Yahwism by dealing mainly with daily human experience in the world created by God. Its perspective is derived more from *general revelation* (as opposed to *special revelation*) in exploring the themes of creation, the meaning of life, order versus disorder, and the journey of faith.[8]

At the same time, the wisdom tradition has an enormous number of intertextual connections with other parts of the OT.[9] The expressions of Proverbs about the path to life and death (Prov 3:1–2; 4:10–19) mirror Deuteronomy's language of blessing and curse (e.g. Deut 5:16; 11:26–28).[10] The designation of "the Holy One" (Prov 9:10; 30:3) echoes the prophets (e.g. Isa 1:4; 41:14; 60:9, 14). The creation language of Proverbs 8:22–31 and Job 38–41 reflects the OT's language about God's creation (e.g. Gen 1–2; Ps 8). There is also a quote from Deuteronomy 23:21–23 in Ecclesiastes 5:4–6 about regulating oaths. Furthermore, the warnings of Proverbs against dishonesty in the workplace (Prov 11:1; 16:11; cf. Lev 19:35–36; Deut 25:13–16), the command to

---

6. Crenshaw, *Old Testament Wisdom*, 9.
7. This essay uses the noun "sages" and "the wise" interchangeably. In Hebrew, they are the *ḥăkāmîm*, from the singular noun, *ḥākām*.
8. The perspective of *special revelation* in the Old Testament focuses on the Abrahamic promises, the covenantal relationship between the Lord and the Israelites, the exodus and revelation at Sinai, and Torah and the Mosaic tradition. All of these are familiar theological themes in the OT.
9. On which see Katharine J. Dell and Will Kynes, eds., *Reading Proverbs Intertextually*, LHBOTS, vol. 629 (Edinburgh: T&T Clark, 2018).
10. Richard L. Schultz, "Unity or Diversity in Wisdom Theology? A Canonical and Covenantal Perspective," *TynBul* 48 (1997): 271–306 (299).

honor parents (Prov 13:1; 15:5; cf. Deut 5:16; 27:16), and the command to shun adultery (Prov 22:14; Deut 5:18; 22:22) are shared between the wisdom literature and the rest of the OT.[11] These intertextual connections illustrate how the wisdom tradition testifies to a common Israelite faith, which should not be dichotomized too neatly into wisdom and covenantal traditions.

1.1.3. The Existence of Wisdom "Schools"

Wisdom needs a cultural setting to live in. There are numerous references in OT wisdom literature to a father and a mother teaching their young ones,[12] as when "my son" is frequently addressed in Proverbs.[13] Parents have full authority in this regard to teach the instructions of the law to the younger generation. This kind of education at home is also a common practice within the Confucian tradition. The primacy of the family in both Confucian and Israelite wisdom is reflected in the pivotal importance of pursuing honor and avoiding shame, both within the family as well as through the impact of these cultural values on the community at large. Families, clans, and community lay at the core of ancient society. In short, home-based schooling has always represented the original environment for wisdom teaching, with the wisdom "schools" of the sages and tradents coming only afterwards.[14]

On this note, *The Analects* of Confucius is one of the most important works of Confucian thought, exercising a significant influence in both ethnic Chinese communities as well as East Asia more broadly.[15] This work is a compilation of conversations between Confucius and his disciples which includes a variety of sayings, dialogues, and observations on human behavior. Like OT wisdom literature, it is also believed to have originated in Confucius' home. It shares the theme with other Confucian literary classics of learning how to become

---

11. Schultz, "Unity or Diversity in Wisdom Theology," 296.
12. E.g. the role of fathers in Proverbs 10:1; 15:20; 20:20; 23:22, 25; 30:11, 17; Ecclesiastes 12:12. Mothers also play a significant role in Proverbs 1:8; 4:3; 6:20; 31:1, 26.
13. E.g. Proverbs 1:8, 10, 15; 2:1; 3:1, 11, 21; 4:10, 20; 5:1, 20; 6:1, 3, 20; 7:1; 19:27; 23:19, 26; 24:13, 21; 27:11.
14. Roland E. Murphy, *The Tree of Life: An Exploration of Biblical Wisdom Literature* (Grand Rapids, MI: Eerdmans, 2002), 4.
15. Confucius (551–479 BCE), whose original name is Kong Qiu, played a fundamental role in shaping Chinese culture by engaging in education, revising classical writings, and communicating his wisdom ideas. Confucius is the Latinized version of his Chinese name Kong Qiu, and he was also called Kong Zi or Kong Fuzi which literally means "Master Kong." This name has been popular since the encounter between Chinese and Western cultures in the sixteenth century. Pertaining to the title, origin and authorship of *The Analects*, numerous theories have been suggested, including multiple authorship. See Bryan W. Van Norden, ed., *Confucius and the Analects* (Oxford: Oxford University Press, 2002), 3.

a noble person (*junzi*) who benefits society at large. Furthermore and as is evident in the Chinese dynastic histories and other literature (e.g. *The Romance of Three Kingdoms*), the royal court would have been the place for more formal training in wisdom. Similarly, in the OT, references to the "men of Hezekiah" (Prov 25:1) and various "counselors" (*yôʿēṣîm*) in the royal court who provide "counsel" (*ʿēṣâ*) indicate the likelihood of a formal class of sages.[16] Political advisors were employed in the ancient world, much as today, to provide advice and strategy for the ruling power. On this note, some kind of formal educational system would have been essential to support the generation and propagation of wisdom. Indeed, the presence of a significant literary corpus which reflects sapiential concerns is evidence that ancient royal courts sought the exceptional faculty of the wise for their instructions and reflections on wise governance.[17]

1.2. Learning Methods

1.2.1. Memorization

In the development of wisdom traditions, it is likely that the textual transmission of wisdom was preceded by a stage of oral communication. In this regard, the use of proverbs which are curated into concise, clever sayings is a standard way of expressing perceived truth and enhancing learning. Such proverbial sayings are found across cultures, together forming a distinct genre of wisdom. The practices of memorization play an especially important part in the oral transmission of proverbs, as in Chinese wisdom literature's injunctions on proper conduct, right attitudes, and virtues such as diligence, honesty, orderliness, eloquence, learnedness, benevolence, and bravery (e.g. *Anal.* 9:29; 12:1–6). Many of these sayings use formulaic language as part of a strategy to

---

16. For more examples, see 1 Samuel 16:20–23; 1 Kings 12:6. "The men of Hezekiah" (Prov 25:1) are also mentioned in the Babylonian Talmud's tractate *Baba Bathra* 15a with regard to their editing of a book. See Daniel J. Estes, *Handbook on the Wisdom Books and Psalms* (Grand Rapids, MI: Baker Academic, 2005), 213.

17. The ancient Near East has a vast wisdom corpus. For example, Egyptian wisdom literature includes *The Instructions of Anii*, *The Instructions of Amenemope*, *The Instruction of Ankhsheshonqy*, and *The Harper's Songs*. See Miriam Lichtheim, *Ancient Egyptian Literature*, 3 vols. (Berkeley: University of California Press, 1975–1980). From Mesopotamia, one finds *The Counsels of Wisdom*, *Ludlul Bēl Nēmeqi*, *The Dialogues of Pessimism*, and *The Aramaic Proverbs of Ahiqar*. See W. G. Lambert, *Babylonian Wisdom Literature* (Oxford: Clarendon, 1960). The ancient Far East also contains vast sapiential collections, with Confucian works in particular being of key importance for Chinese history and culture. For samples, see *The Four Books* (i.e. *The Analects*, *The Great Learning*, *The Doctrine of the Mean*, and *Mencius*, all canonized by Zhu Xi during the Song dynasty); and *The Five Classics* (i.e. *The Book of Songs*, *The Classic of History*, *The Book of Rites*, *The Book of Changes*, and *The Spring and Autumn Annals*, all of which were compiled by Confucius himself).

persuade and reinforce memorization (e.g. *Anal.* 9:4; 11:18; 12:11; 16:4–8). Through terse and memorable wording, these proverbs aim to mold proper behavior and shape desirable character. Many ethnic Chinese people memorize these proverbs from a young age to gain resources for managing their lives and coping with human problems or contingencies. Similar examples of biblical wisdom's rhetoric of instruction and persuasion include the "better" sayings (Prov 16:32; 28:6; Eccl 9:18), the choice between the ways of life and death (Prov 3:16; 14:12), the contrast between wisdom and foolishness (Prov 15:2; Eccl 10:12), and the personification of wisdom. This feature of OT wisdom is one that I wish to explore further in what follows.

1.2.2. Personification of Wisdom

One method that the sages use to enhance pedagogy is that of personifying wisdom as feminine, as enabled by the grammatically feminine gender of *ḥokmâ* ("wisdom"). As a result, wisdom is a "she" in the book of Proverbs. Wisdom thus comes alive as a personal presence in the teaching of the wise. In this regard, Proverbs 1–9 contains four extended poems which extol the virtues of wisdom personified. In Proverbs 1:20–33, Lady Wisdom speaks in the busiest streets and squares of the city rebuking scoffers, fools, and simpletons. Proverbs 3:13–20 prizes Lady Wisdom as better than silver and gold, possessing long life in her right hand, and bearing riches and honor in her left hand. She is the tree of life, and her paths are pleasant and peaceful. Proverbs 8:1–36 is likewise packed with descriptions of wisdom's value. Lady Wisdom appears not only in the royal court, but also at the outset of creation to play a key part when God laid the foundation of the heaven and earth. Proverbs 9:1–18 depicts Lady Wisdom as the host of a sumptuous banquet, extending her invitations of wisdom and life to all people.

The fourth and last wisdom poem in Proverbs depicts Lady Folly as the contrast to Lady Wisdom. Lady Folly prepares food from stolen bread and drink in competing for the same guests. She represents a metaphorical creation of the sages to play the role of wisdom's opposite. Lady Wisdom leads the learners of truth to the path of blessings, while Lady Folly takes the naïve down the path of self-destruction. The theological message of these poems is clear – the one who chooses Lady Wisdom will receive life, whereas the one who follows Lady Folly will suffer death. These symbolic depictions of virtue and vice are unique in the Israelite wisdom tradition. Their creative use of metaphors reflects a form of cultural embodiment – a virtuous woman represents wisdom, while a seductress represents foolishness. In this dialectic of the Israelite sages, Lady Wisdom is far more precious than jewels and an ideal wife to have for oneself (Prov 3:15; 31:10). Therefore, the learners should be motivated to pursue wisdom all the more enthusiastically.

Unlike *The Analects* which usually adds "[a] person" (*zhe*) in its articulations of wisdom to lay emphasis on "a wise *person*" (e.g. *Anal.* 4:2; 6:23; 9:29), wisdom and folly themselves are the ones who are personified in biblical traditions. Wisdom and folly therefore function as rivals in the pedagogy of the biblical sages. In line with this personification, it is profitable to read Ecclesiastes 7:23–8:1 intertextually with Proverbs 31:10–31.[18] The connection between the woman who is "more bitter than death" (Eccl 7:26–29) and she who is "more precious than jewels" (Prov 31:10–31) has long been observed in this regard.[19] For Qoheleth, it is frustrating that wisdom remains beyond his grasp (Eccl 7:23–8:1) despite all his attempts which are recorded in Ecclesiastes. Ironically, Qoheleth's quest of Lady Wisdom has led him into the arms of Lady Folly.[20]

1.2.3. Prescriptive and Descriptive Learning

The sages of the OT also vary their educational methods. As in Confucian wisdom, wisdom in the OT can be attained from both prescriptive and descriptive ways of learning. Prescriptive wisdom comes from direct instructions and admonitions, which aim to shape character and assist in ordering daily life. Descriptive wisdom, by contrast, comes from observation and reflection on life's phenomena, aiming to impart coping strategies for a chaotic world in a more indirect manner.[21] While prescriptive wisdom is prevalent in the book of Proverbs, descriptive wisdom is more characteristic of the books of Job and Ecclesiastes. Since wisdom is didactic in its essence, it is important to strike a balance between its prescriptive and descriptive aspects in the final analysis. Each kind of wisdom reflects a set of "lived experiences" which require critical thinking and empirical observation.

---

18. See my full discussion in Elaine W. F. Goh, "'She Is More Bitter Than Death': Reading Ecclesiastes 7:23–8:1 as an Asian Chinese," in *Reading Ecclesiastes from Asia and Pacifica*, eds. Jione Havea and Peter H. W. Lau (Atlanta, GA: SBL Press, 2020): 115–26.
19. See, for example, A. M. Wolters, *The Song of the Valiant Woman: Studies in the Interpretation of Proverbs 31:10–31* (Carlisle, UK: Paternoster, 2001), 93.
20. Craig G. Bartholomew, *Ecclesiastes*, Baker Commentary on the Old Testament Wisdom and Psalms, ed. Tremper Longman III (Grand Rapids, MI: Baker Academic, 2009), 268.
21. Some use different terms such as *experiential wisdom* (brief proverbial sayings and instructions) and *theoretical wisdom* (philosophical probing of life's inequities or personal reflections on life's meaning). See Crenshaw, *Old Testament Wisdom*, 5.

2. BLESSEDNESS IN BIBLICAL WISDOM

The next part of this essay examines the concept of "blessedness" in biblical wisdom. We first address a common misunderstanding of "the state of blessing[s]" among the ethnic Chinese. As part of this process, it will be necessary to redefine both "blessings" (as a noun) and "blessedness" (as a state) from a biblical perspective. Finally, we will outline how the people of God can live out biblical blessedness according to the pedagogy of OT wisdom.

2.1. "Blessedness" Revisited

"Blessedness" (i.e. the state of having blessings) is a goal to be pursued in OT wisdom traditions (e.g. Prov 5:18; 22:9; Job 42:12). In today's world, definitions of what constitutes blessedness will vary from person to person. Yet common to them all is the commitment to "having a good life." A person is considered "blessed" when he or she has an abundance of daily subsistence, possesses physical and mental health, maintains sufficiency of material possessions as well as financial gain, and has children as well as grandchildren before the end of life comes by natural causes.

Among the Chinese, possession of wealth, social status, longevity, and comfort are generally perceived as the main symbols of having a good life. Furthermore, the Chinese perceive prosperity as the chief reflection of success. The way in which many Chinese greet each other during Lunar New Year is most telling – we bless people to gain "wealth in abundance" (*gongxi facai*), to "possess big money" (*fadacai*), or to "run great fortune" (*xingdayun*). Indeed, the Chinese terms for "blessing" (*fú*, 福) and "wealth" (*fù*, 富) have a pictographic element in common.

It is hence natural for Chinese people to link "blessing" and "wealth" together as the same entity. The purpose of attaining prosperity and wealth drives Chinese people to work harder, leading many to strive to succeed and dare to dream big; some even resort to gambling in an attempt to reap sudden riches. Traditional mindsets about prosperity and success have also penetrated Chinese Christian circles, as when massive church buildings, expanding ministries, huge financial contributions, prosperity gospels, and famous preachers become the signs of success. Some of these pursuits, unfortunately, have also become entangled with scandalous practices which have brought Christians into disrepute. While wealth and success are sometimes attested in the Bible as symbols of God's blessing (e.g. Prov 10:22; Job 42:12), the wise also caution God's people to have a right attitude toward wealth (e.g. Prov 23:4–5; 28:19–20) and to be wary of the consequences that wealth may bring (e.g.

Prov 15:6; Eccl 2:9–11). This mixed picture makes it necessary to reexamine the Hebrew terms for "blessedness" in the understanding of the biblical sages.

2.2. Redefining "Blessedness"

OT wisdom literature uses at least two roots to convey the idea of "blessing," *brk* and *'šr*. In the case of *brk*, the wise pronounce God's "blessing" (*běrākâ*) on those who do not hoard grain in times of need (Prov 11:26), for example. One who is faithful to their spouse is called "blessed" (*bārûk*; Prov 5:18). An inheritance claimed too soon, however, will not be "blessed" (*těbōrāk*) at the end (Prov 20:21). The Lord "blessed" (*bērak*) Job in the latter part of his life more than in his earlier (Job 42:12). Similarly, a faithful person will abound with "blessings" (*běrākôt*; Prov 28:20).

English Bibles use both "happy" and "blessed" to render the Hebrew *'šr*, a root whose forms appear as both *'ešer* and *'āšār*. This verb describes people who find wisdom and gain understanding (e.g. Prov 3:13) as well as those who heed wisdom's instructions (Prov 3:18; 8:32; 29:18). "Happy/blessed" is the one who is kind to the needy (Prov 14:21) and who is generous to share their food with the poor (Prov 22:9). When the righteous lead a blameless life, their children who come after them are also "happy/blessed" (Prov 20:7). In the articulation of Qoheleth, "blessedness" signifies a well-managed life (Eccl 10:17). Furthermore, "happy/blessed" is the one who trusts in Yahweh (Prov 16:20) and the one who always trembles before him (Prov 28:14).

Regardless of whether we use "happy" or "blessed" to render these biblical verses, *brk* and *'šr* are indicative of a particular kind of well-being. Biblical "happiness" departs markedly from prosperity theology's understanding of the term. Many people, the Chinese especially, may think "happiness" means getting one's wishes fulfilled or achieving one's goals in life, especially those associated with wealth and prosperity. Such a misunderstanding of happiness often leads to a lifestyle of indulgence, substance abuse, and ultimately self-destruction. Eventually, such a person will not be "happy" at all (however this word is understood). By contrast, biblical blessedness connotes the idea of inner peace and knowing that one's doing and being invite divine favor and approval (Prov 28:14; Job 1:10). In wisdom pedagogy, "blessedness" is a God-fearing way of life, which is free from the fear of facing negative consequences, such as those resulting from one's wrong behavior and choices in life.

2.3. Blessedness in Wisdom Pedagogy

In developing countries of Asia, many ethnic Chinese strive to survive by taking two jobs, working overtime, or trying to earn a fortune by venturing into business. Regardless of the avenue, countless Chinese aim for prosperity to ensure life-long comfort with a mindset that might appear to reflect Confucius's affirmation that being rich is "good/beautiful" (*mei*; *Anal.* 13:8). However, Confucius also cautions elsewhere about the futility of gaining riches through unrighteous means (*Anal.* 7:16). Therefore, is wealth always to be affirmed in the Chinese/Confucian mind as a sign of blessings? Proverbs 28:20 similarly points out the problem of one's motives: "A faithful person will be richly blessed, but one eager to get rich will not go unpunished."

One of the distinctive contributions of wisdom, whether Confucian or biblical, is drawing people to reassess what truly lies at the core of blessing. Blessedness brings along with it harmony and rectitude, two traits that resonate especially with people who possess affluence yet are insecure or living in fear. Furthermore, biblical blessedness is less about enjoying a wealthy lifestyle and more about having a God-fearing way of life. Rather than living with riches and fortunes while fearing that such a good life may end, the blessed live at ease due to divine approval upon them. Hence, the mark of blessings in wisdom traditions requires a deeper engagement with character formation, a topic that this essay will now elaborate further.

3. CONFUCIAN WISDOM AND *THE ANALECTS*

Raised and educated in Chinese-language schools, a Chinese Christian has typically grown in and been nurtured by the traditions of Confucian wisdom in addition to biblical wisdom. The resulting fusion of the two traditions shapes a person as uniquely Chinese and Christian at the same time. This section therefore brings biblical wisdom and Confucian wisdom into dialogue, with special attention to character formation.

3.1. Confucian Wisdom

The emphasis of wisdom on human conduct has its roots not only in the ancient Near East. Confucian learning aims at self-cultivation (*xiushen*), which gives rise to managing one's family (*qijia*) and then building up the nation (*zhiguo*) and bringing stability under heaven (*pingtianxia*). Biblically, self-cultivation is also not only important, it is imperative for holiness. And culturally, from a Chinese perspective, individual self-cultivation is the expected ethos of the Chinese community.

Education, Learning, and Wisdom

Wisdom is thus a cross-cultural phenomenon. In this regard there have been many attempts to establish a common framework of wisdom thinking between the Hebraic and Confucian cultures.[22] Confucian thought has shaped both Chinese civilization in Asia and many other Asian cultures. Since Confucius was himself a teacher and a sage who accentuated the role of ethics,[23] Confucian sages have common ground with the ancient Israelite sages – they also lay great weight on the moral dimensions of education.[24] Confucian wisdom thus embraces both knowledge and conduct since "the sense of right and wrong is the beginning of wisdom."[25] This notion resonates with Israelite sages in Proverbs 1:7 and 9:10. The Chinese rendering of "wisdom" (*zhi*) in Proverbs is also one of the virtues that characterizes the Confucian ideal of a "noble person" (*junzi*). Learning to gain knowledge will thus lead to the attainment of wisdom and becoming a "saint/holy person" (*shengren*).

The pedagogy of *The Analects* is to nurture wise living through acceptable conduct. Confucius lays down a number of specific ways to be considered among the "wise."[26] Like the biblical sages, *The Analects* advocates humility (2:17), virtue (4:1), and enjoyment in life (6:23; cf. Eccl 5:18–20 [Heb. 5:17–19]). Just as the wisdom of ancient Near East points toward the choice between the path of the righteous and the path of the wicked, *The Analects* distinguishes the way of the "noble" (*junzi*) and the way of the "inferior" (*xiaoren*) using a similar rhetoric of contrasts (e.g. 7:37; 13:23, 26; 14:23). The "noble" represents the person who follows the proper way of moral cultivation, embracing the qualities of virtue (*de*), benevolence (*ren*), civility (*li*), and righteousness (*yi*), and so forth. The "inferior" represents just the opposite. In communicating such distinctions between wisdom and foolishness, *The Analects* urges readers and listeners to choose the way of the wise.

---

22. For example, Xinzhong Yao, *Wisdom in Early Confucian and Israelite Traditions* (Burlington/Hants: Ashgate Publishing, 2006), ix. Also among recent endeavors in this regard is Elaine Wei-Fun Goh, *Cross-Textual Reading of Ecclesiastes with the Analects: In Search of Political Wisdom in a Disordered World*, Contrapuntal Readings of the Bible in World Christianity Series, eds. K. K. Yeo and Melanie Baffes (Eugene, OR: Pickwick Publications, 2019).
23. Kurt Rudolph, "Wisdom," *The Encyclopedia of Religion*, 2nd ed., ed. Mircea Eliade, trans. Matthew J. O'Connell, vol. 14 (New York: Thompson Gale, 2005), 9752–53.
24. See Lawrence Boadt, "Wisdom, Wisdom Literature," *Eerdmans Dictionary of the Bible*, ed. David Noel Freedman (Grand Rapids, MI: Eerdmans, 2000), 1380–82, here 1380. See also Yao, *Wisdom in Early Confucian and Israelite Traditions*, 6.
25. Words of Feng Youlan quoted in Rudolph, "Wisdom," 9753.
26. Xinzhong Yao, "From 'What Is Below' to 'What Is Above': A Confucian Discourse on Wisdom," *Journal of Chinese Philosophy* 33 (Sept 2006): 349–63, 351.

3.2. Confucian and Biblical Wisdom in Dialogue[27]

On character formation, Confucian pedagogy essentially encompasses the following concepts: benevolence (*ren*), ritual propriety or decency (*li*), rightness/righteousness (*yi*), knowledge/wisdom (*zhi*), trustworthiness (*xin*), morality (*de*), and the like. Most of these concepts are virtues that are actively promoted by biblical sages in wisdom pedagogy. As hinted earlier, these Confucian terms are also used in Chinese Bible translations, as when the Chinese Union Version (CUV) at Proverbs 20:6 renders Hebrew *ḥesed* as *ren*, similarly to the English terms "unfailing love" (NIV) and "goodness" (KJV). Likewise, Hebrew *'ĕmûn* becomes Chinese *xin* in denoting "trust." Moreover, the CUV Bible translates *ṣedek* as *yi* ("righteousness, right"; e.g. Prov 2:9; Job 29:14) and *ḥokmâ* as *zhi* ("wisdom"; Prov 1:2; Job 28:12; Eccl 1:17), both being familiar Confucian terms.

In this connection, space limits us to exploring only "benevolence/humanness" (*ren*) and "trustworthiness/trust" (*xin*). The former virtue is especially prized in the world of *The Analects* with regard to human behavior and character. In its etymology, this Chinese term for "humanness/benevolence" (*ren*) is a cognate of "human" (*ren*). In its functions, *ren* has a multi-faceted role in various interpersonal relationships. Since it is the basis that intrinsically connects all of Confucian ethics, *ren* overtakes kinship and family connections in favor of having a love for all people (*Anal.* 12:22). Character formation in Confucian tradition springs from a fundamental emphasis on *ren*. Similarly, the idea of "trustworthiness/trust" (*xin*) in *Analects* covers a complementary aspect of character formation. Its etymology points to a person who stands by one's word, and such a person is deserving of "trust." In *Analects*, a political leader who is trustworthy will receive the sincerity of the people in return (*Anal.* 13:4). When a nation stands by its word, people from other states will be attracted to it (*Anal.* 13:16).[28] The idea of trust is thus regarded as one of the fundamental building blocks of relationships.

The interpersonal notions of "humanness/benevolence" (*ren*) and "trustworthiness/trust/faithfulness" (*xin*) are sometimes the targets of cynicism in biblical wisdom (e.g. Prov 20:6). In my work on Ecclesiastes, however, I have found that even Qoheleth sighs at the usual absence of *ren* and lack of *xin*. He sees wickedness stemming from human choices, ironically in places where

---

27. This section is adapted from Goh, *Cross-Textual Reading*, 151–53.
28. Reading from the literary sequence of *Analects* 13:15–16. Some passages in *Analects* connect to the main idea of the text before or after, like this one.

justice and righteousness should be (Eccl 3:16). Qoheleth is puzzled at times by the value of *ren*, as when a stranger, rather than the next-of-kin, may inherit the fruit of one's wealth, possessions, and honor (Eccl 6:1–2; cf. 4:7–8). Qoheleth also protests against claiming one's reward or praise from another, contra Confucius' advocacy of *ren*. Elsewhere, Qoheleth agonizes over the wicked deeds commonly committed by people against one another rather than the expected *ren* and *xin* under the sun. The oppression of the poor and the violation of justice (3:16–17; 4:1–3) mean that *ren* (humanness) is lacking in civic life and *xin* (trust) is missing in the judicial system.

It is important to note, however, that Qoheleth does not invalidate the ideas of *ren* and *xin*. The rhetorical question in Ecclesiastes 4:8, "For whom am I toiling and depriving myself of good?," implies that one's toil should ideally have a benefit to share with another person.[29] As such, there is actually a creative tension arising between "toiling" and "good" – Qoheleth is saying that there is no use toiling and denying oneself of pleasure if one has nobody to share the benefits with, whether in the present or the future.[30] When another person shares in the fruit of one's labor, however, one's toil gains additional meaning. For this reason, I believe that Qoheleth values the idea of *ren*, though some commentators take Ecclesiastes 4:8 as an ironic or negative statement from Qoheleth.[31]

Further, the numerical proverbs in Ecclesiastes show that Qoheleth affirms the value of partnership over being solitary (Eccl 4:9–12). One who has a companion (i.e. *šěnayim* "two" in the Hebrew, cf. the essence of *ren* that is minimally comprised of "two persons") has a benefit in their toil, and this is considered "good" (Eccl 4:9). Here one sees that the idea of companionship in Ecclesiastes 4:9–12 resonates with the root meaning of *ren* in suggesting a group of at least two people. Qoheleth makes good use of duality in asserting that people are better able to cope with crises if they help one another

---

29. This rhetorical question, as some commentators have pointed out, may be preceded by "he never asks himself" as a hypothetical argument. See Robert Gordis, *Koheleth – the Man and His Word*, 2nd ed. (New York: Bloch Publishing, 1955), 232. Alternatively, Qoheleth may be speaking out of his own experience, as suggested by Michael V. Fox, *A Time to Tear Down and a Time to Build Up: A Rereading of Ecclesiastes* (Grand Rapids, MI: Eerdmans, 1999), 222.
30. Choon-Leong Seow, *Ecclesiastes*, AB (NY: Doubleday, 1997), 188. See also Bartholomew, *Ecclesiastes*, 188–89, who observes Qoheleth's point that the pursuit of wealth by oneself is unfulfilling when a loner finds himself lacking a community (Eccl 4:8).
31. E.g. Ellen F. Davis, *Proverbs, Ecclesiastes, and the Song of Songs*, Westminster Bible Companion (Louisville, KY: Westminster John Knox, 2000), 189–91, who takes Ecclesiastes 4:8 as a result of frenetic labor and overwork, the latter being a form of boredom.

(4:10–12).³² Instead of being selfish, one should gather with companions or turn over a portion of one's possessions to the needy (4:9–12; 11:1–2).³³ Thus, the idea of *ren* reflects part of Qoheleth's pursuit in Ecclesiastes since *ren* has primacy in human relationships. At times, he is merely sighing at its absence in the realities of life. As for *xin*, it is also elusive in the realities of life. The trust of the people toward a ruler either does not endure (as in the case of Eccl 4:13–16) or is unpredictable (as in the case of Eccl 9:13–16).

4. WISDOM'S CONTRIBUTION TO CHINESE AND ASIAN CONTEXTS

The last section of this essay suggests a Chinese and Asian framework for communicating biblical wisdom. It aims to invite dialogue between biblical wisdom and Confucian wisdom in view of the unique contexts of Asia. Due to the convergences between biblical wisdom and Confucian wisdom, I propose that a common sapiential worldview connects biblical wisdom literature with Confucian literature. Regarding their respective approaches to wisdom, it is useful to consider some shared concepts when reading the two textual traditions in parallel since readers of both form their understanding on the basis of a collective fabric of sapiential materials. The use of key terms such as *ṣedeq* ("righteousness") and *mišpāṭ* ("justice") in the biblical wisdom literature will be compared to the Chinese term *yi* ("righteousness") in *The Analects*. In what follows, I first discuss the notion of religion in both biblical wisdom and Confucian wisdom (the latter as based on *The Analects*). This endeavor will address the deeper question of whether Confucian wisdom can be said to contain theology. Subsequently, I suggest three wisdom contributions for Chinese Christians who can benefit from integrating two strands of wisdom pedagogy, one from the Bible and the other from *The Analects*.

4.1. Religious Worldview in Wisdom Thought³⁴

Biblical wisdom refers to God by both generic terms such as *ʾĕlōhîm* and the personal name Yahweh.³⁵ Yahweh is depicted as powerful (Job 38–41), but interestingly in Ecclesiastes, *ʾĕlōhîm* is the one who keeps humans in ignorance (Eccl 3:11). The biblical sages call for obedience and reverence to the divine

---

32. Seow, *Ecclesiastes*, 189.
33. Thomas Krüger, *Qoheleth: A Commentary*, Hermeneia (Minneapolis, MN: Fortress, 2004), 1.
34. A full discussion is found in my work mentioned earlier (Goh, *Cross-Textual Reading*, 163–67).
35. The name by which Yahweh represents and by which Qoheleth abstains from using, reminds us of a covenantal relationship that invokes warmth and closeness.

being while at the same time addressing the issues of oppression, injustice, and governance. Yet the God of the biblical sages is also an active God (Prov 15:3; Job 1–2; Eccl 3:17) and a personal God (Prov 5:21; Job 31:6; Eccl 5:6). Thus, humans are advised to fear *ĕlōhîm* in all that they do (Prov 1:7; Job 37:24; Eccl 12:13).

While biblical wisdom literature upholds the fear of God, *Analects* 16:8 mentions that the *junzi* ("noble person") has "a fear to the destiny of heaven" (*jing tianming*). Confucian thought professes to uphold "reverence for heaven" (*jingtian*). Though the mentions of *tian* are sometimes associated with "fate" or "destiny" (*ming*), the Confucian approach toward the supernatural is probably not agnostic or fatalistic. Scholarly debates continue on whether "heaven/Heaven" (*tian*) refers to a personal divine being or an impersonal cosmic order. Even if *tianming* does not denote a personal relationship between a divine heaven/Heaven (*tian*) and mortal people, there will be a clear point of departure between the biblical and Confucian wisdom – the fear of God as professed by the Israelite sages unmistakably points to the unique Lord who initiated a covenantal relationship with the Israelites. In this regard, the most striking difference between Confucian wisdom and Israelite wisdom possibly lies in this personal relationship that gives rise to "the fear of God."[36]

Even though *The Analects* seldom offer an explicitly theological articulation, some have argued that *The Analects* is fundamentally religious.[37] To begin with, heaven/Heaven (*tian*) clearly has elements of "religious" uniqueness.[38] It represents a supernatural force that guides the order of the universe. *Tian* is described as "great" in *Analects* 8:19. *Tian* is the source wherein moral values and fundamental principles of humans are established. In this regard, *Tian* is sometimes understood in parallel with the Way (*Dao*), namely, the cosmos'

---

36. Yao (*Wisdom in Early Confucian and Israelite Traditions*, 6) maintains that "the Fear of the Lord" is fundamental and distinctive to Israelite tradition, supplying also a key to biblical wisdom literature.
37. See, e.g. Rodney L. Taylor, *The Religious Dimensions of Confucianism* (Albany, NY: SUNY Press, 1990), 1–12. This book presents Confucian tradition as religious by identifying aspects of the tradition that can be described as religious, such as the cultivation of the "sagehood/sainthood" (*sheng*) by religious heroes.
38. Here, heaven/Heaven (*tian*) is understood in a religious peculiarity. Elsewhere in *Analects*, this is understood as a natural phenomenon and represents the cosmos in which humans live and act. *Tian* is regarded in these passages as distinctive from *dao*, especially when *dao* is explained in terms of faculties of human experience, especially humanness (*ren*) and propriety (*li*). The most comprehensive analysis by Yong-Tao Zhang and Shu-You Li classifies *Tian* into four categories of meanings: (1) rightness, (2) virtue, (3) nature, (4) and a willful personal God. See their *Ruxue Yuanliu* [*Origins and Development of Confucianism*] Chinese Classics Series, vol. 1 (Beijing: China Youth, 2000), 186.

decreed way of life. The concept of "the Way of Heaven" (*tiandao*) and "the Mandate of Heaven" (*tianming*) derive from this understanding.[39] As *Tian* shoulders the overarching position of power, all major changes, such as the defeat of an inferior state by a higher political power, derive from the influence and determination of *Tian*.[40] As such, the failure to manifest ethical virtues will lead to the downfall of a ruler.[41] Confucian ethics derive from this cosmic order of *Tian*. Confucius discerns that *Tian* will communicate its course through nature (*Anal.* 17:19), and he also acknowledges that his own virtue was given by *Tian* (*Anal.* 7:23).

Confucius' commitment to the practices of rites and sacrifices further suggests a religious undertone to his sayings in *The Analects*. The Confucian classics' work on rites (*li*) etymologizes this term with sacrificial vessels, meaning that the character has a religious origin. Confucius' speech in *The Analects* reinforces such religious undertones. For instance, he cautions against the superstitions of his time (*Anal.* 2:24). Confucius' attitude towards gods is one of reverence (*jing*), as evident in *Analects* 6:22, spoken against a background of cultic worship in which Confucius found it necessary to caution on the need for proper religious attitudes. Furthermore, Confucius appears open to the idea of "destiny/decree" (*Anal.* 14:36). He comments that anyone who does not know their destiny cannot be a "noble/ exemplary person" (*junzi*; *Anal.* 20:3). To Confucius, humans seem to possess the potential to know the decree of *Tian* and to live accordingly. While the question of whether Heaven/ *Tian* is personal remains open, a religious worldview is clearly embedded in *The Analects'* articulation of ethics.

Both biblical and Confucian wisdom thus have what might be called a "religious" worldview. Although Qoheleth's impression of God and Confucius' impression of *Tian* are somewhat distant, each possesses a religious consciousness which is genuine and sincere. Their wisdom texts express their theological meanings in unique ways, though each acknowledge a higher order of events above the human realm. They both affirm an ultimate order, *'ĕlōhîm* (in the Bible) and *Tian* or *Dao* (in *Analects*). While the understanding of *'ĕlōhîm*

---

39. According to the theory of the "Mandate of Heaven" in ancient China, Heaven gives the mandate to a deserving person as the ruling figure, to govern wisely and humanely. According to Julia Ching, *Chinese Religions* (London: Macmillan, 1993), 45–46, this theory developed with the emergence of classical texts such as the Confucian tradition.

40. Whether Confucius' *Tian* is a personal deity remains debatable till the present day. Most scholars of Confucianism hesitate to claim that *Tian* is a personal deity.

41. Ching, *Chinese Religions*, 46, reasons that the Mandate of Heaven gives justification to the rise and fall of many dynasties in Chinese history.

directs one to a fear of God, Confucius' understanding of *Tian* leads to moral principles. For these reasons, Confucian religious consciousness can be appropriated as conversation partners on how Christians articulate faith and ethics in Asian contexts.

4.2. Life-centered Perspectives

In the wisdom traditions of both the ancient Near East and ancient Far East, there is an overriding interest to address life-centered concerns of one's pragmatic existence. Nurtured by both faith and cultural tradition, Chinese Christians are often reminded to embrace responsible living – doing something practical and transformative here and now, feeding the poor, reaching out to the needy, and reclaiming the stewardship of protecting the earth as well as the living environment of the entire human race. Wisdom teachers focus on the present rather than the time to come. In short, wisdom is "this worldly."[42] In a difficult time like a global pandemic, practical endeavors are preferred to other-worldly assumptions – for example, speculating about whether the end of time is near.

There is a corresponding need to harmonize *The Analects* with biblical-theological principles and reconcile biblical wisdom with *The Analects'* pragmatic ethics. This effort can be made by first appropriating the fear of God (of the biblical sages) as the motive and dynamic of Confucius' vision for change. The fear of God entails an acknowledgment of the divine Being who ultimately judges how humans live in the world. Human effort has its value only in the sight of this supreme ruler and judge. On this account, K. K. Yeo has suggested the idea of "theological ethics,"[43] an intertwined relationship between Confucius' ethics and biblical theology. On this note, the present evil of the global pandemic can be dealt with through the parallel efforts of combining virtuous living with the fear of God. Chinese Christians need to observe *ren* even more, as this is also expected from the people of God. For the common good, then, it is time for Chinese churches to rethink how to build meaningful relationships in the safe-distancing of the pandemic, how to trust one another during a global crisis, how to manage scarcity in resources, and how to cope with the "new normal." Virtuous living and wise management are

---

42. Choon-Leong Seow, "Wisdom as a Canonical Model of Ministry," Wisdom as Practical Theology (guest lecture, Sabah Theological Seminary, Kota Kinabalu, Malaysia, July 25, 2008).
43. A category proposed by Yeo, *Musing with Confucius and Paul,* 88–89, 110–76; see also Goh, *Cross-Textual Reading,* 169–76.

not merely human efforts, but ones undertaken with theological motivations. It is paramount for Chinese Christians to embrace such efforts while discerning God's purposes in times of crisis.

Wisdom is thus a lifelong journey of learning and transforming. Wisdom's tradents seem to reckon that it is all right not to know and understand everything in life. This informs the mission of churches today in the COVID-19 pandemic since one simply does not know when the present crisis will be over. Further, wisdom addresses vividly the issue of divine silence in the midst of suffering. Many have lost their lives or jobs to COVID-19, while even more have lost hope in the midst of hardships and hunger. As a way forward, Proverbs recommends human choice and calculations, Job engages God in searching for truth, while Qoheleth suggests that we see good in life and live in the moment. Likewise, Confucius advocates the pedagogy and self-cultivation and wise governance despite living in a chaotic world, though with a much less explicitly God-centered worldview.

CONCLUSION

The importance of wisdom reminds Asian Christians of the importance of engaging in a contextual approach to Christian ministry. Asia is a continent that is marked by natural disasters, governmental oppression, corruption, poverty, and social injustice. Chinese churches in particular need to adequately consider the perplexed perspective of Job and Ecclesiastes, while at the same time adequately drawing wisdom from Proverbs and *The Analects*. Just as the biblical sages play a part alongside the priests and the prophets in shaping Israel's faith, Chinese Christians can consult wisdom from the Bible as well as from the Confucian tradition. As wisdom invites dialogue and contextual reflections, the holistic wisdom that merges biblical and Chinese resources will generate something distinctively Asian.

In the Bible, Wisdom invites us to reach her, most interestingly in the form of the tree of life in Proverbs 3:16–18. For after the Fall, the tree of life in the Garden of Eden was guarded by cherubim and a flaming sword, preventing humanity from eating from it and living forever (Gen 3:22–24).[44] The tree of life in the wisdom tradition is nevertheless now open to all who wish to grasp it. The portrayal of wisdom as a tree of life in OT wisdom literature recalls

---

44. The intertextual connections between Proverbs 3:13–20 and Genesis 2–3 has been suggested by a handful of wisdom scholars. See, for example, Christine Roy Yoder, "Wisdom is the Tree of Life: A Study of Proverbs 3:13–20 and Genesis 2–3," *Reading Proverbs Intertextually*, 13–17.

the garden of Eden and effects a theological reversal of chaos and de-creation.[45] Wisdom thus invites people back to God's created order with open arms. It need no longer be shame, estrangement, and alienation that characterize life, but rather long life, riches, and honor. This is the vision of true blessedness and wisdom that the tree of life offers to all humanity.

REFERENCES

Bartholomew, Craig G. *Ecclesiastes*. Baker Commentary on the Old Testament Wisdom and Psalms, edited by Tremper Longman III. Grand Rapids: Baker Academic, 2009.

Boadt, Lawrence. "Wisdom, Wisdom Literature." *Eerdmans Dictionary of the Bible*, edited by David Noel Freedman. Grand Rapids: William Eerdmans, 2000): 1380–1382.

Ching, Julia. *Chinese Religions*. London: Macmillan, 1993.

Crenshaw, James L. *Old Testament Wisdom: An Introduction*. Louisville, KY: Westminster John Knox, 1998.

Davis, Ellen F. *Proverbs, Ecclesiastes, and the Song of Songs*. Westminster Bible Companion. Louisville, KY: Westminster John Knox Press, 2000.

Dell, Katharine J., and Will Kynes, eds. *Reading Proverbs Intertextually*. The Library of Hebrew Bible/Old Testament Studies. Vol. 629. Edinburgh: T&T Clark, 2018.

Estes, Daniel J. *Handbook on the Wisdom Books and Psalms*. Grand Rapids, MI: Baker Academic, 2005.

Fox, Michael V. *A Time to Tear Down and a Time to Build Up: A Rereading of Ecclesiastes*. Grand Rapids, MI: Eerdmans, 1999.

Goh, Elaine Wei-Fun. "'She Is More Bitter Than Death': Reading Ecclesiastes 7:23–8:1 as an Asian Chinese" In *Reading Ecclesiastes from Asia and Pacifica*, edited by Jione Havea and Peter H. W. Lau, 115–26. Atlanta, GA: SBL Press, 2020.

———. *Cross-Textual Reading of Ecclesiastes and the Analects: In Search of Political Wisdom in a Disordered World*. Contrapuntal Readings of the Bible in World Christianity, edited by K. K. Yeo and Melanie Baffes. Eugene: Pickwick, 2019.

Gordis, Robert. *Koheleth – The Man and His Word*. 2nd ed. New York: Bloch Publishing, 1955.

Krüger, Thomas. *Qoheleth: A Commentary*. Hermeneia. Translated by O.C. Dean Jr. and edited by Klaus Baltzer. Minneapolis: Fortress, 2004.

Lambert, W. G. *Babylonian Wisdom Literature*. Oxford: Clarendon, 1960.

---

45. Yoder, "Wisdom is the Tree of Life," 17.

Lichtheim, Miriam. *Ancient Egyptian Literature*. 3 vols. Berkeley: University of California Press, 1975–1980.

Murphy, Roland E. *The Tree of Life: An Exploration of Biblical Wisdom Literature*. Grand Rapids, MI: Eerdmans, 2002.

von Rad, Gerhard. *Wisdom in Israel*. Translated by James D. Martin. Nashville, TN: Abingdon, 1972.

Rudolph, Kurt. "Wisdom." *The Encyclopedia of Religion*. 2nd ed., edited by Mircea Eliade. Translated from German by Matthew J. O'Connell. Vol. 14: 9746–54. New York: Thompson Gale, 2005.

Schultz, Richard L. "Unity or Diversity in Wisdom Theology? A Canonical and Covenantal Perspective." *Tyndale Bulletin* 48.2 (1997): 271–306.

Seow, Choon-Leong. "Wisdom as a Canonical Model of Ministry." Wisdom as Practical Theology. Guest lecture, Sabah Theological Seminary, Kota Kinabalu, Malaysia, July 25, 2008.

———. *Ecclesiastes*. The Anchor Bible. New York: Doubleday, 1997.

Taylor, Rodney L. *The Religious Dimensions of Confucianism*. Albany: State University of New York Press, 1990.

Van Norden, Bryan W., ed. *Confucius and the Analects*. Oxford: Oxford University Press, 2002.

Wolters, A. M. *The Song of the Valiant Woman: Studies in the Interpretation of Proverbs 31:10–31*. Carlisle, UK: Paternoster, 2001.

Yao, Xinzhong. "From 'What Is Below' to 'What Is Above': A Confucian Discourse on Wisdom." *Journal of Chinese Philosophy* 33 (2006): 349–63.

———. *Wisdom in Early Confucian and Israelite Traditions*. Burlington/Hants: Ashgate Publishing, 2006.

Yeo, K. K. *Musing with Confucius and Paul: Toward a Chinese Christian Theology*. Cambridge: James Clarke, 2008.

Yoder, Christine Roy. "Wisdom is the Tree of Life: A Study of Proverbs 3:13–20 and Genesis 2–3." In *Reading Proverbs Intertextually*, edited by Katharine J. Dell and Will Kynes, 11–20. Edinburgh: T&T Clark, 2019.

Zhang, Yong-Tao, and Li Shu-You. *Ruxue Yuanliu (Origins and Development of Confucianism)*. Chinese Classics Series. Vol I. Beijing: China Youth, 2000.

CHAPTER 9

OLD TESTAMENT NARRATIVES

Historiography and Historicity

Angukali Rotokha

The Hebrew Bible/Old Testament (HB/OT) has long been read by Jews and Christians as a history of the people of Israel. However, this traditional understanding has undergone a major shift during the last 150 years, especially in scholarly circles. The precritical view that the OT is a straightforward history has given way to the minimalist view that the OT contains no history at all. Between these two extremes lie distinct understandings of "Israel" that overlap to some degree: biblical Israel, historical Israel, and ancient Israel. This bifurcation (and the spectrum between its extremes) reflects differing assessments of the accuracy of the OT record. Particularly in recent decades, critical scholars have mounted many challenges to the historicity of the biblical accounts as core events on which Christian faith stands. Doubts about the historicity of biblical accounts are not new, of course; but while earlier the onus was on those who sought to disprove their historicity, the more recent kind of scholarship is characterized by an extreme skepticism which shifts the burden of proof to the biblical accounts.

This essay explores a way forward regarding the historical value of OT narratives.[1] First, we take a look at concepts that bear upon the genre of OT narrative, such as history, historiography, historicity, fiction, and ideology. These will be briefly discussed in relation to our main point of interest, namely, the nature of OT historiography. Second, the essay compares the general contours of modern and ancient Near Eastern historiography (OT narrative being a species of the latter). This will set the OT narratives alongside contemporary ANE historiographic accounts and provide a better context for assessing the historical value of OT narratives. Third, the essay will assess India's historiographical enterprise vis-à-vis the *Mahabharata*, an ancient Hindu religious text,

---

1. In this chapter, we consider the beginning of the OT historical narratives as particularly, though not exclusively, from Exodus to the end of 2 Kings.

which some in recent years have used as a source to reconstruct the history of ancient India. This exercise will lend greater cross-cultural objectivity on the issue of historicity in ancient texts in the parallel task of reassessing our own Christian scriptures with a better understanding of what is and is not at stake. We begin by examining briefly some of the strands that are interwoven in the issue of biblical narrative as historiography.

1. HISTORY, HISTORIOGRAPHY, AND HISTORICITY

First, a word on the contested terms "history," "historiography," and "historicity." "History" is generally used in two distinct ways. One is history as *event*. History in this sense is the history of happenings located in the past; it is history in the broadest sense and embraces all that has ever been and ever taken place. It may be noted, however, that the reconstruction of history in this sense is unrealistic because exhaustive knowledge of the past is impossible.[2] The second sense is that of history as human perceptions of events and their significance. This is history as an *account* of a "narratively structured understanding of events."[3] This meaning of history is "clearly and exclusively cognitive."[4] The difference between this sense and the first one is that history as event embraces *all* that can be *located* in the past, while history as perception is "what is *known* about *part* of what has existed."[5] It is the human experience and understanding of those events and involves awareness, description, interpretation and narration; it is "a specific kind of human activity,"[6] which is based upon one's perceptions of events and how these perceptions are turned into conceptions of events.

Thus, while the first conception of history asks the question, "What happened?" the second instead asks, "What is known or understood about what happened?" Often these distinctions are lost or overlooked. Before history as event can become history as account, there is a psychological process that must take place – an event comes to mind in the form of *perception* (such as an observation or an act of imagination), after which it solidifies into some form of *knowledge* or *memory*, and only then are the sum of these conveyed (in

---

2. Robert Eric Frykenberg, *Belief and History: The Foundations of Historical Understanding* (Grand Rapids, MI: Eerdmans, 1996), 20–25.
3. Kristen Gjesdal, "History and Historicity," in *The Routledge Companion to Hermeneutics*, eds. Jeff Malpas and Hans-Helmuth Gander (London: Routledge, 2014).
4. Frykenberg, *Belief and History*, 33.
5. Frykenberg, 33, emphasis original.
6. Frykenberg, 33.

verbal, pictorial, or written form) as *descriptions* of events. These descriptions may or may not be explicitly supported by external evidence on the way to becoming an "intrinsic part of our understanding"[7] of that particular event. For instance, the exodus and the events surrounding it as recorded in the book of Exodus happened to a group of Hebrew slaves, who then interpreted and transmitted these memories for future generations of Israel. Therefore, what counts as "history" always involves a degree of human interaction with or experience of the events and not merely the events themselves. What links history as event and history as record, then, is the perception and construction of the events by the historian and their transposition into written or spoken forms.[8]

This art of history writing is called *historiography*, for which Frykenberg gives a comprehensive but complex definition: "The cumulative description of the past events generates histories of historical understandings and those, in turn, generate histories of the writing of history, constituting what we now sometimes call *historiography*."[9] This definition sees the elements of perception, conception, and description of history as central in intelligent history writing. With these concepts in mind, it becomes evident that historiography is distinct from the notion of history as the application and understanding of events located in time and space, as well as history as a merely factual record of such events. The role of the historian becomes more than that of simple reporting. Thus historiography necessarily becomes, to use Philips Long's analogy, more of a painting incorporating the artist's perspective and creativity than a photorealistic reproduction of past happenings.[10]

Related to history writing is the notion of *historicity*, a concept that denotes "the reality of what had actually happened."[11] Georges Augustin Barrois' definition is also apt: "Historicity is that particular quality of documents relative to past events and physical or psychological facts, inasmuch as the memory of such, at first unrecorded, subsequently consigned in writing and eventually gathered in compilations of diverse age, worth and purpose, forms the subject-matter of history."[12] Thus, the skeptic's practice of questioning the historicity of a particular story or account involves challenging whether the

---

7. Frykenberg, 21.
8. V. Philips Long, *The Art of Biblical History* (Grand Rapids, MI: Zondervan, 1994), 69.
9. Frykenberg, *Belief and History*, 256.
10. Long, *The Art of Biblical History*, 20.
11. Frykenberg, *Belief and History*, 193.
12. Georges Augustin Barrois, "The Notion of Historicity and the Critical Study of the Old Testament," *GOTR* 19 (Spring 1974): 7, 12.

events recorded as history actually took place in time and space. This brings us to the related concept of *fiction* which will be investigated next.

2. FICTION

The term "fiction" derives from the Latin word *fictum* ("created"). It is popularly understood as the opposite of fact, reality, truth, or history. In literature, fiction can refer to a literary genre which deals with, in part or in whole, temporally contrafactual events, that is, events that are not true at the time of writing. The application of the term in discussions of OT narrative stems from scholars recognizing the *literary* qualities of OT narratives. In this regard, the rise of literary criticism in biblical studies has provided many tools to understand OT narrative better. With this increasing awareness of literary artistry in the OT, there has also come the skeptical view that the OT as literature is synonymous with fiction, since literary compositions supposedly lack historical *referentiality*, that is, no basis in real events.[13]

However, "fiction" is a bivalent word with another meaning – the literary devices of imagination that writers employ in works of all genres. That is, just as factual history or historical elements (places, people, etc.) are often used in so-called "fictional" genres to create a historicized fiction (as in movies and novels), similarly, the literary devices of fiction can be used in the writing of history, resulting in "fictionalized" history.[14] For instance, Herodotus' work, *Histories*, is an account of the wars between Greece and Persia (499–479 BCE) and is considered by scholars to be a historical source. At the same time, he not only recounts the events but seeks also to explain why the wars were fought and why the Greeks won. He often inserts direct speeches and dialogues by leading historical figures to achieve his goal. As Robert Fowler says, "Herodotus has brilliantly manipulated his knowledge of Persian culture in order to fashion a literary account of a people and its rulers that is both compelling and profound."[15] Hence, while history is often viewed as a matter of facts, with fiction as its antithesis, scholars increasingly perceive them as interrelated points along a continuum.

---

13. For instance, Philip Davies of the "minimalism" school takes strong exception to the use of biblical text in historical research for ancient Israel, due to what he perceives as the OT's literary characteristics and ideological interests (*In Search of "Ancient Israel": A Study in Biblical Origins* [Sheffield: Sheffield Academic Press, 1992], 11–36).
14. See Robert Alter, *The Art of Biblical Narrative* (New York: Basic Books, 1981), 22, 33–34. These categories are further explained by Long, *The Art of Biblical History*, 61–63.
15. Robert Fowler, "Herodotus and Persia," in *The Cambridge Companion to Herodotus*, eds. Carolyn Dewald and John Marincola (Cambridge: Cambridge University Press, 2007), 278.

Uneasiness nonetheless remains for evangelicals, since using the label "fiction" for a biblical account seems incompatible with our traditional conceptions of truth. *Factuality* is generally equated with truthfulness, with *fictionality* by definition being fanciful, detached from reality, and hence untrue. Hence, the axiom that anything true needs to be a fact, that is, corresponding strictly to historical reality. However, as mentioned, fiction can also be understood as the literary devices that every author has at their disposal to convey or reconstruct certain truths. Moreover, that there are varieties of truth which are each properly truth-telling according to their own conventions – whether historical, theological truth, or scientific – needs to be taken into consideration. While scientific truth can be empirically tested and historical truth verified to some extent, theological truth cannot be tested or verified since for the believer it stands above both simultaneously and ultimately on the basis of divine revelation.

3. "IDEOLOGY" IN BIBLICAL STUDIES

Another complaint against historicity in the OT is the contention that its narratives are ideologically oriented and hence unable to present an objective account of the past. In this regard, the term "ideology" has acquired numerous definitions and has steadily gained currency in biblical scholarship. Its origin can be traced back to the influence of perspectives and methods from sociology. Destutt de Tracy first used the term *ideology* in 1786 to refer to his own "science of ideas." Four characteristics from Tracy's science of ideas have come to general acceptance: (1) ideology presents a more or less comprehensive theory of society, (2) ideology represents a political program, (3) ideology foresees struggle in the implementation of the program, and (4) ideology envisions leadership by the intellectuals of a society.[16] Implicit in Tracy's conception was a challenge to the establishment, both secular and religious. This challenge came in the form of linking ideology to revolution (as in political activism or extremism), usually leading to a pejorative sense for the term, especially in the hands of Marxists.[17] Since there is still no single definition of ideology,

---

16. *The New Encyclopedia Britannica*, ed. Philip W. Goetz (Chicago: University of Chicago, 1985), s.v. "Ideology".
17. *New Encyclopedia Britannica*, s.v. "Ideology". Carl R. Holladay notes that in reconstructing the history of Israel, biblical scholars appropriated analytical methods and perspectives developed by modern sociologists and radically moved beyond the historical paradigm by proposing "an explicitly ideological reconstruction of Israel's history from the Marxist perspective" ("Contemporary Methods of Reading the Bible," *NIB* 1:135–36).

such objections reflect the comprehensive nature of ideology which results in various definitions that are useful but often incompatible, for even compatible ones cannot be meaningfully grouped together.[18]

When the concept of ideology entered the field of biblical scholarship, there was a similar lack of consensus.[19] Critical scholars, for instance, appropriated the methods and perspectives of modern sociology and moved beyond the historical paradigm by proposing "an explicitly ideological reconstruction of Israel's history from the Marxist perspective."[20] However, other scholars differed in their understanding of "ideology" and considered it inferior to theology, while still others used it in a neutral or even positive sense.[21] Hence, the meaning of "ideology" has undergone a significant metamorphosis since its coinage. It continues to evolve in all disciplines, including biblical scholarship. The difficulty lies not so much in the term's ambiguity as much as its polyvalence, often bearing conflicting connotations. As such, a helpful way to qualify it for our purposes is to describe it vis-à-vis theology.

Although evangelicals are more familiar and comfortable with the label "theology" for the Bible's system or patterns of thoughts and beliefs, it is noteworthy that their use of the term "ideology" is also increasing. This development can be attributed to scholars coming to a greater recognition of the human dimensions that birthed and shaped each biblical tradition in dialogue with a specific set of circumstances. This is the case, for instance, of the OT's royal covenant/theology which may be called royal "ideology" from a sociological perspective. A theological concept functions as an ideology when it serves to invest a certain construction of reality with meaning, and legitimatize

---

18. Terry Eagleton, *Ideology: An Introduction* (London: Verso, 1991), 1–32.
19. James Barr observes three ways in which the term ideology came to be commonly used in biblical scholarship. In the early stages of ideology's entry, it was immediately taken as the antonym for and diametrically opposed to theology, assigning ideology the negative, non-religious connotation. The second route probably arose from the skepticism of some biblical scholars regarding biblical theology, in as much as theology designated a systematized biblical thought which did not seem to fit within the Bible. But the term "theology" could not be easily discarded in discussions and an alternate term ready to be adopted was found in "ideology." Third is the influence of sociological thought and methods on biblical studies. See James Barr, *History and Ideology in the Old Testament: Biblical Studies at the End of the Millennium* (Oxford: Oxford University Press, 2000), 102–140.
20. Holladay, "Contemporary Methods," 135–36.
21. See Barr's explanation of the range of usage by different scholars (*History and Ideology*, 102–40).

its implementation in the present and its continuation to the future.[22] While evangelicals' use of "ideology" in this manner is neutral, the concurrent recognition that biblical texts are not free from ideologizing tendencies has also contributed to non-evangelical challenges to the historiographical nature of the biblical narratives.

4. MODERN UNDERSTANDINGS OF HISTORIOGRAPHY

Modern historiography tends to be characterized by the premium it places on objectivity. In this understanding, history writing is the exact recounting of the events as they actually happened in the past. Its credibility is thus measured by its strict accuracy in portraying events. Occasionally, there is an admission of the inescapability from bias on the part of any historian and the impossibility of knowing for certain what happened in the past, but the goal and the essential definition of history writing remains "telling exactly what happened in the past."[23]

A brief overview of the "history of history" will offer a glimpse into the climate in which the historical value of biblical accounts came under scrutiny. Although the beginning of historiography is usually attributed to the fifth-century BCE Greek historian Herodotus, "the father of history," the idea of history in the modern sense actually originated in the view of his Greek contemporary, Thucydides, that the aim of history writing must be to seek historical truth. Thucydides proposed that "a historian should use only reliable testimonies, avoid supernatural explanations based on miracles and divine intervention, and strive for objective descriptions."[24] Centuries later, the application of these criteria to biblical narratives would be used by critical scholars to undermine their historiographic value.

During the nineteenth century, the major crisis in the history of biblical historiography arrived when the nature of human existence shifted fundamentally from philosophy to science. All knowledge was to be answerable to the rational faculties and withstand empirical and critical examination to qualify as true or real. Particularly by the end of the 1880s, the move away from tradition

---

22. For a more comprehensive explanation on ideology vis-à-vis theology see Bernhard W. Anderson, "Biblical Theology and Sociological Interpretation," *ThTo* 42 (October 1985): 292–306.
23. Steven L. McKenzie, "Historiography, Old Testament." In *Dictionary of the Old Testament: Historical Books*, eds. Bill T. Arnold and H. G. M. Williamson (Downers Grove, IL: InterVarsity 2005), 418.
24. Yairah Amit, *History and Ideology: An Introduction to Historiography in the Hebrew Bible* (Sheffield: Sheffield Academic Press, 1999), 13.

toward freedom of explanation and new theories, as inaugurated by the natural sciences, had become decisive for all scholarly disciplines. This shift brought into serious question all the histories written prior to the nineteenth century because they had "not been produced using proper scientific method."[25] The pressure generated by the dominance of the Enlightenment's "scientific method" sciences resulted in each discipline's quest to become properly academic and "scientific" by abandoning dependence on what was viewed as naïve and precritical tradition.[26] Consequently, historians also attempted to reconstruct Israel's past "as it actually happened" (in the historicist Leopold von Ranke's famous words) over and above tradition's claims as to what happened. The outcome of modernism's skepticism, also known as *logical positivism*, eventually led to the rise of postmodernism and deconstructionism in the twenty-first century.[27]

5. ANCIENT UNDERSTANDING OF HISTORIOGRAPHY

However, logical positivism's overly rationalistic view of history simply did not exist in ancient times. Ancient historiographic texts, such as the OT narrative books, are ill-suited for modern definitions and understandings of history.[28] Instead, the biblical writers had theological and ideological points to make which involved interpreting the meaning of the past for the present more than reporting the past for its own sake. Particularly important is the aspect of God's intervention in history, presented at times using some of the literary devices of fiction (i.e. not in the overly restrictive sense of "historical untruth") to convey their message.[29] I will use several examples from OT narratives alongside other ANE historiographies to demonstrate that ancient historians allowed literary freedom for the incorporation of interpretive and ideological elements in their history writing.[30]

An example of apparent historical imprecision (by modern standards) in ancient history writing can be seen in how the biblical authors report the

---

25. Iain Provan, V. Philips Long, and Tremper Longman III, *A Biblical History of Israel* (Louisville, KY: Westminster John Knox, 2003), 21–22.
26. Provan, Long, and Longman, 23–24.
27. William G. Dever, *What Did the Biblical Writers Know and When Did They Know It?* (Grand Rapids, MI: Eerdmans, 2001), 24–25. Its major premise is that ancient texts have no recoverable intrinsic meaning, the modern interpreter gives it whatever meaning seems appropriate in social context of his/her realm of discourse regardless of what the author's realm might have been.
28. McKenzie, "Historiography," 419.
29. McKenzie, 419.
30. McKenzie, 420.

death of the Assyrian king Sennacherib (2 Kgs 19:37). When reading the OT in the absence of other sources, one would think that Sennacherib died shortly after attempting to attack Jerusalem in 701 BCE. However, the consensus in archaeology is that Sennacherib lived for two more decades and died only around 681 BCE. Here, the biblical author evidently passed over the remaining years of Sennacherib's life in favor of linking Sennacherib's (eventual) death to God's judgment against Assyria as a whole (2 Kgs 19:36–37). For comparison, one can look to Assyrian historiography. One of the historical sources for the reign of Sargon II (722–705 BCE) is an inscription on a large tablet, written as a letter to the god Ashur, which provides an account of Sargon's campaign in 714 BCE.[31]

Another case of ideological motivations can be seen in the royal ideology that is present in both OT and ANE historiographies. In the social sentences, the notion of royal ideology is understood in descriptive terms as a cluster of ideas that shape and support the monarchy, usually involving an invocation of divine sanction. Second Samuel 7 fits this definition as an OT example, while the Eshnunna Prophecy (FLP 1674) and Mari Prophecy (A.1121) can serve as samples from Akkadian historiographies.[32] In the former, 2 Samuel 7 supplies the foundational biblical passage for understanding kingship in Israel as Yahweh's promise to David of an eternal dynasty.[33] This divine promise plays a crucial role in legitimating the Davidic dynasty during Israel's crucial transition from a non-centralized tribal system to monarchy. Comparable elements are present in both the Eshnunna and Mari prophecies as well. The Eshnunna Prophecy is addressed to King Ibalpiel by goddess Kititum, while

---

31. Albert Ten Eyck Olmstead, *Assyrian Historiography: A Source Study* (Colombia, MO: University of Missouri, 1916), 37.
32. For the Eshnunna Prophecy see Maria deJong Ellis's translation, "The Goddess Kititum Speaks to King Ibalpiel: Oracle Texts from Ishchali," *MARI* 5 (1987): 258–66. For the Mari Prophecy see Abraham Malamat, *Mari and the Bible*, SHCANE, vol. 12 (Brill: Leiden, 1998), 106. The relevant Mari documents are of the Old Babylonian period, the first half of the eighteenth century BCE (if we use the Middle Chronology).
33. In the case of Israel's history, the united monarchy was once considered the most secure period, enjoying a rare scholarly consensus about its general reliability for historical reconstruction. This consensus collapsed at the end of the twentieth century, with scholars calling into question even the existence of Saul and David. For instance, minimalists proposed that David and Solomon and their empire are fictional, while others object that the traditional material about David is ideological and programmatic in favor of defending Davidic assumption of power and hence have no historical value. For further discussion, see Provan, Long, and Longman, *A Biblical History of Israel*, 216; Iain W. Provan, "Ideologies, Literary and Critical: Reflections on Recent Writing on the History of Israel," *JBL* 114 (1995): 586; and Bruce C. Birch, "The First and Second Books of Samuel," *NIB* 2:1254.

that of Mari is addressed to King Zimrilim by Adad, Lord of Kallassu. In all three ANE texts, there is a divine speech addressed to the king which presents the current king as receiving divine approval to rule, while the king is promised prosperity and military success that are conditioned on his loyalty.

It is common, then for ANE historiographies to have theological, ideological, and pedagogical intentions which do not have historical precision as their highest aim or as a goal in itself. This is not to say that the OT contains propaganda, for OT historiography remains distinct in the ANE for openly critiquing the flaws of Israel's kings and other major personalities. Yet this cultural uniqueness must not be allowed to obscure how OT narratives are still historiography which accords with the standards of ANE historiography.

In short, the relationship in OT historiography between history, theology, and religion is hotly contested. As Bible-believing Christians, we are rightly eager to defend the Bible's precision in maximal terms. At times, however, this view of biblical authority can result in demanding that the Bible meet certain standards of exactitude which are inappropriate for its time and place. For this reason, we need a perspective to sacred texts that can take the historiography of the OT on its own terms rather than ours. Such a perspective can be gained from a different but parallel enterprise of examining India's use of a religious text for historical reconstruction. In what follows, this exercise will give us an outsider's view of the complexities of searching for historical data in ancient historiography when those texts are also part of a living religious tradition.

6. ANCIENT INDIAN HISTORIOGRAPHY

In India, the use of an ancient text for historical reconstruction can be seen in the attempts to link the *Mahabharata* to certain accounts of its past. The *Mahabharata* is an ancient Indian Sanskrit epic of over 100,000 verses, making it longer than the combined length of Homer's *Iliad* and *Odyssey*. It is important both as a piece of literature as well as for its influence on culture and life in India (and anywhere else Hinduism is practiced). Although the *Mahabharata*'s genre is that of epic and not narrative, the text itself claims to be "history" (*itihasa*). It thus has several points in common with the OT with respect to our investigation. Also, similar to the OT, the *Mahabharata* is a religious text which originated before the rise of modern historiography, yet is being used to reconstruct a certain view of history for the sake of a present agenda (in this case that of religio-politics in contemporary India). Before exploring the relevance of the *Mahabharata* for these issues, it is necessary to summarize its content.

Old Testament Narratives

The *Mahabharata* narrates the rivalry between two group of cousins, the Pandavas and the Kauravas, which culminated in the war of Kurukshetra (also known as the *Mahabharata*), which involved both gods and mortals. It also contains several works of Hindu philosophy and devotion, including the *Bhagavad Gita*, an important religious text in Hinduism, as well as an abbreviated version of the *Ramayana*, another important Sanskrit epic. The sage Veda Vyasa is traditionally considered the author of the *Mahabharata*, dating to 3102 BCE in the Vedic Period. However, others scholars date it to various points between the fifteenth and ninth centuries BCE on the basis of archaeological evidence.[34]

Study of the historical basis of the *Mahabharata* coincided with Europeans taking interest in the Indian culture and law during the eighteenth century, when India came under British rule. The British portrayal of India's history was generally negative, however, providing the impetus for the rise of Indian historians in the early nineteenth century CE who were eager to reconstruct their history on different terms. Some of them took a rationalist approach, while others were more nationalist such as Hemchandra Raychaudhuri, who dated the *Mahabharata* to the tenth century BCE and used it as the starting point for his reconstruction of the history of India.[35] While the *Mahabharata* is often referenced in history books on ancient India,[36] the amount of reliable historical data in *Mahabharata* is unlikely to be determined anytime soon. Some Indian historians have argued that, at the most, the battle of ten kings described in the *Rig Veda* (the oldest known Vedic Sanskrit text, dated to around 1500–000 BCE) may have formed the original, historical nucleus of the *Mahabharata*.[37] Others view it as containing some historical information

---

34. Vinay Kumar Gupta, "Historicity of the *Ramayana* Versus the *Mahabharata*: An Analysis," in, *Pura Jagat: Indian Archaeology History and Culture: Latest Researches in Honour of Late Shri Jagat Pati Joshi*, ed. C. R. Margabandhu et al. (Delhi: Bharatiya Kala Prakashan, 2012), 558; S. S. N. Murthy, "The Questionable Historicity of Mahabaharata," *Electronic Journal of Vedic Studies* 10 (2003): 1.
35. Hemchandra Raychaudhuri, *Political History of Ancient India: From the Accession of Parikshit to the Extinction of the Gupta Dynasty* (Calcutta: University of Calcutta, 1923). On the contours of the historiographical enterprise in India, see R. S. Sharma, *India's Ancient Past* (New Delhi: Oxford University Press, 2005), 6–12.
36. For example, Upinder Singh, *Ancient Delhi* (Oxford: OUP, 1999); Bujor Avari, *India: The Ancient Past: A History of the Indian Sub-continent from c. 7000 BC to AD 1200* (London: Routledge, 2007), 69; Romila Thapar, *The Past Before Us: Historical Traditions of Early North India* (Harvard: Harvard University Press, 2013).
37. For similarities between these two accounts, see Murthy, "Questionable Historicity," 1–14.

regarding the geography, culture, and social aspects of India,[38] while Indian archaeologists such as B. B. Lal are more optimistic.[39]

On this note, Lal was the first to attempt a historical reconstruction of India using the *Mahabharata* itself as a starting point. Some early attempts at historical reconstruction of ancient India based on the *Mahabharata* was undertaken in the 1950's under the leadership of B. B. Lal. He conducted several excavations in the 1950s that sought to uncover the archaeological remains of the places mentioned in the *Mahabharata*.[40] And as recently as November 2019, India opened nine heritage sites in various states of India for excavation, some of which had been previously excavated. This included the *Purana Qila* (Urdu for "Old Fort"), a sixteenth-century CE stone fort built by the Mughal emperor Humayun and the Afghan, Sher Shah Suri. The excavation at Purana Qila occurred at the supposed site of Indraprastha, the capital of the Pandavas in *Mahabharata*.[41] Past excavations at the Purana Qila (in the 1950s, 1970s, and 2010s) had uncovered artifacts such as painted greyware dating back to around 1200 BCE, although none of them conclusively linked the site to the *Mahabharata*. In 2018, at an excavation at Sanuali (a site 68 kms from Delhi), archaeologists discovered artifacts such as a war chariot, a burial site, and other artifacts, which raised the possibility of pushing the date of the *Mahabharata* to 2000–1500 BCE. However, final analysis of the discoveries is still pending.[42]

The issue of the *Mahabharata*'s historicity is even more varied and complex than presented here, as Indian historians generally recognize that the *Mahabharata* is not historiography in the modern sense. What is noteworthy, however, is that, as ancient historiographies and *at merely the level of their lowest common denominator*, the OT narratives and the *Mahabharata* both reflect customs and practices of particular historical periods. Also embedded within each of them are various kinds of cultural, religious, political, and socio-economic

---

38. Avari, *India: The Ancient Past*, 100.
39. Lal was the Director General of the Archaeological Survey of India from 1968–1972 and has served as Director of the Indian Institute of Advanced Studies, Shimla.
40. Madhur Tankha, "Mahabharat Sites Continue to Have the Same Names Even Today: B. B. Lal," *The Hindu*, May 19, 2016, https://www.thehindu.com/news/cities/Delhi/mahabharat-sites-continue-to-have-the-same-names-even-today-b-b-lal/article5776270.ece.
41. "Purana Qilla May Have Been the Site of Mahabharata's Indraprastha: ASI to Carry Out Another Round of Excavations," November 12, 2020. https://www.opindia.com/2019/11/asi-archeological-survey-delhi-purana-qilla-mauryan-mahabharata-indraprastha/.
42. Vasudha Venugopal, "Mahabharata much older, say ASI Archaeologists," *The Economic Times* (October 20, 2019), https://economictimes.indiatimes.com/news/politics-and-nation/mahabharata-much-older-say-asi-archaeologists/articleshow/71658119.cms.

information. In these respects, OT narratives and the *Mahabharata* are both good examples of ancient historiography.

That said, there are two caveats that are necessary in comparing the *Mahabharata* to OT narrative. The first is the difference in the amount of archaeological evidence that respectively corroborates the records of the *Mahabharata* and the OT narratives. As discussed above, the ongoing efforts to place the *Mahabharata* on a historical foundation have not found conclusive archaeological data to date. The names of the people in the *Mahabharata* do appear in the *Vedas*, but the lack of other shared descriptors makes it difficult to conclude that the corresponding names point to the same person. The names of some of the places in India today, like Indraprastha (the name of an area in present-day Delhi), are identical to or possibly derived from names of the cities in *Mahabharata*. For the archaeologist B. B. Lal, that "the sites associated with the mythological epic continue to have the same nomenclature even till this day" points to the historicity of *Mahabharata*.[43] Again, however, a match of names between *Mahabharata* and a modern Indian toponym is insufficient to prove that these refer to the same places. Hence, archaeological evidence that explicitly supports the claim of historicity for *Mahabharata* has been scanty at best.

However, in the case of OT historical narratives, numerous archaeological evidences support the notion of their historicity. To cite a few, the "house of David" is mentioned in the Tel Dan Inscription (ninth century BCE) and in fragments of the victory stele from the site identified as Dan.[44] Further, the Jehu and Omride dynasty of northern Israel are known from the Assyrian royal inscription known as the "Black Obelisk." Also, the Babylonian record shows that Jehoiachin, the exiled king of Judah, received rations from the Babylonian royal court as recorded in 2 Kings 25:30, while Sennacherib's attack on Jerusalem recorded in 2 Kings 18–19 (and in Isaiah 36–37) are documented in significant detail in the Assyrian annals as well.[45] Not every single datum is a match at the current state of scholarship, but it is significant that these extrabiblical sources are contemporaneous to the OT and lend credence to the historicity of the OT characters and events mentioned. Even though gaps between the OT and archaeology remain, there is a strong case for the

---

43. Tankha, "Mahabharat Sites Continue to Have the Same Names Even Today."
44. Avraham Negev and Shimon Gibson, eds., *Archaeological Encyclopedia of the Holy Land* (New York: Continuum, 2001), 131–32.
45. Davies, *In Search of Ancient Israel*, 21.

historicity of these people and events. The "minimalist" tendency to make sweeping statements about the biblical account's supposed lack of historicity is thus misguided.

The second caveat is that India's quest for historical rootedness has its motivations in a strongly religio-political ideology. The present government of India is led by a nationalist party that advocates a worldview known as *Hindutva*. The outlook of Hindutva proposes, among other things, to redefine Indian national identity on the basis of religious interpretation of the past. "Indian" becomes synonymous to "Hindu," to the exclusion of all others who are not Hindus but self-identify as Indians. Locating *Mahabharata* in the ancient historical past thus serves to project present-day Hindus as the original children of the soil. As such, the current ruling party's efforts involving *Mahabharata* are but one of many steps towards that goal, such as replacing key people in the education ministry and revising curriculums and textbooks, especially history textbooks.[46] In the crisis that has resulted in the relations between state, society, and religion, it should be noted that the present government's goals render suspect any attempt to reconstruct India's history on the basis of *Mahabharata*. In these respects, the efforts of Christians in confirming the historical veracity of the OT differ for being primarily an attempt to use the archaeological data available to support the truth claims that are necessary for Christian faith. At the same time, it is noteworthy that current efforts in India to claim historicity for the Mahabharata on the basis of insufficient evidence offer a mirror to the unwise lengths that Christians sometimes go to in trying to defend the OT's historicity.

7. REFLECTIONS

Some points for consideration emerge in light of the preceding discussion. First, OT narratives need to be recognized for the *ancient* historiography that they are. As such, they are not purely or merely objective, historically accurate records of past events. While we need not concede that the biblical texts only

---

46. This is the second time that this party has been in power in the history of independent India. The first time was in 1999–2004 as a coalition government, and since 2014 as a parliamentary majority. Both stints in power have seen initiatives to revise history textbooks. See also Marie Lall, "Introduction," and "Globalization and the Fundamentalization of Curricula: Lessons from India," in *Education as a Political Tool in Asia*, eds. Marie-Carine Lall and Edward Vickers (Oxon: Routledge, 2009), 8. For critique, see Christophe Jaffrelot and Pradyumna Jairam, "BJP has been Effective in Transmitting its Version of Indian History to Next Generation of Learners," *The Indian Express* (November 16, 2019) https://indianexpress.com/article/opinion/columns/education-ours-and-theirs-6121982/.

convey theological truth and not historical truth,⁴⁷ we must make space in our reading of the text to acknowledge that historical accuracy by modern standards was not necessarily at the top of the biblical writers' agenda. OT narratives were written as history,⁴⁸ but not merely for the sake of cataloguing events. Instead, the biblical authors employed literary techniques and artistry which included fictionalization (here again understood as a *literary device*) in their history writing. At the same time, recognizing that OT narratives are ancient historiography helps us understand that the biblical writers were not trying to pass off fiction as fact, since what they wrote was very much within the norms of ANE historiography. No deception was intended in the process of choosing not be factually exact in every single detail.

Second, the OT narratives are not purely objective, just as no history or history writing is in any meaningful sense of these words. Absolute objectivity as a goal is neither desirable nor attainable for a historian; we all hold, consciously or unconsciously, fundamental assumptions and therefore even an eyewitness account has their own point of view. To understand history as only an objective record of what happened is misleading since every historian works by means of selection, interpretation, and imagination. For by such a standard, there is no historiography, whether ancient or modern, that can stand the test of absolute objectivity. Interestingly, the recognition that there is no escaping from some degree of interpretive perspective is precisely what redeems objectivity as a useful goal since it has been freed from unreasonable expectations. For OT narratives, the epiphany that they must be understood as ancient historiography (in which not everything can or must be historically proven) enables the sincere and objective study of the historical referentiality

---

47. As in the so-called "postliberal narrative theology" associated with Hans Frei and Yale Divinity School.
48. Scholars have noted Israel's obsession with the past, the text itself exhibits its interest in speaking about Israel's past and readers down the centuries too have perceived it to be so. This historical awareness is exemplified, for one, in the repeated injunction *zākôr* ("Remember!"). Historical awareness is also seen in explicit imperatives to recall or retell to posterity past events in connection to certain festivals, rituals, or objects. For instance, the consecration of the firstborn was connected to the exodus event (Exod 13:6–13), while the setting up of the twelve stones was to prompt a retelling of the crossing of Jordan (Josh 4:6–9, 21–24). Such commands to call their past into remembrance not only testify to the historical awareness of its authors but also to their desire to inculcate such awareness in their audience/readers. Although the reconstruction of the intention of the author must be undertaken with caution it has been considered essential to any concept of genre as a set of expectations between the author and the reader. For Israel's historical consciousness, see Baruch Halpern, cited in Frykenberg, *Belief and History*, 193; H. Butterfield, "Historiography," *Encyclopedia Hebraica*, quoted in Amit, *History and Ideology*, 19; Provan, "Ideologies, Literary and Critical," 596.

that *is* present in the OT, as in the careful use of archaeological data to improve our standards of inquiry.

Third, it is helpful to step outside one's own religious tradition to gain a dispassionate view on the immense difficulties and pitfalls that attend the effort of looking for historicity in ancient religious texts. While the OT narratives have better archaeological support overall than the *Mahabharata*, this essay's look at India's efforts at historical reconstruction of ancient India emphasizes the need to be methodologically disciplined in our reading of the biblical texts, in our interpretation of archaeological data or information, and in our efforts to prove the credibility of the biblical accounts by establishing their historicity. Despite some fundamental differences between India's historical reconstruction with the *Mahabharata* and Christians' examinations of the reliability of OT narratives, a cross-cultural perspective on studying historicity shows us the importance of being meticulous and self-aware rather than adopting the apologetics-oriented approach that has characterized evangelicals at times.

CONCLUSION

In sacred texts that lay claim to both time-bound history and timeless truth, the notions of literariness, ideology, and historicity do not need to be mutually exclusive. For OT narrative in particular, there can be no single answer on whether they qualify as "history" for the simple reason that what history writing is (or ought to be) has been a constantly moving target. Undoubtedly, the OT historical narratives are history inasmuch as they interpret and reinterpret the actual events of the past to inform the present. OT history/historiography was thus dynamic and presented as a coherent story which aims at persuading its readers of certain theological truths. Yet it is not pure history in the modern sense due to its ready incorporation of the supernatural, the divine, and much that lies beyond the realm of empirical proof. It is neither a social-scientific history, nor the humanistic history that modernists would like it to be, but of almighty God and his dealings with humanity. The areas in which it departs from being history in the modern sense does not undermine its historicity.

Thus, it is unwise to follow both the Bible's modernist defenders and its postmodern skeptics in devaluing the whole for its use of literary artistry, particular points of view, and having standards other than mere or pure objectivity (whose attainability is highly doubtful to begin with). Hence, we conclude by saying that the OT historiography is an immanent child of its ANE milieu which needs to be studied on its own terms, as well as the transcendent word of Yahweh who spoke and acted in an incomparable manner which is both historical and defies our inadequate categories of what counts as historical. In this regard, the cultural uniqueness of OT historiography lies in its unique ability to encompass both subjectivity and objectivity without compromising either.

REFERENCES

Alter, Robert. *The Art of Biblical Narrative*. New York: Basic Books, 1981.
Amit, Yairah. *History and Ideology: An Introduction to Historiography in the Hebrew Bible*. Sheffield: Sheffield Academic Press, 1999.
Anderson, Bernhard W. "Biblical Theology and Sociological Interpretation." *Theology Today* 42 (October 1985): 292–306.
Avari, Bujor. *India: The Ancient Past: A History of the Indian Sub-continent from c. 7000 BC to AD 1200*. London: Routledge, 2007.
Barr, James. *History and Ideology in the Old Testament: Biblical Studies at the End of the Millennium*. Oxford: Oxford University Press, 2000.
Barrois, Georges Augustin. "The Notion of Historicity and the Critical Study of the Old Testament." *Greek Orthodox Theological Review* 19 (Spring 1974): 7–22.
Birch, Bruce C. "The First and Second Books of Samuel." *NIB* 2:975–1383.
Davies, Philip. *In Search of "Ancient Israel": A Study in Biblical Origins*. Sheffield: Sheffield Academic Press, 1992.
Dever, William G. *What Did the Biblical Writers Know and When Did They Know It?* Grand Rapids, MI: Eerdmans, 2001.
Eagleton, Terry. *Ideology: An Introduction*. London: Verso, 1991.
Ellis, Maria DeJong, translator. "The Goddess Kititum Speaks to King Ibalpiel: Oracle Texts from Ishchali." MARI: Annales de recherches interdisciplinaires 5 (1987): 235–66.
Fowler, Robert. "Herodotus and Persia." In *The Cambridge Companion to Herodotus*, edited by Carolyn Dewald and John Marincola, 274–289. Cambridge: Cambridge University Press, 2007.
Frykenberg, Robert Eric. *Belief and History: The Foundations of Historical Understanding*. Grand Rapids, MI: Eerdmans, 1996.
Gjesdal, Kristen. "History and Historicity." In *The Routledge Companion to Hermeneutics*, edited by Jeff Malpas and Hans-Helmuth Gander, 299–310. London: Routledge, 2014.
Gupta, Vinay Kumar. "Historicity of the *Ramayana* Versus the *Mahabharata*: An Analysis." In *Pura Jagat: Indian Archaeology History and Culture: Latest Researches in Honour of Late Shri Jagat Pati Joshi*, edited by C. R. Margabandhu et al., 557–46. Delhi: Bharatiya Kala Prakashan, 2012.
Holladay, Carl R. "Contemporary Methods of Reading the Bible." *NIB* 1:125–49.

Jaffrelot, Christophe, and Pradyumna Jairam. "BJP has been Effective in Transmitting its Version of Indian History to Next Generation of Learners." *The Indian Express*, November 16, 2019. https://indianexpress.com/article/opinion/columns/education-ours-and-theirs-6121982/.

Lall, Marie. "Introduction." In *Education as a Political Tool in Asia*, edited by Marie-Carine Lall and Edward Vicker, 1–9. Oxon: Routledge, 2009.

———. "Globalization and the Fundamentalization of Curricula: Lessons from India." In *Education as a Political Tool in Asia*, edited by Marie-Carine Lall and Edward Vicker, 157–178. Oxon: Routledge, 2009.

Long, V. Philips. *The Art of Biblical History*. Grand Rapids, MI: Zondervan, 1994.

Malamat, Abraham. *Mari and the Bible*. Studies in the History and Culture of the Ancient Near East 12. Brill: Leiden, 1998.

McKenzie, Steven L. "Historiography, Old Testament." In *Dictionary of the Old Testament: Historical Books*, edited by Bill T. Arnold and H. G. M. Williamson, 418–25. Downers Grove, IL: InterVarsity 2005.

Murthy, S. S. N. "The Questionable Historicity of Mahabaharata." *Electronic Journal of Vedic Studies* 10/5 (2003): 1–15.

Negev, Avraham, and Shimon Gibson, eds. *Archaeological Encyclopedia of the Holy Land*. New York: Continuum, 2001.

Olmstead, Albert Ten Eyck. *Assyrian Historiography: A Source Study*. Colombia, MO: University of Missouri, 1916.

Provan, Iain W. "Ideologies, Literary and Critical: Reflections on Recent Writing on the History of Israel," *Journal of Biblical Literature* 114/4 (1995): 585–606.

Provan, Iain, V. Philips Long, and Tremper Longman III. *A Biblical History of Israel*. Louisville, KY: Westminster John Knox, 2003.

"Purana Qilla May Have Been the Site of Mahabharata's Indraprastha: ASI to Carry Out Another Round of Excavations." November 12, 2020. https://www.opindia.com/2019/11/asi-archeological-survey-delhi-purana-qilla-mauryan-mahabharata-indraprastha/.

Raychaudhuri, Hemchandra. *Political History of Ancient India: From the Accession of Parikshit to the Extinction of the Gupta Dynasty*. Calcutta: University of Calcutta, 1923.

Sharma, R. S. *India's Ancient Past*. New Delhi: Oxford University Press, 2005.

Singh, Upinder. *Ancient Delhi*. Oxford: Oxford University Press, 1999.

Tankha, Madhur. "Mahabharat Sites Continue to Have the Same Names Even Today: B. B. Lal." *The Hindu*, May 19, 2016. https://www.thehindu.com/news/cities/Delhi/mahabharat-sites-continue-to-have-the-same-names-even-today-b-b-lal/article5776270.ece.

Thapar, Romila. *The Past Before Us: Historical Traditions of Early North India*. Harvard: Harvard University Press, 2013.

Venugopal, Vasudha. "Mahabharata much older, say ASI Archaeologists." *The Economic Times*. October 20, 2019. https://economictimes.indiatimes.com/news/politics-and-nation/mahabharata-much-older-say-asi-archaeologists/articleshow/71658119.cms.

CHAPTER 10

EXODUS AND LIBERATION

Naga Nationalism and the People of God

Angukali Rotokha

The title "the people of Yahweh" belongs to the ancient Israelites in the Old Testament (e.g. Judg 5:11; 2 Sam 6:21; 2 Kgs 9:6), and in the New Testament the Christian church also came to see itself as God's people (e.g. 1 Cor 10:1–4; Col 3:12). Consequently, present-day Christians also consider themselves to be the people of God. This idea of the church today as constituting the people of God has some support in Scripture (e.g. Rom 9:23–26; 1 Pet 2:9–10), although scholars continue to debate regarding who exactly the people of God are,[1] as well as whether Christians have now superseded Israel as God's people.[2]

One such group of Christians who see themselves as God's people are the *Nagas*,[3] a collective of several tribes inhabiting the northeastern parts of India as well as the northwestern parts of Myanmar.[4] They have been striving for an independent state for more than seventy-five years. The struggle for Naga sovereignty seeks to politically reintegrate the Naga-inhabited regions in India and Myanmar and refers to these regions collectively as *Nagalim*.[5] However, the scope of this chapter will be confined primarily to Nagas living in the state of Nagaland in India since this is where I am from. Nagaland is a majority-Christian state, with over 90% of the population identifying as Christian. At the same time, it is also home to what has been called "one of the longest

---

1. For a summary of different views, see Robert Osei-Bonsu, "The Church as the *People of God* and Its Relation to the Church as a Community," *AAMM* 4 (2012), 58–59.
2. The *supersessionist* view holds that Christianity has superseded Judaism and that Christians now constitute the true Israel.
3. The term "Naga" was not initially used by the people to describe themselves, but was a generic term for a conglomeration of tribes, who later adopted it to denote their collective identity.
4. In India, the Nagas mainly inhabit the northeastern state of Nagaland, but also reside in the neighboring states of Manipur, Assam, and Arunachal Pradesh. In Myanmar, they are settled mainly in the north-western parts in the Kachin state and Sagaing Division.
5. "Nagalim," *Unrepresented Nations and Peoples Organization* (April 2019), accessed August 23, 2021, https://unpo.org/members/7899.

ongoing struggles for self-determination in the world."[6] This combination of factors has led to a natural but messy alliance in the region between nationalism and Christianity, while raising some knotty theopolitical questions which this chapter will seek to address. To begin with, a broad outline of the emergence of nationalism and Christianity in Nagaland is necessary.

1. BACKGROUND TO THE NAGA PEOPLE IN INDIA: NATIONALISM AND CHRISTIANITY

The Christian faith first came to the Nagas in December 1872 though Edward Winter Clark, an American missionary under the aegis of the American Baptist Foreign Missionary Society, and Godhula Rufus Brown, an Assamese Indian evangelist.[7] The baptism of the first fifteen converts marked the beginning of Christian work among the Nagas.[8] There were two great waves of Christian revival among the Nagas, one in the 1950s and the other in the 1970s. By 1951, the percentage of Nagas identifying as Christian was at 46%, while by 1961 it was 53%. After India's independence in 1947, all foreign missionaries were forced to leave, with the last departing in February 1955.[9] However, the Naga Christians persevered in their desire to evangelize the whole of the Naga population, and since then over 90% of the Nagas in the Indian state of Nagaland have become Christians.

On the political front, the formative stages of the Naga nationalist movement can be traced back to January 1929, when the Naga Club[10] submitted a memorandum to the Simon Commission. The latter body represented the British government and had come to India to assess its administrative system

---

6. Jelle Wouters, *In the Shadows of Naga Insurgency: Tribes, State, and Violence in Northeast India* (Oxford: Oxford University Press, 2018), 8.
7. Miles Bronson, an American Baptist missionary, first made contact with the Nagas in 1839 but no one came to the Christian faith during this visit.
8. Asangba Tsudir, "Historical Records Prove that Naga Forefathers Wanted a Better World," *The Naga Republic* (Jan 2018), accessed August 23, 2021, http://www.thenagarepublic.com/features/historical-records-prove-naga-forefathers-wanted-better-world/.
9. Chongpongmeren Jamir, "Segmentation, Unity, and a Church Divided: A Critical History of Churches in Nagaland, 1947–2017" (PhD diss., Middlesex University/OCMS, 2019), 2, accessed August 23, 2021, https://eprints.mdx.ac.uk/27960/1/JChongpongmeren%20thesis.pdf.
10. During World War I, the British government sent around 2,000 Nagas to France. Upon returning, they formed the Naga Club in 1918 with some elders and other educated people among them. See discussion in Samudra Gupta Kashyap, "Nagaland erects memorial monolith to mark sacrifice of Naga Labour Corps in World War 1," *The Indian Express* (19 April 2017), accessed August 23, 2021, https://indianexpress.com/article/india/nagaland-erects-memorial-for-100-years-of-naga-labour-corps-in-world-war-1-4619630/.

and make recommendations for constitutional reforms.[11] The Naga Club memorandum protested the inclusion of the Naga Hills into the Reformed Scheme of India that was to be proposed by the Simon Commission and asked the British government to "leave us alone to determine ourselves as in ancient times."[12]

The work of the Naga Club led to the formation of the Naga Tribal Council in 1945, later renamed Naga National Council (NNC). After the British left India in 1947, the NNC continued its demands. The Naga nationalist movement has been led since then by the National Socialist Council of Nagalim (NSCN), which was formed in 1980 after the NNC signed the controversial Shillong Accord with the Indian government in 1975 that agreed to submit to the authority of the Constitution of India.[13] While the last seventy-five years of Naga nationalism are difficult to capture in their complexities and nuances, this overview will suffice for our purposes.[14]

Along the way, nationalism and Christianity became intertwined so that nationalism took on strong Christian overtones. As early as 1953, Robert DeLano, the last missionary to leave Nagaland (in 1955), wrote, "Some of the people who are active in the independence movement are also leaders in our Christian work."[15] Religion and politics were evidently not seen as separate spheres in the early days of Naga nationalism.[16] Many thought it their Christian duty to join in the struggle for independence and to spread the gospel at the same time – prayer cells came together and prayers and prophecies from God were sought to guide them in making decisions.

---

11. R. Vashum, *Nagas' Right to Self Determination: An Anthropological, Historical Perspective*, 2nd ed. (New Delhi: Mittal Publications, 2005), 26.
12. "The Naga Memorandum to Simon Commission," presented in Vashum, *Nagas' Right*, 175–76.
13. "Nagalim," accessed August 23, 2021. The NSCN has since split into factions that have often fought against each other. This chapter will refer to them collectively as NSCN or "Naga nationalists," identifying a particular faction only when necessary.
14. For more on the socio-political angle of the matter, see Vashum, *Nagas' Right*; Chandrika Singh, *Naga Politics* (New Delhi: Mittal Publications, 2004); Wouters, *In the Shadows of Naga Insurgency*. For a more grassroots perspective, see Kaka D. Iralu, *Nagaland and India: The Blood and the Tears – A Historical Account of the 52-year Indo-Naga War and the Story of Those Who Were Never Allowed to Tell It* (Kohima: NV Press, 2003); Nandita Haskar and Sebastian Hongray, *Kuknalim, Naga Armed Resistance: Testimonies of Leaders, Pastor, Healers and Soldiers* (New Delhi: Speaking Tiger Books, 2019).
15. Cited in Arkotong Longkumer, "Bible, Guns, and Land: Sovereignty and Nationalism Among the Nagas of India," *Nations and Nationalism* 24 (2018): 1105.
16. For more on this synergy, see chapter 5 by Annelle Sabanal in the present volume.

Nagas concurrently carried on evangelistic work in the regions of eastern Nagaland which were most unreached by the gospel.[17] It was thought that "it was not only with gun that we must fight for our freedom but also power of our prayers."[18] A. Z. Phizo, one of the presidents of the NNC would say in 1951, "I always have a feeling that God, our Heavenly Father – our Creator – is with us and guiding us. What is there for us to fear?"[19] Thus, as Arkotong Longkumer says, it is this "Christian spirit that drives the Naga cadres to resist the Indian military onslaught."[20] Even today, the NSCN-IM faction, the largest among the nationalist groups, has its own religious wing called the Council of Nagalim Churches (CNC). They have chaplains and hold worship services on their campus, while their rhetoric is permeated with appeals to God and Christianity, as we will see.

At the heart of the nationalism-Christianity nexus is the slogan "Nagaland for Christ." The slogan seems to have been first used in 1958 by the Ao Christian Education and Sunday School Union (Ao being one of the Naga tribes) in an appeal against violence and bloodshed in Nagaland. It was then adopted by the Nagaland Baptist Churches Council (NBCC), the highest body of churches in Nagaland, in their activism against violence and corruption in politics.[21] The slogan was also adopted later by the NNC and continues to be affirmed by the NSCN as part of their manifesto, which reads: "We stand for the faith in God and the salvation of mankind in Jesus, the Christ, alone, this is 'Nagaland for Christ.'"[22] The goal, then, is to create a sovereign nation based on a Christian socialist and spiritual vision of "Nagaland for Christ."[23]

How this slogan came to be the bedrock of the nationalist movement is itself the product of a conflict between the church and the nationalists. During the 1960s, some Naga nationalists went to China to train and to acquire arms.

---

17. For instance, see the testimonies of A. Puni, a former Chaplain at the NSCN Camp who later held other leadership positions in the group, as well as of Avuli Chishi Swu, who served in the Naga army for eight years and later took on civil leadership roles in the group's women's wing (Haskar and Hongray, *Kuknalim*, chapter 4).
18. From the testimony of Unice, see Haskar and Hongray, *Kuknalim*, under "Unice: The Oracle."
19. A. Z. Phizo, as cited in Wouters, *In the Shadows of Naga Insurgency*, xii.
20. Longkumer, "Bible, Guns, and Land," 1108.
21. From the minutes of the NBCC Meeting held in Impur, 4–7 December 1958, and "Statement Issued by the General Session of the Nagaland Baptist Church Council Kohima, 14–17 October 1976." Cited in Jamir, "Segmentation, Unity," 151.
22. Cited in Wouters, *In the Shadows of Naga Insurgency*, 34.
23. Namrata Biji Ahuja, "Bullets and the Bible," *The Week*, April 2017, accessed August 25, 2021, https://www.theweek.in/theweek/cover/national-socialist-council-of-nagaland.html?fbclid=IwAR35kzFN5ulGsS4pIx39wgDQ-5NvwsNip9hMOsFmzJRlF0TjUWlXy0BPjkY.

Seeking help from China did not sit well with the Naga churches, who accused the nationalists of coming under communist and atheistic influences. The NBCC was especially vocal in its suspicion and disapproval of the NSCN's communist ties, while the NSCN leaders in turn denied the accusations and reaffirmed their commitment to faith in their manifesto by rooting the movement and their ideology in Christian faith.[24]

2. PRESENT CONUNDRUM: WHAT CAN GO WRONG?

Given the evident and sincere Christian piety of many Naga nationalists, what can go wrong? The Christianity–nationalism nexus among the Nagas began to some extent as an outgrowth of their duty to stand against injustice and fight for their land and their loved ones, rather than as a strategy to bolster a movement. Jessica Stern, in her four-year investigation of religious extremist groups around the world, similarly concludes that all religious extremists believe (or start out believing) that they were "creating a more perfect world."[25] However it may have started, the Naga nationalist movement now does rely on Christianity, or rather its own understanding of Christianity, to provide the ideological basis for the movement. The Bible and its narratives have been summoned as support for the Naga nationalist movement and are frequently cited in political speeches and discussions, a few instances of which are described below. Such a fraught environment creates the danger of reading the Naga nationalist movement into the OT by appropriating the Israelite narrative for oneself.

On this note, various features in Naga society facilitate the adoption of OT narratives by Nagas. At the present time,[26] the social structure of the Nagas consists of different tribes, with each tribe further divided into clans and families. Oral traditions tell of common ancestors who migrated and settled in their present region, although these are now acknowledged as more mythical than historical.[27] In terms of religion, the various tribes in the Naga confederation are held together by their common worship of God and exist

---

24. See Longkumer, "Bible, Guns, and Land," 1109–10.
25. Jessica Stern, *Terror in the Name of God: Why Religious Militants Kill* (New York: HarperCollins, 2003), 282.
26. This chapter does not address the social and political organization of the various Naga tribes before the advent of Christianity, when each Naga village constituted an independent village-state with their own system of governance which ranged from monarchy to republic. On this issue, see Vashum, *Nagas' Right*, 58–59.
27. For instance, one myth speaks of the origin of the Nagas from six stones that were shaped as male and female reproductive organs (Longkumer, "Bible, Guns, and Land," 1099).

as a Christian minority in India. Historically and politically, the story of the Nagas is one of struggle for independence from India, a much larger nation.

Being thus organized socially, religiously, and politically, the Nagas share certain affinities with the ancient Israelite community which was also a confederation of tribes, claimed a common ancestry, worshiped Yahweh while living among polytheists, and was a small and vulnerable nation among the superpowers of the day. All these commonalities mean that the narratives about Israel are familiar and easily appropriated. However, an uncritical acceptance of such a self-perception can result in blurred lines between ancient Israelites and present-day Nagas as well as a distorted reading of the OT. There are similarities between Israelites and Nagas and perhaps even some continuities, but the discontinuities are just as crucial and need greater attention if Nagas are to better understand who they are, who God is, and what being his people entails. For these reasons, the question to be asked is where Christian Nagas stand in relation to Israel, to Israel's history, and to God. To answer these, three theological concepts need further examination: (1) the concept of covenant as central to being God's people, (2) the land as a gift from God, and (3) the use of violence by God's people.

2.1. Covenant and the People of God

Central to the concept of Israel as God's people is the covenant between Yahweh and the Israelites. It is the basic assumption of the OT that Israel stands in a special relationship with Yahweh, and covenant is the principal image used to portray this distinctive status. Walther Eichrodt, in his influential OT theology (1933–1939), even regarded covenant as the theological center of the entire Old Testament.[28] While Eichrodt's proposal found some support, most scholars such as Gerhard von Rad offered a different theological center for the OT,[29] or denied altogether the possibility of having a center. Whichever stance one takes, it is clear that covenant is an indispensable concept in the history of Israel and its redemption.

The formation of Israel as God's people begins with Yahweh calling Abraham out from Ur and making a covenant with him (Gen 12; 15; 17). The Abrahamic covenant involves Yahweh's solemn oath to bless Abraham with

---

28. Walther Eichrodt, *Theology of the Old Testament*, vol. 1, OTL, trans. J. A. Baker (Philadelphia: Westminster, 1961).
29. Gerhard von Rad, *Old Testament Theology*, 2 vols., trans. D. M. G. Stalker (Edinburgh: Oliver and Boyd, 1962).

descendants as well as the gift of land to them (Gen 15:4–5, 18; 17:7–8). The covenant is sealed in a ritual that involved Yahweh passing between a sacrificial animal that had been cut into two (Gen 15:17). This covenant with Abraham was reiterated with Isaac and Jacob as well (Gen 26:3–4; 28:14–15). It also formed the motivational clauses in statements of God's deliverance of Israelites from Egyptian slavery (Exod 2:24) as well as his later acts of deliverance (Lev 26:40–45; 2 Kgs 13:23).

The covenant is later formalized with all Israel at Mount Sinai to forge a relationship in which Yahweh becomes the God of the nation of Israel and the Israelites are Yahweh's people (Exod 19; 24). According to Steven McKenzie, this covenant at Mount Sinai is "*the* Old Testament covenant" so that it is a continuation of the covenant with the patriarchs (Lev 26:42–45) and is renewed in stages (e.g. Deut 29).[30] Indeed the covenant at Sinai becomes foundational to the Israelite self-understanding as a nation and people owing exclusive allegiance to Yahweh. With the advent of Christ, the NT appropriates this theological status to refer to believers of Jesus Christ. This is based on Jesus's declaration during the Last Supper that his sacrifice on the cross would inaugurate a new covenant (Luke 22:14–23; Heb 8:6–13; cf. Jer 31:31–34) in which all believers partake. Thus, Christians also understand themselves as the people of God through the person and work of Christ.

In the rhetoric of the nationalists, Nagas are God's chosen people much like ancient Israel was.[31] The late Isak Chishi Swu, who was chairman of the NSCN and one of those instrumental in founding it, was quoted as saying, "[God] had chosen the Nagas as he had once chosen the Children of Israel to be his own people . . ."[32] Such claims, especially in the context of a nationalist movement, are difficult to support biblically and have several serious consequences.

---

30. Steven L. McKenzie, *Covenant* (St. Louis: Chalice Press, 2000), 4. The first stage is in Exodus 24:3–8, which recounts a ratification ceremony where the people agree to keep the stipulations of the book of the covenant. The second stage happens in Exodus 32, when Moses descends Mt. Sinai with the two stone tablets only to find the people worshiping the golden calf. The breaking and remaking of the stone tablets with the Ten Commandments marks the second stage. The third stage is recorded in the book of Deuteronomy, when the people confirm their covenant with Yahweh on the plains of Moab prior to entering Canaan (Deut 29).
31. Jamir, "Segmentation, Unity," 152.
32. Cited in Jelle Wouters, "Religion, Politics, and the Problem of Secularism among Upland Nagas," in *Brill's Encyclopedia of the Religions of Indigenous People of South Asia*, ed. Marine Carrin, Handbook of Oriental Studies (Leiden: Brill, 2019), 7.

First, the status of ancient Israel as God's chosen people is unique and unrepeatable in a certain sense.[33] It was a special status that traced back to the covenant with the patriarchs and was accompanied by specific promises of deliverance of his descendants from slavery long before Abraham had any children (Gen 15:12–16). Walter Brueggemann notes that Israel's chosenness is repeated in at least three traditions of the OT: (1) the ancestral tradition of Abraham, (2) the exodus tradition, and (3) the Sinai tradition. This unique identification as God's chosen people was not to be claimed by the Israelites as a right, but was "given by divine declaration that comes without explanation or grounding."[34] It was also exclusive to the one people, the Israelites. God has conferred no such status to the Nagas, and he has made no special covenant that involves a promise to liberate the Nagas from the Indian union or from Myanmar as he did for the Israelites from Egyptian slavery. To the extent that the Nagas are God's people, such a privilege comes from being joined to Jesus Christ through the new covenant (Jer 31:31–34; Luke 22:20). This covenant is not exclusive to the Nagas, but universal in scope for all Christians today.

Second, the new covenant differs from the old covenant even as it continues and consummates the former's relationship that was initiated between God and his people. The emphasis in the new covenant is not descendants and land, but redemption from sin and membership in the kingdom of God; it includes promises not so much of national deliverance from earthly oppressors, but of deliverance from sin. The essence of the new covenant is "God's promise decisively to remove the worshipers' sins even from God's own memory, thus enabling them to approach God's holy presence without fear of being consumed on account of their defilements" (Heb 8:12).[35] Further, Jesus transforms Joshua's inheritance language to refer to the meek who will "inherit the earth" (Matt 5:5). The OT promise of possessing a particular land hereby becomes the hope of inheriting the earth itself and ultimately of "enjoying an entirely re-created earth and heavens" with God (Rev 20–22).[36] God is still on the side of the poor and the oppressed (Jas 2:5), but the Nagas cannot be

---

33. This resembles the important distinction in systematic theology between the history of salvation and the order of salvation.
34. See Walter Brueggemann, *Chosen? Reading the Bible Amid the Israeli-Palestinian Conflict* (Louisville, KY: Westminster John Knox, 2015), 15–16.
35. David deSilva, "Hebrews," in *Hebrews, The General Epistles, and Revelation*, eds. Margaret Aymer et al., Fortress Commentary on the Bible (Minneapolis, MN: Fortress, 2016), 642.
36. Craig L. Blomberg, *Matthew*, NAC, vol. 22 (Nashville, TN: Broadman Press, 1992), 99.

equated with ancient Israel, which was offered an exclusive covenant with the promise of earthly liberation from Egypt.

Finally, covenant is also revelatory in nature. John Walton shows that God has a plan which he is sovereignly implementing in history, the ultimate goal of that plan being relationship. Consequently, if the people are to enter a relationship with God, it becomes imperative that the people know who he is. For this reason, God has "undertaken as a primary objective a program of self-revelation," and this is achieved through covenant with Israel as the means. Walton thus concludes that, "while the covenant is characteristically redemptive, and ultimately soteric, it is essentially revelatory."[37] While Walton is speaking primarily of the covenant between Israel and Yahweh, it remains true that the covenant makes God known to us, his covenant partners. The same can be said regarding the new covenant (whether we agree or disagree with Walton's contention of God's self-revelation being the particular objective of covenant). In the new covenant, God draws near to humanity and allows himself to be known personally in an even deeper way. Thus, if Christians are God's people through the new covenant, knowing him through the covenant is not merely a possibility but an invitation.

In summary, there is both continuity with the earlier revelations of the God of Israel in the new covenant as well as discontinuity due to what is not promised to us. This theological balance is lacking in the context of the Naga nationalist rhetoric which tends towards a blind confidence and optimism with definite similarities to prosperity theology.[38]

2.2. Land of the People of God

Land is one of the three important elements of the covenant triangle between Yahweh, Israel, and the promised land. This is also in keeping with the ancient Near Eastern understanding in which statehood is conceived as a tripartite relationship among a god, a people, and the land which a deity gave to the people as a national estate. Land was thus given as a gift or sign of favor, while its loss was an expression of displeasure by the gods. While the OT view of the promised land is pluriform rather than uniform,[39] Walter Kaiser is certainly

---

37. John H. Walton, *Covenant: God's Purpose, God's Plan* (Grand Rapids, MI: Zondervan, 1994), 25.
38. See chapter 12's discussion of prosperity theology by Huu-Thien Tran N. and Daniel C. Owens.
39. Land is given as a gift but it must be taken, while being given unconditionally but possessed conditionally. In addition, the extent of the borders of the promised land varies between

correct in stating that the promise of the land to Israel and its ancestors is of utmost importance in the OT.⁴⁰ Land was one of the first elements in God's promise to Abraham, being embedded in the call itself: "Go from your country, your people and your father's household to the land I will show you" (Gen 12:1). The promise of the land is then reiterated to Isaac and in the Mosaic tradition as well.⁴¹ The land is perceived as a gift, given as a part of God's commitment to the promise to the patriarchs/ancestors (Gen 12:1; 15:7ff; Deut 7:8; cf. 1:8; 8:1). This land is also to be where Yahweh's people obey him and to enjoy their relationship with him (Gen 17:8).⁴²

Similarly, land is a central issue in the Naga nationalist movement since it is a fight for the right to self-determination. When the British left India in 1947, the Nagas found themselves caught between India and Myanmar. Further, within India itself the state Nagaland was carved out in 1963 without including all the regions inhabited by the Nagas. This omission led to the nationalists' demand for what is called "Nagalim" or "Greater Nagaland," an integrated and sovereign state of Naga-inhabited areas in both India and Myanmar. Such a demand for a unified Naga homeland has naturally met with resistance from Nagaland's neighbors, making it a thorny issue in the Indo-Naga peace talks.⁴³

Land is therefore inextricably tied to the demand for sovereignty and figures prominently in the Naga nationalists' narrative. Their understanding of land is permeated with references to God and "Nagaland for Christ." T. Muivah, the General Secretary of the NSCN-IM faction, explained this slogan in these terms:

Genesis (e.g. Gen 15:18's reference to land from Dan to Beersheba) and the various accounts of conquest and land occupation in the Deuteronomistic History. These voices, however, are not necessarily contradictory and can be reconciled since they all contribute to a multifaceted view of the land.
40. Walter Kaiser, Jr., "The Promised Land: A Biblical-Historical View," *BSac* 138 (July 1981): 302.
41. Brueggemann, *Chosen?*, 28.
42. Alain Marchadour and David Neuhaus, *The Land, the Bible, and History: Toward the Land That I Will Show You* (New York: Fordham University Press, 2007), 16–18.
43. See for instance, Dinakar Peri, "Greater Nagaland Idea Worries Manipur," *The Hindu* (November 2018), accessed August 25, 2021, https://www.thehindu.com/news/national/other-states/greater-nagaland-idea-worries-manipur/article25439535.ece, and "Neighbouring States Oppose 'Greater Nagaland' Demand, Say Territorial Changes Not Acceptable," *The Indian Express* (August 2020), accessed August 25, 2021, https://www.newindianexpress.com/nation/2020/aug/17/neighbouring-states-oppose-greater-nagaland-demand-say-territorial-changes-not-acceptable-2184544.html.

> [T]he Nagas trust in the God-ship of Jesus Christ, the Creator of the heavens and the earth and therefore, they have chosen him to be their God. It is the covenant of God with the Nagas, which was declared in the national Hoho (council) by our pioneers with one voice. We believe in the principle of interrelationship of man, land and God. We know nothing exists by itself. Creations and Creator are inseparably interrelated.[44]

He added in an interview:

> God has created heaven and earth and in this creation a portion for the Nagas is also there because for the most of the people there is homeland and there must be a piece of land for the Nagas which can be called their home. . . . And that portion particularly is this Patkoi range because we were made to settle down there.[45]

Later in the Sixth Naga Peoples' Consultative Meeting, which was held to discuss the proposed extension of a ceasefire between the government of India and NSCN-IM,[46] Muivah was also quoted as saying, "I don't have doubt that God gave Naga land to Naga people. This is God's promise. . . . We can do all things through Jesus Christ. We are not a people without [a] promise." The interviewer, Abraham Lotha, observed that the meeting felt like "a religious meeting rather than a political consultative meeting."[47]

These anecdotes show how the Naga nationalist movement has been influenced by religious convictions and what the leaders believe to be God's plan for the Nagas, that is, a movement towards the establishment of a sovereign Christian nation.[48] The slogan "Nagaland for Christ," by contrast, originated as the church's stand against violence and corruption. But in the hands of the nationalists, it has become the rallying cry for the establishment of a Christian

---

44. Cited in Jamir, "Segmentation, Unity," 151.
45. Abraham Lotha, "The Paradox of Religious Nationalism in the Production of Naga Identity," 12. Paper presentation at a workshop on "Performing Identity: Ethnicity and Ethno-Nationalism in the South-east Asian Borderland region of North-east India" at Georg-August-University, Goettingen, Germany from 15th to 18th December, 2011. https://www.uni-goettingen.de/de/document/download/3b6e499f3bd2b8757381094547584646e.pdf/Paper-Lotha.pdf.
46. The meeting was held at Hebron Camp, Dimapur, Nagaland, on July 27, 2017 (Lotha, "The Paradox of Religious," 15–16).
47. See Lotha, "The Paradox of Religious," 16.
48. The NSCN leadership states, "One of the main objectives of our revolution is to make our lands for Christ and in order to construct a Christian state it needs [an] army who trust in the Lord . . . Nagaland for Christ shall be built by those soldiers who trust in Him." Cited in Wouters, "Religion, Politics," 7.

state, although what such a state would look like in terms of policies and administration remains vague.

Theologically speaking, there are several problems with equating Naga nationalism's struggle for a sovereign homeland with the land promised to Israel by Yahweh in the OT. The first is the impossibility of finding biblical evidence to support the assertion that God has apportioned a particular land for the Nagas. The promise of land to Israel is too specific and historically bound to appropriate by any people merely on the basis of being Christian. In the special case of the promised land, the OT repeatedly underlines that it was Yahweh who initiated the covenant and made the promise of land to Abraham's descendants. In the case of the Naga nationalism, the concept of covenant becomes more a matter of wishful thinking, though at times with a pledge of allegiance to God. Yet God is not obligated to act on such beliefs and (mis)conceptions since the Bible records no comparable covenant that God initiated with the Nagas, as he did with ancient Israel. For these reasons, "Nagaland for Christ" is more of an ideology and inference held by Naga nationalists about their desired homeland rather than a theological position that the OT teaches.

Second, the OT asserts that the land was a place for exhibiting the life Yahweh wanted from his people which was set apart and distinct from their neighbors. A separate land was necessary because ancient Near Eastern kingdoms were typically theocracies – religion was usually a matter of the state, and the deities whom kings venerated largely determined whom the citizens would as well. For ancient Israel, its identity and existence as the faithful people of Yahweh depended on being residents of the land that was Yahweh's own.

With the coming of Christ, however, the concept of land has undergone an important transformation. Land in the OT was where Israelite kingdoms were established for the localized worship of Yahweh, but in the NT it has become the universal kingdom of God which occupies the entire earth. The same lives of holiness, righteousness, and justice that were expected of Israel in the land are now to be lived and practiced in the worldwide kingdom of God, wherever God's people are. Even as there is some continuity with the OT, the significance of the land as it relates to being God's people is extended in the NT to encompass both literal and figurative places, both of which are devoid of ethnic and national boundaries.[49] The coming of Jesus Christ leads

---

49. For a more detailed treatment of the land in the NT, see Marchadour and Neuhaus, *The Land, the Bible, and History*, 63–86.

to the land assuming various spiritual dimensions that are no less real than the fixed, physical land. This shift in the Bible's emphasis undercuts any claim by an ethnic group to ownership of a different land, while at the same time citing God's promise of land to ancient Israel.

2.3. Violence and the People of God

Also connected to land is the issue of violence, both in the history of ancient Israel and the history of the Naga nationalist movement. Initially in the call of Abraham (Gen 12:1–3), the land was only "signified by a promise" rather than clearly defined, but the land as later defined in Genesis 15 is even bigger than the borders of Canaan (Gen 15:18–21).[50] Until then, the only piece of land that the Israelites had possessed in Canaan was the small piece of land that Abraham had bought in Machpelah, near Mamre, as a burial site for Sarah. Jacob was eventually also taken and buried there (Gen 50:12–13), and Joseph also asked to be taken to Canaan (Gen 50:24–25). The land therefore remains largely a future promise within the Pentateuch, as when it closes with God affording Moses a fleeting look at the promised land from Mount Nebo (Deut 34:1–4). It is only when the Israelites cross the Jordan that this anticipation of the land becomes "land acquisition," as Brueggemann observes, and it is then that it becomes evident that the land is not so much given as it is "taken by force of arms."[51] As such, the use of divinely sanctioned violence in Israel's conquest of Canaan makes Joshua one of the difficult books in the OT for a modern reader to understand and accept.[52]

Interestingly, Naga nationalism has found further support for itself in this difficult narrative. In the case of ancient Israel, one reason that God commanded Israel to exterminate the inhabitants of Canaan was to preserve the cultic purity of his own people (Deut 7:1–6). In the case of the Naga nationalist movement, however, Nagas are an ethnic and religious minority wherever they are found,[53] and the nationalists have used this fact to argue for the need to protect their culture and religion from assimilation into Hindu-majority India. Muivah alludes thus to Deuteronomy 7:1–4 as support for the

---

50. Marchadour and Neuhaus, *The Land, the Bible, and History*, 16–18.
51. Brueggemann, *Chosen?*, 31.
52. For more discussion on the OT's theological tension between blessing the nations and destroying them, see the essay on the *missio Dei* by Jerry Hwang (ch. 4) in this volume.
53. Christians constitute approx. 2.3% and 6.2% of the population in India and Myanmar, respectively. "Office of the Registrar General and Census Commissioner, India," accessed August 26, 2021, https://censusindia.gov.in/census_and_you/religion.aspx; "Myanmar Population," accessed August 26, 2021, https://worldpopulationreview.com/countries/myanmar-population.

nationalist movement when he says, "God knew this very well, so he warned the Israelites, 'when you reach Canaan, you have nothing to do with this or that,'" and applies Deuteronomy's teaching about cultic purity as the reason for Nagas to guard themselves from this kind of danger.[54]

Further, the late Isak Swu said, "The rulers of India and Burma will be like Herod (sic) of Egypt. If they don't obey God, it'll be to their own cost. Armies of rats will devour their lands. . . . Just as Joshua captured Jericho by blowing trumpets to summon help, so will your war be, God said."[55] Here he is clearly referring to the exodus and conquest events. Although these narratives are relatively muted in describing Yahweh's command to the Israelites to destroy those living in Canaan, the hostile overtones of Swu's language would not have been missed by his largely Christian hearers who were steeped in biblical language and narratives without always having an adequate grasp of how to appropriate them properly.

As Mark Juergensmeyer observes, however, such an association of religion with violence is hardly novel since "violence has lurked as a shadowy presence. It has colored religion's darker, more mysterious symbols."[56] This is true also of the Naga nationalist movement which, as an armed insurgency, has been engaged in much violence and bloodshed in the past decades through battles with the Indian army, as well as among the various nationalist factions and even against civilians. A ceasefire agreement was signed in 1997 between the Indian government and the NSCN-IM faction, which has been extended and will remain in effect in Nagaland until April 2023. Although the state of Nagaland enjoys some measure of respite as of this writing, the issue of using biblical passages to justify violence remains a fundamental and unresolved problem.

In the OT itself, the apparent contradiction between land *promised* to Israel and *taken* by Israel can be reconciled by noting that Yahweh uses Israel as an agent of judgment in overthrowing the Canaanites. Hence Israel takes possession of the land that was promised to them.[57] Moreover, the use of violence against the Canaanites was not because the people of Canaan belonged to another religion, but because the one true God was judging them for their sins (Deut 9:4–5). He allowed the sins of the Amorites, descendants of one of the

---

54. Lotha, "The Paradox of Religious Nationalism," 17.
55. As cited in Longkumer, "Bible, Guns, and Land," 7.
56. Mark Juergensmeyer, *Terror in the Mind of God: The Global Rise of Religious Violence* (Oxford: Oxford University Press, 2000), 6.
57. Patrick D. Miller, "The Gift of God: The Deuteronomic Theology of the Land," *Int* 23 (1969): 455.

sons of Canaan (cf. Gen 10:16), to reach their full measure before punishing them (Gen 15:16). Further, the Canaanites practiced human sacrifice which was detestable to God, so the Israelites were to steer clear from such forms of worship (Deut 12:31; cf. Lev 18:21) and the instruments of such pagan practices (cf. Jer 19:4–5; Ezek 20:31). In sum, the judgment on the Canaanites came from God himself; he alone decreed that their sins needed to be dealt with. While such wars waged with pseudo-theological rationale have come to be called "holy wars," it is God alone who reserves the right of judgment; this has simply not been given to us. The danger of assimilation by a stronger religious "other" remains inadequate on its own as justification for violence.

Moreover, the NT's teachings and perspective on violence are definitive for Christians in both belief and conduct, and as such it is necessary to outline its perspective on the subject of violence. The time and context in which Jesus lived has some similarities, in fact, with the situation in which the Nagas now find themselves. During the first century CE, the Jews were an ethnic and religious minority living under the Roman Empire. Messianic expectation among the Jews was intense since "messiah" was a political concept first and foremost. The Jews were waiting for someone to liberate them and restore their political kingdom. They were not just waiting passively, as attested in various armed rebellions around the time of Jesus, such as the Maccabean revolt (167–164 BCE) when the Jews were able to take control of Judea and established the Hasmonean dynasty (167–37 BCE), as well as a series of Jewish Wars (66–135 CE).[58]

On this note, it is useful to consider the Jewish sect known as the Zealots, the term for members of one of the Jewish freedom movements that is mentioned by Josephus and the rabbinic tradition. The NT has four references to "Zealots" due to the presence of Simon the Zealot (Matt 10:4; Mark 3:18; Luke 6:15; Acts 1:13). The emergence of this freedom movement can be traced back to Judas the Galilean (6 CE) until its decline in the course of the Jewish Wars. The fundamental conviction of the party founded by Judas the Galilean was the demand for theocracy, leading to a radical clash with the Roman emperor's claim to sovereignty. The demand was partly rooted in the perception that eschatological liberation of Israel would begin in their struggle

---

58. Lester L. Grabbe, *Judaism from Cyrus to Hadrian, vol. 1: The Persian and the Greek Period* (Minneapolis, MN: Fortress, 1992), 288; George W. E. Nickelsburg, *Jewish Literature Between the Bible and the Mishnah: A Historical and Literary Introduction* (Minneapolis, MN: Fortress, 2005), 69.

with the Roman oppressor. The zeal of Phinehas and Elijah for the honor of Yahweh in the OT were their models (Num 25:6–13) and served as the roots for the rise of the radical and militant wing of the Pharisees which became known as the "Zealots."[59]

A deep religious motivation lay behind this name, which can be best explained as "zeal for God and his law." The original understanding of the idea of piety was commendable, but by the time of Jesus, it had taken on violent forms as expressed in the readiness to take any means necessary "to preserve the integrity of God's law and his sanctuary, often sacrificing their own lives in the process."[60] The characteristics that the Naga nationalists seem to hold in common with this Jewish freedom movement are their vision of the rule of God, and what one historian calls the latter's "unconditional readiness to fight against all the internal and external enemies of God and of Israel and therefore a readiness to die as a martyr."[61]

In the NT, there are no explicit references to the Zealots except for the four mentioned above. Jesus never addresses the Zealots explicitly or any Jewish freedom fighters in general. As Martin Hengel notes, this was a cultural norm seen frequently in Judaism which "avoids openly naming the opponents."[62] At the same time, one cannot escape the political overtones in Jesus's teachings about the kingdom and claims to be the Messiah, nor the fact that there are certain points of contact between the teachings of Jesus and the Zealots (Matt 5:10; 10:37–39; Mark 3:31–35; Luke 6:21, 25). Thus, there seems to be incidents which might have the Zealots or Judas's movement as a backdrop, such as the question of payment of tax to Caesar (Luke 20:20–26).[63] Ironically, Naga nationalism's adoption of a Zealot-like paradigm is similar to the falsehoods about Jesus being a messianic pretender which culminated in his unjust condemnation and crucifixion.

---

59. See Martin Hengel, *The Zealots: Investigation into the Jewish Freedom Movement in the Period from Herod I Until 70 A.D.* (Edinburgh: T&T Clark, 1989), 377.
60. Hengel, *The Zealots*, 182–83.
61. Hengel, *The Zealots*, 377.
62. Hengel, *The Zealots*, 339.
63. During 6–7 CE, there had been rioting and rebelling in Palestine due to the imposition of a taxation structure, though of course there is also reason to be cautious about this connection. See discussion by John Nolland, *Luke 18:35–24:53*, WBC, vol. 35c (Dallas, TX: Word, 1998), 957. It is possible that "the spies" expected a negative answer from Jesus, and their further emphasis on his love for truth, fearlessness, and obedience to God marked their suspicion of him as a Zealot. Thus they "asked him a question which would make a true 'Zealot' confess his convictions" (Hengel, *The Zealots*, 193–94).

Indeed, the chasm between Jesus and the Zealots was unbridgeable. The Sermon on the Mount, for example, clearly contains and expresses ideas of the kingdom of God and its code of behavior that run contrary to Zealot ideas about cultural engagement. Further, although Jesus called for obedience to God's will in a manner that the Zealots would have supported, he does not approve of his disciples' use of violence (John 18:10–11). By placing the command to love (not only God and our neighbors, but even one's enemies) as the heart of Christian living, Jesus brought "absolute contrast to the idea of 'zeal of God' in the violent sense, which appears only marginally in the NT,"[64] as when he cleared the Temple (John 2:13–16).

Similarly, in the Great Commission, the global vision and mission of Christianity at the end of the age seem to require human participation (Mark 13:10), not through violence, but in going, preaching, teaching, and baptizing (Matt 28:19). This rejection of the Zealot ideal of theocracy reaches its ultimate climax in Jesus's reply to Pontius Pilate: "My kingdom is not of this world. If it were, my servants would fight to prevent my arrest by the Jewish leaders. But now my kingdom is from another place" (John 18:36). Jesus's response to Pilate clearly excludes any affirmation of the Zealots' attempts to bring about the kingdom of God by means of violence and extremism. For these reasons, freedom movements in Judeo-Christianity can easily land on the wrong side of salvation history when they seek to establish a sovereign Christian nation and theocracy, as Naga nationalists hope to do.

If Nagaland is to be "for Christ" in the truest sense, then the path of non-violence needs to be considered much more seriously. The identity of Nagas "in Christ/him" (one of the NT's most frequent descriptions of the Christian life, e.g. Rom 8:1; 1 Cor 1:2; Gal 1:22) must take precedence over their ethnic identity, especially when the two come into conflict. The decontextualizing of OT texts and narratives by recontextualizing them within one's own goals can be a dangerous enterprise which needs careful examination in light of the transformation that Jesus's life and teaching bring on these texts.

CONCLUSION

Our main contention has been that the Scripture, especially the OT narratives of exodus and liberation concerning Israel's formative stages as a nation, have been selectively appropriated to provide direct ideological undergirding for the Naga national movement. While attempts to ground the movement

---

64. Hengel, *The Zealots*, 379.

in faith and the use of Scripture were likely well-intentioned, over time the understanding and application of these teachings by Naga nationalists became deficient and even destructive.

On the one hand, biblical Christianity requires all spheres of life to come under its influence without compartmentalization into Christian and non-Christian spheres. Hence it is no surprise that the spirit of Naga nationalism was incorporated within the framework of cultural Christianity. At the same time, a lack of biblical understanding among Naga nationalists has often led to skewed understandings of God, faith, culture, and self.

As a Naga Christian myself, I humbly suggest that one way forward is to acknowledge the theological discontinuities between Israelites and Nagas more honestly. Nagas can begin by disabusing themselves of the notion that they are God's chosen people in the same way as ancient Israel was. Israel was specially chosen for a specific task which, Israel having failed, was fulfilled by Jesus Christ as the perfect "new Israel." The status of the Nagas as God's people is thus derived from the new covenant inaugurated in Christ, but without being exclusive since it does not come with Israel's one-time promises like that of a guaranteed homeland.

If the Naga struggle for independence is historically and politically legitimate, it should stand on its own merits without needing cultural Christianity as a crutch. And if we are to fight for it, as Naga *Christians*, then we need to gain skill in biblical interpretation and stop justifying violence, since the life and teaching of Jesus have already pointed the non-violent way forward. It is time to fashion ourselves after Christ rather than ancient Israel. The injustices of history mean that our struggle for a sovereign homeland will likely continue, but we should begin by living as the citizens of God's countercultural kingdom that we claim to be.

REFERENCES

Ahuja, Namrata Biji. "Bullets and the Bible." *The Week*, April 2017. Accessed August 25, 2021. https://www.theweek.in/theweek/cover/national-socialist-council-of-nagaland.html?fbclid=IwAR35kzFN5ulGsS4pIx39wgDQ-5NvwsNip9hMOsFmzJRlF0TjUWlXy0BPjkY.

Blomberg, Craig L. *Matthew*. New American Commentary. Vol 22. Nashville, TN: Broadman Press, 1992.

Brueggemann, Walter. *Chosen? Reading the Bible Amid the Israeli-Palestinian Conflict*. Louisville, KY: Westminster John Knox, 2015.

deSilva, David. "Hebrews." In *Hebrews, The General Epistles, and Revelation*, edited by Margaret Aymer et al., 625–53. Fortress Commentary on the Bible. Minneapolis, MN: Fortress, 2016.

Eichrodt, Walther. *Theology of the Old Testament*, vol. 1. Old Testament Library. Translated by J. A. Baker. Philadelphia: Westminster, 1961.

Grabbe, Lester L. *Judaism from Cyrus to Hadrian, vol. 1: The Persian and the Greek Period*. Minneapolis, MN: Fortress, 1992.

Haskar, Nandita, and Sebastian Hongray. *Kuknalim, Naga Armed Resistance: Testimonies of Leaders, Pastor, Healers and Soldiers*. New Delhi: Speaking Tiger Books, 2019.

Hengel, Martin. *The Zealots: Investigation into the Jewish Freedom Movement in the Period from Herod I Until 70 A.D.* Edinburgh: T&T Clark, 1989.

Iralu, Kaka D. *Nagaland and India: The Blood and the Tears – A Historical Account of the 52-year Indo-Naga War and the Story of Those Who Were Never Allowed to Tell It*. Kohima: NV Press, 2003.

Jamir, Chongpongmeren. "Segmentation, Unity, and a Church Divided: A Critical History of Churches in Nagaland, 1947–2017." PhD diss., Middlesex University/OCMS, 2019. https://eprints.mdx.ac.uk/27960/1/JChongpongmeren%20thesis.pdf.

Juergensmeyer, Mark. *Terror in the Mind of God: The Global Rise of Religious Violence*. Oxford: Oxford University Press, 2000.

Kaiser Jr., Walter C. "The Promised Land: A Biblical-Historical View." *Bibliotheca Sacra* 138 (July 1981): 302–12.

Kashyap, Samudra Gupta. "Nagaland erects memorial monolith to mark sacrifice of Naga Labour Corps in World War 1." *The Indian Express*, April 19, 2017. Accessed August 23, 2021. https://indianexpress.com/article/india/nagaland-erects-memorial-for-100-years-of-naga-labour-corps-in-world-war-1-4619630/.

Longkumer, Arkotong. "Bible, Guns, and Land: Sovereignty and Nationalism Among the Nagas of India." *Nations and Nationalism* 24 (2018): 1097–116.

Lotha, Abraham. "The Paradox of Religious Nationalism in the Production of Naga Identity." 1–25. Paper presentation at a workshop on "Performing Identity: Ethnicity and Ethno-Nationalism in the South-east Asian Borderland region of North-east India" at Georg-August-University, Goettingen, Germany from 15th to 18th December, 2011. https://www.uni-goettingen.de/de/document/download/3b6e499f3bd2b875738109454758464e.pdf/Paper-Lotha.pdf.

Marchadour, Alain, and David Neuhaus. *The Land, the Bible, and History: Toward the Land That I Will Show You*. New York: Fordham University Press, 2007.

McKenzie, Steven L. *Covenant*. St. Louis: Chalice Press, 2000.

Miller, Patrick D. "The Gift of God: The Deuteronomic Theology of the Land." *Interpretation* 23 (1969): 451–65.
"Myanmar Population." Accessed August 26, 2021. https://worldpopulationreview.com/countries/myanmar-population.
"Nagalim." *Unrepresented Nations and Peoples Organization*, April 2019. Accessed August 23, 2021. https://unpo.org/members/7899.
"Neighbouring States Oppose 'Greater Nagaland' Demand, Say Territorial Changes Not Acceptable." *The Indian Express*, August 2020. Accessed August 25, 2021. https://www.newindianexpress.com/nation/2020/aug/17/neighbouring-states-oppose-greater-nagaland-demand-say-territorial-changes-not-acceptable-2184544.html.
Nickelsburg, George W. E. *Jewish Literature Between the Bible and the Mishnah: A Historical and Literary Introduction*. Minneapolis, MN: Fortress, 2005.
Nolland, John. *Luke 18:35–24:53*. Word Biblical Commentary 35c. Dallas, TX: Word, 1998.
"Office of the Registrar General and Census Commissioner, India." Accessed August 26, 2021. https://censusindia.gov.in/census_and_you/religion.aspx.
Osei-Bonsu, Robert. "The Church as the People of God and Its Relation to the Church as a Community." *Asia-Africa Journal of Mission and Ministry* 4 (2012): 57–73.
Peri, Dinakar. "Greater Nagaland Idea Worries Manipur." *The Hindu*, November 2018. Accessed August 25, 2021. https://www.thehindu.com/news/national/other-states/greater-nagaland-idea-worries-manipur/article25439535.ece.
von Rad, Gerhard. *Old Testament Theology*. 2 vols., translated by D. M. G. Stalker. Edinburgh: Oliver and Boyd, 1962.
Singh, Chandrika. *Naga Politics*. New Delhi: Mittal Publications, 2004.
Stern, Jessica. *Terror in the Name of God: Why Religious Militants Kill*. New York: HarperCollins, 2003.
Tsudir, Asangba. "Historical Records Prove that Naga Forefathers Wanted a Better World." *The Naga Republic*, January 2018. Accessed August 23, 2021. http://www.thenagarepublic.com/features/historical-records-prove-naga-forefathers-wanted-better-world/.
Vashum, R. *Nagas' Right to Self Determination: An Anthropological, Historical Perspective*. 2nd ed. New Delhi: Mittal Publications, 2005.
Walton, John H. *Covenant: God's Purpose, God's Plan*. Grand Rapids, MI: Zondervan, 1994.
Wouters, Jelle. "Religion, Politics, and the Problem of Secularism among Upland Nagas." In *Brill's Encyclopaedia of the Religions of Indigenous People of South Asia*. Edited by Marine Carrin et al., 652–71. Leiden: Brill, 2021.
———. *In the Shadows of Naga Insurgency: Tribes, State, and Violence in Northeast India*. Oxford: Oxford University Press, 2018.

CHAPTER 11

KINSHIP, PATRONAGE, AND CORRUPTION

Peter H. W. Lau

This chapter discusses three connected subjects prevalent in both the Old Testament and Asia today. The first is *kinship*, on which the focus will be three factors contributing to its importance in the Old Testament. The second is the institution of *patronage*, which is embedded in kinship. The term is not found in the OT, but the concept is. At the same time, we will need to be careful in applying sociological models of patronage to OT texts. The third is *corruption*, a popular topic in research and the media. We will mainly focus on the issue of bribery, while considering why it is common in many patronage cultures, untangling the teaching of the OT, and differentiating between a gift and a bribe.

1. KINSHIP

The central social institution in the ancient Near East was *kinship*, as generally in Asia today. The *family*, a smaller kinship unit, is found in all societies, making the study of the family an important part of any attempt to understand a culture.[1] Individual Israelites were members of various kinship groups, each of which entailed various roles and responsibilities. The example of Saul displays the full complement of kinship groups (1 Sam 9:1; 10:20–21).[2] The

---

1. Carol L. Meyers, "The Family in Early Israel," in *Families in Ancient Israel*, ed. Leo G. Perdue et al. (Louisville, KY: Westminster John Knox, 1997), 1.
2. See also Joshua 7:16–18; Judges 6:15. For further discussion on kinship groupings in the pre-exilic period, see especially Shunya Bendor, *The Social Structure of Ancient Israel: The Institution of the Family (beit 'ab) from the Settlement to the End of the Monarchy*, Jerusalem Biblical Studies 7 (Jerusalem: Simor, 1996); Joseph Blenkinsopp, "The Family in First Temple Israel," in *Families in Ancient Israel*, ed. Leo G. Perdue et al. (Louisville, KY: Westminster John Knox, 1997), 49–57; Baruch Halpern, "Jerusalem and the Lineages in the Seventh Century BCE: Kinship and the Rise of Individual Moral Liability," in *Law and Ideology in Monarchic Israel*, ed. Baruch Halpern and Deborah W. Hobson (Sheffield: JSOT Press, 1991), 49–59; Meyers, "Family," 1–47, and classically, Norman K. Gottwald, *The Tribes of Yahweh: A Sociology of the Religion of Liberated Israel, 1250–1050 BCE* (Maryknoll, NY: Orbis, 1979), 237–337.

narrator of 1 Samuel introduces his lineage using the following categories, in descending order of specificity:

People/Nation	'*am*	Israel
Tribe	*šēbet/ matteh*	Benjamin
Clan	*mišpāḥâ*	Matrite
Father's House	*bêt 'āb*	Abiel
Individual	*'ish/geber*	Saul the son of Kish

The first two kinship groups of "people/nation" and "tribe" held the greatest social and economic significance for an ancient Israelite. The smallest kinship unit, by contrast, was the "father's house."[3] It comprised all those living within the household of a living male ancestor, and would include his wife, his sons, and their wives, as well as their sons and wives and unmarried daughters. The "father's house" (*bêt 'āb*) referred to blood relations, while the broader "household" (*bêt*) of which it was a part would include Israelites and non-Israelites (e.g. servants, resident aliens) as well as household possessions (Exod 20:17).[4] The kinship level above the "father's house" was the "clan," a group of related households, such as those named after Jacob's grandsons. Israelite villages would consist of several clans sharing the same natural resources (Josh 13–19).[5] It was a protective association of families with social, economic, judicial, and military obligations to one another. The next highest kinship grouping was the "tribe," as named in Israel after the sons of Jacob. Its main significance was territorial landholding, although it also functioned to defend against foreigners or other Israelite groupings (e.g. Judg 12; 20–21). At the top of the kinship hierarchy was the grouping of all the tribes which the OT describes as "all [of] Israel." It had similarities to the modern understanding of a "nation" (cf. Josh 3–4).[6]

---

3. Only occasionally is the family unit referred to as a "mother's house" (Gen 24:28; Ruth 1:8; Song 3:4; 8:2).
4. See Tony H. K. Sher, "'Father's House' (*bêt 'āb*) in the Old Testament: Family or Household?," *Hill Road* 14 (2011): 3–19 (Chinese). Compare Hoffner, "*bayit*," *TDOT* 2:113–15.
5. Victor H. Matthews and Don C. Benjamin, *Social World of Ancient Israel 1250–587 BCE* (Peabody, MA: Hendrickson, 1993), 9.
6. See Steven E. Grosby, *Biblical Ideas of Nationality: Ancient and Modern* (Winona Lake, IN: Eisenbrauns, 2002), 13–27; Stuart D. E. Weeks, "Biblical Literature and the Emergence of Ancient Jewish Nationalism," *BibInt* 10 (2002): 144–57; David M. Goodblatt, *Elements of Ancient Jewish Nationalism* (Cambridge: Cambridge University Press, 2006); Doron Mendels, *The Rise and Fall of Jewish Nationalism: Jewish and Christian Ethnicity in Ancient Palestine* (Grand

Kinship, Patronage, and Corruption

The central importance of family in ancient Israelite culture derives from three key components.[7] First are *honor* and *shame*, the two core values that relate to a person's social standing within a community.[8] Honor is publicly acknowledged worth, while shame is a claim to worth that is publicly denied. Honor is primarily a group value, whereby an individual shares in the group's honor. Kinship groups inherit honor from honorable ancestors, which is maintained and defended in the current generation. Males achieve honor in public contests, while females maintain honor through privacy and integrity (personal and sexual). Parents command respect and obedience (Exod 20:12; Deut 21:18–21; Prov 30:17). Threats to family honor are taken seriously, leading to strong disapproval (e.g. Gen 9:20–27) and sometimes to acts of vengeance (e.g. Gen 34). As is most of Asia today, ancient Near Eastern culture was collectivist. The social standing and well-being of the group was of greater importance than the individual.[9]

The second component of the family is *tradition*.[10] Children should honor their parents because it is commanded (Exod 20:12; Deut 5:16) and also since they have given them life. Parents pass on time-tested communal wisdom to their children which carries on the faith and forms the basis of their culture (Deut 6:7, 20–25). In doing so, they establish a circle of societal formation in that tradition informs family structure, while family structure in turn perpetuates tradition.[11] For instance, respect and authority for judges, kings, priests, and prophets (Deut 16:18–18:22) all derive from respect and authority for parents.[12] From this biblical culture also arises a certain exclusiveness (Exod

---

Rapids, MI: Eerdmans, 1997); Mark G. Brett, "Nationalism and the Hebrew Bible," in *The Bible in Ethics*, ed. John W. Rogerson, Margaret Davies, and M. Daniel Carroll (Sheffield: Sheffield Academic Press, 1995), 136–63.

7. Mark McVann, "Family-Centeredness," in *Handbook of Biblical Social Values*, ed. John J. Pilch and Bruce J. Malina (Eugene, OR: Cascade, 2016), 64–66.

8. For a summary, see Joseph Plevnik and John J. Pilch, "Honor and Shame," in *Handbook of Biblical Social Values*, ed. John J. Pilch and Bruce J. Malina (Eugene, OR: Cascade, 2016), 89–96.

9. For an overview of collectivism and individualism, see Harry C. Triandis, "Individualism and Collectivism," in *The Handbook of Culture and Psychology*, ed. David R. Matsumoto (Oxford: Oxford University Press, 2001), 35–50.

10. McVann, "Family-Centeredness," 64–65. My thanks to Paul Barker for some of the insights in this paragraph (personal correspondence, February 28, 2021).

11. There are family traditions that should not be passed on such as the repeated condemnation of "the sin[s] of Jeroboam, son of Nebat" in 1–2 Kings.

12. This is based on the understanding that the order of laws in Deuteronomy broadly follows the Decalogue. See John H. Walton, "Deuteronomy: An Exposition of the Spirit of the Law," *GTJ* 8 (1987): 213–25.

19:4–6) which forms the basis for the understanding that Israel is a family descended from Abraham, Isaac, and Jacob (Gen 48:15–49:27).

In this manner, the nation replicates the family on a large scale. Authority in the larger kinship groupings is shaped by the model provided by the father's house; for instance, people in God's kingdom should respect and obey him as they would a parent (e.g. Deut 8:1–6). Of course, tradition can only be passed down if there is a next generation. Hence the importance in the OT of continuing the family line through children, especially sons. An Israelite's existence continued in some sense through their descendants, and childlessness or death of children meant one would be "cut off" (Num 27:4; 1 Sam 24:21 [Heb. 22]; Isa 56:5). Tradition remains a key component in most Asian cultures today.

The third component of family is *land*.[13] God was the landowner who gave the land to Israel as an inheritance (Lev 25:23; Josh 1:6). The land provided the framework in which honor/shame and tradition were knitted together, and was where the people experienced their covenant relationship with God (Deut 30:15–20).[14] Control and maintenance of land (family inheritance and national borders) were matters of honor/shame and tradition (Deut 19:14). The ancestral inheritance was where ancestors were to be buried, and an Israelite would then be "gathered to them" (Gen 25:8; 35:29; Num 27:13).[15] In addition, land was vital to the economic survival of each family. Expulsion from the land meant the destruction of tradition and family (Ps 137); restoration to it was a cause for rejoicing (Ps 126). The ideal was the continuation of one's "name" on the ancestral inheritance (Deut 25:5–10; Ruth 4:5, 10).

In sum, ancient Israel resembled most of Asia today in that the family was the most important kinship unit. Israel's theological understanding of the family is found in several aspects: (1) its narratives about "father's houses," (2) depictions of God in metaphors of social roles drawn from the family, (3) laws and instructions that shape and direct behavior within the family, and (4) theological reflection found in divine references in law, moral instructions, and prophecies.[16] The family thus held a central place in OT theology

---

13. McVann, "Family-Centeredness," 65.
14. Compare Christopher J. H. Wright, *Old Testament Ethics for the People of God* (Leicester: InterVarsity, 2004), 339, whose triangle of relationships places God, the land, and Israel at the vertices, and the family in the center.
15. For a recent discussion of ancient Israelite burial with references, see Steffan Mathias, *Paternity, Progeny, and Perpetuation: Creating Lives after Death in the Hebrew Bible*, LHBOTS, vol. 696 (London: T&T Clark, 2020), 71–79.
16. Leo G. Perdue, "The Household, Old Testament Theology, and Contemporary Hermeneutics," in *Families in Ancient Israel*, ed. Leo G. Perdue, et al. (Louisville, KY: Westminster

and ethics. Indeed, it was "one of two major social institutions that shaped theological reflection and discourse . . . and the . . . formation of its theological traditions."[17]

2. PATRONAGE

Patronage and benefaction were embedded within kinship, taking on the form of *fictive* kinship. This is the use of kinship terminology to refer to non-kinship relationships. Kinship thus remained the overarching social structure, with the values of honor and shame informing the interaction of families and individuals, while the institutions of patronage and benefaction were embedded within kinship and informed by honor and shame.[18] Patronage and benefaction thus worked with the values of honor and shame, for without the importance attached to accruing honor and avoiding shame, patronage and benefaction would not have existed in the forms or to the extent they did.

The term *patronage* is not actually found in the OT. In Roman history, a *patronus* was an aristocrat who had loyal followers who were called *clientes*. Nonetheless, anthropologists have identified patron-client relations as a widespread phenomenon in both ancient and contemporary Mediterranean societies. Since the 1960s, interest in patronage and patron-client relations has expanded from anthropology to other social sciences, including political science, economics, and sociology.

There are at least seven basic characteristics of *patron-client relations*:[19]

1. Hierarchy and inequality between the two parties
2. The selective provision of benefits and resources to individuals or groups of people
3. A relationship shaped according to the particular traits of the partners

---

John Knox, 1997), 224.
17. Perdue, "The Household," 225. The other was the monarchy.
18. Zeba A. Crook, *Reconceptualising Conversion: Patronage, Loyalty, and Conversion in the Religions of the Ancient Mediterranean*, BZNW, vol. 130 (Berlin: de Gruyter, 2006), 68.
19. Louis Roniger, "Patron-Client Relations, Social and Anthropological Study of," in *International Encyclopedia of the Social and Behavioral Sciences*, ed. James D. Wright (Amsterdam: Elsevier, 2015), 604; S. N. Eisenstadt and Louis Roniger, "Patron-Client Relations as a Model of Structuring Social Exchange," *Comparative Studies in Society and History* 22 (1980): 49–50. See also S. N. Eisenstadt and Luis Roniger, *Patrons, Clients and Friends: Interpersonal Relations and the Structure of Trust in Society* (Cambridge: Cambridge University Press, 1984).

4. The simultaneous exchange of two different types of resources: instrumental (for example, economic) and promises of solidarity and loyalty
5. The undermining of group solidarity among both clients and patrons, especially the latter because of the vertical nature of the relationship between individuals or networks of individuals, rather than between organized corporate groups
6. A favoritism that implies that people are excluded from patron-client relations or are only related to them intermittently
7. Connections that are based on informal and tightly bound understandings, but which are neither contractual nor legal.

These characteristics create an inherently contradictory and tenuous situation in five ways:[20]

1. Asymmetrical power and inequality combined with promises of solidarity
2. The coexistence of potential or actual coercion and exploitation because of the dual voluntary and obligatory nature of the attachment
3. Maintenance of the patron-client relations structure of limiting payoffs only by making payoffs
4. An informal and unregulated character which is used to project public claims over social resources and to bolster public images of power and reputation
5. Patron-client relations are characterized by instability and perpetual contest, resource manipulation, and instability.

There has been a trickle of studies applying the patronage model to ancient near Eastern and OT texts. Niels Peter Lemche was an early proponent of the patronage model in OT studies of the mid-1990s.[21] He argued that

---

20. Roniger, "Patron-Client Relations," 604; Eisenstadt and Roniger, "Patron-Client Relations," 50–51.
21. Niels P. Lemche, "Kings and Clients: On Loyalty between the Ruler and the Ruled in Ancient Israel," *Semeia* 66 (1994): 119–32; Lemche, "From Patronage Society to Patronage Society," in *The Origins of the Ancient Israelite States*, ed. Volkmar Fritz and Philip R. Davies (Sheffield: Sheffield Academic Press, 1996), 106–20. These articles have been collated in Niels Peter Lemche, *Biblical Studies and the Failure of History* (London: Taylor & Francis, 2014), from which I quote.

ancient Israelite society was "organized according to lines following patron-client relationships."²² We will critique his conception of patronage below, but biblical scholars can be thankful that he brought some attention to patronage in the OT.

Yet writing in 2005, Raymond Westbrook bemoaned the disregard for patronage in studies of the ancient Near East or the assumption of patronage without providing textual evidence of its existence.²³ He provided two reasons for this neglect. First, the lack of a dedicated terminology. Kinship terms such as "father" and "son" are used for a range of social relations. Similarly, terms for "gift," "love," and "friend" appear in a variety of contexts, relating to both patronage and non-patronage relations. Second, the nature of the sources. Most primary sources from the ancient Near East record formalized relationships, which excludes patron-client relations. Westbrook then provided textual evidence of primary and intermediary patronage, drawing from ancient Near Eastern texts from the second and first millennia, including the OT. Westbrook's essay was more exploratory than comprehensive; his main contribution was his application of strict criteria to examine texts.

Westbrook's more rigorous approach is echoed by Zeba Crook in his essay published in the following year, 2006.²⁴ Westbrook critiques Lemche for seeing patronage "in every unequal power relationship and in every isolated act of granting benefit,"²⁵ while Crook argues that Lemche wrongly identifies covenant as a form of patronage. Crook identifies the studies of Hannes Oliver and Ronald Simkins as also falling into the same trap as Lemche in conflating covenant with patronage. Crook rightly argues that covenant and patronage are different forms of asymmetrical exchange. The formal, legally binding elements of covenant exchange are lacking in patronage (the seventh basic

---

22. Lemche, *Biblical Studies and the Failure of History*, 205.
23. Raymond Westbrook, "Patronage in the Ancient Near East," *Journal of the Economic and Social History of the Orient* 48 (2005): 210–33. For the latter problem, he cites J. David Schloen, *The House of the Father as Fact and Symbol: Patrimonialism in Ugarit and the Ancient Near East*, Studies in the Archaeology and History of the Levant 2 (Winona Lake, IN: Eisenbrauns, 2001), 72, 110, 310; Matthews and Benjamin, *Social World*, 120–22, 59–60; Barry J. Kemp, *Ancient Egypt: Anatomy of a Civilization* (London: Routledge, 1989), 219, and T. Thompson, "'House of David': An Eponymic Referent to Yahweh as Godfather," *SJOT* 9 (1995): 59–74, who applies the criteria set out by Lemche. From scholarship pre-2005, I would add Walter J. Houston, "What's Just about the Jubilee?: Ideological and Ethical Reflections on Leviticus 25," *Studies in Christian Ethics* 14 (2001): 34–47.
24. Zeba A. Crook, "Reciprocity: Covenantal Exchange as a Test Case," in *Ancient Israel: The Old Testament in Its Social Context*, ed. Philip Francis Esler (Minneapolis, MN: Fortress, 2006), 78–91.
25. Westbrook, "Patronage," 216.

characteristic of patron-client relations mentioned above). Crook cautions that the patronage model of exchange, which is drawn from a Graeco-Roman setting needs to be adapted for the ancient Near East. With the caveat that the categories are fluid – familial and patronal exchange overlap, as do gift exchange and patronage – he presents the following model:[26]

Familial Exchange	Symmetrical Exchange	Asymmetrical Exchange	Negative Exchange
Kinship based	Non-kin based	Non-kin based	Non-kin based
Egalitarian (relative to non-kin); open-ended reciprocity, selfless giving	Balanced social status and balanced value of exchange	Unequal social status; unequal social exchange (repayment not in-kind)	Social status not relevant, treatment of enemies, opponents, and strangers
Examples: exchanges within households, between households in clans, and between clans in tribes	Examples: gift exchange, loan and loan repayment, buying/selling, trading	Examples: patronage (teacher/student, patron-client), benefaction (imperial benefactions, euergetism), covenant exchange (treaties, oaths)	Examples: bartering, cheating, stealing

While there has been a recent explosion of interest in patronage from a ministry and missiological perspective,[27] rigorous academic application to OT texts remains sparse. For instance, Tarah Van De Wiele's 2016 article presumes the existence of an Israelite "patronage economy in emerging urban conditions" without providing evidence for its existence.[28] However, W. Dennis Tucker Jr's

---

26. Crook, "Reciprocity," 91.
27. Werner Mischke, *The Global Gospel: Achieving Missional Impact in Our Multicultural World* (Scottsdale: Mission ONE, 2015), 122–40; Jayson Georges, *Ministering in Patronage Cultures: Biblical Models and Missional Implications* (Downers Grove, IL: InterVarsity, 2019); E. Randolph Richards and Richard James, *Misreading Scripture with Individualist Eyes: Patronage, Honor, and Shame in the Biblical World* (Downers Grove, IL: IVP Academic, 2020), 64–110; Jayson Georges, *Ministering in Honor-Shame Cultures: Biblical Foundations and Practical Essentials* (Downers Grove, IL: IVP Academic, 2016), 138–61.
28. Tarah Van de Wiele, "What Rights get Wrong about Justice for Orphans: An Old Testament Challenge to a Modern Ideology," *Studies in Christian Ethics* 29 (2016): 69–83. See also Emanuel

2007 article is an exception.²⁹ He examines some communal laments in the psalter and notes features of patronage, using aspects of S. N. Eisenstadt and Louis Roniger's model (see above).³⁰ Nonetheless, further work remains to be done in applying the patronage model to the rest of the OT. Such application would be beneficial, not only in enhancing exegesis and interpretation, but also in making the biblical text more easily relatable to the Asian context.

On this note, patronage is common in Asia with its societies that are characterized by mutually reciprocal links and reinforced by family connections. These relationships require the regular exchange of gifts and favors, and, while patronage is a neutral institution, it can also encourage biased decision making of various kinds. For example, in Thailand *chao pho* ("godfathers") use their informal networks to obtain government permissions, gain freedom from harassment, or to sway the election results.³¹ When patronage is thus protected by the state (monarchy, military, and judiciary) and sanctioned by tradition, it can prove difficult to curtail, as we will now discuss.³²

3. CORRUPTION

The practice of *corruption* can be defined as "dishonest or fraudulent conduct by those in power, typically involving bribery"³³ or simply as "the abuse of entrusted power for private gain."³⁴ It is found in all countries, including Asian ones, and has recently gained attention as a key issue in accounting for poor economic growth and underdevelopment.³⁵ I will outline this issue from a macroperspective of politics and economics in order to prepare for a focus on

---

O. Pfoh, "Genesis 4 Revisited: Some Remarks on Divine Patronage," *SJOT* 23 (2009): 38–45.
29. W. Dennis Tucker, Jr., "Is Shame a Matter of Patronage in the Communal Laments?," *JSOT* 31 (2007): 465–80.
30. See also Alexandra Grund, "'Schmähungen der dich Schmähenden sind auf mich gefallen': kulturanthropologische und sozialpsychologische Aspekte von Ehre und Scham in Ps 69," *Evangelische Theologie* 72 (2012): 174–93, who mentions patron-client relations in an excursus (pp. 183–87).
31. John Walsh, "Corruption: 1900 to Present: East and Southeast Asia," in *Cultural Sociology of the Middle East, Asia, & Africa: An Encyclopedia*, ed. Andrea L. Stanton, Edward Ramsamy, and Peter J. Seybolt (Thousand Oaks, CA: SAGE, 2012), 253–55.
32. For a description of kinship, patronage, and corruption in one South Asian country, see Anatol Lieven, *Pakistan: A Hard Country* (London: Penguin, 2012).
33. "Corruption," Lexico, accessed February 4, 2021, https://www.lexico.com/definition/corruption.
34. "What is Corruption," Transparency International, accessed February 4, 2021, https://www.transparency.org/en/what-is-corruption.
35. See especially Mauro Paolo, "Corruption and Growth," *The Quarterly Journal of Economics* 110 (1995): 681–712.

one type of corruption – *bribery*.³⁶ Since bribery is a major and systemic issue in most of Asia, I will examine the OT's teaching on bribery, then consider one particularly thorny practical issue: how to differentiate between a gift and a bribe.

Corruption is mainly caused by three intersecting causes.³⁷ The first is the reality of *incentives* such as low salaries, monopoly power, discretion, and lack of accountability. The second is the presence of *institutions* and their political structure, legal structure, rule of law, and culture. Third and finally, there is the issue of *personal ethics*. In what follows, we will focus on the macro factor of *governance regimes* as institutions which fall under the second category.

The various working definitions of corruption rest on the presumption that it is wrong to use public office for private gain.³⁸ Yet societies today that are characterized by a *collectivistic*, not individualistic, culture do not necessarily value a distinction between public and private. Relational connections are then used to personalize one's transactions with the state, with a multitude of such transactions occurring daily. In such a context, the head of state and high-level government officials can institute policy in favor of interest groups in exchange for receiving benefits from them. That is, they act as *patrons*, with rulers treating the state as their patrimony. In such countries, personal autonomy and political participation – the indicators of a society's ability to constrain rulers – are generally low.

The key question for a society, then, is whether *particularism* (treating a person not as an individual but according to ties or group affiliations) is the norm or a deviation. If the norm, these practices will also typically be found: (1) vertically-structured favoritism (*patronage/clientelism*), (2) horizontally-structured particularism (negative social capital networks, old boys), (3) *kinship*-motivated particularism (nepotism, ethnic favoritism), *bribery*, and (4) extortion. In a word, *corruption* is an indicator of the lack of the institutionalization of market economy and democracy.

---

36. Other types of corruption include extortion, exchange of favors, nepotism, cronyism, judicial fraud, accounting fraud, electoral fraud, public service fraud, embezzlement, kleptocracy, influence peddling, and conflicts of interest; Susan Rose-Ackerman and Bonnie J. Palifka, *Corruption and Government: Causes, Consequences, and Reform*, 2nd ed. (Cambridge: Cambridge University Press, 2016), 8–9.
37. Rose-Ackerman and Palifka, *Corruption and Government*, 27–28.
38. The following two paragraphs summarize Alina Mungiu-Pippidi, "Corruption: Political and Public Aspects," in *International Encyclopedia of the Social and Behavioral Sciences*, ed. James D. Wright (Amsterdam: Elsevier, 2015), 13–14.

Kinship, Patronage, and Corruption

On this note, the following table summarizes current theories of governance regimes and how they regard traits such as power, autonomy, and access:[39]

Governance Trait	Limited access order			Open access order (universalism)
	Patrimonialism	Competitive particularism	Borderline	
Power Distribution	Hierarchical with monopoly of central power	Stratified with power disputed competitively	Competitive with less stratification	Citizenship equality
State autonomy	State captured by ruler	State captured by election winners	Archipelago of autonomy and captured "islands"	State autonomous from private interest
Public resources	Particular and predictable	Particular but unpredictable	Particular and universal	Ethical universalism
Separation of public-private	No	No	Poor	Sharp
Relation formal/informal institutions	Informal institutions substitutive of formal ones	Informal institutions substitutive of formal ones	Competitive and substitutive	Complementary
Mentality	Collectivistic	Collectivistic	Mixed	Individualistic
Government accountability	No	Only when no longer in power	Occasional	Permanent
Rule of law	No; sometimes "thin"	No	Elites only	General; "thick"

In reality, the borders between these types are not so distinct. All Asian countries fall into at least one of these types, with the majority of them categorized as "competitive particularism." Hence, we find one macro factor contributing to corruption which is ubiquitous in Asia.

Based on the prevalence of collectivistic cultures in Asia, which are characterized by strong kinship bonds, patronage, and gift exchange, it is not surprising that bribery is also pervasive. Hwa Yung observes that "the line between

---

39. Mungiu-Pippidi, "Corruption: Political and Public Aspects," 15.

a gift and a bribe is not always easy to draw" and suggests that further work needs to be done within an Asian context.[40] Also for the OT, scholars often perceive an ambivalence in the OT teaching on bribery and gift-giving. John T. Noonan, Jr. likewise finds a linguistic ambiguity in ancient Near Eastern texts and presents it as evidence that a clear understanding of what constituted bribery was not developed in ancient Israel.[41] J. J. Finkelstein also presents evidence that said ambiguity was found in Israel's surrounding cultures,[42] while Michael Goldberg notes that in the ancient Near East "the practice of taking gifts from litigants [was] perfectly moral and absolutely legitimate."[43] Hwa Yung, following Bernard T. Adeney, states that in the six references to bribery in Proverbs, three condemn it (15:27; 17:23; 22:16), but three "extol it in positive terms" (17:8; 18:16; 21:14)![44] Yet, a closer examination of the OT's key terminology will show that its stance on bribery is not as ambiguous as it might seem.[45] There are five Hebrew terms/idioms worthy of comment:

1. Although the noun *šōḥad* has two meanings in the lexica – both "gift" and "bribe"[46] – its twenty-three occurrences in all major sections of the OT overwhelmingly mean the latter.[47] While bribery might have been treated ambivalently in the ancient Near East, OT law clearly condemns it (Exod 23:8; Deut 16:19; 27:25).[48] In narrative texts, bribes pervert justice (1 Sam 8:3), and in a

---

40. Hwa Yung, *Bribery and Corruption: Biblical Reflections and Case Studies for the Marketplace in Asia* (Singapore: Graceworks, 2010), 25. Compare Hwa's further reflections in *Asian Christian Ethics: Evangelical Perspectives* (Carlisle, UK: Langham, 2022).
41. John T. Noonan Jr., *Bribes* (New York: Macmillan, 1984), 13–30.
42. J. J. Finkelstein, "The Middle Assyrian Šulmānu-Texts," *JAOS* 72 (1952): 77–80.
43. Michael L. Goldberg, "The Story of the Moral: Gifts or Bribes in Deuteronomy?," *Int* 38 (1984): 16.
44. Hwa, *Bribery and Corruption*, 36; Bernard T. Adeney, *Strange Virtues: Ethics in a Multicultural World* (Downers Grove, IL: InterVarsity, 1995), 152: "Such equivocation [about bribery] in the Old Testament seems to reflect a recognition of the power differential between a poor person who gives a gift in order to stave off injustice and the rich who uses his power to exploit the poor. The powerful and the powerless are not judged by the same abstract absolute, but by the relationships and intentions of their situation."
45. This word list and some of the ideas that follow are from David J. Montgomery, "'A Bribe Is a Charm': A Study of Proverbs 17:8," in *Way of Wisdom: Essays in Honor of Bruce K. Waltke* (Grand Rapids, MI: Zondervan, 2000), 136–42.
46. BDB, 1005; HALOT, *šōḥad*, 4:1457.
47. Cf. *TDOT*, "*šōḥad*," 14:556. See also Mark W. Hamilton, "Bribery at the Boundaries of Gift Giving in the Hebrew Bible," *BN* 187 (2020): 39–58.
48. See David L. Baker, *Tight Fists or Open Hands?: Wealth and Poverty in Old Testament Law* (Grand Rapids, MI: Eerdmans, 2009), 215–22.

military context, the "present" is not a disinterested "gift," but is given to prompt military intervention (1 Kgs 15:19; 2 Kgs 16:8).[49] Prophetic texts denounce bribery (Isa 1:23; 5:23; Ezek 22:12; Mic 3:11), while psalms and wisdom texts also view bribery negatively (Ps 15:5; 26:10; Prov 17:23; Job 15:34). Although Proverbs 17:8 seems to view bribery positively, the crucial phrase within the verse is its apparent goodness "in the eyes of" the one who gives it. In Proverbs, this outlook on the world denotes "a fool's state of self-delusion."[50]

2. The noun *mattān* holds a broader range of meaning than *šōḥad*. Generally, it is morally neutral, denoting "gifts" with (Gen 34:12) and without (Gen 25:6; Esth 9:22; Ezek 46:16, 17) any expectation of reciprocation. Theologically, God gives humankind "gifts" (Ps 68:18 [Heb. 19]) and people give God "gifts" or "offerings" (Exod 28:38; Lev 23:38; Num 18:11; Ezek 20:26). A negative connotation, however, can sometimes be detected in the motivation behind the *mattān* (Prov 15:27; 19:6; 21:14; Eccl 7:7).

3. Probably deriving from the root "to cover over," the noun *kōfer* means "price of a life" or "ransom."[51] A ransom was permitted under the law (Exod 21:30), but not in all cases (Num 35:31, 32). Negatively, the *kōfer* could be used to pervert justice (Job 36:18; Amos 5:12) or to cover up an offense (Prov 6:35).

4. The expression *nāsa' pānîm*, "lift up the face," can denote either a physical action (2 Kgs 9:32) or have a figurative meaning.[52] Positively, it means "to show consideration or favor" (Gen 19:21; 32:20 [Heb 12]; 1 Sam 25:35; Mal 1:8); negatively, it means "to show partiality" (Lev 19:15; Ps 82:2; Prov 18:5) and is condemned as an injustice, often as a result of bribery (Prov 6:35). God is impartial and does not accept bribes (Deut 10:17; Job 34:19; compare Mal 2:9).

---

49. So also BDB, 1005; *pace* HALOT, "*šōḥad*," 4:1457, "gift to show one's allegiance (2 Kgs 16:8)."
50. Bruce K. Waltke, *The Book of Proverbs: Chapters 15–31*, NICOT (Grand Rapids, MI: Eerdmans, 2005), 49.
51. BDB, 497.
52. Simian-Yofre, "*pānîm*," *TDOT* 11:600–601.

5. The closely connected concept of extortion is covered by two Hebrew words. The noun *'ōšeq* is a more general term for oppression or extortion (Jer 6:6; 22:17; Ezek 22:7; 22:12; Ps 62:10 [Heb. 11]; 73:8; Eccl 7:7).[53] The verbal root of *beṣaʿ* can have a neutral connotation, "cut off" or "die."[54] But its more common noun form predominantly has a negative meaning; normally referring to extortion or unjust gain, often involving bloodshed.[55]

While there is some lexical ambiguity, the overall biblical witness on bribery is clear. The Hebrew word *šōḥad* holds negative moral connotations as a "bribe," while *mattān* is used for both a "gift" and a "bribe." The latter are distinguished according to the context and the motivation. If a gift is given with the expectation of profit or gain, it is a bribe and thus to be rejected (Prov 15:27). A *mattān* might avert anger (21:14), but its concealed nature is problematic, as we will soon see, and it will ultimately bring trouble on the giver (15:27). Indeed, such a *mattān* corrupts the heart (Eccl 7:7).

Most scholars agree that *variance bribes* (i.e. those given to pervert the course of justice) are condemned in the OT, but this does not necessarily extend to *transactional bribes* (i.e. those given to facilitate a process, also known as "grease money"). Yet a *mattān* can be akin to a transactional bribe if it grants the giver access to "the presence of the great" (Prov 18:16), and hence should be denounced.[56] And similar to Proverbs 17:8 (see above), while Proverbs 19:6 might seem to be commending gift-giving to curry favor with a nobleman or benefactor, but the immediate context does not support such a reading. The earlier aphorism in Proverbs 18:24 says that a true friend "sticks closer than a brother"; friendship is not based on selfish interests (19:6).

The modern concept of a "pay-off" is found in the word *kōfer*. For instance, if Proverbs 13:8 describes the kidnapping or blackmailing of a wealthy

---

53. BDB, 799.
54. D. Kellermann, "*beṣaʿ*," *TDOT* 2:206–08.
55. P. J. Harland, "betsa: Bribe, Extortion or Profit?," *VT* 50 (2000): 310–22.
56. Antonio Argandoña, "Private and Public Corruption: Facilitating Payments," in *The Changing Face of Corruption in the Asia Pacific*, ed. Marie dela Rama and Chris Rowley (Amsterdam: Elsevier, 2017), 77, describes "facilitating payments" (transactional bribes, paid to obtain regular, nondiscretionary service) from a secular perspective: they are "not a minor nuisance in the functioning of the public administration and companies but a cancer that has harmful consequences. The burden they create is borne mostly by low-income citizens and small businesses; they lessen efficiency, hamper economic development, disrupt income distribution, create social malaise, and eventually become large-scale corruption."

person,[57] his family can "pay off" the kidnapper or blackmailer.[58] In any case, a *kōfer* was often a deceitful practice to avoid a just punishment. The OT primarily condemns the person receiving bribes, but those giving bribes are also condemned (1 Kgs 15:19; 2 Kgs 16:8; Prov 6:35). Victims of extortion are not condemned.

In sum, the main reason that the OT denounces bribery is because of the holy character of God. He hates bribery and does not show partiality based on a person's gifts or place in society (Deut 10:17). He gives gifts, and our gifts or offerings to him, unlike in other religions, should not spring from a desire to manipulate him. Bribery is also denounced because it perverts the course of justice (Prov 17:23), it has a destructive effect on wider society (1 Sam 8:1–3; cf. 12:1–5), it favors those who can pay (Prov 18:16), and it is counter-productive (Prov 15:27).

While the OT's stance on bribery is unambiguous, more needs to be said about the difference between a gift and a bribe. Noonan is worth quoting in full for his summary of the complexities:

> A bribe expresses self-interest, a gift conveys love; a bribe subordinates the recipient to the donor, a gift identifies the donor with the recipient. A gift brings no shame, a bribe must be secret. A gift may be disclosed, a bribe must be concealed. The size of a gift is irrelevant; the size of a bribe, decisive. A gift does not oblige, a bribe coerces.[59]

Mark Hamilton's recent article echoes some of Noonan's ideas and adds specificity. After an analysis of the OT instances of *šōḥad*, Hamilton defines a bribe as "a gift exchange through which a subordinate person influences a superior to exercise judicial or political power in a way that benefits the gift giver to the detriment of a third party."[60] In such an exchange of goods and services, the parties agree to prices, generally (but not always) without the presence of

---

57. Tremper Longman III, *Proverbs*, BCOTWP (Grand Rapids, MI: Baker Academic, 2006), 286. Waltke, *The Book of Proverbs: Chapters 15–31*, 558, suggests that the person is guilty rather than being blackmailed.
58. Yet the second half of the proverb undermines the benefit of wealth since the poor are not subject to such crimes.
59. Noonan Jr., *Bribes*, 697.
60. Hamilton, "Bribery," 51. Cf. Noonan Jr., *Bribes*, xi: "an inducement improperly influencing the performance of a public function meant to be gratuitously exercised."

personal feelings or the desire for a long-term relationship.[61] In a non-market gift exchange, by contrast, there is a desire for a longer-lasting relationship. The bribe, however, is yet a third category: it is not based on a fair exchange of goods or services, and it does not build a long-term relationship. Hamilton then draws from the classic ideas in Marcel Mauss' influential and widely translated French work *Essai sur le don*,[62] along with that of Mediterranean anthropologist Julian Pitt-Rivers. Mauss highlighted the obligatory nature of gift-giving, of reciprocity, while Pitt-Rivers noted that since this is the case, the gift giver must carefully judge the character and actions of a potential partner.[63]

Herein lies the problem: a bribe neither allows for the limits of economic exchange nor leads to a friendship inviting ongoing reciprocity.[64] Rather, it potentially creates ill will, violence, and social disruption in order to produce some gain for the exchange participants. Hamilton argues that an important part of the OT's aversion to bribes is that such a gift crosses the boundary that distinguishes gift exchange from other sorts of commodity transfer. Central to this is the hiding of information – in short, the problem of *secrecy*. In any exchange of goods and services, knowledge by outside parties may (or must) be limited. In a licit gift exchange, the parties have full knowledge of the gift value because they must negotiate the reciprocal relationship that the gift creates and symbolizes. With a bribe, however, relevant knowledge remains obscured from the concerned parties (though paradoxically, the bribe is sometimes hidden while everyone knows it has taken place). Thus, bribery is an outlier for being neither an economic transaction nor a proper gift exchange. "It is an illicit act at the boundary of the two."[65] It disrupts social relations and shields or fosters violence. The "reciprocity" it invokes actually harms both parties without establishing a stable and trusting relationship between them. Ultimately, bribery exposes the participants' lack of confidence in the system to reach a just solution to their problems, thereby calling into question the conception of justice and/or the moral integrity of the justice system as a whole.

---

61. In some instances of market exchange, there might be a secondary desire for long-term relationship. In the ancient Near East, social relationships shaped some market forces and vice versa; see Daniel M. Master, "Economy and Exchange in the Iron Age Kingdoms of the Southern Levant," *BASOR* 372 (2014): 81–97.
62. Marcel Mauss, *The Gift: The Form and Reason for Exchange in Archaic Societies*, trans. W. D. Halls (London: Routledge, 1990), 72.
63. Julian Pitt-Rivers, "The Paradox of Friendship," trans. Matthew Carey. *HAU: Journal of Ethnographic Theory* 6 (2016): 449.
64. This paragraph draws from Hamilton, "Bribery," 53–55.
65. Hamilton, "Bribery," 55.

Kinship, Patronage, and Corruption

We can apply these ideas to Asian contexts in which gift-giving and reciprocity are part and parcel of the culture. That is not to say, however, that Asian societies are incapable of discerning between a gift and a bribe (as Western observers sometimes suggest). Malaysian sociologist Syed Hussein Alatas denies such cultural relativism and argues that leaders violating norms throughout history have always known about those local norms. Cultural practices are (mis)used for the purpose of corruption rather than being the cause of corruption itself.[66] On this note, the problem of gift-giving in patronage cultures transgressing the boundary to corruption and bribery also still plagues more "developed" Asian countries. South Korea has a strong gift-giving culture, for instance, with three of the last four South Korean presidents implicated in corruption.[67] Countries such as Singapore and Hong Kong share similarities with gift-giving, while they have managed to reduce corruption and bribery (although this has taken many years of effort).[68]

Certainly, collectivist-dominant cultures will exhibit the relational ties and the expectation of reciprocal gift-giving which create more situations for transgressing the gift-exchange boundary. Along with this often resides a more intense temptation to do so due to a sense of obligation.[69] This set of cultural traits has been noted in many Asian countries, such as Indonesia,[70] Cambodia,[71] and the Philippines. In the last country, the concept of *utang na loob* ("debt of gratitude") is morally neutral, but has often been used manipulatively in bribery, extortion, and nepotism.[72]

And certainly, the OT reflects some lexical ambiguity on the differences between "gift" and "bribe." Yet, we must remember that the OT was written in a collectivist-dominant culture to a collectivist-dominant audience, similar to

---

66. Syed Hussein Alatas, *Corruption and the Destiny of Asia*, rev. ed. (Selangor Darul Ehsan: Prentice Hall, 1999), 28–42, 70–71.
67. My thanks to Hwa Yung for this example (personal correspondence, January 20, 2021).
68. These are the two highest-ranking Asian countries (third and eleventh, respectively) in "Corruption Perception Index: 2020," Transparency International, accessed February 11, 2021, https://www.transparency.org/en/cpi/2020/index/nzl. South Korea is ranked thirty-third.
69. Nina Mazar and Pankaj Aggarwal, "Greasing the Palm: Can Collectivism Promote Bribery?," *Psychological Science* 22 (2011): 843–48, conducted a study showing that collectivism promotes bribery by mitigating an individual's perceived responsibility for their actions, but it focused on offering bribes in an international (that is, outgroup) business exchange. See also Ahmed Seleim and Nick Bontis, "The Relationship between Culture and Corruption: A Cross-National Study," *Journal of Intellectual Capital* (2009): 165–84.
70. Cf. Julius Ary Mollet, "Corruption and Asian Value's in Indonesia: The Case of The Suharto Family Business," *Journal of Social and Political Sciences* 1 (2018): 316.
71. Arun Sok Nhep, "A Christian Perspective on Corruption," *Honeycomb* 4 (2003): 52–53.
72. Richard Langston, *Bribery and the Bible* (Singapore: Campus Crusade Asia, 1991), 76.

Asian cultures today. Gift-giving and reciprocity is an inherent and legitimate part of social interactions which can easily be corrupted into bribery. The OT unambiguously denounces bribery, and biblical teaching is clear about what is an acceptable gift, and in what circumstances and with which motivations it is not acceptable. There is no biblical basis to argue that a gift and a bribe are indistinguishable. Indeed, the OT can only prohibit bribery on the basis that people can distinguish between a gift and a bribe.

The web of cultural values that impact bribery will vary from one Asian country to the next. Nonetheless, there are at least two factors that can be taken into consideration when differentiating between a gift and a bribe. First, the *motivation*: if the gift is given to influence or manipulate the receiver so the giver receives preferential treatment, it is a bribe. After a bribe, there is no further sense of obligation. Second, the *context*: a bribe is given to secure preferential treatment, such as ensuring a favorable verdict in a court case. Gifts given after favorable treatment are generally not considered bribes, such as tips.[73] Also, as mentioned above, bribes have the trait of *covertness*. They are a form of secretive exchange without public disclosure. Although larger-value gifts are normally used for bribery (often but not restricted to money), the value of the gift is not a decisive factor because any gift, no matter how small, can be used as a bribe.

Theological reflection on the OT's teaching yields further differences between a gift and a bribe. A gift is consistent with God's character, while a bribe is not. He gives based on his grace and mercy to establish a personal relationship, first with Israel, and now with all people who trust in Israel's Messiah. He shows us favor by paying the ransom to set us free (Mark 10:45; 1 Tim 2:5–6). God is thus consistent in showing his mercy to the undeserving – first to the Jew, now to all (Rom 9–11).[74] Our response to God's gift of his Son is

---

73. Because of the dynamic nature of relationships and its various cultural expressions, there will be some overlap between the three categories of proper gift exchange, economic transaction, and bribe. For instance, in some Asian countries a gift may be given to a service provider to establish or maintain a relationship with the hope of better future service. The three categories and two main factors can guide decision making, but wisdom is required to apply them to specific situations.

74. John M. G. Barclay, *Paul and the Gift* (Grand Rapids, MI: Eerdmans, 2015), 72–73, describes this as *incongruity* in grace (a gift given without regard to the worth of the recipient). God shows no favoritism in that he accepts "from every nation the one who fears him and does what is right" (Acts 10:34–35). Nonetheless, in the OT he chose Israel as his people to reveal himself to the nations and ultimately to produce the savior for all nations. In other words, God brings about *universal* blessing through *particular* people; see Richard Bauckham, *Bible and Mission: Christian Witness in a Postmodern World* (Grand Rapids, MI: Baker Academic, 2003).

to reciprocate with faith and love and obedience out of gratitude. God gave of himself to us because he knew we could not cover our sin, although he knew we could not fully repay him. We can therefore give freely (Matt 10:8), knowing that since God has already given us his Son, he will give us all that we need (Rom 8:32).[75] If we trust in a just God who will right all wrongs, if not in this life but certainly in the next (Rom 12:19), we need not try to pervert justice for our own benefit.

REFERENCES

Adeney, Bernard T. *Strange Virtues: Ethics in a Multicultural World*. Downers Grove, IL: InterVarsity, 1995.

Alatas, Syed Hussein. *Corruption and the Destiny of Asia*. Rev. ed. Selangor Darul Ehsan: Prentice Hall, 1999.

Argandoña, Antonio. "Private and Public Corruption: Facilitating Payments." In *The Changing Face of Corruption in the Asia Pacific*, edited by Marie dela Rama and Chris Rowley, 71–79. Amsterdam: Elsevier, 2017.

Baker, David L. *Tight Fists or Open Hands?: Wealth and Poverty in Old Testament Law*. Grand Rapids, MI: Eerdmans, 2009.

Barclay, John M. G. *Paul and the Gift*. Grand Rapids, MI: Eerdmans, 2015.

Bauckham, Richard. *Bible and Mission: Christian Witness in a Postmodern World*. Grand Rapids, MI: Baker Academic, 2003.

Bendor, Shunya. *The Social Structure of Ancient Israel: The Institution of the Family (beit 'ab) from the Settlement to the End of the Monarchy*. Jerusalem Biblical Studies 7. Jerusalem: Simor, 1996.

Blenkinsopp, Joseph. "The Family in First Temple Israel." In *Families in Ancient Israel*, edited by Leo G. Perdue et al., 49–57. Louisville, KY: Westminster John Knox, 1997.

Brett, Mark G. "Nationalism and the Hebrew Bible." In *The Bible in Ethics*, edited by John W. Rogerson, Margaret Davies, and M. Daniel Carroll, 136–63. Sheffield: Sheffield Academic Press, 1995.

"Corruption Perception Index: 2020." Transparency International. Accessed February 11, 2021. https://www.transparency.org/en/cpi/2020/index/nzl.

"Corruption." Lexico. Accessed February 4, 2021. https://www.lexico.com/definition/corruption.

---

75. We can even give to those who cannot give back materially, such as the poor, knowing that God will reciprocate. For the poor recipients of gifts can "bless you" (invoke God's blessing on the donor), so that the gift "will be regarded as a righteous act in the sight of the Lord your God" (Deut 24:13). Similarly, Jesus says we can give to the needy in secret because our reward will be from God in the future (Matt 6:1–4; Luke 14:13–14).

Crook, Zeba A. "Reciprocity: Covenantal Exchange as a Test Case." In *Ancient Israel: The Old Testament in Its Social Context*, edited by Philip Francis Esler. 78–91. Minneapolis, MN: Fortress, 2006.

———. *Reconceptualising Conversion: Patronage, Loyalty, and Conversion in the Religions of the Ancient Mediterranean*. Beihefte zur Zeitschrift für die neutestamentliche Wissenschaft 130. Berlin: de Gruyter, 2006.

Eisenstadt, S. N., and Louis Roniger. "Patron-Client Relations as a Model of Structuring Social Exchange," *Comparative Studies in Society and History* 22 (1980): 42–77.

———. *Patrons, Clients and Friends: Interpersonal Relations and the Structure of Trust in Society*. Cambridge: Cambridge University Press, 1984.

Finkelstein, J. J. "The Middle Assyrian Šulmānu-Texts." *Journal of the American Oriental Society* 72 (1952): 77–80.

Georges, Jayson. *Ministering in Honor-Shame Cultures: Biblical Foundations and Practical Essentials*. Downers Grove, IL: IVP Academic, 2016.

———. *Ministering in Patronage Cultures: Biblical Models and Missional Implications*. Downers Grove, IL: InterVarsity, 2019.

Goldberg, Michael L. "The Story of the Moral: Gifts or Bribes in Deuteronomy?" *Interpretation* 38 (1984): 15–25.

Goodblatt, David M. *Elements of Ancient Jewish Nationalism*. Cambridge: Cambridge University Press, 2006.

Gottwald, Norman K. *The Tribes of Yahweh: A Sociology of the Religion of Liberated Israel, 1250–1050 BCE*. Maryknoll, NY: Orbis, 1979.

Grosby, Steven E. *Biblical Ideas of Nationality: Ancient and Modern*. Winona Lake, IN: Eisenbrauns, 2002.

Grund, Alexandra. "'Schmähungen der dich Schmähenden sind auf mich gefallen': kulturanthropologische und sozialpsychologische Aspekte von Ehre und Scham in Ps 69." *Evangelische Theologie* 72 (2012): 174–93.

Halpern, Baruch. "Jerusalem and the Lineages in the Seventh Century BCE: Kinship and the Rise of Individual Moral Liability." In *Law and Ideology in Monarchic Israel*, edited by Baruch Halpern and Deborah W. Hobson, 49–59. Sheffield: JSOT Press, 1991.

Hamilton, Mark W. "Bribery at the Boundaries of Gift Giving in the Hebrew Bible." *Biblische Notizen* 187 (2020): 39–58.

Harland, P. J. "*betsa*: Bribe, Extortion or Profit?" *Vetus Testamentum* 50 (2000): 310–22.

Houston, Walter J. "What's Just about the Jubilee?: Ideological and Ethical Reflections on Leviticus 25." *Studies in Christian Ethics* 14 (2001): 34–47.

Hwa, Yung. *Bribery and Corruption: Biblical Reflections and Case Studies for the Marketplace in Asia*. Singapore: Graceworks, 2010.

Kemp, Barry J. *Ancient Egypt: Anatomy of a Civilization*. London: Routledge, 1989.
Langston, Richard. *Bribery and the Bible*. Singapore: Campus Crusade Asia, 1991.
Lemche, Niels Peter. *Biblical Studies and the Failure of History*. London: Taylor & Francis, 2014.
Lieven, Anatol. *Pakistan: A Hard Country*. London: Penguin, 2012.
Longman III, Tremper. *Proverbs*. Baker Commentary on the Old Testament Wisdom and Psalms. Grand Rapids, MI: Baker Academic, 2006.
Master, Daniel M. "Economy and Exchange in the Iron Age Kingdoms of the Southern Levant." *Bulletin of the American Schools of Oriental Research* 372 (2014): 81–97.
Mathias, Steffan. *Paternity, Progeny, and Perpetuation: Creating Lives after Death in the Hebrew Bible*. The Library of Hebrew Bible/Old Testament Studies 696. London: T&T Clark, 2020.
Matthews, Victor H., and Don C. Benjamin, *Social World of Ancient Israel 1250–587 BCE*. Peabody, MA: Hendrickson, 1993.
Mauss, Marcel. *The Gift: The Form and Reason for Exchange in Archaic Societies*, translated by W. D. Halls. London: Routledge, 1990.
Mazar, Nina, and Pankaj Aggarwal. "Greasing the Palm: Can Collectivism Promote Bribery?" *Psychological Science* 22 (2011): 843–48.
McVann, Mark. "Family-Centeredness." In *Handbook of Biblical Social Values*, edited by John J. Pilch and Bruce J. Malina, 64–66. Eugene, OR: Cascade, 2016.
Mendels, Doron. *The Rise and Fall of Jewish Nationalism: Jewish and Christian Ethnicity in Ancient Palestine*. Grand Rapids, MI: Eerdmans, 1997.
Meyers, Carol L. "The Family in Early Israel." In *Families in Ancient Israel*, edited by Leo G. Perdue et al., 1–47. Louisville, KY: Westminster John Knox, 1997.
Mischke, Werner. *The Global Gospel: Achieving Missional Impact in Our Multicultural World*. Scottsdale: Mission ONE, 2015.
Mollet, Julius Ary. "Corruption and Asian Value's in Indonesia: The Case of The Suharto Family Business." *Journal of Social and Political Sciences* 1 (2018): 314–25.
Montgomery, David J. "'A Bribe Is a Charm': A Study of Proverbs 17:8." In *The Way of Wisdom: Essays in Honor of Bruce K. Waltke*, 136–42. Grand Rapids, MI: Zondervan, 2000.
Mungiu-Pippidi, Alina. "Corruption: Political and Public Aspects." In *International Encyclopedia of the Social and Behavioral Sciences*, edited by James D. Wright, 12–20. Amsterdam: Elsevier, 2015.
Nhep, Arun Sok. "A Christian Perspective on Corruption." *Honeycomb* 4 (2003): 49–55.
Noonan Jr., John T. *Bribes*. New York: Macmillan, 1984.

Paolo, Mauro. "Corruption and Growth." *The Quarterly Journal of Economics* 110 (1995): 681–712.

Perdue, Leo G. "The Household, Old Testament Theology, and Contemporary Hermeneutics." In *Families in Ancient Israel*, edited by Leo G. Perdue et al., 223–57. Louisville, KY: Westminster John Knox, 1997.

Pfoh, Emanuel O. "Genesis 4 Revisited: Some Remarks on Divine Patronage." *Scandinavian Journal of the Old Testament* 23 (2009): 38–45.

Pitt-Rivers, Julian. "The Paradox of Friendship," translated by Matthew Carey. *HAU: Journal of Ethnographic Theory* 6 (2016): 443–52.

Plevnik, Joseph, and John J. Pilch. "Honor and Shame." In *Handbook of Biblical Social Values*, edited by John J. Pilch and Bruce J. Malina, 89–96. Eugene, OR: Cascade, 2016.

Richards, E. Randolph, and Richard James. *Misreading Scripture with Individualist Eyes: Patronage, Honor, and Shame in the Biblical World*. Downers Grove, IL: IVP Academic, 2020.

Roniger, Louis. "Patron-Client Relations, Social and Anthropological Study of." In *International Encyclopedia of the Social and Behavioral Sciences*, edited by James D. Wright, 603–6. Amsterdam: Elsevier, 2015.

Rose-Ackerman, Susan, and Bonnie J. Palifka. *Corruption and Government: Causes, Consequences, and Reform*. 2nd ed. Cambridge: Cambridge University Press, 2016.

Schloen, J. David. *The House of the Father as Fact and Symbol: Patrimonialism in Ugarit and the Ancient Near East*. Studies in the Archaeology and History of the Levant 2. Winona Lake, IN: Eisenbrauns, 2001.

Seleim, Ahmed, and Nick Bontis. "The Relationship between Culture and Corruption: A Cross-National Study." *Journal of Intellectual Capital* 10 (2009): 165–84.

Sher, Tony H. K. "'Father's House' (*bêt 'āb*) in the Old Testament: Family or Household?" *Hill Road* 14 (2011): 3–19 (Chinese).

Thompson, T. "'House of David': An Eponymic Referent to Yahweh as Godfather." *Scandinavian Journal of the Old Testament* 9 (1995): 59–74.

Triandis, Harry C. "Individualism and Collectivism." In *The Handbook of Culture and Psychology*, edited by David R. Matsumoto, 35–50. Oxford: Oxford University Press, 2001.

Tucker Jr., W. Dennis. "Is Shame a Matter of Patronage in the Communal Laments?" *Journal for the Study of the Old Testament* 31 (2007): 465–80.

Van de Wiele, Tarah. "What Rights get Wrong about Justice for Orphans: An Old Testament Challenge to a Modern Ideology." *Studies in Christian Ethics* 29 (2016): 69–83.

Walsh, John. "Corruption: 1900 to Present: East and Southeast Asia." In *Cultural Sociology of the Middle East, Asia, & Africa: An Encyclopedia*, edited by Andrea L. Stanton, Edward Ramsamy, and Peter J. Seybolt, 253–55. Thousand Oaks, CA: SAGE, 2012.

Waltke, Bruce K. *The Book of Proverbs: Chapters 15–31*. New International Commentary on the Old Testament. Grand Rapids: Eerdmans, 2005.

Walton, John H. "Deuteronomy: An Exposition of the Spirit of the Law." *Grace Theological Journal* 8 (1987): 213–25.

Weeks, Stuart D. E. "Biblical Literature and the Emergence of Ancient Jewish Nationalism." *Biblical Interpretation* 10 (2002): 144–57.

Westbrook, Raymond. "Patronage in the Ancient Near East." *Journal of the Economic and Social History of the Orient* 48 (2005): 210–33.

"What is Corruption." Transparency International. Accessed February 4, 2021. https://www.transparency.org/en/what-is-corruption.

Wright, Christopher J. H. *Old Testament Ethics for the People of God*. Leicester, UK: InterVarsity, 2004.

CHAPTER 12

PROSPERITY THEOLOGY IN ASIA

Description and Evaluation in Light of the Old Testament

Huu-Thien Tran N. and Daniel C. Owens

Prosperity Theology (hereafter PT) is a global phenomenon, from its roots in America to its offshoots and developments in places around the world as diverse as São Paulo, Sydney, Seoul, and Lagos. Although not represented exclusively by a single denomination or organizational structure, PT shares many common beliefs and practices. This chapter seeks to describe and evaluate PT in light of the Bible and particularly the Old Testament, from which the PT movement draws much of its inspiration. This chapter also draws from our experiences in Vietnam and beyond to address the various issues that PT raises.

1. AN OVERVIEW OF PROSPERITY THEOLOGY IN ASIA

Christianity in Asia has been influenced by Western Christianity since Western missionaries arrived and began spreading the gospel. PT is rooted in the West and is "one of the fastest growing religious movements in the world."[1] The message of PT promoted in Asia is similar to what is preached in the West.[2] It has been taught across Asia, including countries such as Vietnam,[3] the

---

1. P. J. Buys, "Paying Unpaid Debts. Reformational Antidotes for Some of the Challenges Posed by Prosperity Gospel Theology," in *Reformed Theology Today: Practical-Theological, Missiological and Ethical Perspectives*, eds. Sarel P. Van der Walt and Nico Vorster (Durbanville, South Africa: AOSIS, 2017), 106.
2. Wonsuk Ma, "Pentecostal Worship in Asia: Its Theological Implications and Contributions," *Asian Journal of Pentecostal Studies* 10 (2007): 150.
3. Vince Le, *Vietnamese Evangelicals and Pentecostalism: The Politics of Divine Intervention*, Global Pentecostal and Charismatic Studies, vol. 29 (Leiden: Brill, 2018), 109–10.

Philippines,[4] Malaysia,[5] Indonesia,[6] Singapore,[7] China,[8] Korea,[9] and India.[10] For example, in Vietnam, books by prominent American prosperity teachers such as Joyce Meyer, Kenneth Hagin, and Joel Osteen have been translated and published in Vietnamese. Joyce Meyer even maintains a Vietnamese website through which her ministry distributes her books and sermons.[11] Examples in other countries could be multiplied, but is it possible to characterize the movement as a whole? What unites the varieties of PT, which also go by other names such as the "prosperity gospel," "health and wealth gospel," "word of faith movement," "positive confession theology," "name-it and claim-it gospel," and "gospel of success"?[12] Broadly speaking, PT claims that all believers with true faith in Jesus Christ can turn spiritual power and blessings into material realities. True faith is manifested in wealth and health, which the Lord will bestow upon those who practice tithing (also known as *sowing and gaining*) and positively confessing the faith in the name of Jesus Christ in their prayers.[13]

---

4. Katharine L. Wiegele, "The Prosperity Gospel among Filipino Catholic Charismatics," in *Pentecostalism and Prosperity: The Socio-Economics of the Global Charismatic Movement*, eds. Katherine Attanasi and Amos Yong (New York: Palgrave Macmillan, 2012), 175–76.
5. Denise A. Austin and Lim Yeu Chuen, "Critical Reflections on the Growth of Pentecostalism in Malaysia," in *Asia Pacific Pentecostalism*, ed. Denise A. Austin, Jacqueline Grey, and Paul W. Lewis, Global Pentecostal and Charismatic Studies, vol. 31 (Leiden: Brill, 2019), 202.
6. Gani Wiyono, "Pentecostalism in Indonesia," in *Asia Pacific Pentecostalism*, 261.
7. Mathew Mathews, "Pentecostalism in Singapore: History, Adaptation and Future," in *Asia Pacific Pentecostalism*, 275.
8. Nanlai Cao, "Urban Property as Spiritual Resource: The Prosperity Gospel Phenomenon in Coastal China," in *Pentecostalism and Prosperity*, 153.
9. Joel Tejedo, "Asian Perspectives on Prosperity Theology, Simplicity and Poverty," in *Prosperity Theology and the Gospel: Good News or Bad News for the Poor?*, ed. J. Daniel Salinas, Lausanne Library (Peabody, MA: Hendrickson Publishers, 2017), 136.
10. Jonathan D. James, "Global, 'Glocal' and Local Dynamics in Calvary Temple: India's Fastest Growing Megachurch," in *Handbook of Megachurches*, ed. Stephen Hunt, Brill Handbooks on Contemporary Religion, vol. 19 (Leiden: Brill, 2019), 309.
11. "Joyce Meyer Ministries – Vietnamese," accessed August 15, 2021, https://tv.joycemeyer.org/vietnamese.
12. David W. Jones and Russell S. Woodbridge, *Health, Wealth, and Happiness: How the Prosperity Gospel Overshadows the Gospel of Christ* (Grand Rapids, MI: Kregel Publications, 2011), 15; C. J. P. (Nelus) Niemandt, "The Prosperity Gospel, the Decolonisation of Theology, and the Abduction of Missionary Imagination," *Missionalia* 45 (2017): 210.
13. Kate Bowler, *Blessed: A History of the American Prosperity Gospel* (New York: Oxford University Press, 2013), 7, 129–32, 187–88; Valdir Steuernagel and Maicon Steuernagel, "Historical Overview: Cape Town and Our Mission," in *Prosperity Theology and the Gospel*, 56.

In response, critics of the movement charge PT with misinterpreting the Bible,[14] misrepresenting the gospel of Jesus Christ,[15] and misunderstanding God's purposes for Christians in this life.[16] As a result, many contemporary teachers who are labeled as prosperity theologians deny that they are spreading PT. For example, the Singaporean pastor Joseph Prince claims that he has not preached any form of the prosperity gospel, though he does teach that material blessings must be the result of Jesus's gospel.[17] American Joel Osteen also states, "I don't really know what the prosperity gospel is," but he believes that in this life God wants all Christians to prosper in business, flourish in their careers, relationships, and family, and enjoy good health.[18] Although prosperity teachers may reject the label of PT, their theologies share four main themes (which they support using the Bible passages in parentheses):

1. The Abrahamic covenant promises material blessings to Christians through redemption in Jesus Christ (Gen 12:1–3; Gal 3:13–14).
2. Jesus's redemption through his death on the cross provides physical health and healing (Isa 53:5; 1 Pet 2:24).
3. Positive confession in prayer is the means for the believer to receive prosperity from God (Prov 18:20–21; Jas 4:2).
4. Tithing and generous giving are avenues to gain abundant material returns from God (Mal 3:10; Mark 10:29–30).[19]

Despite the controversies over PT mentioned above, Asian Christians are naturally drawn to PT for several reasons. Many Asians live in underdeveloped

---

14. Numerous examples of prosperity teachers' misreading the Bible will be found at Ken L. Sarles, "A Theological Evaluation of the Prosperity Gospel," *BSac* 143 (1986): 337–47; Douglas J. Moo, "Divine Healing in the Health and Wealth Gospel," *TJ* 9 (1988): 201–9; Femi Adeleye, "The Prosperity Gospel and Poverty: An Overview and Assessment," in *Prosperity Theology and the Gospel*, 13–15.
15. Adeleye, "The Prosperity Gospel and Poverty," 16; J. Daniel Salinas, "Mainline Churches and Prosperity Theology in Latin America," in *Prosperity Theology and the Gospel*, 115–22.
16. Prabo Mihindukulasuriya, "Prosperity Theology," in *South Asia Bible Commentary: A One-Volume Commentary on the Whole Bible*, ed. Brian Wintle (Grand Rapids, MI: Zondervan, 2015), 637; Tejedo, "Asian Perspectives," 140; Steuernagel and Steuernagel, "Historical Overview," 63.
17. Jayeel Cornelio and Erron Medina, "The Prosperity Ethic: The Rise of the New Prosperity Gospel," in *Routledge International Handbook of Religion in Global Society* (London: Routledge, 2020), 71.
18. Michelle A. Vu, "Interview: Joel Osteen on Prosperity Gospel, Crystal Cathedral, and Jesus," The Christian Post, accessed August 14, 2021, https://www.christianpost.com/news/interview-joel-osteen-on-prosperity-gospel-crystal-cathedral-and-jesus.html.
19. Jones and Woodbridge, *Health, Wealth, and Happiness*, 82–102; Tejedo, "Asian Perspectives," 139.

and developing countries, and they face poverty and struggle for daily physical survival. Such people seek a holistic solution and hope from the gospel. Wonsuk Ma states,

> Most of such under-developed and developing areas are in the non-western world, where worldviews tend to be holistic. The demarcation between the material and spiritual realms in such places is not as clear as in the western world. Christianity cannot simply be restricted to religious matters such as sin, forgiveness, eternal life, etc., while physical and material concerns are assigned to different mission programs such as development, education, hospitals, etc. Only after a life can survive physically, will the soul have a chance to learn of spiritual matters.[20]

Amos Yong observes that some Asians believe in Jesus Christ because they have experienced divine healing or have witnessed others being healed. Other Asians have experienced God in terms of not only spiritual salvation, but also through the material realm of his provision of jobs and support for their financial needs. For both groups, the gospel is holistic in that it speaks both to spiritual and physical needs,[21] as is true for believers in Vietnam. For example, many Vietnamese drug addicts have been healed from their addiction through faith in Jesus Christ. As of 2018, fifty-two drug rehab centers have been established in Vietnam by churches, and more than 1,900 drug addicts have experienced complete healing through their ministries. Even the Vietnamese government has recognized this outstanding work,[22] for the rate of successful healing from drug addiction in those drug rehab centers is 55.1%.[23] This phenomenon of PT's attractiveness for addressing physical and material matters is evident in other parts of Asia as well.[24] Joel Tejedo thus acknowledges

---

20. Wonsuk Ma, "David Yonggi Cho's Theology of Blessing: Basis, Legitimacy, and Limitations," *ERT* 35 (April 2011): 147.
21. Amos Yong, "A Typology of Prosperity Theology: A Religious Economy of Global Renewal or a Renewal Economics?," in *Pentecostalism and Prosperity*, 23.
22. Chu Thanh Vân, "Đồng bào tôn giáo gắn bó với dân tộc, đồng hành cùng đất nước," December 24, 2018, https://baotintuc.vn/news-20181224172939140.htm.
23. "Bộ Công an Ngỏ ý Muốn Quản Lý Trung Tâm Cai Nghiện Ma Túy," accessed September 8, 2021, https://www.rfa.org/vietnamese/in_depth/should-the-ministry-of-public-security-manage-drug-addiction-centers-11132020120749.html.
24. Tejedo, "Asian Perspectives," 137; Austin and Chuen, "Critical Reflections," 202; Vinay K. Samuel, "A Biblical Ethical Assessment of Prosperity Teaching and the Blessing Movement," in *Prosperity Theology and the Gospel*, 80.

that PT gives hope to people struggling with poverty or sickness, though he maintains that this theology is unbiblical.[25]

The remainder of this chapter will examine some common misreadings of the Bible by PT teachers and outline a better biblical theology of prosperity that is simultaneously faithful to the Bible and brings hope to Asians in poverty, suffering, and illness. Three aspects will be explored. First, we will see that God's blessings are not always embodied through wealth, and in fact the Bible even warns God's people about the dangers of wealth. Since faithful believers may not always be blessed with prosperity, we will also see that suffering is an inevitable part of the Christian life on the earth, even as believers experience hope in the midst of adversity. Finally, prayer for physical healing in PT needs to be tempered by a more biblical understanding of the atonement, the fear of the Lord, and the eschatological realities of life on this side of the return of Christ.

2. PROSPERITY AND SUFFERING IN BIBLICAL PERSPECTIVE

Biblical teaching regarding prosperity is more nuanced than the claim by prosperity teachers that God will grant the blessings of prosperity (including wealth and physical healing) to all believers who positively confess their faith. The claims of prosperity teachers are simply insufficient to account for the fullness of the Bible's teaching on these matters. The problem begins with an inadequate understanding of the Abrahamic Covenant. In addition, PT lacks a complete account of the Bible's teaching about wealth and suffering.

2.1. Prosperity Theology's Misinterpretation of the Abrahamic Covenant

That the Abrahamic covenant promises prosperity to Christians through redemption in Jesus Christ (Gen 12:1–3; Gal 3:13–14) is generally recognized as "an important component of prosperity theology."[26] This theme is the source of other themes such as positive confession as well as giving and reaping.[27] Prosperity teachers argue, for instance, that God's covenant with Abraham brought him many material blessings (Gen 12:1–3; 13:2). Pointing to Paul's statements in Galatians that "Christ redeemed us from the curse

---

25. Tejedo, "Asian Perspectives," 137, 146; C. Rosalee Velloso Ewell, "Can We Offer a Better Theology? Banking on the Kingdom," in *Prosperity Theology and the Gospel*, 162.
26. Jones and Woodbridge, *Health, Wealth, and Happiness*, 92.
27. Dennis P. Hollinger, "Enjoying God Forever: An Historical/Sociological Profile of the Health and Wealth Gospel," *TJ* 9 (1988): 132.

of the law in order that the blessing given to Abraham might come to the Gentiles through Christ Jesus" (Gal 3:13–14), and "if you belong to Christ, then you are Abraham's seed, and heirs according to the promise" (Gal 3:29), PT preachers claim that Christians are Abraham's heirs through Christ who are also destined to receive the prosperity promised in the Abrahamic covenant.[28] Just as Abraham received the blessings of this covenant by faith and by tithing, which is itself an act of faith (Gen 12–15), Christians today supposedly receive these blessings through faith (Rom 4:2–5, 13–14; Gal 3:11–14)[29] and through tithing (Gen 14; Heb 7:1–22).[30] In addition, prosperity teachers point to several other biblical passages that make certain affirmations about wealth and material blessings (e.g. 3 John 2; Deut 8:18; Mal 3:10; Prov 19:17; Mark 10:25–30; Luke 6:38).[31]

To what extent do such ideas strike an accurate balance regarding the Bible's teaching about material prosperity in the life of God's people? Prosperity teachers rightly indicate that the Abrahamic covenant promised material blessings to Abraham and his descendants (see these promises in Gen 12:1—13:2). These promises were indeed fulfilled in Abraham's material prosperity during his own lifetime, God's provision for his descendants to become a nation, and their inheritance of the land of promise in later generations.

At the same time, prosperity teachers misread Galatians 3:13–14 and 3:29 by ignoring their literary context. According to the second half of Galatians 3:14, the blessing that Abraham's heirs receive is the blessing of the Holy Spirit, not material blessings.[32] Moreover, the whole of Galatians 3 aims to explain the blessing of justification for Gentiles. Like Abraham, who believed in God and was reckoned as righteous (Gal 3:6), Gentiles who have faith in Jesus Christ are justified before God in Christ, not by works of the law (Gal 3:1–13). The Gentiles' justification by faith in Christ fulfills God's covenant with Abraham, which states that Gentiles would be blessed in Abraham and

---

28. Kenneth Copeland, *The Laws of Prosperity* (Fort Worth, TX: Kenneth Copeland Publications, 1974), 43–44; Copeland, *The Blessing of the Lord: Makes Rich and He Adds No Sorrow With It* (Fort Worth, TX: Kenneth Copeland Publications, 2011), 95–97, 194; Kenneth E. Hagin, *Redeemed from Poverty, Sickness and Spiritual Death*, 2nd ed. (Tulsa, OK: Faith Library Publications, 1995), 8–9.
29. Copeland, *The Blessing of the Lord*, 250–52.
30. Kenneth E. Hagin, *The Midas Touch: A Balanced Approach to Biblical Prosperity* (Tulsa, OK: Faith Library Publications, 2000), 76–77.
31. Copeland, *The Laws of Prosperity*, 44–58; Oral Roberts, *Seed-Faith 2000: Spiritual, Physical, and Financial Increase Through the Power of Seed-Faith* (Tulsa, OK: Oral Roberts, 1999), 35–44; Hagin, *The Midas Touch*, 79–90; Hagin, *Redeemed from Poverty*, 8–13.
32. Sarles, "A Theological Evaluation of the Prosperity Gospel," 347.

become Abraham's heirs (Gen 12:3; Gal 3:14–29). For these reasons, prosperity teachers are mistaken in understanding Galatians 3 to mean that all who have faith in Jesus Christ will enjoy material prosperity. On this note, a different epistle of Paul describes his life of faith in Jesus Christ not in terms of physical prosperity, but rather physical sufferings such as persecution, torture, lack of food, water and clothing (2 Cor 11:22–29). Hebrews 11:36–39 likewise states that many who had great faith in God did not enjoy material prosperity. Therefore, the PT vision of all Christians experiencing material prosperity overlooks the Bible's broader depiction of Christians under the Abrahamic covenant and its blessings.

2.2. Key Biblical Corrections to PT's View of Wealth and Suffering

The PT view of wealth and suffering is also undermined by an inadequate understanding of wealth and suffering. A fuller account of the biblical data leads to two key corrections: (1) Not all of God's people are granted wealth, and (2) Suffering is an inevitable part of the life of God's people.

2.2.1. Not all of God's people are granted wealth

To understand wealth in the life of the believer, we need to look at the bigger picture that the Bible offers. In the covenant with Israel made at Sinai, material prosperity was a blessing promised by God to a chosen people who were to fear him and obey his laws (e.g. Deut 11:13–15; Lev 26:3–13; Pss 1:1–3; 112:1–3; Prov 10:22). Although godly Israelites were promised material blessings, Yahweh also warned his people about several dangers of wealth. First, wealth itself is neutral, but may become a temptation. This is why God prohibits greed (Exod 20:17). Later passages elaborate on the Decalogue by saying that the desire for wealth and the love of money is a root of all kinds of evil (Ps 10:3; 1 Tim 6:9–10; Heb 13:5), so that those who exploit others and hoard wealth are condemned (Jas 5:1–6).

Second, Deuteronomy 8:17–18 warns that wealth can lead God's people to trust in human power instead of him. This warning also reverberates in many psalms. For example, Psalm 10:3–6 describes the wicked person whose wealth leads to pride and a heart that does not seek the Lord (cf. Ps 52:7). The speaker in Proverbs 30 similarly acknowledges the danger of wealth and asks the Lord to support his daily needs, as receiving the gift of riches may become a temptation for him to disown the Lord (vv. 8–9).

Since wealth may be dangerous for people, Jesus Christ followed in the same line when he taught that "life does not consist in an abundance of possessions" (Luke 12:15). Indeed, the promise of material prosperity to godly Israelites was in keeping with the physical nature of God's covenant which envisioned life in the promised land. This promise was not straightforwardly transferred to the church under the new covenant. While PT motivates believers by supposedly biblical promises of wealth, the NT also indicates that faithful believers in Jerusalem and Macedonia were poor (Rom 15:26; 2 Cor 8:1–2), while emphasizing the spiritual nature of the blessings promised to all Christians (Eph 1:1–14). Certainly, the presence of the kingdom of God in the ministry of Jesus provides a foretaste of the eventual material wholeness and prosperity of the Kingdom. However, OT passages such as Isaiah 11:1–9, Isaiah 65:17–25, and a NT passage such as Revelation 21 locate the experience of that wholeness and prosperity most fully in the return of Christ and the reign of the Lord.

Since wealth is not promised to every believer, is it the case that God does not bless Christians with wealth at all? Although the Bible speaks of the dangers of wealth, it does not deny altogether the value of possessions. Instead, it urges the rich to use their money and treasure to help those in need. The OT highlights the value of working hard to obtain wealth (Prov 10:4; 12:27; 21:5), partly to help people in need (Deut 24:19–21). This principle can also be found in the NT, as when God's people are urged to work hard, earn a sufficient living, and even have surplus for the needy (2 Cor 8:1–15; Eph 4:28; 2 Thess 3:11–13; Jas 2:14–17; 1 John 3:17–18). God is willing to enrich his people in every way for them to exhibit an abundance of good works that glorify him (2 Cor 9:6–15). For this reason, Wonsuk Ma is among those who rightly indicate that Christians must examine their motives for seeking material blessings. He notes that it is correct to ask God to bless our hard work to sustain us and enable us to serve others, but it is wrong to ask for his blessings merely to satisfy our own desires.[33]

Many Asian contexts reflect this biblical picture of people following Christ and experiencing spiritual blessings and God's gracious work in the midst of economic hardship. For instance, when Western missionaries came to Vietnam, they found that Vietnamese people were characterized both by "dire poverty"

---

33. Wonsuk Ma, "David Yonggi Cho's Theology of Blessing," 158–59.

and being "spiritually lost."³⁴ After a century of evangelism, most Vietnamese Christians have not become rich, yet have experienced the spiritual blessings of knowing Christ so that they are no longer spiritually lost. At the same time, Vietnamese Christians have experienced God's provision for their daily life, as in the great famine of 1944–1945 during World War II. A food shortage in northern Vietnam led to the deaths of two million Vietnamese people. According to a reliable account, however, "not a single member of the Evangelical Church in the north died of starvation in spite of their well-known poverty."³⁵ In sum, Vietnamese Christians have not become rich after conversion, but God has been at work among the Vietnamese Christian community to help them overcome adversity.

Moreover, Vietnamese Christians are like the Christians of Macedonia who were poor but still gave generously to support Christians needier than themselves (2 Cor 8:1–15). For instance, several clubs of Vietnamese Christian workers have been established, such as the CBMC Vietnam (Connecting Business and Marketplace to Christ) and the A&B (Aquila & Beritsin (Priscilla) Christian clubs. These clubs encourage Vietnamese Christians of all denominations to uphold integrity in their financial gain, use their surplus to give to needy people, and contribute generously to the work of God. Ministry thus also happens in the marketplace when Vietnamese Christians who are blessed by God seek to become God's blessing to others.

2.2.2. *Suffering is an inevitable part of the life of God's people*

God indeed does not always bless Christians with material prosperity, for a far greater number of his people face suffering of some kind. C. S. Song observes that for Asians, "suffering is first and foremost a physical reality."³⁶ In a study that compares Christians across the world, it is estimated that one in twelve Asian Christians regularly face significant suffering.³⁷ Such an experience mirrors the OT's teaching that the approach of the day of the Lord will

---

34. R. H. Glover, "Principles of Christian Missions," *Alliance Weekly*, February 12, 1921, 730. Quoted in Quynh-Hoa Le Nguyen, "Tin Lành: The Bible and the Construction of an Evangelical Vietnamese Christian Identity (1975–2007)" (PhD diss., Claremont Graduate University, 2013), 174.
35. Le Hoang Phu, "A Short History of the Evangelical Church of Vietnam (1911–1965)" (PhD diss., New York University, 1972), 283.
36. Choan-Seng Song, *The Compassionate God* (Maryknoll, NY: Orbis Books, 1982), 162.
37. Kar Yong Lim, "A Theology of Suffering and Mission for the Asian Church," in *Asian Christian Theology: Evangelical Perspectives*, ed. Timoteo D. Gener and Stephen T. Pardue (Carlisle, UK: Langham Global Library, 2019), 181.

bring severe suffering, including terror, disaster, destruction, hardship, war, injury, diseases, sickness, persecution, oppression, loss of property, failure of crops, starvation, killing, and death (Isa 2:12–21; 24:1–23; 26:20–21; Zech 14:1–21; Matt 24:1–51; Luke 17:20–37; 21:5–28). The aforementioned list of passages indicates that this will be the case for all people, including God's people. Indeed, the Bible teaches that the Lord uses suffering, whether suffering for sin or innocent suffering, for the benefit of his children and his glory.[38]

The balanced character of the Bible's teaching on suffering deserves further comment. On the one hand, God uses suffering as the means to discipline his people so that they might repent of their sins. This is God's purpose as indicated, for example, in Leviticus 26:14–33. This passage outlines the covenant theology that God will bring suffering on his people if they do not repent, while suffering will cease when they do. Many narratives in the OT demonstrate this retribution principle (e.g. Judg 3:7–4:24; 6:1–8:35), which is found in the NT as well (e.g. John 5:14; 1 Cor 11:27–34; Col 3:25). Thus, suffering for sin is one means that God uses to bring people back to him.

The concept of suffering for sin is familiar in Asian cultures. Adherents of certain Eastern religions share the concept of *karma* (a key belief within Buddhism, Hinduism, Jainism, and Sikhism) which hold that suffering is always the consequence of sin. However, the concept of karma (which literally means "action" in Sanskrit) is different from the biblical understanding of suffering for sin. In these religions, karma holds that people suffer in this life because of their bad actions (i.e. bad karma) in a previous life, while good actions in this life (i.e. good karma) will deliver them from the cycle of rebirth and suffering in a next life.[39]

Traditional Vietnamese also believe in the connection between sin and suffering, though the traditional culture and religions of the Vietnamese people are a mixture of animism, Buddhism, Taoism, and Confucianism.[40] This means that Vietnamese ideas about suffering are different from the concept of karma. Traditional Vietnamese believe that when people pass away, they arrive at a place in an outside world called "yellow stream" (or "the nine streams")

---

38. Contrast Kenneth E. Hagin, *The Key to Scriptural Healing*, Fourteenth printing (Tulsa, OK: Faith Library Publications, 1995), 17, who states, "God is glorified through healing and deliverance; not through sickness and suffering."
39. John Arun Kumar, "Karma and Fatalism," in *South Asia Bible Commentary: A One-Volume Commentary on the Whole Bible*, ed. Brian Wintle (Grand Rapids, MI: Zondervan, 2015), 1051.
40. Reg Reimer, *Vietnam's Christians: A Century of Growth in Adversity* (Pasadena, CA: William Carey Library, 2011), 13. Only 16% of Vietnamese identify as Buddhist (accessed September 8, 2021. https://vn.usembassy.gov/vi/irfreport2018/).

rather than experiencing reincarnation (as in Buddhism).⁴¹ Consequently, the Vietnamese do not hold that sins or bad actions in this life relate to their next life as claimed in reincarnation but rather to their children's lives. This belief is demonstrated in a Vietnamese folk saying, "*Doi cha an man, doi con khat nuoc*" ("the sins of the fathers are visited upon the children").⁴² This is similar to the Israelite proverb that the OT prophets quote in order to debunk, "The parents eat sour grapes, and the children's teeth are set on edge" (Jer 31:29; Ezek 18:2). Moreover, traditional Vietnamese understand retribution to be the experience of negative outcomes for evil actions in the present life rather than a previous life (as in karma). As another Vietnamese folk saying states, "*Qua bao nhan tien*" ("retribution appears before one's eyes"). This belief is similar to God's principle of discipline already mentioned in Leviticus 26:14–33 (cf. Deut 28:15–68).

But whether for Israelites, the Vietnamese, or any people who hold to divine retribution, the key question is whether people can ever guarantee that they have accomplished enough good to deliver them from suffering. On this note, Isaiah 64:6 declares, "All of us have become like one who is unclean, and all our righteous acts are like filthy rags" (cf. Rom 3:23). The prophet Jeremiah also asserts that people's hearts are deceitful and beyond cure, so we all will be under God's examination and judgment (Jer 17:9–10; cf. Heb 9:27). Thus, the Bible not only shares with Asian religions the belief that people suffer because of their sin, but goes further in revealing that suffering for sin is also a means for God to turn people back to him. The previous section already mentioned that the Abrahamic blessings are for both Gentiles and Israelites in terms of spiritual blessings (Gen 12:1–3; Gal 3:13–29). This principle resonates with the experience of Vietnamese Christians, among whom there is a consensus that non-Christians who have a personal crisis or experience suffering are more likely to open their hearts to the gospel and turn to Jesus Christ as their Savior.⁴³ So suffering can play a key role in bringing people closer to God.

On the other hand, it is also true that righteous and godly people in the Bible endured much suffering without always bearing blame for the fact that they were suffering. This contrasts starkly with PT teaching that suffering is a sign of a lack of faith or God's favor. Regarding this kind of suffering by the

---

41. Truong Van Thien Tu, "*Mệnh Trời*: Toward a Vietnamese Theology of Mission" (PhD Diss., The Graduate Theological Union, 2009), 158. Tu indicates, "There is no evidence that traditional Vietnamese people believed in reincarnation before Buddhism came to Vietnam."
42. Traditional Vietnamese ideas have been demonstrated in many folk stories and sayings.
43. Le, *Vietnamese Evangelicals and Pentecostalism*, 67.

innocent, the author of Psalm 73 laments that the wicked are always at ease and prosperous (Ps 73:3–11), while the faithful suffer (Ps 73:13–14). Many OT passages similarly indicate that when faithful and righteous people endure innocent suffering, those afflictions help them to grow in their faith since the Lord uses adversities to test, teach, and purify them according to God's will (Job 23:10; Ps 66:10; Isa 48:10; cf. Jas 1:2–4; 1 Pet 1:6–7).

This is precisely what happened to the church in Jerusalem during the apostolic era. In the midst of poverty, they were forced to depend on support from other churches for their survival (Rom 15:25–27; 2 Cor 9:1–5). Jesus foretells that believers should expect trouble and suffering (John 16:33) since they enter a narrow path to reach life (Matt 7:13–14). Paul also highlighted this principle when he stated in Romans that "we also glory in our sufferings, because we know that suffering produces perseverance; perseverance, character; and character, hope" (Rom 5:3–5). Likewise, the Lord did not take away the thorn in Paul's flesh, though he prayed earnestly three times. Instead, God used this suffering to keep Paul from becoming conceited and to help him grow in endurance through his weakness (2 Cor 12:7–10). In sum, faithful Christians will be encouraged in the midst of suffering since the Bible affirms that they share in Christ's sufferings and the hope of sharing in his glory (Phil 3:8–10; 1 Pet 4:12–13).

By contrast, Asians who believe in the concept of karma and face innocent suffering are often hopeless and helpless in the face of suffering as they consider it the outcome of their bad karma in a previous life.[44] According to this understanding, the hope that they have been good people in this life cannot change their fate in the same life because their good deeds affect only their next life. Conversely, those who trust in God can have hope and joy through innocent suffering because of God's justice and God's good will for them through suffering. Joseph was one such believer in Yahweh who experienced God's good will for both him and many others through his innocent suffering. While Joseph's brothers expected retribution from him, he instead summarized his experience in terms of God's sovereignty: "You intended to harm me, but God intended it for good to accomplish what is now being done, the saving of many lives" (Gen 50:20). Many psalms of lament and reorientation demonstrate this same profession of faith (e.g. Pss 10; 12; 13; 17; 28; 35; 44; 56; 86; 88; 140–143).

Similarly, Vietnamese Christians have experienced God's good will through suffering. God has used the suffering of the church in Vietnam to sift and

---

44. Kumar, "Karma and Fatalism," 1051.

purify her. Thousands of Vietnamese people who did not have genuine faith in the Lord fell away during the war of independence (1945–1954) and again after the end of the civil war in 1975.[45] Yet, the Church was purified since both remaining members and new ones were tested through their suffering and proved to be true believers. Truly, suffering has resulted in perseverance, character, and hope in the lives of Vietnam's faithful Christians (cf. Rom 5:3–5).

Besides ethnic Vietnamese Christians who have learned these lessons, the Hmong are a minority who have similarly often coped with severe persecution and poverty after conversion to Christianity. Despite their suffering, many of them have faithfully followed Jesus Christ and persisted in studying the Bible and sharing the gospel because they have been taught and encouraged to join in suffering with the early church for the sake of the gospel, by the power of God (2 Tim 1:8).[46] In contrast, Vietnamese non-believers usually doubt God's justice, complain, and moan when they suffer and do not know why.[47] In summary, both biblical teaching and the testimony of Vietnam's Christians refute the PT position's view that suffering does not glorify God.[48] He is sovereign to use either suffering for sins or innocent suffering for the benefit of his people.

3. PRAYER AND HEALING IN BIBLICAL PERSPECTIVE

Just as wealth and suffering must be kept in proper biblical perspective, the same applies to prayer, healing, and sickness. In much of rural Vietnam, where quality medical care is not always ready to hand, Christians do not usually think first to seek medical care when loved ones fall ill or are injured. Their first response is instead to pray and to ask the community to pray for healing. While this faith-filled response honors God, there is likely also some influence from PT's teaching (with perhaps sometimes a worldview that naturally seeks first for spiritual power rather than medical technology for solutions to physical problems). On this note, it is less than clear whether PT leads believers rightly by directing them *merely* to pray for healing. The broad influence of this teaching can be seen in many Asian evangelical churches when believers pray and claim Isaiah 53:5d as God's promise that "by his stripes we are healed!" The next section will explore and critique the presuppositions of the PT movement's understanding of prayer which expects healing as part

---

45. Reimer, *Vietnam's Christians*, 37, 57–58.
46. Reimer, *Vietnam's Christians*, 76.
47. Truong Van Thien Tu, "*Mệnh Trời*: Toward a Vietnamese Theology of Mission," 153.
48. Cf. Hagin, *The Key to Scriptural Healing*, 17.

of the atonement, uses positive confession to claim it, and assumes a highly realized eschatology.

3.1. Prosperity Theology's Misguided Theology of Prayer for Healing

First, undergirding prayer for healing in the PT movement is an *overly expansive view of the atonement*. According to this position, Christ purchased the guarantee of healing through his cross so that healing is ready to be claimed as a *legal* right for believers in the present age. As hinted, advocates of this understanding base their expectation on a literal understanding of Isaiah 53:5d as referring to physical healing. The Singaporean pastor Joseph Prince explains,

> At the cross, God also took all our sicknesses and diseases and put them on Jesus' originally perfect and healthy body, so that we can walk in divine health. That is why the Bible says by his stripes, we are healed (Isa 53:5, 1 Pet 2:24).[49]

The American pastor Kenneth Hagin likewise insists, "Nothing is left out of the redemptive work of Christ: not a headache, not a stomachache, not any kind of cancer, nor any kind of heart trouble."[50] Although Pentecostals usually affirm that the atonement provides for our healing,[51] PT teachers go further and assert that both healing and an end to poverty are *guaranteed* by the death and resurrection of Christ.[52] As an Asian pastor-theologian who is also a Pentecostal himself, the Indian writer David Prasanna Kumar Mende affirms divine healing, but warns against the PT view that believers can therefore *expect* healing.[53] So in contrast to mainstream Pentecostalism, PT argues that if the atonement provides for it, then we should claim it. In effect, God's power has become God's will.

Second, PT teaches the practice of *positive confession*. Popularly known as "name-it and claim-it" theology, positive confession is characterized by "the

---

49. Joseph Prince, "The Power of The Holy Communion," *Joseph Prince Ministries*, accessed August 9, 2021, https://www.josephprince.org/blog/articles/the-power-of-the-holy-communion.
50. Kenneth E. Hagin, "Does God Want Me to Be Sick?," *Rhema*, June 22, 2017, accessed August 9, 2021, https://events.rhema.org/is-it-gods-will-to-heal/.
51. Wolfgang Vondey, *Pentecostalism* (London: Bloomsbury, 2013), 102; "Assemblies of God 16 Fundamental Truths," Assemblies of God, accessed August 9, 2021, https://ag.org/Beliefs/Statement-of-Fundamental-Truths.
52. Bowler, *Blessed*, 95.
53. David Prasanna Kumar Mende, "A Biblical Analysis of the Main Teachings of the Prosperity Gospel, with Special Reference to the Preachers of Hyderabad, India," *Journal of Asian Evangelical Theology* 23 (March 2019): 27.

idea that faith requires verbal declaration, and that the faithful receive what they claim by their vocal declaration of faith."[54] Positive confession derives its intellectual roots from the "New Thought" of E. W. Kenyon, who ministered in the United States about the time that American Pentecostalism was born. Kenyon believed that the atonement gave believers a legal authority to demand health and wealth in the name of Jesus.[55] Building on Kenyon, the American writer Fred F. Bosworth reasoned that positive confession *forces* God to act to fulfill his promises. One thus needs to speak the demand to obtain it.[56] Kenneth Hagin also described this as "the law of faith" which is the spiritual analogue to natural forces like gravity, by working invisibly to actualize God's promises of health and wealth in the real world.[57] Whether known as the "prayer of faith" or "positive confession," PT advocates assert that this practice claims the results that Christ achieved on the cross. By the act of speaking, believers claim what is already theirs in Christ. Any failure to receive is consequently a failure of faith.

Third, PT adds to its understanding of the atonement and positive confession with a *highly realized eschatology*. Kenyon contrasted hope with faith: hope looks for a result in the future, but faith claims the reality now.[58] Believers in the PT tradition will even praise God for something they have not yet experienced as if it were already so.[59] The title of American pastor Joel Osteen's famous book, *Your Best Life Now* (2004), captures the eschatology of the movement in brief, namely, that the fullness of human flourishing is for those who would seize it now. Or framed in biblical terms, PT would say that the blessings of the kingdom of God are not for some future time, but for the present age, for believers to claim now.

3.2. Key Biblical Corrections to PT's View of Prayer and Healing

What does the OT say about this quasi-magical approach to prayer and healing? Certainly, healing in response to prayer is attested in the OT. This is the case, for example, in the raising of the Shunammite's son (2 Kgs 4:8–37) and

---

54. Vondey, *Pentecostalism*, 102.
55. Bowler, *Blessed*, 20.
56. Bowler, 21.
57. Bowler, 45.
58. E. W. Kenyon, *The Two Kinds of Faith: Faith's Secret Revealed* (Lynnwood, WA: Kenyon's Gospel Publishing Society, 1942), 7.
59. Bowler, *Blessed*, 143.

the healing of Naaman (2 Kgs 5), both of which find their NT counterparts in the healing of many during the ministries of Jesus and the apostles. However, these events were extraordinary. Most fitting for Christians who must consider the entirety of the biblical witness, it is imperative to examine the expectation of healing as based on the atonement. Reading in the literary context of Isaiah 53, does Isaiah 53:5d really speak about physical healing? The verse reads:

> But he was pierced for our transgressions,
>   he was crushed for our iniquities;
> the punishment that brought us peace was on him,
>   and by his wounds we are healed. (Isa 53:5)

Ironically, the wounds inflicted on the Servant are what bring healing to a certain "us" (both Isaiah's own Israelite community as well as Christian believers today). But healing from what? And how can wounds on another bring healing to us?

The four poetic lines of Isaiah 53:5 build in intensity from beginning to end. In the first two lines, the reason for the Servant's suffering is "our transgressions" and "our iniquities."[60] Even from the beginning of the book that bears his name, Isaiah has worked toward the resolution wrought by the Servant for human rebellion against God. The metaphors in Isaiah 53:4–5 of being "stricken" and "wounded" are similar to those of Isaiah 1:5–6, describing the weight of God's discipline on Israel.[61] God laid his "punishment" or "discipline" on the Servant to bring us peace and healing. The Servant suffers vicariously for our sin. The final two lines of Isaiah 53:5 encapsulate the result, namely, a restoration of peace with God. The fundamental work of the atonement to address the sin that brought judgment and thereby heal humanity's severed relationship with God. Read in context, then, Isaiah 53:5d is a rather slim foundation upon which to build expectations for immediate physical healing. While the atonement in its fuller NT understanding paves the way for a restoration of sinners to the abundance of the Kingdom (thus anticipating a reversal of the curse from Genesis 3), it does not in the first instance concern physical healing. The language of healing in Isaiah 53:5 is more of a metaphor.

However, PT proponents may rightly point out Matthew 8:17, which applies the expectation of the Servant in Isaiah 53:4 to Jesus, "He took up

---

60. So also Ken Mbugua, "Misunderstanding the Bible," in *Prosperity?: Seeking the True Gospel* (Bukuru Jos, Plateau State: ACTS Kenya, 2016), 19.
61. John Oswalt, *The Book of Isaiah: Chapters 40–66*, NICOT (Grand Rapids: Eerdmans, 1998), 397.

our infirmities and bore our diseases." It is important to keep in mind that Matthew is describing the actions of Jesus during his Galilean ministry, not prescribing or mandating the experience of future believers. Instead, Jesus was doing something special. Through his healing ministry, Jesus showed that the dawning of the kingdom of God had come (Matt 4:17). Although Isaiah 53:4 does refer to the action of the Servant to bear the diseases of the people, the crucial point is that Jesus's healing ministry culminates in the cross, which deals with the sin that causes disease and brings forgiveness.[62] In his ministry, Jesus gave us a foretaste of the physical wholeness we can expect in the New Creation, but he did not heal everyone. And he did not teach that Christians should *expect* immediate physical healing *whenever* they pray.

If immediate physical healing is not the entitlement of God's children (even if healing is our earnest prayer), what can we expect? As outlined above, the OT, like the NT, is practical in its outlook about suffering. It is a fact to be brought to God for prayer. In one psalm, for example, David juxtaposes suffering and salvation in a stark way:

> The righteous person may [or "will," both are viable
>   renderings] have many troubles,
> but the LORD delivers him from them all. (Ps 34:19; cf.
>   John 16:33)

As with any of the psalms of praise or thanksgiving, David is often exuberant about God's mighty deeds in his life, but just as often David is near to despair in his lament. In this one verse, he brings together praise and lament – the two polarities of the Psalter. The OT expectation of the life of the faithful thus includes *both* suffering *and* deliverance. Most poignant of all on this theme is Psalm 89:49:

> Lord, where is your former great love,
>   which in your faithfulness you swore to David?

If anyone had a concrete promise of deliverance, it would have been David and his descendants. While PT sees sickness as a temptation and healing as dependent on the faith of the believer, the biblical picture of the faithful consistently lies in seeking God in prayer for healing.[63] We should thus not be surprised when the faithful fall ill. Positive confession denies this realism about

---

62. Brian J. Tabb, *After Emmaus: How the Church Fulfills the Mission of Christ* (Wheaton, IL: Crossway, 2021), 171–72.
63. Mende, "Prosperity Gospel," 23–25.

suffering and is not only theologically incorrect, but also pastorally dangerous since it risks victimizing the poor and ill in the name of faith.[64]

In addition, positive confession confuses the role of the creature in relationship to the Creator. Isaiah 66:2 describes the appropriate posture of reverence that finite beings should display toward their Maker: "These are the ones I look on with favor: those who are humble and contrite in spirit, and who tremble at my word." The fear of the Lord precludes demanding that God act in the manner and timing of our choice, as a spoiled child would in demanding candy from his or her mother. The OT certainly leaves room for passionate lament with urgent prayers in seeking to move God to action, but the attitude must always be one of trust and humility that befit a creature seeking the favor of the Creator.

Finally, PT rightly highlights the holistic abundance of God's kingdom, but its highly realized eschatology gets the timing wrong. Isaiah envisioned a future in the new heavens and new earth where weeping and premature death would be no more (Isa 65:19–20; cf. 25:6–8). In the NT, Revelation 21:1–4 takes up the Isaianic hope but places the full presence of God's kingdom *after* the return of Christ.[65] PT thus fails to see the fulfillment of the kingdom in terms of its proper and final referent. They want to see the consummated abundance of the kingdom *now.* Would that it were so! But such is not the plan of God as revealed in Scripture. PT's highly realized eschatology is analogous to the situation in the early sixth century BCE when, in the face of foreign domination, the false prophet Hananiah preached that God would break the yoke of Babylon. Jeremiah replied, "Amen! May the LORD do so!" (Jer 28:6), but such was not the word of the Lord for that moment. Although the new creation will do away with disease and poverty, God has not promised such abundance in this age.

Those who hold out false expectations of this sort are false prophets. God is free and acts according to his own timing and will rather than to our demands. So, we should pray for healing with desperate pleas for mercy and even reminders of the promises of God that are meant to motivate him to act, but in the end the decision belongs to God.

---

64. Christopher J. H. Wright and Lausanne Committee for World Evangelization, "Lausanne Theology Working Group Statement on the Prosperity Gospel," *ERT* 34 (2010): 101.

65. Even granting that John's visions of Revelation may not be in strict temporal order, it is noteworthy that advocates of all views concerning the book recognize that chapters 21–22 are concerned with the final state.

CONCLUSION

PT is a movement that scratches the powerful itch of fallen sinners to be delivered from their poverty, suffering, and disease. Believers in Vietnam and across Asia all share such a longing for wholeness and prosperity. Ultimately, this desire reflects the universal human longing for the kingdom of God. However, PT offers a vision of the Christian life that neither does justice to the complexity of how the Bible treats wealth, suffering, and healing, nor fits the lived experience of God's people through the ages. Although God does affirm the principle that those who work hard will experience his blessings of surplus to help the needy, not all of God's people become rich in the manner envisioned by PT. Suffering is an inevitable part of the Christian life, and the blessings guaranteed to all Christians are always spiritual and only sometimes material in nature. Likewise, prayer for healing is a godly practice for Christians who desire to live whole and healthy lives by the grace of God, who sent Jesus to heal, cast out demons, and inaugurate his kingdom of God on earth. However, the atonement in biblical perspective (both through Isa 53:5 and elsewhere) deals with the heart of the matter – *sin*. It also paves the way for the new creation when God will swallow up death once and for all (Isa 25:8). As Christians wait for the return of Christ, they should fervently seek the grace of healing in the fear of the Lord, who freely gives such healing out of his kindness and mercy rather than as a legal right to be demanded through positive confession. Like the OT saints who looked forward to the coming of the Christ, NT believers can also say with the apostle John, "Amen. Come, Lord Jesus" (Rev 22:20).

REFERENCES

Adeleye, Femi. "The Prosperity Gospel and Poverty: An Overview and Assessment." In *Prosperity Theology and the Gospel: Good News or Bad News for the Poor?*, edited by J. Daniel Salinas, 5–22. Lausanne Library. Peabody, MA: Hendrickson, 2017.

"Assemblies of God 16 Fundamental Truths." Assemblies of God. Accessed August 9, 2021. https://ag.org/Beliefs/Statement-of-Fundamental-Truths.

Austin, Denise A., and Lim Yeu Chuen. "Critical Reflections on the Growth of Pentecostalism in Malaysia." In *Asia Pacific Pentecostalism*, edited by Denise A. Austin, Jacqueline Grey, and Paul W. Lewis, 195–216. Global Pentecostal and Charismatic Studies. Vol. 31. Leiden: Brill, 2019.

"Bộ Công an Ngỏ ý Muốn Quản Lý Trung Tâm Cai Nghiện Ma Túy." Accessed September 8, 2021. https://www.rfa.org/vietnamese/in_depth/should-the-ministry-of-public-security-manage-drug-addiction-centers-11132020120749.html.

Bowler, Kate. *Blessed: A History of the American Prosperity Gospel.* New York: Oxford University Press, 2013.

Buys, P. J. "Paying Unpaid Debts. Reformational Antidotes for Some of the Challenges Posed by Prosperity Gospel Theology." In *Reformed Theology Today: Practical-Theological, Missiological and Ethical Perspectives*, edited by Sarel P. Van der Walt and Nico Vorster, 87–106. Durbanville, South Africa: AOSIS, 2017.

Cao, Nanlai. "Urban Property as Spiritual Resource: The Prosperity Gospel Phenomenon in Coastal China." In *Pentecostalism and Prosperity: The Socio-Economics of the Global Charismatic Movement*, edited by Katherine Attanasi and Amos Yong, 151–70. New York: Palgrave Macmillan, 2012.

Copeland, Kenneth. *The Blessing of the Lord: Makes Rich and He Adds No Sorrow With It.* Fort Worth, TX: Kenneth Copeland Publications, 2011.

———. *The Laws of Prosperity.* Fort Worth, TX: Kenneth Copeland Publications, 1974.

Cornelio, Jayeel, and Erron Medina. "The Prosperity Ethic: The Rise of the New Prosperity Gospel." In *Routledge International Handbook of Religion in Global Society*, edited by Jayeel Cornelio et al., 65–76. London: Routledge, 2020.

Ewell, C. Rosalee Velloso. "Can We Offer a Better Theology? Banking on the Kingdom." In *Prosperity Theology and the Gospel: Good News or Bad News for the Poor?*, edited by J. Daniel Salinas, 161–65. Lausanne Library. Peabody, MA: Hendrickson, 2017.

Hagin, Kenneth E. *Redeemed from Poverty, Sickness and Spiritual Death*, 2nd ed. Tulsa, OK: Faith Library Publications, 1995.

———. *The Key to Scriptural Healing.* Fourteenth printing. Tulsa, OK: Faith Library Publications, 1995.

———. *The Midas Touch: A Balanced Approach to Biblical Prosperity.* Tulsa, OK: Faith Library Publications, 2000.

———. "Does God Want Me to Be Sick?" *Rhema*, June 22, 2017. Accessed August 9, 2021. https://events.rhema.org/is-it-gods-will-to-heal/.

Hollinger, Dennis P. "Enjoying God Forever: An Historical/Sociological Profile of the Health and Wealth Gospel." *Trinity Journal* 9 (1988): 131–49.

James, Jonathan D. "Global, 'Glocal' and Local Dynamics in Calvary Temple: India's Fastest Growing Megachurch." In *Handbook of Megachurches*, edited by Stephen Hunt, 302–22. Brill Handbooks on Contemporary Religion 19. Leiden: Brill, 2019.

Jones, David W., and Russell S. Woodbridge. *Health, Wealth, and Happiness: How the Prosperity Gospel Overshadows the Gospel of Christ*. Grand Rapids, MI: Kregel Publications, 2011.

"Joyce Meyer Ministries – Vietnamese." Accessed August 15, 2021. https://tv.joycemeyer.org/vietnamese.

Kenyon, E. W. *The Two Kinds of Faith: Faith's Secret Revealed*. Lynnwood, WA: Kenyon's Gospel Publishing Society, 1942.

Kumar, John Arun. "Karma and Fatalism." In *South Asia Bible Commentary: A One-Volume Commentary on the Whole Bible*, edited by Brian Wintle, 1051. Grand Rapids, MI: Zondervan, 2015.

Le, Vince. *Vietnamese Evangelicals and Pentecostalism: The Politics of Divine Intervention*. Global Pentecostal and Charismatic Studies 29. Leiden: Brill, 2018.

Lim, Kar Yong. "A Theology of Suffering and Mission for the Asian Church." In *Asian Christian Theology: Evangelical Perspectives*, edited by Timoteo D. Gener and Stephen T. Pardue, 181–98. Carlisle, UK: Langham Global Library, 2019.

Ma, Wonsuk. "David Yonggi Cho's Theology of Blessing: Basis, Legitimacy, and Limitations." *Evangelical Review of Theology* 35 (April 2011): 140–51.

———. "Pentecostal Worship in Asia: Its Theological Implications and Contributions." *Asian Journal of Pentecostal Studies* 10 (2007): 136–52.

Mathews, Mathew. "Pentecostalism in Singapore: History, Adaptation and Future." In *Asia Pacific Pentecostalism*, edited by Denise A. Austin, Jacqueline Grey, and Paul W. Lewis, 271–94. Global Pentecostal and Charismatic Studies. Vol. 31. Leiden: Brill, 2019.

Mbugua, Ken. "Misunderstanding the Bible." In *Prosperity?: Seeking the True Gospel*, edited by Michael O. Maura, et al., 15–32. Bukuru Jos, Plateau State: ACTS Kenya, 2016.

Mende, David Prasanna Kumar. "A Biblical Analysis of the Main Teachings of the Prosperity Gospel, with Special Reference to the Preachers of Hyderabad, India." *Journal of Asian Evangelical Theology* 23 (March 2019): 19–35.

Mihindukulasuriya, Prabo. "Prosperity Theology." In *South Asia Bible Commentary: A One-Volume Commentary on the Whole Bible*, edited by Brian Wintle, 637. Grand Rapids, MI: Zondervan, 2015.

Moo, Douglas J. "Divine Healing in the Health and Wealth Gospel." *Trinity Journal* 9 (1988): 201–9.

Nguyen, Quynh-Hoa Le. "Tin Lành: The Bible and the Construction of an Evangelical Vietnamese Christian Identity (1975–2007)." PhD diss., Claremont Graduate University, 2013.

Niemandt, C. J. P. (Nelus). "The Prosperity Gospel, the Decolonisation of Theology, and the Abduction of Missionary Imagination." *Missionalia* 45 (2017): 203–19.

Oswalt, John. *The Book of Isaiah: Chapters 40–66*. New International Commentary on the Old Testament. Grand Rapids: Eerdmans, 1998.

Phu, Le Hoang. "A Short History of the Evangelical Church of Vietnam (1911–1965)." PhD diss., New York University, 1972.

Prince, Joseph. "The Power of The Holy Communion." *Joseph Prince Ministries*. Accessed August 9, 2021. https://www.josephprince.org/blog/articles/the-power-of-the-holy-communion.

Reimer, Reg. *Vietnam's Christians: A Century of Growth in Adversity*. Pasadena, CA: William Carey Library, 2011.

Roberts, Oral. *Seed-Faith 2000: Spiritual, Physical, and Financial Increase Through the Power of Seed-Faith*. Tulsa, OK: Oral Roberts, 1999.

Salinas, Daniel. "Mainline Churches and Prosperity Theology in Latin America." In *Prosperity Theology and the Gospel: Good News or Bad News for the Poor?*, edited by J. Daniel Salinas, 115–22. Lausanne Library. Peabody, MA: Hendrickson, 2017.

Samuel, Vinay K. "A Biblical Ethical Assessment of Prosperity Teaching and the Blessing Movement." In *Prosperity Theology and the Gospel: Good News or Bad News for the Poor?*, edited by J. Daniel Salinas, 77–87. Lausanne Library. Peabody, MA: Hendrickson, 2017.

Sarles, Ken L. "A Theological Evaluation of the Prosperity Gospel." *Bibliotheca Sacra* 143 (1986): 337–47.

Song, Choan-Seng. *The Compassionate God*. Maryknoll, NY: Orbis Books, 1982.

Steuernagel, Valdir, and Maicon Steuernagel. "Historical Overview: Cape Town and Our Mission." In *Prosperity Theology and the Gospel: Good News or Bad News for the Poor?*, edited by J. Daniel Salinas, 53–65. Lausanne Library. Peabody, MA: Hendrickson, 2017.

Tabb, Brian J. *After Emmaus: How the Church Fulfills the Mission of Christ*. Wheaton, IL: Crossway, 2021.

Tejedo, Joel. "Asian Perspectives on Prosperity Theology, Simplicity and Poverty." In *Prosperity Theology and the Gospel: Good News or Bad News for the Poor?*, edited by J. Daniel Salinas, 136–47. Lausanne Library. Peabody, MA: Hendrickson, 2017.

Tu, Truong Van Thien. "*Mệnh Trời*: Toward a Vietnamese Theology of Mission." PhD diss., The Graduate Theological Union, 2009.

Vân, Chu Thanh. "Đồng bào tôn giáo gắn bó với dân tộc, đồng hành cùng đất nước." December 24, 2018, https://baotintuc.vn/news-20181224172939140.htm.

Vondey, Wolfgang. *Pentecostalism*. London: Bloomsbury, 2013.

Vu, Michelle A. "Interview: Joel Osteen on Prosperity Gospel, Crystal Cathedral, and Jesus." The Christian Post. Accessed August 14, 2021. https://www.christianpost.com/news/interview-joel-osteen-on-prosperity-gospel-crystal-cathedral-and-jesus.html.

Wiegele, Katharine L. "The Prosperity Gospel among Filipino Catholic Charismatics." In *Pentecostalism and Prosperity: The Socio-Economics of the Global Charismatic Movement*, edited by Katherine Attanasi and Amos Yong, 171–88. New York: Palgrave Macmillan, 2012.

Wiyono, Gani. "Pentecostalism in Indonesia." In *Asia Pacific Pentecostalism*, edited by Denise A. Austin, Jacqueline Grey, and Paul W. Lewis, 243–70. Global Pentecostal and Charismatic Studies. Vol. 31. Leiden: Brill, 2019.

Wright, Christopher J. H., and Lausanne Committee for World Evangelization. "Lausanne Theology Working Group Statement on the Prosperity Gospel." *Evangelical Review of Theology* 34 (2010): 99–102.

Yong, Amos. "A Typology of Prosperity Theology: A Religious Economy of Global Renewal or a Renewal Economics?" In *Pentecostalism and Prosperity: The Socio-Economics of the Global Charismatic Movement*, edited by Katherine Attanasi and Amos Yong, 15–33. New York: Palgrave Macmillan, 2012.

CONTRIBUTORS

Mona P. Bias (PhD, Dallas Theological Seminary) is a missionary with Cru-Philippines, but is on-loan as a faculty member at the International Graduate School of Leadership (IGSL) where she last served as the Academic Dean (2016–2020) and continues to teach in the Biblical Studies Department. She co-authored a commentary on the Book of Job that was published in 2011, and she is currently rewriting this for ATA/Langham. She contributed articles and essays related to contextualization with the *Journal of Asian Mission*, *Principalities and Powers: Reflections in the Asian Context*, *Gospel in Culture: Contextualization Issues through Asian Eyes*, and *Jian Dao*. Most recently, she started to have teaching stints at schools that were started by IGSL alumni or where these alumni are currently teaching in Asia.

Havilah Dharamraj (PhD, University of Durham) serves as the Head of the Department of Old Testament and as the Academic Dean at the South Asia Institute of Advanced Christian Studies in Bengaluru, India. One of her research interests is Old Testament narrative. Here, she sees storytelling as a vehicle for developing narrative theology in South Asia. A second research interest is comparative literature, in which biblical texts can be placed into conversation with parallel non-Christian sacred texts. A work-in-progress is a comparative thematic study of the Song of Songs and the Gita Govinda, a Hindu sacred poem. Besides these, she explores innovative assessment methods in higher theological education and in training for ministry. Her publications include *Altogether Lovely: A Thematic and Intertextual Reading of the Song of Songs (South Asian Theology)* (Fortress, 2018); *Challenging Tradition: Innovation in Advanced Theological Education* (ed.) (Langham Publishing, 2018); *South Asia Bible Commentary: A One-Volume Commentary on the Whole Bible* (ed.) (Langham Publishing/Zondervan, 2015); and *A Prophet Like Moses? A Narrative-Theological Reading of the Elijah Stories* (Paternoster, 2011).

Bayarjargal Garamtseren (PhD, University of Cambridge) is Manager of the Mongolian Standard Version Project, Mongolian Union Bible Society, and pastor of Life Community Church in Ulaanbaatar, Mongolia. He is a founding member of the Mongolian Research Institute for Christianity and serves on its board. In addition, he is a Langham Scholar and coordinates Langham Preaching trainings in Mongolia. Along with his wife, he is involved in publishing Christian books in the Mongolian language. His research interests include the Hebrew Bible, Septuagint, Bible translation, and history of Christianity in Mongolia. He has contributed articles and essays in Mongolian and English in various publications, such as "Mongolia," in *Christianity in East and Southeast Asia, Edinburgh Companions to Global Christianity* (Edinburgh University Press, 2020); "Mongolian," *A Guide to Bible Translation: People, Languages and Topics* (United Bible Societies, 2019); "Re-establishment of the Christian Church in Mongolia: The Mongolian Standard Version Translation by National Christians," *Unio Cum Christo* (October 2016); "Mongolia" (co-authored with Hugh Kemp) in *Asian Handbook for Theological Education and Ecumenism* (Regnum Books International, 2013); and "A History of Bible Translation in Mongolian," in *The Bible Translator* (2009). He is married with two sons and two daughters.

Elaine Wei-Fun Goh (ThD, SEAGST/ATESEA Theological Union) is the Dean of Studies at Seminari Theoloji Malaysia (Malaysia Theological Seminary) where she teaches Old Testament studies. She is also the Director of Chinese Theological Education by Extension in the seminary, and has served as co-editor for the recently published work, *From Malaysia to the Ends of the Earth: Southeast Asian and Diasporic Contributions to Biblical and Theological Studies* (Claremont Press, 2021). Her published books include an English title, *Cross-Textual Reading of Ecclesiastes with the Analects: In Search of Political Wisdom in a Disordered World* (Pickwick Publications, 2019), a Mandarin commentary in Hong Kong, *Rediscovering the Bible: The Book of Ecclesiastes* (Logos, 2019), an EPUB commentary titled *Proverbs* (Shenzhou Biblical Commentary at Smashwords, Inc., 2021), and several academic papers. During her sabbatical at Fuller Theological Seminary from January to June 2020, she wrote a collection of biblical reflections on the COVID pandemic titled *Footprints during Covid-19* (Kuala Lumpur: Eternal Wisdom, 2020). She is currently writing a commentary on the Song of Songs in Mandarin, and working on several journal articles. Besides being passionate about teaching the Old Testament, she leads study tours to biblical lands. She is married to Rev. Ng Way Min and they have a daughter, Jolin.

Shirley S. Ho (PhD, Trinity Evangelical Divinity School) is Assistant Professor of Old Testament and Hebrew Language and Dean of School of Pastoral and Missions Studies at China Evangelical Graduate School of Theology in Taoyuan, Taiwan. She is a Filipino-Chinese but resides in Taiwan. Her research interests include Contextual Theology, Embodied Cognition and Intercorporeality, Metaphors and Conceptual Blending, Cultural Trauma, Psalms, and Wisdom

Literature. Her monograph on the Book of Proverbs is currently in review, while several other articles on the same book have already been published. The latest article is entitled "Making Wise the Stranger: Sapiential Hospitality in Proverbs 1–9" (Open Theology Open Access). Another entitled "Cyrenaics and Beyond: The Moral Reasoning of the Fool in the Book of Proverbs" will soon be published in *Journal of Sino-Christian Studies* in 2024. She has been teaching full-time for sixteen years and has loved every moment of it. Shirley has been a Langham scholar since 2001.

Jerry Hwang (PhD, Wheaton College) is Associate Professor of Old Testament and Academic Dean of the School of Theology (English) at Singapore Bible College, where he has served since 2010 and teaches courses in Old Testament and Hebrew. As an OT professor who is also a member of OMF International, his research interests lie at the intersection of Old Testament, contextualization, and Asian theology. In addition to fifty articles, essays, and reviews, his books include a monograph on Deuteronomy (Eisenbrauns, 2012), a Hosea commentary (Zondervan, 2021), a Jeremiah commentary (Crossway, 2022), *Contextualization and the Old Testament: Between Asian and Western Perspectives* (ATA/Langham Publishing, 2022), and a Job commentary (Wipf & Stock, in preparation). He is also a Fellow with Every Voice: A Center for Kingdom Diversity in Christian Theological Education. Prior to teaching at Singapore Bible College, he served in pastoral ministry in the United States in both Chinese and multicultural churches, as well as working in the IT industry for several years before entering pastoral ministry. He is married to Jackie and they have three children.

Koowon Kim (PhD, University of Chicago) is a Research Fellow and Lecturer at the Institute for Research on Early Civilizations in Dankook University. His research area is the comparative study of the Old Testament and ancient Asian texts. He is also interested in the Old Testament as a philosophical text with invaluable ideas which are relevant not only to Christians, but also to those who do not share the same belief in the Bible. He is the author of many articles and books in both English and Korean, including *1 Samuel: A Pastoral and Contextual Commentary* (Langham Publishing, 2018); *A Short Introduction to the Old Testament* (Hongsungsa, 2020); *Song of Songs: A Commentary* (Christian Literature Crusade, 2017); *Incubation as a Type-Scene in the Aqhatu, Kirta and Hannah Stories* (Brill, 2011). His recent essays include "Why is the Woman of Endor Portrayed as a Heroine?" in *The Expository Times* (2018); "When Even the Gods Do Not Know: El's Dream Divination in KTU 1.6 iii" in *Perchance* *to Dream* (SBL, 2018); "Three Kingdoms and David's Rise to Kingship," in *Journal of Asian Evangelical Theology* (2020); "Psalm 1: Structure and Meaning," in *Like Ilu Are You Wise: Studies in Northwest Semitic Languages and Literature in Honor of Dennis G. Pardee* (Oriental Institute Publications, 2022).

Peter H. W. Lau (PhD, University of Sydney) serves with OMF International in Diaspora Returnees Ministry. He is adjunct Old Testament lecturer at Seminari Theoloji Malaysia, Equip Gospel Ministries Malaysia, and Sydney Missionary and Bible College. His publications include *Unceasing Kindness: A Biblical Theology of Ruth* (co-authored with Greg Goswell; IVP, 2016) and *Esther* (Asia Bible Commentary, Langham Publishing, 2018). He co-edited (with Jione Havea) *Reading Ruth in Asia* (SBL Press, 2015) and *Reading Ecclesiastes from Asia and Pasifika* (SBL Press, 2020). A commentary on the book of Ruth (Eerdmans) is forthcoming. At his local church he is involved in preaching, small group leading, and music ministry.

Daniel C. Owens (PhD, Wheaton College) is a professor at Hanoi Bible College in Hanoi, Vietnam, where he teaches primarily Old Testament courses. In addition to his dissertation, published under the title *Portraits of the Righteous in the Psalms: An Exploration of the Ethics of Book I* (Pickwick, 2013), he has written or co-written several works in Vietnamese, including *Sổ Tay Thuật Ngữ Thần Học Anh-Việt* (*Handbook of Theological Terms English-Vietnamese*, NXB Tôn Giáo, 2014); *Ngữ Pháp Căn Bản Tiếng Hê-bơ-rơ* (*Elementary Hebrew Grammar*, NXB Tôn Giáo, 2015); and *Giải Nghĩa Sách Giô-na* (*Commentary on the Book of Jonah*, NXB Tôn Giáo, 2021). He served for three years as an elder at the Hanoi International Fellowship and preaches periodically there, and in Vietnamese churches in and around Hanoi. Prior to coming to Hanoi, he taught as a visiting professor at Singapore Bible College, Singapore, and served in Ho Chi Minh City, Vietnam.

Angukali Rotokha (PhD, South Asia Institute of Advanced Christian Studies) has been teaching the Old Testament for the past ten years at Oriental Theological Seminary, Dimapur, and South Asia Institute of Advanced Christian Studies, Bengaluru. She is currently on a break from teaching and is working on some writing projects as well as on publishing her dissertation. She has written commentaries on 1 Samuel and Daniel in *South Asia Bible Commentary: A One-Volume Commentary on the Whole Bible* (Langham Publishing/Zondervan, 2015). She has been involved in youth ministry in various capacities in the past twenty years and is currently an executive member of her church, where she also preaches and teaches frequently. She is married to Luke Haokip and they reside in Bengaluru, India.

Annelle Sabanal (PhD, University of Edinburgh) serves as the Research Director and Assistant Professor in Old Testament at Asian Theological Seminary in Manila, Philippines. Her interests include the intersection of the Old Testament with Ethics and Political Theology. One of her articles on the topic was recently published by Langham Publishing. Her dissertation entitled "The Motif of Shepherd and Politics in the Hebrew Prophets" will be published by Mohr Siebeck next year.

Huu-Thien Tran N. (PhD, AGST Alliance) is a pastor with the Evangelical Church of Vietnam (South, also known as ECVN). He teaches Old Testament Theology at the ECVN Institute of Bible and Theology and serves as the senior pastor of a local church in Ho Chi Minh City, Vietnam. He is also a Langham scholar. He has authored a commentary on the book of Ruth in Vietnamese (2022) and co-wrote a textbook and workbook of Basic Biblical Hebrew Grammar in Vietnamese (2016). He is currently working on a dictionary of Hebrew-Vietnamese to provide a basic tool for Vietnamese to learn biblical Hebrew, while working on publishing his dissertation, "The Chronicler's Reading of Biblical Sources: A Model for Asian Biblical Hermeneutics." He is married to Lan-Khue and they have two children, Thien-Duc (son) and Thien-Hoai (daughter).

SUBJECT INDEX

A
Abrahamic covenant 190, 233–34
Adam and Eve 13, 32, 41
Akkadian 173
Amaterasu 37
American Baptist Foreign Missionary Society 186
Analects 126, 142, 148, 151, 155–56, 159, 161
ancient Near East 1, 25, 31, 47, 64–65, 82, 86–87, 89–90, 111, 113, 154–55, 161, 165, 173–74, 179, 205, 211, 216
ancient Near Eastern 28, 30, 45, 129, 1330, 165, 193, 196, 207, 211
animistic 10, 13
Arabic jihad 67
Aramaic 7
Ashur 36
Assyrian 173, 177
atheism 25
atheistic 39
atonement 233, 242, 244
Ayodhya 43, 47–48

B
Baal 30, 33, 38
Babylon 75–76
barangay 108
Bhagavad Gita 175
Bible 8–10, 12, 17–18, 20–22, 26
Bible translation 21
blessedness 152
blessing(s) 11, 14, 36, 46, 60–61, 66, 74, 150, 152–53, 233
bribe 216, 218–20, 222
bribery 15, 214–15, 219–20, 222
Buddha 13
Buddhism 10, 12, 18, 238
Buddhist 13, 70

Burkhan 21
Burmese 92

C
Canaanite 7, 25, 29–31
centrifugal 61, 77
centripetal 61, 76
China 34, 37, 66, 68, 82, 91, 230
Chinese 29, 34–35, 38, 125, 127, 148, 150, 152, 154, 158, 161
chosen people 191–92, 202
Christian missionaries 60
clan(s) 63, 148, 189, 206
collectivist 207, 221
collectivistic 214–15
Communist 15
Confucian 124, 142, 145–46, 148, 154, 156, 158
Confucianism 94
Confucius 127, 140, 148, 160
corruption 213, 221
covenant 14, 27, 36, 74, 82, 103, 106, 116, 190, 193, 195–96, 235
creation 8, 29

D
Decalogue 105
Deuteronomic Code 101, 106
Deuteronomic Law 62, 103, 105, 109–11, 113–14
divine council 29

E
East Asia 33
Eden 13, 50, 52, 56
education 2, 148
El 30–31, 33, 38
election 36
eschatology 243, 246

ethics 16, 111, 114, 145, 155–56, 160–61
Eve 56
evil 37–38, 239
exchange 212, 214, 220
exile 85, 88, 117

F
Fall 13, 41
family 108, 148, 156, 207
favor(s) 213, 218
favoritism 210, 214
fear of God 159, 161
fiction 168
Filipino 95, 97, 108, 113

G
gender 46
gift 193, 212, 215–16, 218–19, 222
Golden Age of Missions 66

H
healing 232–33, 241, 243
Hebrew 7, 19
Hindu 48–49
Hinduism 10, 12, 238
historicity 167, 176–77
historiography 165, 167, 171–72, 174, 176, 178
history 166, 171, 174, 179
Hittite treaty 27, 102
Holiness Code 101
holistic 83, 232, 246
Holy war 67
Hong Kong 221
honor 113, 148, 207, 209
household 206

I
Ibaloy 101
Ibaloys 114
ideology 15, 169–70, 173
Ifugao 101, 104
image of God 11, 46

imago Dei 45
Imperialism 72
inayan 117
India 174, 180, 185, 194, 230
Indonesia 230
Islam 10, 18, 83
Islamic 83

J
Jainism 238
Janaka 48
Japan 37, 87
Japanese 33, 37, 69
Judah 74
justice 64, 88, 109, 116, 118, 216, 219–20, 223

K
Kalinga 101, 112
Kalingas 118
Kankana-ey 101
karma 72, 117, 238, 240
kingship 84, 86, 89–90
kinship 156, 205, 209, 211
Koine Greek 19
Korea 25, 230

L
Lakshmana 43
land 114, 193, 196–97, 208
languages 7, 18–19, 23
Lanka 43
law 101
leadership 81, 83–84, 94
learning 145
legalism 141–42
Li 124, 133, 135, 137, 140, 142
liberation 32, 185
liberation theologies 73
literary 168, 172

M
Mahabharata 165, 174, 176–77, 180
Malaysia 230

Subject Index

male and female 41, 46
Mandate of Heaven 82, 91
Manila 96
Marduk 30, 36
Megillah 25
Mencius 35, 91
Mesopotamian 38
Miao 29
missio Dei 60–61, 66, 68, 72, 74, 76
mission 14, 60, 162, 201
missionaries 19–20, 186, 229, 236
Mission of God 14
Mongolia 8, 10, 12, 15, 17–18, 21
Mongolian Standard Version 19, 22
monogamy 56
monolatrous 28, 31, 36
monotheism 25–26, 29, 33–34, 37–38
monotheistic 28, 36
monotheists 37
Muslim(s) 49, 83, 104
Myanmar 92, 185, 192

N
Naga 189
Naga Club 187
Nagaland 185, 187, 194
Nagaland for Christ 188, 194–95
Nagalim 185, 194
Naga National Council 187–88
Nagas 185, 191, 197
nationalism 185–87, 189, 196–97, 200
nationalist movement 186, 189, 194, 197
National Socialist Council of Nagalim 187–88, 191, 195, 198
nations 8, 14, 36, 59–61, 72
Nepal 52, 101, 106
new covenant 191–93, 236
Nihon Shoki 37
northern Luzon 104, 112, 114, 116
North Korea 111

O
objective 178–79
objectivity 171
Opium Wars 66

P
patronage 36, 209, 213
patron-client 209
patrons 214
Pentecost 19
Philippines 82–83, 95, 97, 104, 107–8, 110, 112–13, 230
pluralism 2, 123
polygamy 56
polytheism 25, 37, 123, 130
polytheistic 25, 28, 34
positive confession 242, 245
postcolonialism 73
poverty 63, 110, 162, 232, 236, 240
prayer 233, 241, 243
priests 83, 93
prophecy 73, 90, 173
prophets 86, 90–91
prosperity 152–53, 230, 233
prosperity gospel(s) 37, 152, 230–31
prosperity theology 153, 193, 229, 232–33, 235–36, 239, 241, 245
Protestant 8

Q
Qoheleth 151, 153, 157
Qur'an 18

R
Rama 43, 47, 52
Ramayana 42–43, 47–48, 52, 175
Ravana 43
reciprocity 220, 222
ren 142, 156–57
retribution 238–39
ritual(s) 10, 92, 125, 127, 133, 140
ritualism 141–42
royal ideology 88

S

Sabbath 28
sacrifice(s) 133, 135 142
sage(s) 25, 46, 48, 93, 147–48, 155, 158–59
Scramble for Africa 66
Scripture 2, 7–8, 22
Septuagint 20
serpent(s) 42, 47
shalom 81, 95
shame 113, 148, 207, 209
Shari'ah 83, 104
Shema 27, 105
shepherd 88
Shinto 87
Sikhism 238
Simon Commission 186
Singapore 221, 230
sin(s) 7, 13, 66, 116, 118, 135, 192, 198, 238–39, 244
Sita 43, 47, 52
sons of God 25, 28–29
South Korea 221
spiritual 22, 34, 126, 129
suffering 235, 237, 239
Susanowo 33, 37
syncretism 31

T

Taiwanese 123, 126, 129, 132, 138–39
Taylor, J. Hudson 68
temple 35, 92
Temple 37, 74
Thailand 70, 213
Tibetan Buddhism 12, 18
tradition 207
translation 19–20, 22
tribe 206
Trinity 25

U

Ugaritic 30
Utnapishtim 38

V

Valmiki 44, 47
Vedic Period 175
Vietnam 229
Vietnamese 232, 237–38, 240
violence 197, 199

W

wealth 152–53, 230, 233–36
Western 1, 59, 69, 73, 83, 229
wisdom 94, 146–47, 150, 154, 158, 160, 162
wisdom tradition(s) 93–94, 147, 149, 152, 154, 161
wise 146–47, 149, 155, 161
worldview(s) 47, 70, 83, 123–24, 128–30, 158, 178, 232, 241
worship 12, 92, 106, 123, 130, 133–35, 137–38, 140

X

xin 156–57

Y

Yahweh 26, 31
Yahwism 31
Yunnan 29

Z

Zealots 201

AUTHOR INDEX

A
Abeysinghe, R. T. B. 1
Acoba, E. 104
Adeleye, Femi 231
Adeney, Bernard T. 216
Ahmed, Ishtiaq 83
Ahuja, Namrata Biji 188
Alatas, Syed Hussein 221
Allen, James P. 29
Alter, Robert 168
Amit, Yairah 171, 179
Anderson, Bernhard W. 171
Argandoña, Antonio 218
Austin, Denise A. and Lim Yeu Chuen 230
Avari, Bujor 176

B
Baines, John 86
Baker, David L. 216
Barclay, John M. G. 222
Barrameda, Mary Constancy 118
Barr, James 170
Barrois, Georges Augustin 167
Bartholomew, Craig G. 19–20, 22, 151
Bauckham, Richard 9, 15, 18, 222
Beaver, R. Pierce 13
Bell, Catherine 132–33, 139
Berlin, Adele 115
Berrigan, Daniel 76
Birch, Bruce C. 173
Blakeley, Donald N. 126
Blenkinsopp, Joseph 93, 205
Block, Daniel I. 103–4, 109
Blomberg, Craig L. 192
Boadt, Lawrence 155
Bontis, Nick 221
Borgen, Robert, and Marian Ury 37
Bosworth, David A. 75

Bowler, Kate 230, 242–43
Bravmann, M. M. 48
Brett, Mark G. 207
Brueggemann, Walter 74, 192, 194, 197
Buys, P. J. 229

C
Cabato, Regine 96
Cao, Nanlai 230
Carter, Steven 104
Chang, Hsiao-Ming, Ching-Hui Lin, and Yen-Chen Huang 125
Chapman, Stephen B. 67
Charles, Mark, and Soong-Chan Rah 59
Chaves, João B. 73
Chianeque, Luciano C., and Samuel Ngewa 103, 110
Ching, Julia 83, 160
Chisholm Jr., Robert B. 116
Choon Sup, Bae 25
Chow, Lien-Hwa 123
Clements, Ronald E. 103
Copan, Paul, and Matthew Flannagan 68
Copeland, Kenneth 234
Cornelio, Jayeel, and Erron Medina 231
Cornelio, Jayeel, and Ia Marañon 97
Cotter, David W. 46
Crenshaw, James L. 146–47, 151
Crook, Zeba A. 209, 211–12
Curzer, Howard 128

D
Dallaire, Hélène 60, 66–67
Davies, Philip 168, 177
Davis, Ellen F. 157
Dawkins, Richard 59, 67

Day, John 106
Dell, Katharine J. and Will Kynes 147
deSilva, David 192
Dever, William G. 172
Dillard, Raymond B., and Tremper Longman III 103
Douglas, Mary 135
Dulawan, Lourdes S. 104
Dumbrell, William J. 85
Dyrness, William 105, 112

E
Eagleton, Terry 170
Eichrodt, Walther 190
Eisenstadt, S. N. and Louis Roniger 209–10, 213
Ellis, Maria DeJong 173
Estes, Daniel J. 149
Ewell, C. Rosalee Velloso 233

F
Finkelstein, J. J. 216
Flesher, LeAnn Snow 50
Fowler, Robert 168
Fox, Michael V 157
Frykenberg, Robert Eric 166–67, 179

G
Gabriel, Theodore 1
Gane, Roy 119
Garamtseren, Bayarjargal 21
Georges, Jayson G. 113
Gjesdal, Kristen 166
Glanville, Luke 83, 91
Glover, R. H. 237
Goheen, Michael W. 61
Goh, Elaine Wei-Fun 151, 155–56, 158
Goldberg, Michael L. 216
Goodblatt, David M. 206
Gordis, Robert 157
Gordon, C. H. 47
Gottwald, Norman K. 205
Gowen, Annie 44

Grabbe, Lester L. 84, 199
Grosby, Steven E. 206
Grund, Alexandra 213
Gupta, Vinay Kumar 175

H
Hachalinga, Passmore 117
Hagin, Kenneth E. 234, 238, 241–42
Halpern, Baruch 205
Hamilton, Mark W. 216, 219–20
Hamilton, Victor P. 44
Haran, Menahem 93
Harland, P. J. 218
Haskar, Nandita, and Sebastian Hongray 187–88
Hays, J. Daniel 115
Heiser, Michael S. 28, 129–30
Hengel, Martin 200–1
Heschel, Abraham J. 70–71
Hiers, Richard H. 101–2, 106, 109
Hilber, John W. 91
Holladay, Carl R. 169–70
Hollinger, Dennis P. 233
Houston, Walter J. 107–8, 110, 116, 211
Hwang, Jerry 74
Hwa, Yung 215-16

I
Iralu, Kaka D. 187

J
Jaffrelot, Christophe, and Pradyumna Jairam 178
James, Jonathan D. 230
Jamir, Chongpongmeren 186, 188, 191, 195
Jenson, Philip 102, 105–6, 119
Jones, David W., and Russell S. Woodbridge 230–31, 233
Juergensmeyer, Mark 198

K
Kaiser Jr., Walter C. 61, 194

Author Index

Kashyap, Samudra Gupta 186
Kellermann, D. 218
Kenyon, E. W. 243
Kitamori, Kazoh 69–70
Kline, Meredith 104
Knight, Douglas A. 102, 104, 109
Korošec, Victor 102
Koyama, Kosuke 69–70
Krüger, Thomas 158
Kugel, James L. 29
Kumar, John Arun 238, 240

L

Lall, Marie 178
Lamb, David T. 68
Lambert, W. G. 149
Lambrecht, Francis 82
Lam, Wing-Hung 124
Langston, Richard 221
Lapsley, Jacqueline E. 112, 115
Lau, D. C. 128, 142
Lau, Peter H. W. 115
Laytner, Anson H. 71
Lemche, Niels P. 210–11
Levenson, Jon D. 38
Le, Vince 229, 239
Lewis, C. S. 54, 57
Lewis, Theodore J. 31–32
Lichtheim, Miriam 149
Lieven, Anatol 213
Lim, Kar Yong 237
Lincoln, Andrew T. 56
Longenecker, Richard N. 51
Longkumer, Arkotong 187–89, 198
Longman III, Tremper 219
Long, V. Philips 167
Lotha, Abraham 195, 198

M

Machinist, Peter 62
Malanes, Maurice 117
Marchadour, Alain, and David
    Neuhaus 194, 196–97
Mark Hamilton W. 219

Markl, Dominik 113–14
Master, Daniel M. 220
Mathews, Kenneth A. 43–45
Mathews, Mathew 230
Mathias, Steffan 208
Matthews, Peter 95
Matthews, Victor H., and Don C.
    Benjamin 206
Mauss, Marcel 220
Ma, Wonsuk 229, 232, 236
Mazar, Nina and Pankaj Aggarwal
    221
Mbugua, Ken 244
McCarthy, Dennis J. 102
McComiskey, Thomas E., and
    Tremper Longman III 117
McConville, J. G. 82, 85, 89, 103, 113,
    118
McDermott, Gerald R. 74
McKenzie, Steven L. 171–72, 191
McVann, Mark 207–8
Mende, David Prasanna Kumar 242,
    245
Mendels, Doron 206
Mendenhall, George E. 102
Merrill, Eugene H. 104
Meyer, Joyce 230
Meyers, Carol L. 205
Mihindukulasuriya, Prabo 231
Miller, Patrick D. 32, 36, 198
Mischke, Werner 212
Mollet, Julius Ary 221
Montgomery, David J. 216
Moo, Douglas J. Moo 231
Moran, William L. 27
Moss, C. R. 104, 114
Muller, A. Charles 126
Munayer, Salim J. 117
Mungiu-Pippidi, Alina 214
Murphy, Roland E. 148
Murray, Donald F. 89

N

Nadeau, Randall L. 87

Negev, Avraham, and Shimon Gibson 177
Neusner, Jacob 51
Ngien, Dennis 70
Nguyen, Quynh-Hoa Le 237
Nhep, Arun Sok 221
Niemandt, C. J. P. (Nelus) 230
Nolland, John 200
Noonan Jr, .John T. 216, 219

O

Oak, Sung-Deuk 35
O'Brien, Peter T. 56
Oliver, Hannes 211
Olmstead, Albert Ten Eyck 173
Ortlund Jr., Raymond C. 50
Osei-Bonsu, Robert 185
Osteen, Joel 230-31, 243
Oswalt, John 244

P

Packer, J. I. 69-70
Paolo, Mauro 213
Pardee, Dennis 30
Pelikan, Jaroslav 81
Perdue, Leo G. 209
Peri, Dinakar 194
Pfoh, Emanuel O. 213
Phan, Peter C. 1
Phu, Le Hoang 237
Pieris, Aloysius 123
Pitt-Rivers, Julian 220
Plevnik, Joseph, and John J. Pilch 207
Prenzler, Tim 109
Prince, Joseph 231, 242
Prior, Michael 73
Provan, Iain W. 173, 179
Provan, Iain W., V. Philips Long, and Tremper Longman III 172
Pungayan, Eufronio L. and Isikias Picpican 107

R

Raabe, Paul R. 72

Rad, Gervard von 67, 146, 190
Rafael, Vicente L. 95
Raychaudhuri, Hemchandra 175
Reimer, Reg 238, 241
Reyes, Portia L. 96
Richards, E. Randolph, and Richard James 113
Römer, Thomas 32
Romila Thapar 175
Roniger, Louis 209-10
Rose-Ackerman, Susan, and Bonnie J. Palifka 214
Roth, Martha 108, 111
Rotz, Margaret Palaghicon Von 82
Rudolph, Kurt 155
Ryken, Leland 115

S

Sabanal, Annelle 88
Salinas, J. Daniel 231
Samuel, Vinay K. 232
Sanneh, Lamin 19-20
Santos, Narry F. 113
Sarles, Ken L. 231, 234
Sarna, Nahum M. 43, 46
Sattar, Arshia 44, 48, 52
Schneider, Laurel C 25
Schultz, Richard L. 147-48
Seow, Choon-Leong 157-58
Sharma, R. S. 175
Shellnut, Kate 92
Sher, Tony H. K. 206
Simkins, Ronald 211
Singh, Chandrika 187
Singh, Upinder 175
Smith, Mark 31
Sohn, Seock-Tae 27
Sommer, Benjamin D. 26, 28, 30
Song, Choan-Seng 237
Stein, Robert H. 53
Stern, Jessica 189
Steuernagel, Valdir, and Maicon Steuernagel 230-31
Sumayao, Marco 96

Author Index

T
Tabb, Brian J. 245
Tankha, Madhur 176–77
Taylor, Rodney L. 159
Tejedo, Joel 230–33
Thompson, T. 211
Tigay, J. H. 31
Triandis, Harry C. 207
Trible, Phyllis 45, 51
Trick, Bradley R. 53
Trimm, Charlie 67
Tsudir, Asangba 186
Tucker Jr., W. Dennis 213
Tu, Truong Van Thien 239, 241

V
Vân, Chu Thanh 232
Van de Wiele, Tarah 212
Van Leeuwen, Raymond C. 22
Van Norden, Bryan W. 148
Vashum, R. 187, 189
Venugopal, Vasudha 176
Verora, L. P. 101
Vogt, Peter T. 110
Vondey, Wolfgang 242–43
Vriezen, Theodorus C. 90
Vu, Michelle A. 231

W
Walls, Andrew F. 20
Walsh, John 213
Waltke, Bruce K. 217, 219
Walton, John H. 28–29, 45, 83, 193, 207
Walton, John H., and J. Harvey Walton 68, 130
Weeks, Stuart D. E. 206
Weinfeld, Moshe 102, 105–6
Wei, Xiao-hong, and Qingyuan Li 127
Wenham, Gordon J. 45–47, 50, 111, 115
Westbrook, Raymond 211
Westermann, Claus 116

Whybray, R. N. 93
Wiegele, Katharine L. 230
Wigram, Christopher E. M. 68
Williamson, H. G. M. 107
Witherington III, Ben 53
Wiyono, Gani 230
Wolters, A. M. 151
Wouters, Jelle 186–88, 191
Wright, Christopher J. H. 14, 16, 61, 68, 102–4, 108, 208, 246

Y
Yang, Lihui, and Deming An. 29, 38
Yao, Xinzhong 155, 159
Yee, Gale 85
Yeo, K. K. 161
Yoder, Christine Roy 162–63
Yong, Amos 232
Yung, Hwa 216

Z
Zhang, Yong-Tao and Li Shu-You 159

SCRIPTURE INDEX

OLD TESTAMENT

Genesis
1 .... 29, 46–47, 51, 55
1:1 130
1:2 29
1–2 .... 41, 147
1–3 41
1–11 53
1:11–12, 21, 24–25 46
1:26 45
1:26–27 130
1:27 .... 11, 45
1:28 46
2 50
2–3 46
2:5, 7, 15 46
2:8, 10, 15 133
2:16 50
2:18 50
2:19–20 47
2:21–25 10
2:24 .... 10, 47, 49
3 .... 13, 41, 44
3:1 32
3:2 50
3:14–15 42
3:16 42
3:16a 43
3:17–19 44
3:22–24 162
3:23 50
5:3 45
8:20 133
9:20–27 207
11 19
12:1 194
12:1–3 .... 36, 60, 66, 197,
231, 233, 239
12:1–3; 13:2 233

12:1–13:2 234
12:3 235
12:3a–b 74
12:7, 8 133
12–15 234
12; 15; 17 190
14 234
14:22 32
15:4–5, 18 191
15:7ff 194
15:16 .... 67, 199
15:17 191
15:18–21 197
17:1 74
17:6 64
17:7–8 191
17:8 194
18:23–33 71
19:21 217
21:33 31
22:16 74
25:6 217
25:8 208
26:3–4 191
26:22 32
28:14–15 191
29:14 49
32:20 217
33:20 32
34 207
34:12 217
35:11 64
35:29 208
48:15–49:27 208
50:12–13 197
50:20 240
50:24–25 197

Exodus
2:23–24 32
2:24 191
3 84
3–4 90
5:1 81
6:2–3 31
6:3 32
6:7 72
7:5 72
10:2 72
13:6–13 179
14:4 72
14:30 61
15:2 61
19:4 61
19:4–6 208
19:5 62
19:5a 61
19:5b–6a 61
19:6 36
19–20 61
19; 24 191
20:2 .... 32, 61
20:4 12
20:5 11
20:12 207
20:17 .... 206, 235
21:30 217
23:8 216
24 103
24:3–8 191
25:8 133
25–40 133
28:38 217
31:3 35
31:3–6 146
32 191

32:11–14 71	14:24 35	6:21 62
34:6–7 72	18:11 217	6:22 62
34:14 11	25:6–13 200	6:23 62
35:25 146	25:11 11	6:24–25 62
36:1–2 146	27:4 208	7:1–4 197
	27:13 208	7:1–11:32 105
Leviticus	35:31–32 217	7:1–26 105
1:4 134		7:2 60
1:5, 11 134	**Deuteronomy**	7:2–3 67
1:9, 13 134	1:5 103	7:7–8 .... 62, 106
2:9, 16 134	1:8; 8:1 194	7:8 194
3:2, 8, 13 134	1:10–11 81	8:1–6 208
3:17 134	1:13–15 94	8:1–20 105
4:5–6, 25 134	1:31 62	8:5 62
4:15, 24, 29, 33 134	4:1–2 65	8:17–18 235
5:9 134	4:6 .... 61, 146	8:18 234
6:16, 18, 23, 29 134	4:7 61	9:1–29 105
6:27 134	4:8 .... 61, 103	9:4–5 74
7:14, 26–27 134	4:32–34, 36–38 62	9:4–5 198
7:16, 23 134	4:35, 39 .... 25, 62	9:5 67
7:30, 34 134	4:41–43 112	10:1–22 105
8:21 134	5:1–11:32 .... 104, 118	10:17 .... 217, 219
8:24 134	5:6–15 105	11:1–32 105
10:1–20 134	5:6–21 105	11:13–15 235
11–15 134	5:7 105	11:23 67
12–15 134	5:8 105	11:26–28 147
18–20 134	5:11 105	12:1–26:15 .... 104, 106, 118
18:21 199	5:16 .... 105, 147–48, 207	12:4 106
18:24–30 67	5:16–21 105	12:31 .... 106, 199
19:15 217	5:17 105	13:1–5 106
19:35–36 147	5:18 .... 105, 148	13:6–11 106
23:37 134	5:19 105	13:12–18 106
23:38 217	5:20 105	14:1 62
25:23 208	6:4 25	14:2 62
26:3–13 235	6:4–5 .... 27, 105	14:27–29 110
26:12 71	6:4–9 105	15 66
26:14–33 238–39	6:5 143	4 63
26:40–45 191	6:6–9 105	5 63
26:42–45 191	6:7 207	6 63
26:46 134	6:10–15 105	7–8 63
27:34 134	6:16–19 105	15: 1–3 63
	6:19 67	15:7–8 110
Numbers	6:20 62	16:18–18:22 207
3 61	6:20–25 105	16:18–20 108

Scripture Index

16:19 216	26:18 62	2:11–22..........................114
17 ....66, 86	27:3 103	3:7–4:24..........................238
16–17 65	27:16 148	5:11 185
18–19 65	27:17 114	6:1–8:35..........................238
17:2–7 106	27:25 216	6:15 205
17:6 109	28:64–68..........................116	8:22–23..........................85
17:8–13 108	28:1–14..........................116	9:2 49
17:14–20 ....85, 108	28:15–68..............116, 239	17:6 85
17:15 64	28:36–37..........................116	18:1 85
17:18 103	28:61 103	19:1 85
17:20 65	28:63–68..........................103	21:25 85
18:1–8 108	29 191	
18:9–12 107	29:1 103	**Ruth**
18:9–22 108	29:14–15..........................17	1:8 115
18:15–18 ....84, 90	29:29 103	2:8–9 115
18:20 109	30:1–9 117–18	2:11 115
19:1–13 ....109, 112	30:1–10..........................103	2:11–12..........................115
19:4–13 109	30:11–20..........................103	3:9–12..........................115
19:13; 21:1–9 109	30:15–20..........................208	3:10 115
19:14 ....114, 208	31:11 103	3:11 115
19:16–19 109	32:39 25	3:11–16..........................115
19:19–20 109	32:46 103	4:1–12..........................94
20–25 207	34:1–4 197	4:5, 10 208
21:1–9 109		4:17 115
21:15–17 114	**Joshua**	
21:18–21..........108–9, 207	1:6 208	**1 Samuel**
21:21 109	1:9 60	2:12–17..........................134
22:8 112	2:9–11 67	8 84
22:13–21 109	2:10 75	8:1–3 219
22:15 94	4:6–9 179	8:3 216
22:22 148	6:17 75	8:10–18..........................85
22:22–23 109	7:16–18..........................205	9:1 205
23:15–16 111	9:24–25..........................67	10:11 83
23:19–20 113	10:1 75	10:20–21..........................205
23:21–23 147	10:39–40..........................67	11:1–4..........................94
23:24–25 113	21–24 179	12:1–5..........................219
24:6; 10–11..........................110	23:3–13..........................67	12:6–8..........................84
24:7 109	23:5 67	13 89
24:15 110	23–24 84	15 89
24:19–21 236	24:31 114	16:4b 94
24:19–22 110		16:20–23..........................149
25:1–4 113	**Judges**	18:10 83
25:5–10 208	1–2 67	24:21 208
25:13–16..........................111, 147	1:33 67	25:35 217

2 Samuel
5	89
5:1	49
6:21	185
7	89, 173
7:5–9	75
7:7–8	71
7:14	36
7:23	27
13:3–5	146

1 Kings
3	94
5:3–4	89
8–9	133
8:29–30	35
10:6	146
12:1–19	94
12:6	149
15:19	217, 219
22	30

2 Kings
4:8–37	243
5	244
9:6	185
9:32	217
13:23	191
16:3–4	67
16:8	217, 219
17:7–8	67
18–19	177
19:36–37	173
19:37	173
25:3	177

1 Chronicles
22:8	89

Nehemiah
8	35

Esther
9:22	217

Job
1:1	29
1–2	159
1:6	25
1:10	153
15:34	217
23:10	240
28:12	156
29:14	156
31:6	159
34:19	217
36:18	217
37:24	159
38–41	158
38–41	147
41:1–11	30
42:12	152–53

Psalms
1:1–3	235
2	87
2:7	36
5:7	137
8	147
9:15–20	72
9; 99	81
10	240
10:3	235
10:3–6	235
12	240
13	240
15:5	217
17	240
20	92
24:1–2	135
24:8–10	87
26:10	217
26:12	136
28	240
28:2	136
29:1	25
29:3–4, 10	135
34:19	245
35	240
35:13	137
40:6	142
44	240
46:8–10	67
47	72
47:1	136
48	72
51:17	137
52:7	235
56	240
62:10	218
66:10	240
68:18	217
72	87
73:3–11	240
73:8	218
73:13–14	240
74:12–17	38, 135
74:13–15	30
78:10	102
82	131
82:2	217
82:6–8	30
84:5–7	135
86	240
86:4	137
86:8–10	132
88	240
88:9	136
89:9–10	135
89:49	245
95:6	137
96	131–32
2–3	131
9	131
10, 13	131
11–12	131
96:4–5	131
96:5	130
97:1–6	72
97:7	131
104:26	30
105:10	102
107:22	138

Scripture Index

107:43 146
110:4 90
112:1–3 235
115:2–8 10
115:15 130
116:17 138
117:1 132
118:23 136
119:18, 82 136
119:48 136
120–134 135
121 136
123:1 136
123:2 137
126 208
134:2 136
136:5–9 130
137 208
138:2 137
139:7–12 11
140–143 240
141:2 .... 135–36, 138
143:8 137
148 132
148:1–14 130

Proverbs
1:2 156
1:2–7 145
1:7 .... 155, 159
1:8 145
1:8, 10, 15 148
1–9 150
1:20–33 .... 145, 150
1:22 146
2:1 148
2:9 156
3:1–2 147
3:1, 11, 21 148
3:13 153
3:13–20 .... 150, 162
3:15 151
3:16 150
3:16–18 162

3:18 153
4:10–19 147
4:10, 20 148
5:1, 20 148
5:18 152–53
5:21 159
6:1, 3, 20 148
6:35 .... 217, 219
7:1 148
8:1–36 150
8:22–31 147
8:32 153
9:1–18 150
9:10 .... 147, 155
10:1 148
10:4; 12:27; 21:5 236
10:22 .... 153, 235
11:1 147
11:26 153
13:1 148
13:8 218
13:22 114
14:12 150
14:21 153
15:2 150
15:3 159
15:5 148
15:6 153
15:20 148
15:27 216–19
16:11 147
16:20 153
16:32 150
17:8 216–18
17:23 .... 216–17, 219
18:5 217
18:16 .... 216, 219
18:20–21 231
18:24 218
19:6 217–18
19:17 234
19:27 148
20:6 156
20:7 153

20:20 148
20:21 153
20:26 146
21:11 146
21:14 216–18
22:9 152–53
22:14 148
22:16 216
23:4–5 153
23:19, 26 148
23:22, 25 148
24:13, 21 148
25:1 149
27:11 148
28:6 150
28:14 153
28:19–20 153
28:20 153–54
29:11 146
29:18 153
30:8–9 235
30:3 147
30:11, 17 148
30:17 207
30:24 146
31:1–9 145
31:10 151
31:10–31 151

Ecclesiastes
1:1 145
1:17 156
2:9–11 153
3:11 158
3:16 157
3:16–17 157
3:17 159
4:1–3 157
4:7–8 157
4:8 157
4:9 157
4:9–12 157–58
4:10–12 158
4:13–16 158

5:4–6 147	41:13 81	25:9 75
5:6 159	41:14 147	26:2–6 74
5:18–20 155	42:1 34	27:3–5 75
6:1–2 157	42:1–4 85	27:6 75
7:7 217–18	44:12–20 10	28:6 246
7:23–8:1 151	45:5 25	29:4–7 77
7:26–29 151	45:7 37	31:20 69
7:27 145	48:10 240	31:29 239
9:13–16 158	51:9–11 135	31:31–34 191–92
9:18 150	52:13–53:12 85	31:33 102
10:12 150	53 244	33:21–22, 26 75
10:17 153	53:4 244–45	40:2–3 76
11:1–2 158	53:4–5 244	46:26 76
12:9 145	53:5 ....231, 242, 244, 247	48:30–31 76
12:12 148	53:5d 241–42, 244	48:47 76
12:13 159	56:5 208	49:6, 39 76
	56:7 35	

Song of Songs
7:10 43

Isaiah
1:3 81
1:4 147
1:11–17 142
1:23 217
2:1–4 67
2:12–21 238
5:23 217
6 30
9:7 85
10:13 146
11:1–9 236
11:7–9 53
19:12 146
19:22 71
19:25 71
24:1–23 238
25:6–8 246
25:8 247
26:20–21 238
27:1 ....30, 135
36–37 177
40:1–2 118
40:18 31

60:9, 14 147
63:15 69
65:19–20 246
66:2 246

Jeremiah
1:5 ....74, 76
1:10 74
2:11, 28 74
3:17 76
4:2 74
6:6 218
7:6 74
7:9–10 74
7:23 27
9:1 75
9:23–24 77
10:3–16 10
10:9 146
17:9–10 239
18:7–11 75
18:18 147
19:4–5 199
21:4–5 75
22:1–10 75
22:17 218
23:5–6 85

Lamentations
4:16 94

Ezekiel
7:26–27 94
18:2 239
20:26 217
20:31 199
22:7 218
22:12 217–18
27:8 146
34:23–24 85
36:27 34
46:16–17 217

Daniel
4:37 77
8:16 37
10:13 37

Hosea
1:9–10 71
6:6 142
8:1 ....102, 116
8:13 116
11:8–9 69
14 117

Scripture Index

14:4–8 117–18

Joel
2:29 34

Amos
2:7 116
3:9–10 116
5:12 .... 116, 217
5:24 116
6:12 116
8:11–12 116

9 117
9:8 117
9:1–4 116
9:11, 13–15 117

Micah
3:11 217

Habakkuk
3:2 71

Haggai
2:5 34

Zechariah
4:6 34
14:1–21 238

Malachi
1:8 217
2:8 102
2:9 217
3:10 .... 231, 234

NEW TESTAMENT

Matthew
4:17 245
5:5 192
5:10 200
6:10 98
7:13–14 240
8:17 244
10:4 199
10:8 223
10:37–39 200
22:23–28 53
22:30 53
24:1–51 238
28:19 201
28:20 60

Mark
1:1 36
3:18 199
3:31–35 200
10:25–30 234
10:29–30 231
10:45 222
12:25 53
13:10 201

Luke
6:15 199
6:21, 25 200

6:38 234
17:20–37 238
20:20–26 200
20:34–35 53
21:5–28 238
22:14–23 191
22:20 192

John
2:13–16 201
3:4 72
4:2 72
4:24 139
5:14 238
16:33 245
18:10–11 201
18:36 201

Acts
1:13 199
2 19

Romans
4:2–5, 13–14 234
5:3–5 240–41
8:1 201
8:20–22 53
8:32 223
9–11 222

9:23–26 185
11:11–24 17
12:1 142
12:19 223
13:1 97
15:25–27 240
15:26 236

1 Corinthians
1:2 201
1:23 77
1:31 77
10:1–4 185
10:1–6 17
11:27–34 238

2 Corinthians
8:1–2 236
8:1–15 236–37
9:1–5 240
9:6–15 236
11:22–29 235
12:7–10 240

Galatians
1:22 201
3 235
3:1–13 234
3:6 234

3:11–14 234
3:13–14 .... 231, 233–34
3:13–29 239
3:14–29 235
3:29 234

Ephesians
1:1–14 236
4:28 236
5:21 56

Colossians
3:12 185
3:25 238

Hebrews
5:17–19 155
7:1–22 234
8:6–13 191
8:12 192
9:27 239
11 218
11:13 77
11:36–39 235
12:2 136
13:5 235
19 217
22 208

James
1:2–4 240
2:5 192
2:14–17 236
4:2 231
5:1–6 235

2 Thessalonians
3:11–13 236

1 Timothy
2:5–6 222
6:9–10 235

2 Timothy
1:8 241
3:16–17 35

1 Peter
1:1 77
1:6–7 240
2:9–10 185
2:24 .... 231, 242

1 John
3:17–18 236

3 John
2 234

Revelation
1:8 31
20–22 192
21 236
21:1–4 246
22:20 247

Asia Theological Association
54 Scout Madriñan St. Quezon City 1103, Philippines
Email: ataasia@gmail.com Telefax: (632) 410 0312

OUR MISSION

The Asia Theological Association (ATA) is a body of theological institutions, committed to evangelical faith and scholarship, networking together to serve the Church in equipping the people of God for the mission of the Lord Jesus Christ.

OUR COMMITMENT

The ATA is committed to serving its members in the development of evangelical, biblical theology by strengthening interaction, enhancing scholarship, promoting academic excellence, fostering spiritual and ministerial formation and mobilizing resources to fulfill God's global mission within diverse Asian cultures.

OUR TASK

Affirming our mission and commitment, ATA seeks to:

- **Strengthen** interaction through inter-institutional fellowship and programs, regional and continental activities, faculty and student exchange programs.
- **Enhance** scholarship through consultations, workshops, seminars, publications, and research fellowships.
- **Promote** academic excellence through accreditation standards, faculty and curriculum development.
- **Foster** spiritual and ministerial formation by providing mentor models, encouraging the development of ministerial skills and a Christian ethos.
- **Mobilize** resources through library development, information technology and infra-structural development.

To learn more about ATA, visit www.ataasia.com or facebook.com/AsiaTheologicalAssociation

Langham Literature, along with its publishing work, is a ministry of Langham Partnership.

Langham Partnership is a global fellowship working in pursuit of the vision God entrusted to its founder John Stott –

> *to facilitate the growth of the church in maturity and Christ-likeness through raising the standards of biblical preaching and teaching.*

Our vision is to see churches in the Majority World equipped for mission and growing to maturity in Christ through the ministry of pastors and leaders who believe, teach and live by the word of God.

Our mission is to strengthen the ministry of the word of God through:
- nurturing national movements for biblical preaching
- fostering the creation and distribution of evangelical literature
- enhancing evangelical theological education

especially in countries where churches are under-resourced.

Our ministry

Langham Preaching partners with national leaders to nurture indigenous biblical preaching movements for pastors and lay preachers all around the world. With the support of a team of trainers from many countries, a multi-level programme of seminars provides practical training, and is followed by a programme for training local facilitators. Local preachers' groups and national and regional networks ensure continuity and ongoing development, seeking to build vigorous movements committed to Bible exposition.

Langham Literature provides Majority World preachers, scholars and seminary libraries with evangelical books and electronic resources through publishing and distribution, grants and discounts. The programme also fosters the creation of indigenous evangelical books in many languages, through writer's grants, strengthening local evangelical publishing houses, and investment in major regional literature projects, such as one volume Bible commentaries like the *Africa Bible Commentary* and the *South Asia Bible Commentary*.

Langham Scholars provides financial support for evangelical doctoral students from the Majority World so that, when they return home, they may train pastors and other Christian leaders with sound, biblical and theological teaching. This programme equips those who equip others. Langham Scholars also works in partnership with Majority World seminaries in strengthening evangelical theological education. A growing number of Langham Scholars study in high quality doctoral programmes in the Majority World itself. As well as teaching the next generation of pastors, graduated Langham Scholars exercise significant influence through their writing and leadership.

To learn more about Langham Partnership and the work we do visit **langham.org**

www.ingramcontent.com/pod-product-compliance
Lightning Source LLC
Chambersburg PA
CBHW071813230426
43670CB00013B/2446